CITIZENSHIP AND THE LAW
SERIES

General Editor
ROBERT BLACKBURN

RIGHTS OF CITIZENSHIP

Edited by

ROBERT BLACKBURN

MANSELL

First published 1993 by
Mansell Publishing Limited. A Cassell Imprint
Villiers House, 41/47 Strand, London WC2N 5JE, England
387 Park Avenue South, New York, NY 10016–8810, USA

British Library Cataloguing-in-Publication Data
A catalogue record for this book is available from the British Library.
ISBN 0–7201–2124–8

Library of Congress Cataloging-in-Publication Data
Rights of citizenship/edited by Robert Blackburn.
     p.   cm. — (Citizenship and the law series)
Includes bibliographical references and index.
ISBN 0–7201–2124–8
  1. Citizenship — Great Britain.   I. Blackburn, Robert, 1952–   .
II. Series.
KD4050.R54   1993
342.41'083 — dc20
[344.10283]

Printed and bound in Great Britain by
Biddles Ltd, Guildford and King's Lynn

Contents

Contributors

ANDREW ASHWORTH has been the Edmund-Davies Professor of Criminal Law and Criminal Justice at King's College, University of London, since 1988. He previously taught at Manchester and Oxford Universities. He is Editor of the *Criminal Law Review*, and between 1989 and 1992 was Chairman of the Council of Europe Select Committee on Sentencing. Two recent books of his are *Principles of Criminal Law* (1991) and the *Sentencing and Criminal Justice* (1992).

GEOFFREY BINDMAN is a practising solicitor, and the senior partner of Bindman and Partners, which he founded in 1974. He was formerly Legal Adviser to the Race Relations Board 1966–76 and to the Commission for Racial Equality 1976–83. He has represented bodies including the International Commission of Jurists and Amnesty International in human rights missions in several countries. He has contributed many articles in the national and legal press on human rights, anti-discrimination laws and the legal profession, and his books include (with Anthony Lester) *Race and Law* (1972), and as editor *South Africa: Human Rights and the Rule of Law* (1989). He is a Visiting Professor of Law at University College London, and an Honorary Fellow in Civil Legal Process at the University of Kent.

PATRICK BIRKINSHAW is Professor of Law at the Law School of the University of Hull and the Director of that school's Institute of European Public Law. His publications include *Grievances, Remedies and the State* (1985, 2nd edn 1994), *Freedom of Information: The Law, the Practice and the Ideal* (1988), *Government and Information: The Law relating to Access, Disclosure and Regulation* (1990) and *Reforming the Secret State* (1991). He co-authored *Government by Moonlight: The Hybrid Parts of the State* (1990) with Norman Lewis and Ian Harden.

ROBERT BLACKBURN is Senior Lecturer in Law at King's College, University of London. He has written extensively on constitutional law and subjects in British politics as both an author and a journalist. He is a solicitor and since 1983 has acted as a legal consultant to the Council of Europe Directorate of Human Rights. He has been Director of the Centre of British Constitutional Law and History at King's College since 1987, and Deputy Director of the British Institute of Human Rights (whose President is Lord Scarman) in London since 1985. Among his recent publications are *The Meeting of Parliament* (1990) and *Human Rights for the 1990s* (co-editor with John Taylor 1991). He is General Editor of the Citizenship and the Law book series published by Mansell.

MARGARET BRAZIER is Professor of Law and Director of the Centre for Social Ethics and Policy at the University of Manchester. She is the author of *Medicine, Patients and the Law* (1992), and editor of *Street on Torts* (1989) and *Clerk and Lindsell on Torts* (1990). She has written widely on legal issues relating to health care and has a particular interest in the role of the state in the regulation of health care professionals.

TREVOR BUCK is Lecturer in Law at Leicester University. He is a section editor of 'Ombudsman's decisions' in the *Journal of Social Welfare Law*, and has published widely in the field of social welfare and family law. At present he is the Course Director of the LLM Welfare Law programme at Leicester University, and has recently been appointed as legal adviser to the UK Social Fund Commissioner.

PAUL CRAIG is Reader in Law in the University of Oxford and Fellow of Worcester College. He has written widely in the field of public law, including *Administrative Law* (1989) and *Public Law and Democracy in the United Kingdom and the United States of America* (1990).

KEITH EWING is Professor of Public Law at King's College London; he formerly taught at the Universities of Cambridge and Edinburgh. He is a prolific writer in the fields of civil liberties and labour law, and among his publications are *The Right to Strike* (1991), (with Conor Gearty) *Freedom under Thatcher: Civil Liberties in Modern Britain* (1990) and (with P. Elias) *Trade Union Democracy: Members' Rights and the Law* (1988).

CONOR GEARTY is Senior Lecturer in Law and Director of the Civil Liberties Research Unit at King's College London. He is the author of *Terror* (1991) and (with Keith Ewing) *Freedom under Thatcher: Civil Liberties in Modern Britain* (1990).

JULIAN LONBAY is Senior Lecturer in Law and Director of the Institute of European Law at the University of Birmingham. He has published many articles on educational matters, especially in a European context, and (with others) *Training Lawyers in the European Community* (1990) and (with L. Spedding) *International Professional Practice* (1992).

JOHN McELDOWNEY is Senior Lecturer in Law at the University of Warwick. He is the author of various articles in the field of public law, a textbook on *Public Law* (1993), and co-editor with Patrick McAuslan of *Law, Legitimacy and the Constitution* (1985). His interests include legal history, the role of the jury and the control of public expenditure.

ANDREW NICOL is a practising barrister, at Doughty Street Chambers in London. He is the author (with A. Dummett) of *Subjects, Citizens, Aliens and Others* (1990), and a member and former chair of the Immigration Law Practitioners' Association.

KATHERINE O'DONOVAN is Professor of Law at the University of Kent Law School and Professeur Invité at the University of Paris X. Born and educated in Dublin, she has taught at universities in Belfast, Addis Ababa, Kuala Lumpur and Hong Kong. She is the author of *Sexual Division in Law* (1985), *Family Law Matters* (1992), and co-author of *Equality and Sex Discrimination Law* (1988). Her current research is concerned with family rights under the European Convention on Human Rights.

MARTIN PARTINGTON is Professor of Law at the University of Bristol. He has written extensively on housing law, including *Landlord and Tenant* (1975, 2nd edn 1980), (with Andrew Arden) *Housing Law* (1983, 2nd edn forthcoming) and (with Jonathan Hill) *Cases and Materials on Housing Law* (1991). He was, for a number of years, an academic adviser to the Education Committee of the Institute of Housing. He has also given many lectures to legal practitioners on housing law and, more recently, has been involved in training programmes for judges and recorders organized by the Judicial Studies Board.

ROBIN WHITE is Professor of Law and Dean of the Faculty of Law at the University of Leicester. He is the author of *The Administration of Justice* (1992) and editor of the *European Law Review*. He was a member of the JUSTICE Committee which prepared the report *Justice and the Individual*. He is a solicitor and sits as a part-time Chairman of the Disability Appeal Tribunals and Social Security Appeals Tribunals.

Introduction: Citizenship Today

ROBERT BLACKBURN

The 1990s are witnessing a renaissance in the interpretation of national progress in terms of citizenship. Britain in the past has had some difficulty in finding a generally acceptable language for individual rights, and this has been aggravated by the absence of any codified body of civil or political rights in British law to which to refer. The terminology of civil liberties has tended to be confused with radical causes in Britain, which is perhaps ironic given the relative respectability of civil rights claims elsewhere in Western Europe and in the United States of America, and so too has the term human rights, which has the additional problem of possessing too international a flavour to be adopted generally in domestic British political speaking. But all of a sudden the language of the citizen's rights and responsibilities – or 'citizenship' – has come to be embraced by our politicians and in academic research as the yardstick against which to judge our national progress and national efficiency.

All the British political parties went into the April 1992 general election with public policy programmes expressly designed and presented in terms of enhancing the quality of citizenship and a citizen's rights. This was reproduced in their manifestos, before which, in preparation for the election, the three main parties first produced their major policy statements on the subject virtually simultaneously in the month of July 1991. First came the Labour Party's *Citizen's Charter*, then there followed the Liberal Democrats' *Citizens' Britain*, and finally (and most sensationally in the press) the Conservatives' *The Citizen's Charter* was published as a Government White Paper.[1] A close inspection of the three party documents not surprisingly discloses substantial differences in their approach to the concept of citizenship. Indeed some party spokesmen have alleged that either or

1

both of the other parties are not addressing genuine issues of citizenship at all, but abusing the true meaning of an appealing-sounding term. Although Labour and the Liberal Democrats have more comprehensive programmes for promoting citizenship than that of the present Government in terms of dealing with a far wider spectrum of public policy issues, most notably on constitutional affairs and employment rights, it is in large measure precisely because of the Conservative leader John Major's own personal interest and enthusiasm for citizen's charters, and the accompanying publicity that only he as Prime Minister can arrange and deliver, that the whole citizenship debate has been galvanized and brought to the forefront of politics today. Whether or not one accepts that Mr Major's Citizen's Charter, and the spawning of smaller citizen's charters across the public sector from education to London Underground transport, is in fact dealing with genuine issues of citizenship, not even his most critical political opponents can deny that he has tapped into a strain of thinking that is very powerful – and delivers votes.

Citizenship means different things to different people. Rights of citizenship today are of a widely diverse nature, and certainly go far beyond the rights of a purely constitutional nature dealt with, for example, by A. V. Dicey in a book of a similar title to this one published back in 1912.[2] Earlier Western theorists had even narrower notions of citizenship, including Aristotle, for whom a citizen was simply one who had as share in 'both the ruling and being ruled'.[3] Today it is fundamental that citizenship and democracy are mutually defined, and among the most basic of our accepted moral rights are those to be found in the international treaties which the UK has played a leading role in formulating this century, in particular the United Nations Declaration of Human Rights[4] and the European Convention on Human Rights.[5] Historically there may be said to have been three waves in the acquisition and assertion of citizens' rights, broadly corresponding to civil rights in the eighteenth century, political rights in the nineteenth, and social and economic rights in the present century. These three elements of our modern citizenship were described by T. H. Marshall, in his classic essay 'Citizenship and social class', in the following way:

> The civil element is composed of the rights necessary for individual freedom – liberty of the person, freedom of speech, thought and faith, the right to own property and to conclude valid contracts, and the right to justice. The last is of a different order from the others because it is the right to defend and assert all one's rights on terms of equality with others and by due process of law. This shows us that the

institutions most directly associated with civil rights are the courts of justice.

By the political element I mean the right to participate in the exercise of political power, as a member of a body invested with political authority or as an elector of the members of such a body. The corresponding institutions are Parliament and councils of local government.

By the social element I mean the whole range from the right to a modicum of economic welfare and security to the right to share to the full in the social heritage and to live the life of a civilised being according to the standards prevailing in the society. The institutions most closely connected with it are the education system and the social services.[6]

It is true that defining citizenship is itself a political activity. The particular interpretation of citizenship taken by each person will reflect his or her own ideology in general about the proper relationship between the individual and society. Similarly the particular interpretation taken by each political party reflects the dominant political ideology within the party and its programme of public policy generally. The rights with which the present Government has been concerned in promulgating its charters since 1991 have been principally restricted to the economic sphere, and more particularly, in the Treasury Minister Francis Maude's words, to the 'principles that will govern the way in which every public sector organisation treats those who use their services'.[7] The four main goals to be achieved, the Government's Citizen's Charter declares, are improvement in the quality of public services, to give the citizen the choice between competing providers in public services, to ensure the citizen knows what standard of service he or she can expect, and for the citizen as taxpayer to receive value for money from public services. In the achievement of these goals, the charter states, every citizen is entitled to expect standards, openness, information, choice, non-discrimination, accountability and a complaints procedure.[8] William Waldegrave, the Minister responsible for implementing the Citizen's Charter, has commented as follows:

Much to the disappointment of those, including – dare I say it – some academics and management consultants who would love to complicate the concept so that they can make it their business to explain it to the rest of us, the Citizen's Charter is rather a simple idea. And simple ideas are almost invariably the best. The Charter is a way of making sure that the pressures which would be brought to bear to the user's advantage in competitively provided services are also brought to bear on public services where little or no competition is available.[9]

3

The Citizen's Charter contains no declaration of rights traditionally understood as being of a civil or political nature. Certainly there is no mention of constitutional improvements, and this reflects the general policy of the Conservative Party leadership, which is formally opposed to the enactment of a Bill of Rights or any other major constitutional change. John Patten, the Education Secretary, articulated this view in July 1991 (the same month the charter was published) in a much-publicized lecture to the Conservative Political Centre, when he observed with approval that 'we have in the United Kingdom a culture which is individual-based and rights-based – but rights protected not by imposed constitutional constructs, but rather by the people themselves'.[10]

By contrast, the most striking feature of the Liberal Democrats' *Citizens' Britain* is its emphasis upon reform of the political structure, a matter to which they – and the Liberal Party and SDP before them – have attached the highest priority over the past ten years. In the view of their leader, Paddy Ashdown, 'Full citizenship requires political reform to produce a nation of citizens, not subjects. That means a bill of rights, a fair voting system, and full integration into a democratic political union in Europe.'[11] Other reforms of a con-stitutional nature mentioned in the document are for a Freedom of Information Act, devolution and strengthening of local government democracy. The charter's package of reforms was drawn from the pro-posals of a working party under Robert Maclennan, the former SDP leader, for a written Constitution, and subsequently these were also adopted for its 1992 election manifesto.[12]

The historical purpose of the Labour Party has always been to work towards social justice for each citizen, and in particular to help bring about the social integration of its disadvantaged citizens, notably the poor, the unemployed and the homeless. Its own *Citizen's Charter* issued in 1991 gave equal emphasis to 'consumers' and 'citizens'. The document is sub-titled *Labour's Better Deal for Consumers and Citizens*, and in its introduction it says, 'Our Charter recognises that we are both consumers and citizens, citizens and electors, electors and tax-payers, and contributors.' Holding Labour out as the natural party of the consumer and citizen, the charter then cites the former Labour leader Neil Kinnock's redefinition of these words in terms of

> an individual freedom that is not nominal but real; a freedom
> that can be exercised in practice: because the school is good;
> because the hospital is there; because the alternative work is
> available; because the law is fair; and because the street is safe.[13]

The nine rights laid down in the Labour charter are a right to choose, a right to quality, a right to safety, a right to be treated equally, a right to swift and fair redress, a right to citizen's action (i.e. legal remedy), a right to a voice, a right to know and a right to advocacy (i.e. advice and representation).[14]

There is no doubt of the tendency on the right and left in British politics to see human nature rather differently, and in particular human motivation. All parties speak of the advancement and fulfilment of Britain's citizens, but whereas Conservatives give greater emphasis to the individual's natural desire for independence and self-reliance, Labour has given greater stress to the individual's need for society and compassion for those who cannot help themselves. Contrast these two extracts from words delivered on the subject by John Major and Labour's Tony Blair, both in June 1992. Speaking to the Adam Smith Institute, Mr Major said:

> The instinct for independence is a basic human instinct. Any parent knows that. Among too many people in this country – people who take the easy choices of prosperity and privilege for granted – there is still an arrogance which assumes that people who have little, or are dependent on public services, cannot be trusted with choice. Over the years, government at all levels has been stiff with that attitude. But not only government. It can still be found in some of the professions, in universities, and in the media. I was brought up among people who had little. Yet they – we – were no different from the next man or woman. We had our own ideas, our own hopes, our own ambitions. Just because you have little money, it does not follow that you need little choice, that you are fit only to follow where others lead. People in those circumstances long to have choices. They want to be independent, not dependent on town hall or benefit offices. They want a share in this country – a hand up, not a hand-out.
>
> This then must be the next phase of Conservatism: to shift the balance of choice in society more radically than ever before into the hands of ordinary people. In the 1990s we mean to widen the avenue to choice and freedom. We mean to empower not just the enterprising, but all people – the least well-off – those most dependent on public services as well.[15]

Whereas in Mr Blair's view of citizenship,

> The distinctive contribution of the Labour Party to British democracy is to place the well-being of the individual within that of society, to link the individual's prosperity to that of

the broader community. Its inspiration is justice. Its purpose is the empowerment of the individual. Its means is through people acting together to achieve what they cannot do on their own . . .

To operate successfully a society must act on the basis of justice, the right to fair treatment, without which citizenship will be an unrealistic goal. A society that is unjust cannot bind its people together. Yet people are held back: by lack of decent education, poverty, immobility, vested interests. From these they must be released. The idea of empowerment is stronger than that of liberty.[16]

But whatever their ideological reasoning, everyone supports improving the quality of public services. And if it comes more naturally for Labour to stress that 'we depend upon good public services', the Minister responsible for implementing the goals of the Conservatives' Citizen's Charter, William Waldegrave, nevertheless recently told the Institute of Directors that 'Public services serve some of our most fundamental needs and it is rightly considered to be the sign of a civilised society that its citizens should have access to decent services.'[17]

What interpretations of democracy underpin the contemporary meanings of citizenship? It is here that MPs belonging to the opposition parties, with more overt policies on constitutional affairs, have most vehemently attacked the Government's Citizen's Charter for being devoid of constitutional and democratic principle. Many commentators, including Labour and Liberal Democrat politicians, have attacked the Conservatives' charter as an exercise in consumerism, rather than citizenship. They have suggested that what Mr Douglas Hurd started as Home Secretary in May 1988 by promoting the concept of the 'active citizen', meaning good neighbourliness and participation in the community, has been twisted into a party propaganda exercise that has virtually nothing in substance to do with civil, political or social rights of citizenship, simply to challenge the left's monopoly of the word 'citizen' in political rhetoric.[18] The day after publication of the Conservatives' Citizen's Charter, Neil Kinnock dismissed the document for saying 'nothing about basic citizens' rights'.[19] According to Mr Ashdown, speaking for the Liberal Democrats, they had 'taken citizenship and pasteurised the politics out of it. They have confused consumerism with citizenship.'[20] And a veteran backbencher in the Commons said from the left: 'The Citizen's Charter has nothing to do with people's real rights. It is an attempt to mobilise public opinion against the public services.'[21]

It is a mistake, however, to write off the Citizen's Charter as mere Conservative enthusiasm for privatization and the market, devoid of democratic principle. So what precisely do John Major and William Waldegrave mean when they say the charter is all 'about giving more power to the people'?[22] The answer lies in the belief shared by all three main parties today in the close correlation between economic and political power, which has a fundamental bearing on the meaning of citizenship today. The idea that civil and political rights are determined by and dependent upon the economic infrastructure of society has been a leading principle of socialism. This was especially so until the revisionism of the 1950s and 1960s, epitomized in Anthony Crosland's *The Future of Socialism*,[23] which ironically emerged at exactly the same time that the brand of libertarianism which became Thatcherism and the New Right in the 1980s was being developed by conservative writers such as Michael Oakeshott and Enoch Powell. The conservative definition of citizenship has its roots embedded in the ideology of the market, and in its civil and political virtues, as well as economic merit:

> The market decentralises power right down to every individual consumer, so that a grand, continuous general election is in progress the whole time, a vote being cast whenever a share or a security of an article or a service is bought and sold. This is an economic democracy in which there are no privileges – everybody's dollar is as good as everybody else's dollar – and where the mightiest of corporations and capitalists have had to bow to the collective wishes of the humblest citizens.[24]

It is more on the formal constitutional aspects of citizenship that the greatest divergence of opinion between the political parties becomes evident. The Government stoutly defends the British Constitution as it now stands, but Labour and the Liberal Democrats have moved towards a large measure of agreement in principle on a substantial number of reforms designed to promote individual rights and democracy. Some of these policies concern the machinery of government and elections, most notably a Scottish Parliament, an elected second chamber in place of the House of Lords, and a review of the method for electing Members of Parliament. Others seek to extend legally assertable rights in such areas as personal privacy, freedom of information and discrimination upon new grounds, such as homosexuality and disablement. Labour's level of commitment to constitutional reform was illustrated by its preparation in advance of the 1992 election of detailed legislation for a Scottish Parliament Bill and a Right to Information Bill, which were ready to go on the statute book immediately it took office.[25]

Both Labour and the Liberal Democrats as part of their 1992 election campaigns promised a bill of rights. Labour's chief spokesman in the House of Lords, Lord Cledwyn, presented the party's position shortly after the election was announced: 'As regards a bill of rights, as I have said on a previous occasion, we favour a freedom of information act ..., an individual's right to prohibit or restrict the collection of personal information ..., the equal treatment of all citizens of this country irrespective of their sex or racial origin ..., equal access to the law as well as equal treatment before the law. We would also introduce a Bill of Rights to incorporate the European Convention on Human Rights'.[26] Despite continuing resistance from the Government to the incorporation of the Convention into British law, a large number of the Conservatives' own backbenchers now support this measure, including the present chairman of the Home Affairs Select Committee, Sir Ivan Lawrence. It was a Conservative MP, Sir Edward Gardner, who introduced draft legislation to incorporate the European Convention on Human Rights in 1987, which failed to proceed further than a second reading debate for lack of parliamentary time.[27] Within the country at large, opinion polls have consistently indicated popular majority support for a bill of rights based on the European Convention,[28] and the leader writers of *The Times*, *The Independent* and *The Guardian* newspapers have all strongly urged such a policy on the Government within the past few years.[29] Even senior present members of the judiciary are now expressing public support for incorporation of the Convention, including the new head of the civil division of the Court of Appeal, the Master of the Rolls Sir Thomas Bingham. As the Labour leader John Smith has put it, our 'antique and antiquated' constitution needs a bill of rights based upon the European Convention: 'we need a new constitution for a new century'.[30]

The study of citizens' rights and freedoms at our universities is an old one. It has been regarded as an essential component of a liberal education in the social sciences and law ever since the modern university system was founded during the nineteenth century. It is of particular significance, however, that whereas from the 1940s to the end of the 1970s the central concern of the social sciences tended to be the exploration of the new phenomenon of state intervention, in the 1980s and 1990s there has been a huge revival of interpreting society in terms of the individual. So far as the study of law is concerned, this has led to a blossoming of new courses, some devoted to citizens' rights and freedoms generally, called 'The individual and the state' or 'The law relating to civil liberties' or 'Human rights law', and other more specialized options on particular rights, such as 'Race relations law', 'Women and the law' or 'International human rights law'. This has been accompanied by a emerging body of literature on the subject, and the year 1980 provided a particular landmark with the publication of two major student cases and materials books on civil liberties law, one edited by Paul O'Higgins of King's College London, and the other by Messrs Bailey, Harris and Jones of Nottingham University.[31] Previously, apart from the general constitutional law books, the only available legal work solely devoted to individual rights was *Freedom, the Individual and the Law* (1963) by Professor Harry Street at Manchester University.[32] And now, for the 1990s, Mansell becomes the first publishing house to launch a book series devoted to the analysis and improvement of citizenship in Britain today.

A decision was taken at the outset of this project not to impose upon contributing authors a straitjacket definition of citizenship to which all must conform. It was made clear that the question of the rights of the individual within Britain's society in the 1990s was the subject of this book, and that such rights were drawn from across the whole range of citizenship, including questions of political liberty, civil rights and freedoms, and social and economic rights. But otherwise the editor's request to each contributing author was simply to write for this book on rights of citizenship on a particular subject, be it sexual equality, freedom of expression, housing or medical services, and within each chapter to link the subject to the concept of citizenship, developing selected topical strands for analysis and discussion, and finally giving suggestions for improvement in the quality of citizenship within the field with which they are concerned. By leaving open a partisan political and intellectual definition of citizenship today, it is intended that this book should display a diversity of opinion, and it is hoped that precisely how each individual contributor has approached the subject, and the common denominators and differences that may be displayed across the book, will prove more instructive than any tightly drawn, single definition could provide. For readers seeking further elaboration of the politics and philosophy of citizenship, a bibliography is appended and special attention is drawn to the recent contributions on the subject from the *Report of the Speaker's Commission on Citizenship*, and a new collection of essays on *The Welfare of Citizens* from the Institute for Public Policy Research.[33]

It is hoped that collectively these articles, which form the first title in the new 'Citizenship and the Law' series, will serve to further the debate about values in citizenship and how improvements can be made in the practical quality of citizens' rights and freedoms as we approach the twenty-first century. The editor expresses his gratitude to each of the contributing authors for their support and helpful cooperation in the publication of this book.

NOTES AND REFERENCES

1 *Citizen's Charter: Labour's Deal for Consumers and Citizens* (1991); *Citizens' Britain: Liberal Democrat Policies for a People's Charter* (1991); *The Citizen's Charter: Raising the Standard*, Cm 1599 (1991).

2 *Rights of Citizenship: A Survey of Safeguards for the People* (1912).

3 *The Politics* (Penguin edn, 1951), see especially Book III, pp. 167–85.

4 *Universal Declaration of Human Rights: International Covenant on Civil and Political Rights; International Covenant on Economic, Social and Cultural Rights* (United Nations, 1992).

5 *Convention for the Protection of Human Rights and Fundamental Freedoms* (Council of Europe, 1991).

6 T. H. Marshall, 'Citizenship and social class', in T. H. Marshall, *Class, Citizenship and Social Development* (1977), p. 78.

7 HC Deb., Vol. 198, 15 November 1991, Col. 1333.

8 pp. 4 and 5.

9 'A revolution in Whitehall', Speech given to The Institute of Directors, 20 July 1992.

10 *Political Culture, Conservatism and Rolling Constitutional Change*, (1991) p. 9.

11 *The Independent*, 21 May 1991.

12 *We the People: Towards a Written Constitution* (1990). For a different and more comprehensive model of reform involving a written constitution, see Institute for Public Policy Research, *A Written Constitution for the United Kingdom* (Mansell, 1993).

13 p. 8.

14 pp. 11–33.

15 From extract published in *The Guardian*, 17 June 1992.

16 Article in *The Guardian*, 30 June 1992.

17 *Op. cit.*

18 See, e.g., Peter Kellner, 'Suddenly we're citizens, but what does it mean?', *The Independent*, 19 June 1991.

19 *The Independent*, 24 June 1991.

20 *Ibid.*, 12 July 1991.

21 Tony Benn, HC Deb., Vol. 198, 15 November 1991, Col. 1396.

22 *The Citizen's Charter*, p. 2.

23 Published in 1956.

24 P. Douglas and J. E. Powell, *How Big Should Government Be?* (1968), p. 68.

25 The Right to Information Bill was formally introduced into the House of Commons, receiving a formal First Reading: HC HC Bill [1991–92] 79. See also the Labour Party's policy statement, *The Charter of Rights* (1990).

26 HL Deb., Vol. 536, 11 March 1992, Col. 1337.

27 Human Rights Bill [1986–87] 19, on which see Robert Blackburn, 'Parliamentary opinion on a new Bill of Rights', *The Political Quarterly* (1989), p. 469.

28 See, e.g., *British Public Opinion*, Vol. VII, June 1985, p. 4; MORI, *State of the Nation* (1991); Patrick Dunleavy and Stuart Weir, 'They want to see it in writing'. *The Independent*, 2 October 1991, which disclosed that 79 per cent of respondents supported a bill of rights.

29 Most recently, see 'British rights', *The Times*, 18 August 1992 ('Nothing would do more to protect the rights of the citizen. . . . More than three centuries after the last bill of rights, the time has come for Britain to adopt the European Convention as its own. Without citizens' rights, a citizen's charter means little.')

30 Interview in *The Independent*, 18 July 1992; article in *New Statesman & Society*, 15 May 1992.

31 Paul O'Higgins (ed.), *Cases and Materials on Civil Liberties* (1980); S. H. Bailey, D. J. Harris and B. L. Jones (eds), *Civil Liberties: Cases and Materials* (1980, 3rd edn, 1991).

32 Since Professor Street's death in 1984, the barrister Geoffrey Robertson QC produced a sixth edition of the book in 1989. For a recent new commentary on civil liberties law, see Keith Ewing and Conor Gearty, *Freedom under Thatcher: Civil Liberties in Modern Britain* (1990).

33 Report of the Speaker's Commission on Citizenship, *Encouraging Citizenship* (1990); Anna Coote (ed.), *The Welfare of Citizens: Developing New Social Rights* (1992).

1

Gender Blindness or Justice Engendered?

KATHERINE O'DONOVAN

In his classic paper on citizenship rights Marshall identified three elements: civil, political and social.[1] Viewing this conceptualization through gendered glasses leads to questions at a variety of levels. Challenges can be issued to the choices, priorities and content of Marshall's vision, and as to whether citizens do have these rights on an equal basis. Current debates about citizenship often assume that a universal model can be devised; that is, which abstracts from specific characteristics of race, gender, ethnicity and class. The reasons for universality are evident, but getting to such a model may not be easy. It is to this question that the chapter addresses itself. The discussion is largely confined to political aspects of citizenship, an aspect relatively underdeveloped and taken for granted in Marshall's essay.

Who is the abstract person, the citizen, under discussion in current debate? What qualities are attributed to, what connections are assumed about, *notre citoyen(ne) d'aujourd'hui*? I want to suggest that Marshall's citizen is of the male gender and, further, that the legal subject seen in current laws often defies neutrality. There is enough evidence of the projection of a particular perspective in law-making to sustain the charge that the middle-class male heterosexual is most often the privileged legal subject, and that he masquerades as the abstract individual.[2] What does this have to do with the citizenship debate? It provides a cautionary tale. It raises questions about the search for a universal model *citoyen(ne)* abstracted from particular characteristics and communities.

WHO IS THE LEGAL INDIVIDUAL?

Recent work on political philosophy,[3] and on jurisprudence,[4] argues that women continue to be excluded as full legal subjects despite changes in the law from the mid-1970s. Sets of syllogisms implicate language, concepts, theories, social arrangements, the ways in which we see ourselves. The contribution of Carole Pateman takes us back to the origins of social contract theory, a story told in political philosophy to justify current state organization.[5] The interest of her argument for this chapter is that she indicts the notion of the free individual who contracts freely into the social contract, asserting that this hypothetical individual is patriarchally constructed. Dealing with the original exclusion of women from the political life, and their location in the private sphere of the family under patriarchal power, Pateman implicates social contract theory as omitting women's unfreedom, and leaving a legacy of problems about women's incorporation as citizens, and their status as free individuals. Although some may see this as an attack on a historical and contingent omission of women, rather than on Rawlsian contractarians, the immediate relevance of Pateman's work is her argument that the notion of the free individual is a male construct.

> The conclusion is easily drawn that the denial of civil equality to women means that the feminist aspiration must be to win acknowledgement for women as 'individuals'. Such aspiration can never be fulfilled. The 'individual' is a patriarchal category.[6]

According to the cautionary tale, the danger is that real live men will be smuggled 'into the seemingly innocent and abstract universals that nourish political thought. The "individual" or the "citizen" are obvious candidates for this form of gendered substitution.'[7] The example which follows, drawn from criminal law, is of the concealment of a male perspective in the defences to the common law crime of homicide and in the term 'reasonable man' used in legal discourse as an objective standard.

It is in the family that we first learn about gender. The family reproduces the sex/gender system from generation to generation. Experiences of family life are gendered; they may also vary according to factors such as social class, sexuality, ethnicity and race. But it is unlikely that the gender factor will be denied. This being so, how does the law react to the case of the battered woman who kills her partner after enduring continued physical abuse, termed cumulative violence? Is her perspective, perhaps one of self-help, admitted by the law? I suggest that the defences of self-defence and provocation which

13

justify or partially excuse homicide are limited to male definitions and behavioural patterns, and that the defence of diminished responsibility is often interpreted in gendered terms.[8]

In the past the killing of a wife by a husband led to a homicide charge, whereas the wife who dared to kill her husband suffered the more serious charge of petty treason.[9] Although this double standard no longer applies it is evidence of the cultural context in which the law evolved, of male authority and female subordination. And when the law changed to bring wives under the crime of homicide, their particular needs and reactions seem to have been ignored. The fact that many more killings are done by men than by women has also affected the development of the law. Given women's lesser participation in court cases as killers, it is likely that the law of self-defence evolved in the context of male patterns of behaviour. Where a violent attack takes place, the victim must be in imminent danger, and respond with force proportionate to the attack, if self-defence is to be successfully pleaded.[10] The problem for the victim of cumulative violence is that no particular attack may constitute imminent danger, and yet the victim feels herself under threat to her being – whether physical or psychological. Furthermore, as women are on average of smaller size than men, and are less likely to have training in controlled aggression, the requirement of reasonable force in countering an attack may be inappropriate.

Under the Criminal Law Act 1967, where force is used for the prevention of crime there is immunity from prosecution. But the action taken must be reasonable – a requirement which overlaps with the common law on self-defence. The common law cases on reasonable force in response to an attack will apply to give guidance. Again, these cases have been subjected to the criticism that they are culturally specific to men and not to women.[11] Thus fears of violence, and responses to it on a gendered basis, are overlooked. The current literature on masculinity as a rationalistic culture posits preparation for killing and responding to violence as part of male socialization.[12] It is not the purpose here to suggest that women should be so prepared, but rather that the law of self-defence has in its gaze a male subject. Cumulative violence rather than life-threatening attack, response when the abuser is quiet or asleep, uncontrolled response rather than reasonable and proportional response, these characterize the battered-woman-turned-killer cases. Women's socialization in violence has not been the same as men's. We belong to various sub-cultures, but men are better prepared for bodily protection. Given the content of the law of self-defence it is not surprising that it is not successfully pleaded in these cases,[13] although it is a complete defence which exonerates the killer.

Arguing that the deceased provoked the killing by his conduct might seem a more fruitful line of defence, and where this succeeds it reduces the offence from murder to manslaughter. But again the prolonged violence, the apparent initial tolerance by the victim and her failure to respond with immediate violence pose problems in relation to the current definition of provocation in English law. According to the decision in *Duffy*[14] there must be some act or series of acts done by the deceased which would cause in any reasonable person 'a sudden and temporary loss of self control'. This is partially excused by the defence of provocation as happening 'in the heat of passion'. But what I want to suggest is that the self-controlled individual, losing control briefly in response to the act of the deceased, is male. This can be supported by empirical evidence from cases[15] and by reference to theories of the social construction of masculinity.[16]

What the cases show is that not only is the model of sudden and temporary loss of self-control more applicable to male patterns of behaviour, but also behaviour denoted provocative varies according to gender, with sympathy shown to jealous husbands.[17] As with self-defence the response must be immediate; waiting is denoted 'revenge'. Women do tend to wait; writers suggest that this is because of a process known as the 'slow burn' in which rage builds up in the powerless.[18] Delay, the product perhaps of nervousness and timidity, is generally fatal to pleas of provocation or self-defence. Paradoxically, to be 'reasonable' in law's parlance is to lose one's self-control immediately and in a violent fashion. The identification of masculinity with notions of self-control and self-domination is a cultural construct, according to recent theorists.[19] Law makes a concession in permitting a temporary aberration of loss of temper. To so argue is not a denial of the importance of the right to life and bodily integrity of legal subjects, who need the protection of the criminal law, but to query the form this takes in law. Self-domination, the repression of feelings and emotions, characterize the strong male who is partially excused if he loses control temporarily: 'a gentleman is a man who never strikes his wife without provocation'. To be able to lose control and strike immediately is an indication of a sense of power. On the whole it is the boss who shouts at his subordinates. Timidity, lack of power and socialization as a passive receiver may inhibit such direct loss of control. Women's rage has to be repressed.

Pleas of diminished responsibility have been successful in cases of killings following cumulative violence. According to Hilary Allen, interpretations of the Homicide Act 1957 s.2 vary according to cultural factors, of which gender is significant.[20] A woman who wishes to make such a plea is advised to conform to a sterotypical gender role and enlist the sympathy of the court. Demonstrating anger or independence may be viewed as threatening. Work on magistrate's courts supports this, showing that conformity to gender role, being a dependent woman with children or a man supporting a family, leads to a lighter sentence for offences against the law.[21] It can be understood from the above that the question of who the legal individual is operates at a number of levels. There is the projection of an abstract person in legislation, of the reasonable man in common law. There is an interpretive stage at which the participants in the legal drama, lawyers and judges, bring their understandings of human nature to bear on the trial, and where pleas of mitigation are often based on gender and family responsibilities. There is the projection of common sense by the jury. Law, legal interpretation, jury discussion, and finally judgment and sentence by the court occur in the context of a culture which is gendered. This is hardly surprising. But the problem remains of abstraction from the particular and from difference in the creation of that universal individual – the citizen. At the same time the creative process must be viewed from perspectives unseen in the past.

WHAT RELATIONSHIPS DOES THE CITIZEN HAVE?

The universal model citizen, abstracted from characteristics and communities, poses problems in relation to sexuality and family. Sarah Benton asks whether there can be fraternity/sorority when women are so often sex objects for men and not equal subjects. This applies to political discourse as much as to legal. Even if some basis can be found for the admission of the 'virtuous women', the wives, mothers and sweethearts to citizenship, what of the sexual women, the prostitutes, the male homosexuals?[22] Political man must sacrifice his self-interest 'in the interest of creating the city, and within that city he is "public man"'.[23] He is vulnerable, his status is not secure, he can be called to account by his fellow men and exiled for betraying the brotherhood of public life. His sexual desires are problematic. So he has constructed a private space in which he can be free. There he splits the objects of desire in two: there are those over whom he has authority, his family; and there are those who are objects of erotic fantasies – whores, sluts, all children, homosexuals. In Benton's description of the *polis* prostitutes and homosexuals are outside the law, and therefore cannot be subjects; nor can 'good women', for like nature they are non-political. Of course this is a description of the *polis* as it now is. It can change. Women are not only fighting their way to the city, but challenging its rules on their way. The important problem that Benton locates is one of history and tradition.

The history and tradition of political discourse is of a brotherhood from which women and some men were excluded. I do not wish to suggest a unitary brotherhood, for this has not been so. Challenging exclusion and changing the rules of the political club are part of the battle for women and some men. Nevertheless from at least the seventeenth century a fundamental political problem has been how to draft the social contract so as to retain individual freedom and yet to surrender power to the state for the common wealth. The civil freedoms of the individual listed by Marshall and so highly prized by men, such as freedom from arbitrary arrest or freedom of speech, must be shown to be equally valued by women. Whereas men's freedoms lie in the construction of a private life free from the interference of the state, women often need the state to enter this domain to rid them of its tyrannies. Public life is imprinted with the colours of the private. The injustices present in the domestic realm are reproduced in public.

The history of women's demands against the state is a history of achievement: married women's property Acts, the vote, equal parental rights, divorce on equal terms and, more recently, a degree of control over sexuality and reproduction, and legislation on equality and against discrimination. It might therefore seem that women have changed the agenda. But closer inspection reveals that the conditions of entry were set by those already in the club. The early claims by women were for the allocation of rights, privileges and power on a formally equal basis with men, and not for a radical alteration of values. But more recently these claims have been for a priority to be given to women's definitions of civil freedom. For example, a curtailing of men's freedoms in relation to pornography and physical and sexual abuse is primary for some groups; to 'reclaim the night', that is, to walk the streets, to make them free for women, through a male curfew, is primary for others. Further, it has been argued that freedom of speech that permits the circulation of pornography denies women's subjectivity as they are turned into objects in these images and texts. If this is so women's citizenship is threatened, for as objects their personhood is denied. And if liberty is one of the principles into which we contract, then pornographic images and stereotypes of women restrict their freedom to be and to become. 'Women and men constitute continuous threats against each other's freedoms.'[24]

The problem of the private relationships of citizens presents itself in a variety of guises. Critiques of political theory as ignoring the domestic realm and failing to theorize the relation between family and politics have become common.[25] But what that relationship might be in the ideal world of citizenship is not clear, or agreed. There is also the problem of what we mean by family. Which relationships are recognized and legitimated, which fall outside the law? In discussing this we are not only drawn to explain the legal privileging of marriage, but also the privileging of heterosexual males. On the

17

married couple as a unit the state builds policies concerning housing, taxes, social security, children and inheritance; it is true that heterosexual cohabiting partners may also have some of these privileges extended to them. But homosexual relationships are outwith the law and receive no recognition.

The right to marry is denied not only to homosexual couples, but also to post-operative transsexuals.[26] Marriage law requires a union between one male and one female, so determined biologically, and not already married to someone else. The European Court of Human Rights has upheld 'traditional marriage' in applications by transsexuals for an interpretation of the right to marry contained in the European Convention to cover them.[27] The combination of English law with the jurisprudence of the Court indicates a particular relationship between family and state. But does it have to be so? Danish law permits the registration of partnership by homosexual monogamous partners; the conventional incidents of marriage are attached to this relationship, with some exceptions.[28]

The male legal subject is a heterosexual. The preferred form of sexuality attributed to him is a goal-oriented penetrative act committed with the phallus, on the body of a woman. This is reified in the law on consummation of marriage. One of the reasons why post-operative transsexuals cannot marry is that they are assumed incapable of such an act, *in veritas*, either as male or female partner; for even surgery on a male cannot 'produce a person who is naturally capable of performing the essential role of a woman in marriage'.[29] Once a male, always a male is the law's motto. Citizenship operates on sex as a biological category; all citizens belong in an essentialist fashion to one of two categories and marriage is constituted by a particular form of sexual act performed actively by one category on the other. Will the *citoyen moyen sensuel* of the future be a male heterosexual?

Identities are presented in the literature on citizenship as a problem of abstraction from differences to a universal hypothesis. What I am raising here is the problem of stigmatized identities whose differences are outwith the law. In the construction of citizenship are these differences to be given a place? Are same-sex partnerships to be registered? Are prostitutes to be accepted as full citizens? Will masculinity and femininity cease to be constructed as polar opposites? Will the sex/gender system with all its injustices continue to be reproduced in the family? These are important questions for *égalité*.

What goes on in the home is the focus of criticism of the relationship between family and *polis*. At present we live with the sexual division of labour and the constitution of the economic and domestic spheres as separate. As Bill Jordan points out, there is nothing necessarily wrong in that. 'What is wrong is that men and women do not enter the two systems on equal term.'[30] The family is a problem: one does not enter a family through full consent; one is born into relationships unwilled and unchosen by oneself, where roles and power are preordained. There one learns that being born female or male will dictate the course of one's life. One may offer a prayer of thanksgiving daily that one was not born a woman. This in itself is a reflection on justice. By contrast citizenship upholds the ideal that differences of birth are irrelevant in the *polis*. Justice in the family and justice in citizenship seem two different conceptions.

For women too the family is a problem. We are taken to have chosen a role which is prescribed for us. Because of what happens in the family citizens will not enter the city on equal terms. This may be one reason why political philosophy forgets the domestic realm. But, as Okin points out, political theorists have ignored the internal inequalities of the family since their fundamental assumption is that the patriarchal separation of the private/natural sphere from the public/civil realm is irrelevant to theories of justice and to political life.[31] What goes on in the family affects women not only as adults but also as children, because their conceptions of self and their life chances are limited. This is true to a lesser extent of boys; the models of masculinity transmitted to them, while extolling dominance, are confining.

What goes on in the family is crucial to political life, for it is there that our future citizens are produced; it is there that their moral development including a sense of justice takes place. Given the gender stratification of present arrangements, what kind of place is the family to bring up children? The past exclusion of women from the public/civil realm means that the practices that produced the individual are contaminated by patriarchal subordination. All may be well in the ideal city, but today's individual continues to be constructed in law, in the 'psy discourses' of psychology and psychiatry, in medico-legal language, in political speech; and this individual has a gender, and gender difference is a badge of inferiority for some. Past exclusions inform present practices. History is not yet abolished. Family law plays a part in ordaining family roles. Its discourse constructs two individuals, masculine and feminine. On to these two prototypes are projected qualities in a binary system of opposition, with polar differences mirrored in economic, social and political power. Examples can be found in juridical discourse on family relations, for it is in marriage, with its essentialist insistence on biological difference, that these oppositions are crystallized.

Masculinity is associated with being a breadwinner, providing for family, contract, self-control, rationality. Femininity is associated with dependence, status of wife, emotionality, irrationality. Judicial reasoning in family law cases exemplifies this:

It is a totally artificial situation to bring about to have a father giving up his work, which is his career and will be something which he will need to follow for the rest of his working life, to live on social security to look after two small children when the mother is fully available to look after them.[32]

I shall take a great deal of convincing that it is right that an adult male should be permanently unemployed in order to look after one small boy.[33]

It is natural for young children to be with mothers, but where there is a dispute it is a consideration not a presumption.[34]

It is not being suggested that members of the judiciary are alone in imposing these prescribed roles on persons. It is true that they are drawn, almost exclusively, from a particular class, gender and racial group. But they speak from a particular heritage, from a culture, which although imposed is widely shared. Thus, when considering whether children should be brought up in lesbian households, or whether a stable homosexual relationship constitutes a family, terms such as 'common sense', the 'reasonable man', 'unusual household' and 'normality' are used in discussion.[35] This form of reference to popular morality should worry those non-citizens standing at the gates of the city. For it is a guarantee of continued stigmatization as 'not normal'; or, for women, as binary opposites of 'masculine'. Too often this leads to a denial of subjectivity, to discrimination or classification as inferior.

In lineage, descent, the patrilineal system, inheritance, surname, the monarchy, succession to title and nobility, men define the family. Being constructed as breadwinner gives power, although it carries the meaning of not being good at emotional relations or with children. There is a nexus – masculinity, authority, paterfamilias, public representative of the family. In feminist theory the division between the domestic sphere and the 'rest' is the equivalent of the division between private and public, whereas in traditional political theory the domestic sphere is forgotten and the public/private distinction is between state and civil society. This has meant that the individual who is 'seen' is male. In the past, difference, whether social, biological or familial, has often resulted in discrimination against the less powerful. We need to find a language to discuss this in non-hegemonic terms.

PRIVATE RELATIONS AS A MODEL FOR CITIZENSHIP?

Difference is 'the joker in the citizenship pack',[36] which we need to recognize and yet transform. The debate is about how this is to be done. It is not simply a matter of maintaining the old structures in which the 'subject' had his being, while recognizing differences. Nor is it about incorporating the hitherto powerless. Those persons and groups, stigmatized as 'the Other' in the past, have a positive contribution to make. Their experiences give them understandings denied to the powerful. Some among them have even proposed that they might show the way. An example comes from women's writings. I want to consider the contribution of feminist theory to debates about justice and see whether there is a lesson for us. In Susan Glaspell's short story, 'A jury of her peers',[37] a farmer is found dead, apparently strangled in his home. The widow is suspected and taken off to jail. The sheriff, Peters, the man who found the body, Hale, and the county attorney return to the scene of the crime to investigate further. The first two men are accompanied by their wives, who remain downstairs while the men investigate the bedroom in which the body was found. In the kitchen, that place from which women never quite escape, where the men have not thought to search for clues, the women discover the evidence of the wife's guilt: the body of a pet bird with its neck broken. Mrs Hale immediately understands what has happened. In this bleak cheerless place the only comfort for a lonely, childless woman with the hard life of the farm was her pet bird, which the husband – a cold man – killed. In return she has strangled him. Despite some doubts expressed by Mrs Peters, it is agreed that the men must not be told.

The story points up the complacent, patronizing attitude of the men who do not contemplate that the women might have uncovered something hidden from them. But there is another point, which can be used to illustrate arguments in feminist jurisprudence about women's alternative conceptions of justice.[38] Mrs Hale and Mrs Peters are willing to excuse a killing and to withhold evidence because they see the breaking of the bird's neck as provocation. They are less committed to a version of justice which is couched in abstract rules and look to the context of what has happened. Carol Gilligan advances the thesis that male reasoning adheres to a formalistic set of neutral legal principles couched in impersonal objective rules, an 'ethic of rights', whereas female reasoning is discretionary and person-orientated, couched in equitable principles, with a flexibility that looks to the spirit of the law and an 'ethic of care'.[39] Not all feminist theorists accept Gilligan's typology. Some have argued that women's present values are the product of oppression and that we cannot know what women's authentic voices will be like until they cease to be subordinate.[40] It is possible for lawyers to reformulate these two 'ethics' in terms of the distinction between law and equity, both of which inform justice. So it appears that the gendered female voice

21

identified by Gilligan already speaks in law. Yet other writers object that the presentation of two very different voices, and the attachment of gender to them, is the continued reification or dualisms from which we are trying to escape. As long as the male–female dichotomy remains in place the female will be constituted as inferior.[41]

There is lively contention that we can learn from mothering and other female gender activities. Robin West emphasizes that women's experiences of relationships are different from those of men, because of connectedness in pregnancy and breast-feeding, and because they are penetrated rather than penetrating in sexual intercourse.[42] However, whether this is the basis for an alternative sense of justice, or for a broader standard encompassing women's experiences, or whether this corresponds to the experiences of all or many women remains in debate. To this may be added the fact that girls are raised primarily by a parent of the same sex, whereas boys have to separate themselves from the nurturer to achieve their individuality.[43] On this has been built a theory of different psyches. Women's sense of self is different from, and their sense of connection to others is greater than, that of men. Therefore, the argument goes, women's sense of justice, their understanding of relationships, provides an alternative model for citizenship to men's. My own position is that these perceived differences are not essential, but cultural. Furthermore, a claim to privilege women's experiences as superior runs the danger of leaving present dichotomies and inequalities in place. But all experiences must be welcomed in political discourse where they have something to add to the conversation.

All this may seem a long way from discussion of *notre citoyen(ne) idéal(e)*. But is the claim that mothers have a capacity for empathy which should inform political life to be taken seriously? Although this is often referred to as maternal thinking, it is not claimed that it is biologically based, but that it arises from experience. In Sara Ruddick's view maternal thought is not just a different set of values or commitments but a different way of thinking altogether, giving 'priority to preserving vulnerable life' and honouring a moral 'style' that makes central the values of humility, good humour and attentiveness to others.[44] Jean Elshtain argues that maternal thinkers might transform public values, and create an ethical polity that will displace the individualism of political discourse.[45] There is reason for scepticism at this vision, especially when placed alongside the prescriptive and implicitly moral language of the judiciary in child custody cases, and of politicians on mothers' duties in the home. But does the vision offer something none the less?

I have already argued that current family structures are unfair, excluding those who want to create family relationships but are denied the capacity to do so legally, perpetuating an unfair sex/gender system, and educating children in injustice. It is true that a close relationship with children, the possibility of becoming a maternal thinker, is women's compensation for subordination. But surely if nurturing has something to offer citizenship, men should be encouraged to do it too. To argue otherwise is to return to a biologistic position. As Jean Grimshaw says, what is likely is 'that the principles on which they [women] act are not recognised (especially by men) as valid or important ones', but not that women's moral reasoning is sharply opposed to that of men.[46] If experiences gained from nurturing are to alter political life it is likely to be on the basis of conceptions of equality and liberty which recognize that the content of these principles is not given, but open to debate, and that women's understandings of vulnerabilities, based on their own experiences, may give them concerns that must be of equal account.

Cultural feminism of the 'pro-family' variety is not without its critics. Mary Dietz has argued that mothering is the wrong model for citizenship as it is based on an inequality of power between the helpless infant and the nurturer. If *égalité* is what we seek, then citizenship is an activity where

> human beings can collectively and inclusively relate to one another not as strong over weak, fast over slow, master over apprentice, or mother over child, but as equals who render judgments on matters of shared importance, deliberate over issues of common concern, and act in concert with one another.[47]

But in her concern with democratic citizenship Dietz overlooks the reordering of priorities which is the advantage that a focus on nurturing might bring to political deliberations. It is also not clear how we are to be transformed into equals. Must maternal thinkers learn to think in another way? How will this help the attainment of equality? If we go along with Dietz in rejecting mothering as a model for citizenship, we are still left with the present problem of inequality. Furthermore, the idea that experiences of mothering can bring to political life qualities at present lacking remains in play; for if mothers' voices are heard in debate their values may become recognized.

FINDING OR FIGHTING OUR WAY TO THE CITY?

Thus far this chapter might seem to have entered a bind. On the one side gender perspectives are relevant, mothering might teach us new priorities, alternative feminist conceptions of justice have been valorized. On the other side gender has been a source of injustice, the

traditional legal family form is indicted as exclusionary of other relationships, the construction of individuals as belonging to biologically
opposed categories, and of masculine and feminine ascribed characteristics, has been criticized. The issue of the relevance of gender is still
inscribed. With one bound can we break out of the bind? A way out,
advocated from time to time, is a society in which gender has no more
significance than eye colour.[48] A practical political programme to
give effect to this has been sketched out by theorists and is summarized below.

A minimally gendered society will be one in which prescriptions as
to sex/gender roles are not made. Intimate relationships to which
partners wish to give legal effect will be recognized on an agreed and
voluntary basis. Shared parental responsibility for children will be
assumed and facilitated. Employers will no longer assume that workers
have no family responsibilities, and labour law policies will reflect
a new understanding. Schools will not only cooperate with shared
parenting, but will educate children both as participating citizens and
to value women equally with men.[49] Power, it is believed, will be
shared by partners with a consequent elimination of wife and child
abuse. Values derived from parenting will be recognized by most people. But this utopian vision is not necessarily shared by all victims of
the present sex/gender system.

Critics of standard concepts of Western political thought have, for
some time, been asking, 'whose justice?', 'whose consent?'. One root
of such questions is the experiences women have of domestic life
and child rearing, which are not valorized, and the experience of
sex discrimination in the public worlds of work, politics and law. In
gendered society women are likely to develop different conceptions of
duty, obligation, of all the virtues. The old taunt was that women
were truncated beings whose reason was defective. Cultural feminism
has succeeded in making us see that what is at issue here is conceptions
of self which challenge much of modern Western political writing,
particularly that based on a binary system of oppositions between
body and mind, emotion and reason, private and political, object and
subject. The association of women with the first part of these dualities
and the negative valuing of body, emotion and nature lead to calls for
an integrated self. While different conceptions of selves emerge, there
is also emphasis on the shared experiences, understandings and values
of women as collectives. Giving up women's shared cultures to become
a neutral *citoyenne* in a genderless (or almost) society is not necessarily
seen as practical or desirable by cultural feminists, particularly those
who claim that their vision is superior. But does this have to be? A
debate has developed between those who believe that citizens will
pursue general concerns and those who believe that citizenship will be

about groups working together while retaining their perspectives and identities.[50]

I am not sure that we can achieve general legislation and court decisions which take account of rainbow perspectives, that is which include the viewpoints of those excluded by past practices. First we must listen. On the road to citizenship there has to be a forum in which the silent can be heard. Otherwise, as Iris Young points out, universal citizenship will repeat women's past experiences of being 'incorporated' in the body politic.

> In a society where some groups are privileged while others are
> oppressed, insisting that as citizens persons should leave
> behind their particular affiliations and experiences to adopt a
> general point of view serves only to reinforce that privilege;
> for the perspectives and interests of the privileged will tend to
> dominate this unified public, marginalising or silencing those
> of other groups.[51]

Given the differentiation of society we have to be careful about ideas of the universal. There are some problems here for law, which claims its authority from its general applicability. Scepticism about the generality of present laws and law-making, and consequently about neutrality and universality, is a feature of current legal theory. Whereas the modern era was characterized by belief in the feasibility of the rule of law, with its claims to generality, what we are hearing now is late modern scepticism. The fragmentation of identity that characterizes the recent past creates difficulties of generalization. From this follow doubts about a universal, portmanteau self as the legal individual.

The debate that has taken place on gender among political theorists has come up with some tentative answers. Iris Young uses the American idea of a 'rainbow coalition' as a model whereby groups can work together while retaining their identity, and not be absorbed into the 'establishment view'. In her version of the conversations of citizenship we shall acknowledge others as of equal account, in our common membership of a shared community, while maintaining a group identity. Young's proposal does not insist on universalizability; rather she anticipates claims made on difference, on special needs. These would be agreed upon as a form of compromise, but not necessarily on the basis of some universal application. Whether law, with its tradition of categorization, definition, positivism and generalization, can open up to these conversations remains in question. Such a proposal marks a break with formal notions of equality under the law, although, as we have seen, this formality has not been observed in practice. What it means is the abolition of the ideal of a universal standard, of a unitary model of citizenship and of claims about a single legal subject. The virtue of this approach is that it precludes the smuggling in of one point of view in the voice of the many and questions the existence of a universal model *citoyen(ne)* abstracted from particular characteristics and communities.

The rainbow coalition ideal is contrastable with ideas of abstraction currently used by other theorists to escape the dilemmas of difference and fragmentation. Abandoning the Kantian imperative of universal principles to guide conduct will go hard with philosophers and lawyers. Moving to a level away from individual concerns is the traditional answer. It is sometimes proposed that citizenship should include an obligation of abstraction: a stepping outside one's commitments and seeing one's point of view as one among many; a juxtaposing of other points of view.[52] In this version each person is assumed capable of the virtue of empathy and the judgment of Portia. Putting self-interest aside will be a mark of the citizen. The universalization principle will be retained. This presupposes an Archimedean point of view; someone, most likely a judge, who can decide between competing viewpoints, empathy notwithstanding.

An additional step in the effort to retain universalizability is to a collective sphere of justification in which actions can be challenged, when an infringement of liberty or equality is in question, even though the action stems from personal belief or takes place in private. This, it is suggested, will lead to universalizability.[53] It is true that the ideal of a collective sphere of justification is one way of dealing with the thorny issues of personal belief and conduct in the private sphere. It also moves the discussion away from court-centredness to a political forum. Iris Young[54] and Anne Phillips[55] argue that there should be certain aspects of our lives that we are entitled to treat as private, such as our sexual lives, but that 'we should also be entitled to demonstrate publicly on all sexual issues, and none should be excluded from public discussion as inappropriate or trivial or better suited to the public domain'.[56] It may be that a public calling to account for dominance and cruelty will facilitate generality, as might empathizing with the views of the Other. And the idea that this should be part of general political debate is welcome. But how is the collective standard for judgment to be arrived at? Participants may call upon liberty and equality and base their claims on these. Both concepts may be valued but conceptions thereof may clash. As Steven Lukes says, 'the abstract unity often serves to conceal, and thus tame, real disagreements'.[57] But in public discussion, such as is envisaged to lead to generalization, these disagreements over the meanings of liberty and equality will be out in the open.

The debate that is under way about citizenship, however it is resolved or not resolved, is healthy. We have come some way from dominance and separatism, particularly in the recognition that what goes on in private is relevant to theories of justice. But the issue of the universal against group rights remains unresolved, as is the question of the place of debate: what kind of public forum is in view, or is this a disguised form of court talk? The debate itself has created a space for discussion, a way of opening up concerns such as that of who the legal individual is. For the present there is a gap between the developing language of citizenship and the critique of subjecthood as currently constituted in law and politics. That gap must be closed before citizens can be born.

NOTES AND REFERENCES

This chapter was written during the academic year 1991–92 when I was a Jean Monnet Fellow at the European University Institute, Florence. I wish to thank the Director of the European Cultural Centre and its members for their hospitality. Another version of the work was presented at the meeting of the Interdisciplinary Working Group on Women's Studies in November 1991, coordinated by Dr Valeria Russo. Thanks also to Maurice Glasman and Jeff Weintraub, colleagues at the Social Contract Seminar for reading and commenting on this version.

1 T. H. Marshall, 'Citizenship and social class', in T. H. Marshall, *Class, Citizenship and Social Development*, 1977, p. 78.
2 Not only did Marshall cast civil citizenship in terms of traditional freedoms of speech and property rights, he also did not show any awareness of gender as a problem. For criticisms of the projection of a male perspective in law-making, see K. O'Donovan, 'Defences for battered wives who kill', *Journal of Law and Society*, 1991, Vol. 18, p. 219; N. Naffine, *Law and the Sexes*, 1990.
3 See, for example, J. B. Elshtain, *Public Man, Private Woman: Women in Social and Political Thought*, 1981; S. M. Okin, *Women in Western Political Thought*, 1979; C. Pateman and E. Gross (eds) *Feminist Challenges: Social and Political Theory*, 1987.
4 See, for example, C. MacKinnon, *Feminism Unmodified*, 1987; K. O'Donovan, 'Engendering justice: women's perspectives and the rule of law', *University of Toronto Law Journal*, 1989, Vol. 39, p. 127.
5 C. Pateman, *The Sexual Contract*, 1988.
6 *Ibid.*, p. 184.
7 A. Phillips, 'Citizenship and feminist theory', in G. Andrews (ed.) *Citizenship*, 1991, p. 76.
8 See O'Donovan, note 2. A successful plea of self-defence means that the defendant is considered by the jury to have been justified in killing the deceased. Provocation reduces the offence to manslaughter as a partial excuse. Diminished responsibility

is defined as 'suffering from such abnormality of mind (whether arising from a condition of arrested or retarded development of mind or retarded development of mind or any inherent causes or induced by disease or injury) as substantially impaired his responsibility for his acts or omissions in doing or being a party to the killing', Homicide Act 1957, s.2.

9 W. Blackstone, *Commentaries* (1st edn, 1769, repr. 1966), Book IV, Chapter 14.

10 I have found no examples of successful pleas of self-defence by physically abused wives who kill.

11 C. Wells, 'Domestic violence and self-defence', *New Law Journal*, 1990, Vol. 140, p. 127.

12 V. Seidler, *Rediscovering Masculinity*, 1989; L. Segal, *Slow Motion: Changing Masculinities, Changing Men*, 1990; R. Chapman and J. Rutherford (eds) *Male Order: Unwrapping Masculinity*, 1988.

13 There has been more success in pleading self-defence in American law, which shares a common base with English law. For examples see E. Schneider, 'Describing and changing: women's self-defence work and the problem of expert testimony on battering', *Women's Rights Law Reporter*, 1986, Vol. 9, p. 198.

14 *R. v. Duffy* (1949) 1 All ER 932.

15 In the recent case of *R. v. Thornton, The Independent*, Law Report, 30 July 1991, the court of Appeal (Criminal Division) confirmed that the approach taken in *Duffy* (note 14) would be adhered to.

16 For example, Seidler (note 12) argues that self-control and masculinity have been identified in Western culture since the Enlightenment, and this is a form of separation of intellect and body, of domination of feelings and emotion, of instrumentalism in activities. See Chapter 4 on control.

17 Criminal law has traditionally been sympathetic to jealous husbands who killed their wives or their wives' lovers. But this sympathy was not extended to jealous wives until the case of *Holmes* v. *DPP* (1946) 2 All ER 124, whereas the case of *Regina v. Madding* 83 Eng. Rep. 112 (1793) is evidence of judicial identification with a jealous husband from 250 years earlier. A gender difference, overlooked in the reporting of this discrepancy of judicial sympathy, is that women and men tend to kill their partners for different reasons. For adultery to inspire killing there has to be a notion of proprietory rights over the partner.

18 L. J. Taylor, 'Provoked reason in men and women: heat of passion manslaughter and imperfect self-defence', *University of California Law Review*, 1986, vol. 33, p. 1679.

19 See note 12.

20 H. Allen, *Justice Unbalanced*, 1987.

21 M. Eaton, *Justice for Women? Family Court and Social Control*, 1986.

22 S. Benton, 'Gender, sexuality and citizenship', in G. Andrews (ed.) *Citizenship*, 1991, p. 151.

23 *Ibid.*, p. 155.

24 *Ibid.*, p. 160.

25 C. Pateman, 'Feminist critiques of the public/private dichotomy' in C. Pateman, *The Disorder of Women: Democracy, Feminism and Political Theory*, 1989; J. B. Elshtain, note 3; for law see K. O'Donovan, *Sexual Division in Law*, 1985.

26 For a summary of the human rights implications of the current law and the

argument that it is contrary to the International Covenant on Civil and Political Rights, see P. R. Ghandhi and E. Macnamee, 'The family in UK law and the International Covenant on Civil and Political Rights 1966', *International Journal of Law and the Family*, 1991, vol. 5, p. 104.

27 *Rees* v. *UK* Series A no 106; *Cossey* v *UK* Series A no 184.

28 L. Nielsen, 'Family rights and the "registered partnership" in Denmark', *International Journal of Law and the Family*, 1990, vol. 4, p. 297.

29 *Corbett* v *Corbett* (1971) P 83 at p. 106.

30 B. Jordan, *The Common Good*, 1989, p. 30.

31 S. M. Okin, *Justice, Gender, and the Family*, 1989, Chapter 7.

32 *Plant v Plant* (1983) 4 FLR 310.

33 *B v. B* (1985) FLR 166 at p. 173.

34 *Re S* (1991) 2 FLR 388 at p. 390.

35 See D. Bradley, 'Homosexuality and child custody in English law', *International Journal of Law and the Family*, 1987, Vol. 1, p. 155, at pp. 177–85.

36 S. Hall and D. Held, 'Citizens and citizenship', in S. Hall and M. Jacques (eds) *New Times*, 1989, p. 177.

37 1917. See R. Posner, *Law and Literature*, 1988, Chapter 2.

38 S. Sherry, 'Civic virtue and the feminine voice in constitutional adjudication', *Virginia Law Review*, 1986, Vol. 72, p. 543.

39 C. Gilligan, *In a Different Voice: Psychological Theory and Women's Development*, 1982.

40 C. MacKinnon, as a participant in a debate at which C. Gilligan was present, said: 'Why do women become these people, more than men, who represent these values? For me, the answer is . . . the subordination of women . . . . I'm not saying that taking these values seriously would not transform discourse, which would be a good thing under any circumstances of gender. She has also found the voice of the victim – yes, women are a victimized group.' From 'Feminist discourse, moral values, and the law – a conversation', *Buffalo Law Review*, 1985, Vol. 34, p. 50.

41 S. J. Hekman, *Gender and Knowledge*, 1990, Chapter 1.

42 R. West, 'Jurisprudence and gender', *University of Chicago Law Review*, 1988, Vol. 55, p. 1.

43 N. Chodorow, *The Reproduction of Mothering: Psychoanalysis and the Sociology of Gender*, 1978.

44 S. Ruddick, 'Maternal thinking', *Feminist Studies*, 1980, No. 6.

45 Note 3.

46 J. Grimshaw, *Philosophy and Feminist Thinking*, 1986, p. 210.

47 M. Dietz, 'Citizenship with a feminist face: the problem with maternal thinking', *Political Theory*, 1985, No. 13.

48 A. Jagger, 'On sexual equality', *Ethics*, 1974, No. 84, p. 285.

49 Okin, note 31.

50 Dietz, note 47; I. Young, 'Polity and group difference: a critique of the ideal of universal citizenship', *Ethics*, 1989, No. 99, p. 250; Phillips, note 7.

51 Young, note 50, at p. 257.

52 S. Lukes, Seminar on Rawls, 6 March 1992, European University Institute, Florence.

53 M. Glasman, Seminar on Rawls, 6 March 1992, European University Institute, Florence.

54 I. M. Young, 'Impartiality and civic public', in Benhabib and Cornell (eds), *Feminism as Critique*, 1987.

55 Phillips, note 7.

56 Phillips, note 7, at p. 85.

57 S. Lukes, *Moral Conflict and Politics*, 1991, p. 66.

2

Citizenship and Privacy

PATRICK BIRKINSHAW

PROBLEMS ABOUT PRIVACY

What problems do the concept and practice of 'privacy' pose for citizenship? In my view, they pose considerable problems for democratic states, particularly the British state. Citizenship connotes a bundle of rights and duties, obligations and privileges. The source of these rights and duties is the state, that institution representing the official and public side of our human affairs. The formal content of the state is represented by such bodies as the Crown, the Government, Parliament, the army, the police and so on. The body that provides these rights may also invade these rights. If citizenship is to mean anything, then there should be adequate protection against such invasion unless it is clearly justified. For this reason we commonly provide a private space, a sphere of inviolability which is ours alone unless we choose to share it or allow others to enter. In contradistinction to this private sphere, there is a public sphere to our existence in which our collective or community interests are debated, selected, implemented, acted upon and enforced. This public sphere, which we may term government, consistently claims that it has its own private sphere which those over whom it exercises its public power, citizens, have either no right to enter or the right to enter only on terms strictly defined by itself. Simply expressed, the argument of government, or governors, is that people's citizenship does not give them the right to be informed about the private government of public business.

Citizenship involves a sense of community and one's membership of that community – a community bounded by space, territorial extent and cultural and traditional heritage. In a community there are limits to each individual's potential or actual isolation from others, for

'No man is an island, entire of itself.'[1] There are practical limits to the realization of the desire to be 'let alone'. Enforcement of laws and the genuine public interest may well necessitate an invasion of the private sphere; conversely, to treat individuals not as citizens but as mere subjects whose private sphere only exists at the grace and favour of a sovereign power is to deprive citizenship of any, or any worthwhile, integrity or meaning. Nor does the threat to the private sphere only come from those acting under the sovereign power. Invasion of another's private sphere may be profitable, or worthwhile, for other private, i.e. non-state actors. This is especially so where there are items of, or which foment, salacious gossip and scandal and where the prurient interest of a sector of the community can be fanned by an intrusive and irresponsible press and media in their search for financial profit. Or invasion may simply be motivated by malice.

The privacy of citizens in their private spheres, and the privacy of government in the public sphere, do not exhaust our inquiry. An additional important concern is the need to expose to scrutiny the private sphere of those who conduct the public business of government, not so that the process of government is exposed but rather so that they are exposed; that their fitness for office is beyond question and seen to be so. In their case, it may be argued, invasion is necessary in a manner which would not usually be justified in the case of a citizen's private sphere. We want to ensure, or to be assured, that they are capable and fit to conduct public business at the level of office to which they have been appointed.

Around all these 'publics' and 'privates' various problems fasten. First, how satisfactorily has British law protected that sphere of inviolability which elsewhere is known as a right to privacy? Second, has the law drawn a suitable distinction between such a right and the public's right to know about a private life – to invade the private sphere? Third, is there sufficient access to the private sphere of activity carried out on behalf of the public, i.e. government? I will deal with these questions in this order, concentrating upon the first and third questions.

PERSONAL PRIVACY

English law allows no remedy for an invasion of privacy *per se*. The fact that no remedy is given means that there is no right to privacy. Our Government has bound itself to international agreements which provide some protection to privacy as well as access to information – most notably Articles 8 (privacy) and 10 (information) of the European Convention on Human Rights (ECHR) and the Recommendation of the Committee of Ministers of the Council of Europe on Access to

Information Held by Public Authorities (Rec. No. R (81) 19). As other contributors point out, the provisions of international law are invoked by our courts as aids to interpret domestic legislation and to develop common law, but they do not override domestic legislation or common law. British judges, at least, have been unpersuaded by the arguments put forward over one hundred years ago by the American jurists Warren and Brandeis that the precedents, many of them English, established a right to privacy as a discrete item of common law.[2] Their work had a seminal impact in encouraging the development of the tort of invasion of privacy in the USA and other common law jurisdictions. As we are so often reminded by English judges, they prefer a pragmatic and incremental development of common law, not a sudden, albeit rational, development or exposition of principle. In its own way, and although no one would deny that privacy is a particularly thorny concept for law to grapple with, the failure adequately to address the problem of privacy reveals contemporary English common law at its weakest, both in terms of technique and as a protector of civil liberties.

Both these deficiencies are related to a concept of property determining legal development. Insofar as privacy may be protected, such protection has been seen as a corollary of a property right, unlike the law of confidentiality, which possesses hybrid property and personal features. The particular concept of property is one fashioned to protect real estate and tangibles, not a person's – any person's – integrity.[3] The property right is developed from the notion of trespass. So, for instance, even when the Secretary of State wished, through his servant Carrington, to seize an individual's papers at will and randomly, the common law would not interpret an unspecified or general warrant to enter, search and seize as authority for such action. A right to such invasion was unknown to the common law. The judgment of Lord Camden in *Entick* v *Carrington*[4] was a proud statement; today, it appears as a swan-song, as Parliament has provided statutory powers to give what the common law refused,[5] and indeed the judiciary have interpreted statutes in a manner to provide such powers.[6] Cases involving improper use of the highway, nuisance and damage to one's property rights in the form of copyright, 'passing off' or damage to reputation or good name under defamation or malicious falsehood afford degrees of protection to proprietary rights, but they are not directly concerned with privacy.[7] In terms of civil liberties, this is a striking example of the common law's inability to protect those civil rights which are not in proprietary form. Indeed, it is a dramatic illustration of the residuary nature of civil liberties in Britain; what the law does not prohibit an individual may do – even if that means an invasion of another's privacy.[8]

33

The problem, which accounts in Britain at least for the judicial reluctance to fashion a remedy for wrongful invasion of privacy, has been the complexity of the subject, a subject which has spawned a variety of official reports and numerous Private Member's Bills. Sir Nicolas Browne-Wilkinson (Calcutt, Cm.1102 para. 12.10, 1990) put the matter well when he said:

> I think it is extremely difficult for a legal system to apply a general concept of privacy, because it is hard to distinguish what is meant by it. On the other hand, it seems to me impossible to draw a comprehensive list of those things which, in any one society, are to be treated as private. As a legal technician, I would be unhappy dealing with the law of privacy.

This has not prevented the United States, in the *Restatement, 2d, Torts*, para. 652A, defining a right of privacy as follows:

(1) One who invades the right of privacy of another is subject to liability for the resulting harm to the interests of the other.
(2) The right of privacy is invaded by
    (a) unreasonable intrusion upon the seclusion of another . . .; or
    (b) appropriation of the other's name or likeness . . .; or
    (c) unreasonable publicity given to the other person's life . . .; or
    (d) publicity that unreasonably places the other in a false light before the public.

For a judge who adjudicated on so many claims of breach of confidentiality, it is a little surprising that Sir Nicolas felt such reluctance in what is often a cognate area to privacy, albeit one protected by pre-existing duties, express or implied, rather than by a more overt appeal to *ex post facto* ratiocination.[9] However, it is not only British judges who feel a reluctance to fashion appropriate remedies for invasions of privacy. Government-appointed committees have thought the subject an inappropriate topic to define in general terms as a basis for legislative protection. This was the view of the Younger Committee (Cmnd 5012, 1972), which was concerned with the private sector, and the Calcutt Committee of 1990, which was primarily concerned about the excesses of the press following numerous abuses and a variety of 'last chance' warnings from Parliament to get its own house in order. 'A general wrong of infringement of privacy . . . would give rise to an unacceptable degree of uncertainty' (Calcutt, Cm. 1102, para. 12.12). However, Calcutt gave some support to the possibility of a tort of invasion of privacy that was specifically related to the unauthorized publication of personal information, including photographs.

> Personal information could be defined in terms of an individual's personal life, that is to say, those aspects of life which reasonable members of society would respect as being such that an individual is usually entitled to keep them to himself, whether or not they relate to his mind or body, to his home, his family, or to other relationships, or to his correspondence or documents. (para. 12.17)

The committee had strong reservations about a general defence of public interest – although one exists in the law of confidentiality – preferring the defence for 'justified disclosure' to be specifically and tightly drawn and for the definition of personal information to be developed by judicial interpretation. Interestingly, Calcutt did not believe that such a development would be the thin end of a wedge whereby a government could introduce censorship through the pretext of privacy protection. Neither was there any need to introduce a Freedom of Information Act to balance protection of privacy, or to provide a guarantee for freedom of speech. In fact, the committee was anxious to persuade its audience that investigative journalism would not be inhibited and Article 10 of the ECHR – which protects free-dom of speech and the right to impart and receive information – would not operate against a right to privacy. It is, however, difficult to reconcile investigative journalism with the English tradition of 'prior restraint' – preventing publication by judicial order – and the Committee's reference to case law in defamation where prior restraint was not usually imposed is not really to the point. A more precise analogy would be with the law of confidentiality, not defamation.[10] In confidentiality, the courts are more favourably inclined to allow interim injunctions to preserve a status quo, i.e. to enforce prior restraint on publication.[11] Calcutt also recommended the creation of specific criminal offences related to the concept of trespass, which would be aimed at an over-intrusive press.

In the light of the Committee's support for a self-regulatory scheme, and its lack of enthusiasm for a general right to privacy, the Govern-ment opted not to introduce any criminal amendments but preferred a 'last chance' for the press to regulate itself. A probationary period of non-statutory self-regulation would last until July 1992, after which the position would be reviewed. Under self-regulation – and it can take many forms – both sides are seen to win: the Government in that it extracts a commitment from the interest concerned under pain of the threat of legislation if the self-regulatory scheme does not prove satisfactory; the interest group insofar as it is still left with a large degree of autonomy in the conduct of its own business, in the maintenance of standards and in its control over, and enforcement of, discipline – it is still seen to be its own master. The interest is then left to devise, or to accept, a code of practice which it enforces. Self-regulatory schemes are staple fare in the British state and fall under the general legal rubric of reflexive legal processes, whereby the role of formal law as set out in legislatures and applied by the courts fulfils the enabling and residuary task of recognizing and approving the existence of organized self-regulatory groups and ensuring that they adopt *modi operandi* which are proper and above board in the manner in which they regulate their allotted spheres.[12] This development raises interesting constitutional and civil liberties questions as many of the most important decisions affecting our interests are decided not by government but by 'hybrids' operating between the state and civil society, very often as a consequence of government encouragement and effective delegation of public tasks. I have no doubt that the terms of such delegation and the accompanying 'deals' raise items in which citizens have a profound interest; such matters are all too frequently regarded, however, as private compacts and not as subjects in which the public has any rights, let alone a right to know.

The press, then, operates under a non-statutory Press Complaints Commission established in 1991, which enforces a Code of Practice. This it applies in the spirit as well as the letter. It goes well beyond the existing law. 'All members of the Press', it rather piously intones, 'have a duty to maintain the highest professional and ethical standards.' Editors are responsible for the actions of their journalists and they must ensure that material obtained from non-staff members was obtained in accordance with the code. The code stipulates duties: to be accurate, to provide a fair opportunity of reply, to distinguish between comment, conjecture and fact, to invade privacy only when justified in the public interest (see p. 41 on 'celebrities'); on how to deal with patients in hospitals, on misrepresentation and harassment, intrusion into grief or shock, identifying innocent relatives and friends, interviewing or photographing children, treatment of children in cases of sexual abuse and their identity, not to identify victims of crime and avoidance of discrimination.

The success of the special pleadings of the press may be assessed by the fact that although the Chairman is independent, the press or press-influenced bodies easily outweigh those without such links in its membership. Any person may complain to the Commission, but it does not conduct oral hearings and there is no formal conciliation procedure.

Furthermore, two specific proposals of Calcutt were rejected: the 'hotline' procedure and the 'fast track' procedure. In the former it was envisaged that complainants would have access to editors via the Commission, and in the latter case significant factual errors could be corrected expeditiously. The Commission has no power to fine a newspaper or to award compensation and it has no power to insist that newspapers publish an adverse 'adjudication' – its powers are restricted to censuring a newspaper or a journalist. If the non-statutory regime does not work, the Government has threatened to establish a statutory body (but see p. 50). The Broadcasting Complaints Commission is a statutory body that deals *inter ilia* with complaints of unwarranted infringements of privacy by broadcasters. It must be remembered, of course, that except in the case of direct satellite broadcasting, broadcasters have to be franchised and licensed by the Independent Television Commission or the Radio Authority, or, in the case of the BBC, chartered by the Crown.[13]

Privacy and Access to Personal Documents

In several common law jurisdictions, a Privacy Act or similar legislation allows individuals a right of access to personal information held upon them by public authorities. The Conservative Governments of 1979–92 were stubbornly resistant to a general right of access by a 'subject' to documents held on him or her where they take manual form[14] – whether held by public or private bodies. It should be noted that in the USA, Canada and Australia, access laws only cover the public sector. One of the most controversial aspects of this subject concerns the activities of those bodies that collect and sell information on prospective employees so that they can be blacklisted by prospective employers.[15] Much of the public sector, and certainly central government, is not covered by legislation, so individuals have no right of access to such records. In some areas, a specific right exists under legislation: health records, school records, housing records and social service records, for example.

The position is different when we come to computerized personal records. Our international obligations forced upon the Government – with dire commercial consequences if they had not legislated – the Data Protection Act 1984 (DPA). This imposes on both the public sector and the private sector, certain duties in relation to those who hold computerized information about identifiable individuals. Data users have to register with the Data Protection Registrar (DPR). Copies of the register are maintained in major public libraries on microfiche. This contains information about the identity of the user, the personal data held and the purposes for which they are held or used, the sources from where the user may obtain the information in the data, persons to whom the data may be disclosed and overseas countries or territories to which the data may be transferred. Holding personal data without registration is a criminal offence. The DPR is empowered to require data users to comply with the Data Protection Principles, which cover the obtaining, use, processing and holding of data. The DPR is a regulator, an ombudsman and an enforcer of the law and data principles. Subjects have rights of access to the data held on them and a variety of remedies where the data are inaccurate or in breach of the law and guidelines. There are three classes of exemption for data, which may result in data being excluded completely from the Act, exemptions from the non-disclosure provisions, i.e. data can be disclosed to persons other than identified recipients, and subject access exemptions. Users, but not subjects, may appeal to the Data Protection Tribunal against adverse decisions of the DPR.

I stated above that the DPA was not introduced to strengthen civil liberties; its origins were pragmatism and commercial necessity. The law seems certain to be modified, in some respects rather substantially, by the Draft European Directive on Data Protection (Com. (90) 314 final SYN 287 and 288). This, the Commission optimistically hoped, would be applied by 1 January 1993; it has been followed in fact by a further draft. It raises very important questions about protection of privacy in the single European market and beyond; in fact, the USA is very concerned about the Directive's implications for its own privacy protection laws, which will need considerable amendment if the USA is to receive personal data from EC states. It seeks to harmonize DP law, providing a strict and comprehensive DP law to be followed in each member state.

The Directive has two objectives: the protection of privacy of individuals in relation to the processing of personal data, and ensuring that member states shall neither restrict nor prohibit the free flow of personal data between themselves for reasons to do with the protection afforded to individuals. The further draft of 1992 (Com. (92) 422 Fin., SYN 287) drops the formal distinction between the rules applying in the public and private sectors and expands the provision on the procedures for notification to the supervisory authority and on codes of conduct. The DPR has said that the Directive as drafted introduces the concept of privacy, which is not used in the DPA and which, furthermore, is not a part of British law; it would give more knowledge to individuals about how information on them was used; it would give greater control to individuals over the collection and control of information concerning them; and it would introduce compensation rights greater than those under the Act. 'The result would be to provide enhanced protection for individuals.' The DPR felt that the original draft goes too far, as it will apply extensively to manual data whereas the British approach has been 'piecemeal', and that there was unnecessary bureaucracy attached to registration provisions; the movement in the UK, the DPR observed, was to relax registration. Furthermore, the proposal to notify the subject whenever data were given to a third party was too onerous. Finally, codes of practice had been drawn up by various organizations under the DPA. The DPR was concerned that proposals to allow the Commission to endorse codes of practice were acceptable if following that model; if, however, they were allowed to act as surrogates and replacements for statutory schemes, that was not acceptable.[16]

The DPA is entering an interesting phase. The subject access provisions have been operative for over four years and complaints to the DPR amounted to 2698 in 1988–9, and 2419 in 1989–90. There are over 160,000 registered user entries. However, only 38 per cent of the public had heard of the Act and the awareness of the fact that registration was required had from 1986 decreased among small company users quite significantly: 70 per cent in 1986, only 51 per cent in 1990 and an increase to 62 per cent in 1991.[17] Crucially, decisions of the DPR on enforcement are coming up on appeal to the tribunal and in these decisions a more subject-sympathetic approach is being taken than is envisaged in the Preamble to the DPA, which talks of regulation of automatically processed data relating to individuals without reference to protection of individuals, as in the draft Directive.[18]

The DPR's report gives a good idea of the problems posed by an increasingly obtrusive state and the balance that has to be struck between privacy protection and investigation. Of particular interest are the plans for a DNA database from genetic material which could be recorded in the same way as fingerprints; the Home Affairs Committee of the Commons has suggested a DNA profile database on the whole male population, a suggestion supported by the Metropolitan Police Commissioner. Under the Child Support Act 1991, which seeks to ensure that fathers contribute to the maintenance of their children, the Child Support Agency and Child Support Officers will have wide powers to gather information under regulations. It will not be subject to the first DP principle, i.e. obtained lawfully and processed fairly and lawfully.

More generally, the state has invaded the privacy of the client and professional adviser in areas as diverse as auditing, banking, medicine and social work.[19] Parliament has removed, subject to judicial control, any privilege that may have existed between a journalist and an informer in specified circumstances.[20] Where serious fraud investigations and insolvency investigations take place under the Criminal Justice Act 1987 and the Insolvency Act 1986, the person investigated has lost the right against self-incrimination by remaining silent.[21] A right of this nature under English law was claimed in dramatic circumstances by the Maxwell brothers when they were questioned by the Commons Social Security Committee about unlawful interference with employees' pension funds by Robert Maxwell.[22] Only the legal profession and their clients possess a privileged relationship. No Fourth Amendment, or its equivalent, exists to prevent prosecutors putting forward evidence seized unlawfully; it is a matter of judicial discretion.[23] On the more positive side, though it is heavily qualified, interception of phone calls and correspondence, and surveillance involving trespass and what would otherwise constitute criminal acts by the Security Service, have to be authorized by warrant under statute, and the information acquired by the Security Service has to be collected and used according to safeguards under legislation.[24] In all these cases, the reason why such invasions of privacy are authorized, if I may call them such, is obvious. National security and prevention of serious crime may justify emergency measures. Emergency measures require safeguards. While safeguards have improved, we are still left in too many cases with inadequate protection, not least in relation to the absence of democratic oversight of the activities of the security, intelligence and Special Branch services.[25] This is undoubtedly a result of our version of citizenship not taking rights seriously, or more correctly taking our liberties too easily.

GETTING TO KNOW YOU BETTER

Under what circumstances, and with what safeguards, are we justified in invading privacy not to investigate crime or threats to public order, national security or economic well-being, but rather to protect the vulnerable or to protect citizenship generally? Or as Article 8 of the European Convention on Human Rights has it, to protect health or morals, or to protect the rights and freedoms of others. Article 8 in effect stipulates that there shall be no interference by a public authority with the right to privacy, except to the extent that interference is in accordance with the law and is necessary in a democratic society to protect those things which constitute the necessary foundations of democracy.

The formulation in Article 8 makes sense and is a useful starting point. The Commission and Court have emphasized the balance that has to be struck between a right to privacy and the wider rights of the community or other individuals, so that, for instance, restrictions on a right to abortion are not necessarily an *interference* with a right to respect for one's private life. Indeed, the Commission has held that Article 8 was wider than the Anglo-Saxon and French concept of privacy, i.e. a right to live as far as one wishes, protected from publicity. It also comprises 'to a certain degree, the right to establish and to develop relationships with other human beings, especially in the emotional field for the development and fulfilment of one's own personality'.[26]

The regulatory state requires ever more information and intrusive investigation into individuals in sensitive, vulnerable, corruptible or responsible positions. Compulsory drug-testing for train drivers, airline pilots, public vehicle drivers or other public employees has been supported as a justifiable practice. In the United States, for example, random urine analysis tests have been upheld against constitutional challenges based upon the right to privacy and Fourth Amendment safeguards.[27] What of vetting procedures for security officials and other classes of civil servants – procedures which were in fact changed in July 1990?[28] Independent judicial safeguards, under both domestic and European law, offer very limited protection against adverse vetting decisions, although the safeguards in Articles 8 and 10 have to be established to the satisfaction of the Commission and Court of Human Rights.[29] These contain provisions allowing at wide margin of appreciation for respondent states in balancing national security and individual privacy. However, one should not overlook Article 17, which, although it is rarely resorted to, can allow a significant escape route for respondent states. This denies protection to actions that are aimed at the destruction of any of the rights and freedoms under the Convention, or their limitation to a greater extent than is otherwise provided for in the Convention. Vetting for individuals who work with children involves a system of police checks that started in 1988 and takes up to twelve weeks.[30]

Do we possess adequate information on those who serve in public office? The courts do seem to accept that those in the public spotlight have exposed themselves to additional attention and must accept the glare of public scrutiny.[31] Is there any reason, on the other hand, why public figures should not have their privacy protected in the same manner, and to the same extent, as those who are not in the limelight? We should recall that in Britain there is inadequate protection for the latter. In the run-up to the 1992 general election, the Chairman of the Press Complaints Commission urged the press to recognize 'the dangerous consequences in the pre-election period of mixing political reporting with irrelevant commentaries upon the private lives of political figures'.[32] The press sensed a danger here. The fact that a leading politician is having, or had, an adulterous affair is a newsworthy item in a way that it would not be where it concerns an unknown individual. Certainly, a more robust view had been adopted by the Commission previously over revelations involving MPs. The Commission's Code of Practice states that enquiries into a person's

41

private life without consent are justifiable on the grounds of public interest. When Clare Short MP complained in 1991 of an invasion of privacy, the Commission stated:

> the circumstances in the life of an MP may bear on her
> conduct of that office or fitness for it. The Commission agrees
> that it is proper for such matters to be inquired into and
> published in the public interest. Mere passage of time, even
> for many years, does not necessarily diminish their relevance
> or the justification for publication.

It is not entirely clear how the Code's definition of public interest squares with this ruling. Clause 4 of the Code defines the public interest as 'detecting or exposing crime, serious misdemeanour or anti-social conduct, protecting public health, and preventing the public from being misled'. The only possible protection for the individual might then be resort to the law of confidentiality and defamation.

Interestingly, the Court of Appeal has revealed a more liberal attitude to freedom of the press in a case, not involving a public figure, which shows quite clearly the influence of the European Convention on Human Rights on freedom of speech. The case concerned an application by a local authority for an injunction to restrain a newspaper publishing a story about a fifteen-year-old ward of court, who had been subjected to persistent homosexual abuse and who had subsequently been fostered with two homosexual men who had a long-standing and stable relationship. The Court of Appeal overruled the judge at first instance and allowed a national newspaper to publish a story of these events, even to the extent of publishing the identity of the local authority but not of the parties concerned. Even in a matter as sensitive as the placing of a ward, the court none the less had to balance the great importance attaching to freedom of the press – especially as influenced by the ECHR Article 10 – and restrictions imposed to protect children. The Court held that it

> will weigh the need to protect the ward from harm against
> the right of the press (or other outside parties) to publish or
> to comment. An important factor will be the nature and
> extent of the public interest in the matter which it is sought
> to publish. A distinction can be drawn between cases of mere
> curiosity and cases where the press are giving information or
> commenting about a subject of genuine public interest.[33]

The Court was prepared to accept this even though it might lead to limited local knowledge of the parties involved and to distress in the child. Only in exceptional circumstances would the latter be sufficient to restrain publication.

Article 10's liberalizing spirit upon the common law was also evidenced in *Derbyshire CC* v. *Times Newspapers Ltd*, when both the Court of Appeal and the House of Lords held that public bodies may not sue for libel but rather should be open to uninhibited public criticism.[34] The House of Lords, however, placed less emphasis upon Article 10 than did the Court of Appeal.

In terms of individuals in public office, there should be a right to reveal that which it is in the public interest to know, not that which is of idle interest to the public. It is in the public interest where it reveals unfitness for office, or raises serious questions about fitness if facts remained secret, in that the person is a liar or a cheat, or prone to blackmail or illegitimate influence, or is seriously lacking in judgment or necessary ability. And here, let it be noted, the Lord Chancellor has stated that he does not have a policy not to appoint homosexual judges: 'their sexual orientation and behaviour is a matter of the individual circumstances'.[35]

The processes behind judicial appointments are particularly discreet, not to say opaque, in England. The spectre of Clarence Thomas before the Senate Judicial Committee hearings, which were examining his Presidential nomination to the US Supreme Court in 1991, may have been a particularly American episode in openness and political melodrama, almost as if fashioned to rivet prime-time TV. The Establishment view on this side of the Atlantic was that the proceedings lacked decorum and taste and were singularly inappropriate for eminent judicial candidates. Such proceedings are, however, beneficial to ensure that candidates of the right calibre are put up for office. This prompts the thought that the Thomas episode was really about a lack of trust between President and Congress, and improper sounding out of Supreme Court candidates between the branches of government. This resulted in distrust and recrimination when the Senate felt it was asked to approve a candidate whose record, many suggested, did not justify such an elevated position. Crucially, the procedure adopted helped to expose these reservations.

Finally, and with a brevity belittling the importance of the topic, are we provided with adequate information about our elected representatives? Should we have compulsory statutory registers of interests for MPs as there are provisions for a register for councillors in local goverment? Are we sufficiently informed about lobbyists' connections in Parliament?[36]

FREEDOM OF INFORMATION AND OPEN GOVERNMENT

The third question I posed at the outset was the extent to which citizens had a right of access to government information, or, putting it another way, to what extent can government claim that the business of running the country is a private affair? Is the quality of citizenship in any way impaired by the absence of access to information legislation? Are people being treated as less than full citizens in being denied access to information or by not being permitted to observe governmental processes?

I have long taken the view that the existence of such legislation, or its absence, is an insight into how seriously a society takes democracy. The view that the democratic process begins and ends with the ballot box is acceptable if a society has recently progressed from a state of affairs where even that safeguard was not present. It is a poor realization of democracy, however, if that is the only justification and legitimization for the exercise of power over others. That the British political system is notoriously secretive is a much repeated truism, as is the assertion that Britain is not a very democratic state. All governments are prone to secrecy, Britain's more transparently so than most. The reform of the Official Secrets Act in 1989 confirmed the degree to which the Government placed greater faith in the maintenance of secrecy rather than the provision of information to those whom it governs. Our feudal legacies and prerogatives have ensured unelected tiers of government in crucial areas of our public life, irrespective, of course, of the vast array of non-departmental bodies or quangos and advisory bodies that occupy the space between the ceremonially public sector and civil society.

Many countries that are at comparable stages of economic and social development to our own have enacted laws allowing citizens, and indeed non-nationals, access to information held by public bodies. What is provided is a presumptive right of access.[37] Surveying the Freedom of Information (FOI) legislation that does exist one can detect common patterns in what is exempted: information damaging to national security, to international relations, jeopardizing the process of criminal investigation or law enforcement, unjustifiable interference with personal privacy, commercial or economic confidences, information which is still 'live' in the policy-making process and so on. What will be useful will be an exploration of the reasons that have been used in a British context to justify the non-introduction of FOI at central government level, and to see how convincing they are and what they tell us about our governors' perception of citizenship.

First, it has been argued, FOI is irrelevant and unnecessary. The argument runs that we have representative democracy, parliamentary government and ministerial responsibility. Information is released all the time through Green Papers, White Papers, press releases, statements and questions in the House, appearances before Select Committees, Ombudsman reports, departmental annual reports and so on. Even assuming that such practices are as open and informative as government claims, the balance is drawn very firmly in the executive's favour. There is no method, all too often, to check the accuracy of answers in the House; the Government refuses to answer an extensive range of topics; the timing of release and the content is at the government's discretion; civil servants have a lengthy list of subjects on which they must not answer questions without reference to their Ministers, who can veto the appearance of civil servants before the Committees and, indeed, in the case of Mrs Thatcher, refuse to attend herself. MPs have no right of access to departmental documents in their individual capacity, nor indeed in their role as Select Committees – they may call for and request papers in Committee, but they cannot compel. Where a committee views papers in a department it does not have the right to take them; in the investigation into the sinking of the *Belgrano* the papers viewed in the Ministry of Defence had to be recollected by the collective memory of the Committee when back in Westminster.[38] More recently – early in 1992 to be precise – witnesses before Committees, both private citizens and civil servants,[39] have frustrated the investigations of Committees by pleading a right to silence, in a manner reminiscent of Colonel Oliver North pleading the Fifth Amendment before the Congressional Committee investigating the Irangate episode. This is a challenge to the idea of parliamentary supremacy but the cumbersome method of enforcing the giving of evidence – basically a vote in support from the whole House – would have become a party political issue long before any such vote was taken.

Furthermore, the movement to executive agencies will have a major impact upon the 'British way' of conducting government. This will take, it was originally predicted, up to 480,000 civil servants (by March 1992, the number was 220,000) away from Westminster and central departments and into executive agencies with devolved responsibilities under a chief executive. Ministerial responsibility will certainly need to be recast as chief executives assume greater responsibility for programme implementation and policy formulation, with the distinct possibility of inadequate constitutional safeguards.[40]

In short, the first argument is not made out. It is true that the Select Committee on the Parliamentary Commissioner for Administration and the Public Accounts Committee are served by expert officers who have almost (although this is more true of the latter) untrammelled access to departmental files. I would not deny that there are occasions when access is best restricted to elected representatives and even to an officer of the House – the Comptroller and Auditor General, for instance, and the Chair of the Public Accounts Committtee alone.[41] But, as things stand, too much turns on the 'grace and favour' of government and its total control over the provision of information to the House.[42]

The second objection would relate to the assertion that FOI would interfere with the efficiency of government and its effectiveness. Quite frankly, this argument has no support from the evidence of those countries where FOI operates. Organizing sections of administration to facilitate responses to requests from citizens for information about their government and its operations is a small price to pay for treating citizens as citizens and not as subjects. In fact, it can have the beneficial effect for government of forcing departments and agencies to index their information efficiently, as Sir Douglas Wass has argued.[43] On the argument from efficiency and effectiveness, I have long taken the view that effectiveness precedes efficiency.[44] The latter is concerned with the relationship between input and output in programme and service delivery – achieving a given level of output for a certain input. Effectiveness concerns the meeting of overall objectives, or, to formulate it differently, meeting a required level of outcome. Being efficiently ineffective is the route to disaster. To assess effectiveness, one has to know the criteria and objectives, how these objectives were established and why they were preferred to other objectives. Effectiveness has to be judged and judged independently and so does efficiency; hence the important debate over systems of inspection and the independence of inspectorates.[45] It is not adequate simply to allow inspectorates access if there is a question over their independence; nor is there any reason in principle why the public, and especially interest groups, should not have access to the data on which inspections are based. Notorious scandals have been uncovered in the USA under FOI legislation and have concerned environmental and commercial regulation. These have been uncovered by the press and the public. No one could seriously argue that this was a denial of the democratic process, rather a vindication of it. Furthermore, a Whistleblower's Charter exists in the USA to protect federal employees who reveal information about waste, corruption, inefficiency and danger to public safety and health in their programmes. They are protected against the disciplinary consequences of their actions, and the laws were reinforced in 1989 after President Reagan's earlier opposition. In other words, the official preserve on information is not paramount as it is in the UK.

The third objection is that FOI subverts the democratic process. This objection can take a variety of forms. The first formulation argues that representative democracy will be undermined. Special interest groups will be equipped more effectively to lobby and press for their causes. The consultation processes involved in the making of regulations and legislation are notoriously opaque and exclusive in the

UK, with none of the safeguards that exist in the USA, such as the Federal Advisory Committee Act or the safeguards against *ex parte* contacts – communications by or with one interested party only to the exclusion of others. There is simply too much scope for privileged access, preferential treatment and lop-sided domination by sectional interests. Any political system is going to face problems arising from effective interest group domination and 'capture' of official organs of government and, in all likelihood, can never eradicate them. This is certainly an issue that needs to be addressed in the European Community, where the Commission encourages interest group representations to be made to it and where processes of consultation operate in confidence and without FOI. Vital committees of the European Parliament sit *in camera* with no provision for public access. These are points which must be addressed, and the Maastricht Treaty has made a start. At least FOI, and related legislation on open government, addresses the problem of what may be termed 'exclusivity' in representative democratic states, i.e. the domination of private interest groups in the political and executive processes. The other side of this argument states that it is simply wrong to allow bodies outside government to amass vast amounts of information from government holdings, and indeed in circumstances where it is better indexed than it was in government hands to the extent that government utilizes the privately held facility.[46] There in no denying that FOI laws, like all laws, can be abused – which is not to say that the previous example constitutes an abuse. But no one can respectably argue that because freedom of speech may be abused, it should therefore be abolished. The remedy is in vigilance, education and satisfactory remedies against abuse. A justifiable measure would include differential charges for the exercise of access rights, so that scholars are charged lesser fees than commercial users, with the press and possibly public interest groups at the lower end of the scale.

The final opposition relates to the cost of implementing FOI. Any estimated cost is vastly exceeded by the amount the UK Government spends on its own publicity exercises. The cost of the US FOI was $71,107,435 for 1989–90 with about 8 per cent of that amount recouped in fees.[47] In 1988–9 the UK Government spent £200 million on its publicity programmes.[48] Canada's access laws cost £10,500,000 per annum – most of this covering access to personal files; Australia's were costed at under £5 million but the legislation saved £266 million when a proposed defence project was shown not to be viable and was cancelled after information was released under its FOI laws. Experience has shown that the savings and benefits of FOI laws vastly outweigh the costs.[49]

The argument of principle in favour of protecting the privacy of government by refusing to give citizens rights of access to government information can only be won at the cost of debasing the concept of citizenship in our contemporary community. To deny a right of access is to assert that citizens are not mature enough or responsible enough to know what government is doing on their behalf, in their name and with their money. It is not a mere accident that the British state, which has only reluctantly and incompletely protected the privacy of individuals, has been one of the last in the Western democratic world to unwrap the privacy surrounding its own business. Change, however, is afoot and was promised by the opposition parties as a priority for reform if elected. Their proposals followed those of the Bill drafted by the Campaign for Freedom of Information in 1992, although the Labour Party published its own Bill, adding reform of official secrecy laws. It was also reported that John Major was proposing greater openness and access to information following his Citizen's Charter proposals.[50]

The FOI Campaign Bill would cover all departments and agencies of central government – regulatory and 'next steps' – nationalised industries, NHS bodies and advisory bodies to government departments and agencies. Access would be to documents in whatever form kept, e.g. disk, tape, microfiche, paper and so on. It would give a right of access to 'any person' as in the US FOI Act, i.e. it includes others besides US nationals. Authorities would be under a duty to assist requesters to identify the type of information they require and to make proper applications. These must be made in writing, stating that they have been made under the Bill, and they must be responded to, which means access must be given to the information, unless an exemption is claimed, within 30 days. The requester must identify the record sought, a task which will be facilitated by a requirement that codes of guidance, and indexes on information held and on information previously released, must be published. Requests may be broad, but the authority may refuse access where a substantial number of items or volumes is sought and 'access would interfere substantially and unreasonably with the authority's work'. Provisions cover transfers of requests between authorities and the running of response times in such cases. The Bill would give acccess to personal records to the subjects of those records. Fees would cover photocopying, reproduction and posting but not processing the request or allowing inspection (see above on commercial and other users). In the case of personal records, records could be corrected where inaccurate and compensation would be allowed for inaccurate information.

Exemptions cover the usual areas, and it should be noted that there is no excluded[51] information as in the US and Canadian laws. A right of appeal exists to the Ombudsman, who can examine all information including the 'exempt' portion. Further appeal would be allowed to an Information Tribunal – the Bill says nothing about further rights of appeal to the courts. Most of the exemptions would only apply where the disclosure would be likely to cause 'significant damage' to a stated interest; the onus would be on the government to establish this. Exempted areas cover information relating to defence, security, international relations, law enforcement, legal professional privilege and policy advice, though not to factual information or its analysis or to expert advice.[52] The purpose of this exemption is to protect the identity of civil servants; it may be drafted in too wide a manner, however, to meet a genuine objection. The exemption should only apply to information relating to 'active' policy-making and not to protection of information once the policy is made.[53] Furthermore, are there not ways to protect the identity of civil servants and the candour of their advice, in their role as advisers to Ministers? In some cases, identity will be a matter of notoriety and, indeed, on some issues leading civil servants have been identified as supporters of a party line, and not simply as independent advisers. In spite of this trend, in a large majority of instances this will not be the case and identity can be protected from public exposure.[54] The Bill would provide a right to information by way of reasons for decisions where a person's right or individual affairs are in question – and then presumably only to that person or their representative. Invasion of privacy is a ground for refusing access and so is a release of information which would cause significant damage to economic and commercial affairs, i.e. premature disclosures of changes in taxation, interest rates, etc., or those that would be damaging to the authority's own legitimate financial or commercial interests as, *inter alia*, trader, contractor or employer. Another exemption covers the competitive position of a third party with provisos to ensure that the exemption is not too easily claimed. The Official Secrets Act 1989 would be redrafted, as it was in the Labour Party's Bill, to protect specified information whose unauthorized leaking would cause 'serious damage' to the interests of the UK.[55]

One final point from the many that could be raised concerns the unauthorized disclosure of exempt information where disclosure is in the public interest. This would be allowed where there is evidence of significant abuse of authority, official negligence, individual injustice, public danger or unauthorized use of public funds. 'The commissioner and the Tribunal should be able to consider whether the public interest justifies disclosing exempt information. They would, however, have to consider not just the possible benefits of disclosure but also any potential damage – and be satisfied that the public interest would be better served by openness.'[56] This bears some similarity to the public interest defence in the law of confidentiality.

As a general comment, the Bill says little about open government, i.e. opening up the decision-making processes of government. In the USA this is known as 'Sunshine' legislation and covers the meetings of many agencies of federal government; federal advisory committees are under similar provisions contained in the Federal Advisory Committee Act 1972.[57] Unlike local government, central government decision-making processes are not exposed to public scrutiny and central government does not take formal decisions in public, although they may be announced in Parliament. As well as providing a more satisfactory forum for major enquiries, opening up consultation processes and public hearings, what scope would there be for the admission of the press and public to more central government meetings?

Public attitudes to information and access thereto show that it is being perceived as an increasingly significant issue. The DPR has reported that 70–73 per cent of the public thought access was very important.[58] A MORI poll in January 1991 revealed that 77 per cent of those sampled favoured a FOI Act, and it had broad cross-party support with voters.[59] These somewhat impressionistic figures reinforce the theme of this chapter: the question of privacy, both in terms of proper protection of individual privacy and in terms of the removal of unnecessary privacy in government business, is an essential feature of contemporary citizenship, just as, one may add, the operation of *habeas corpus*, the reform of libel laws and the extension of the franchise have been in the past.

AN AFTERWORD

It would take a chapter of greater length than the present to recount all the relevant and important developments since the chapter was written. Two points, however, merit attention. The first is the Government's commitment to greater openness under the Citizen's Charter, but not, it seems, to FOI legislation. Secondly, in January 1993, the second Calcutt report was published ahead of schedule after leaks of its contents were published and after disclosure from the Chairman of the Press Complaints Commission that members of the Royal Family had briefed newspapers to advance their side of a story. It was not true to say that they were simply the victims of intrusive journalism. Sir David Calcutt reported that self-regulation of the press had failed. The criticisms centred around his belief that the Commission was not independent, indeed it was too partial in its protection of press 'independence'. Its treatment of complainants was not adequate for a variety of reasons and he was critical of the fact that the 'hotline' to editors for those about whom an imminent article was to be published had not been established. The most striking recommendation, to universal condemnation from the press, was for a statutory tribunal chaired by a High Court judge to impose 'prior restraint' of publications and to impose large fines where a statutory code had been breached. The Government immediately seemed to distance itself from the idea of a statutory tribunal. Sir David also recommended a variety of criminal offences relating to trespass, the obtaining of personal information and the use of surveillance devices, and the photographing and recording of individuals on private property without their consent and with a view to publication. Public interest defences would be available to these offences. The High Court should be empowered to restrain by injunction the publication of any information obtained in contravention of these criminal provisions. Sir David also revived the question of the creation of a law of privacy.

It is fair to say that the report does not give due weight to the fact that in a free society, an effective press will be a nuisance and more to the powerful and influential; that is one of its *raisons d'être*. In this respect the provisions on prior restraint, so much in the English tradition, are to be viewed with alarm. However, there is a great deal in the report which could do much to introduce effective and responsive grievance procedures against irresponsible elements of the press to assist those who have been abused and where no legitimate public interest has been advanced. One should be careful to exaggerate neither the extent of such abuse nor the number of newspapers likely to perpetrate it.

NOTES AND REFERENCES

1 John Donne, *Meditations* XVII.
2 S. Warren and L. Brandeis (1890) 4 Harv LR 193. See R. Wacks, *Personal Information: Privacy and the Law* (1989).
3 On computer disks and criminal damage by altering the content of a disk, see *R.* v. *Whiteley* (1991) 93 Cr. App R 25 (CA).
4 *Entick* v. *Carrington* (1765) 19 State Tr 1029.
5 Most recently under the Security Service Act 1989 which provides a statutory framework for the operations of the Security Service, MI5; see P. Birkinshaw, *Reforming the Secret State*, 1991, Open University Press.
6 *IRC* v. *Rossminster Ltd* [1980] 1 All ER 80 (HL); cf. *McLorie* v. *Oxford* [1982] QB 1290 (DC).
7 *Kaye* v. *Robertson* [1991] FSR 62 (CA). The law relating to breach of confidence may well protect privacy – where it embraces a confidence or a 'secret' – but it is

not concerned with privacy itself, rather what is confidential in a relationship, usually of an intimate, commercial or state sensitive nature; see the references at notes 9 and 11.

8 *Malone* v. *Met. Police Commissioner* [1979] Ch 344 – telephone tapping not unlawful at common law. See the different approach of the European Court of Human Rights: *Malone* v. *United Kingdom* (1985) 7 EHRR l4 applying article 8 of the Convention and finding unanimously that article 8 had been broken insofar as the restrictions on tapping were not in accordance with the law. See *Gaskin* v. *Liverpool City Council* [1980] 1 WLR 1549 (CA) and *Gaskin* v. *UK* (1990) 12 EHRR 36 for the differing analyses of domestic courts and the European Court of Human Rights. Note also *Campbell* v. *UK* (1992) *The Guardian* 3 April.

9 See the Law Commission, *Breach of Confidence*, Cmnd 8388, 1981.

10 *Bonnard* v. *Perryman* [1891] 2 Ch 269; *Gulf Oil (GB) Ltd* v. *Page* [1987] Ch 327; *Femis Bank* v. *Lazar and Another* [1991] 2 All ER 865.

11 *A-G* v. *Guardian Newspapers* [1987] 3 All ER 316 at 343 (HL); *Lord Advocate* v. *Scotsman Publications Ltd* [1989] 2 All ER 852 (HL); *Observer Newspaper and Guardian Newspaper* v. *UK* (1991), *The Times* 27 November (ECHR). P. Birkinshaw, *Government and Information*, 1990, Butterworths, pp. 60–1.

12 G. Teubner, 'Substantive and reflexive elements in modern law' (1983) 17 *Law and Society Review* 239; P. Birkinshaw, I. Harden and N. Lewis, *Government by Moonlight: The Hybrid Parts of the State*, 1990, Unwin Hyman.

13 See T. Gibbons, *Regulating the Media*, 1991, Sweet & Maxwell.

14 Rather than approach the problem from principle, the Government adopted a piecemeal approach.

15 Employment Committee, HC 176 I and II (1990–1) and Reply, HC 406 (1990–1).

16 Seventh Report of the Data Protection Registrar, 1990/1991, HC 553 (1990–1).

17 *Ibid*, p. 40.

18 Napier (1991) NLJ 497. *Op. cit.*, note 16 at p. 18. The case concerned a credit reference agency which had been served with an Enforcement Notice by the DPR, who believed it had been processing data unfairly when carrying out a credit reference search. This, the DPR believed, was contrary to principle 1 because the user extracted information about other people who lived, or had lived, at the same address as the applicant to assess creditworthiness. The Tribunal held that extracting the information by a complex computer program was processing, and not, *pace* the agency, merely 'use' and could be unfair. 'Use', it should be added, is not mentioned in principle 1. The Tribunal believed it was unfair to extract information on an individual unrelated to the applicant financially or in any way. 'Unfairness' was to be decided objectively, not subjectively, and the agency's intentions were not relevant, nor was the predictive value of the data, i.e. the utility of the data in assessing credit risk. In determining what constituted fairness, paramount consideration should be given to the interests of the data subject, not the interests of the data user. However, a subsequent decision of the DP Tribunal ruled that using information on third parties with a 'similar name' to the applicant for credit and living at the same address is permissible: *The Times*, 14 March 1992.

19 Banking Act 1987 s. 47, Financial Services Act 1986 s. 109; Cm 622 ch 5 and App. Q for a list of relevant statutes; *Bank of Tokyo Ltd* v. *Karoon* [1987] 1 AC 45, *Barclays Bank plc* v. *Taylor* [1989] 3 All ER 563; Police and Criminal Evidence Act

1984 ss. 9–14 and Sched. 1; *Birmingham City Council* v. *O* [1983] 1 All ER 497 (HL), *Re W* [1992] 1 All ER 794 (CA).

20 Contempt of Court Act 1981 s. 10 and see *X Ltd* v. *Morgan-Grampian (Publishers) Ltd* [1990] 2 All ER 1 (HL).

21 *In re British and Commonwealth Holdings plc (No 2)* (1991), *The Times* 31 December, *Cloverbay Ltd* v. *Bank of Credit and Commerce International* [1991] Ch 90.

22 HC 61 (1991–2), Social Security Committee.

23 Police and Criminal Evidence Act 1984 s. 78 and ss. 76 and 82.

24 Interception of Communications Act 1985; Security Service Act 1989.

25 P. Birkinshaw, *Reforming the Secret State*, pp. 34–36. I Leigh and L. Lustgarten, 'The Security Service Act 1989' (1989) Mod. LR 801. The Special Branch have been the subject of an inquiry conducted by the Home Affairs Committee: Fourth Report, HC 11 (1984–5).

26 *Bruggerman and Scheuten* v. *FRG* (1977) 3 EHRR. The European Court has ruled that there was no breach of European law when the Irish Republic prohibited the dissemination of information about abortion facilities in another member state, and, on the facts, the case fell outside the provision of article 10 ECHR as no element of European law had been breached: *Society for the Protection of Unborn Children* v. *Grogan* (1991), *The Times* 7 October. See now *Open Door Counselling etc.* v. *Ireland* (1992) *The Times* 5 November (ECt. HR).

27 *Skinner* v. *REA* (1989) S Ct 1402; *NTEU* v. *Von Raab* (1989) S Ct 1384.

28 HC Debs. Vol. 177, cols 159–61 (24 July 1990). No one should be employed in security-sensitive work where they have engaged in activities threatening to national security, have belonged to organizations advocating such activities or have associated with such organizations or its members, are susceptible to pressure from such bodies or foreign intelligence or hostile bodies, or who suffer 'from defects of character which may expose them to blackmail or other influence by any such organisation or by a foreign intelligence service or which may otherwise indicate unreliability'.

29 *Hilton* v. *UK* 12015/86 (Commission); *H and H* v. *UK* 12175/86 (Commission); *Glasenapp* v. *FRG* (1984) 6 EHRR 499, (1987) 9 EHRR 25; *Kosiek* v. *FRG* (1984) 6 EHRR 519, (1987) 9 EHRR 328; *Leander* v. *Sweden* (1985) 7 EHRR 557, (1987) 9 EHRR 433; and see I. Cameron, *National Security and the European Convention on Human Rights*. Internal procedures exist through which an individual who has failed a vetting may challenge the decision – it only applies to existing 'public servants'. See *R.* v. *Secretary of State for the Home Department ex p. Hosenball* [1977] 3 All ER 452; *R.* v. *Secretary of State for Home Affairs ex p. Ruddock* [1987] 2 All ER 518; *R.* v. *Director of GCHQ ex p. Hodges* (1988), *The Times*, 26 July; *R.* v. *Secretary of State for the Home Department ex p. Cheblak* [1991] 2 All ER 319; *CCSU* v. *Minister for the Civil Service* [1985] AC 374. See Security Service Act 1989, s.5 and sched. 1.

30 The procedure is exempted from the provisions of the Rehabilitation of Offenders Act 1974.

31 *Woodward* v. *Hutchins* [1977] 1 WLR 760 (CA); *Lennon* v. *NGN Ltd* [1978] FSR 573 (CA).

32 *The Guardian*, 7 February 1992.

33 *Re W* [1992] 1 All ER 794 (CA). Given the sensitivity of the subject matter, and the fact that it involved a minor and not a public figure, the case is a remarkable example of a more liberal attitude from the courts towards press freedom under the influence of article 10. I personally doubt that this liberalizing tendency would prevail in cases where, to prevent publication, the Government asserted national security: see *Guardian Newspapers, Spycatcher,* and *Scotsman Publications*, note 11.

34 [1993] 1 All ER 1011 (HL). Proceedings for malicious falsehood, criminal libel and at the suit of individuals may be possible.

35 C. Richardson (1991) New LJ 130.

36 See the Select Committee on Members' Interests on *Parliamentary Lobbying* HC 586 (1990–1) and *Registration and Declaration of Members' Interests* HC 388 (1990–1), For councillors, note s. 19 Local Government and Housing Act 1989; this provision is to be implemented by statutory regulations. As of writing, they have not been made and approved.

37 P. Birkinshaw, *Freedom of Information: The Law, the Practice and the Ideal*, 1988, Weidenfeld & Nicolson; on the USA, the same, *Freedom of Information: The US Experience*, 1991 Hull University Law School Studies in Law.

38 Select Committee on Procedure, *Working of the Select Committee System* HC 19 (1989–90).

39 The investigations concerned the Social Security Committee's inquiry into the operation and regulation of pension funds and the Trade and Industry Committee's investigation into the Iraqi supergun affair: HC 61 and HC 86, respectively, both 1991–2.

40 Sir Robin Butler, the Secretary to the Cabinet and Head of the Home Civil Service, has publicly stated that ministerial responsibility may well have to be re-forged to accommodate the changes affecting the civil service, particularly the Next Steps developments: *The Independent* 21 October 1991. On Next Steps, see Cm 1760 and 1761 (1991) and A. Davies and John Willman, *What Next? Agencies, Departments, and the Civil Service*, 1991, IPPR.

41 As occurs with certain sensitive defence procurement contracts. However, this arrangement has not always been complied with on the Government side.

42 See M. Frankel's excellent 'Parliamentary accountability and Government control of information', in N. Lewis (ed.), *Happy and Glorious: The Constitution in Transition*, 1990, Open University Press.

43 See P. Birkinshaw, *Freedom of Information: The Law, the Practice and the Ideal*, note 37, pp. 233–5.

44 P. Birkinshaw, I. Harden and N. Lewis, *Government by Moonlight: The Hybrid Parts of the State*, 1990, Unwin Hyman.

45 Which was dramatically illustrated by the Government's plans for privatizing school inspectorates under the Education (Schools) Bill; these provisions fell in the Lords in March 1991; see now Education (Schools) Act 1992, ss. 9–15.

46 See Birkinshaw, note 37.

47 H. Relyea, *The Administration and Operation of the Freedom of Information Act: An Overview, 1966–90*, 1990, Congressional Research Service (90-500 GOV, CRS).

48 Public Accounts Committee HC 46 (1989–90); and see *R. v. Secretary of State for the Environment ex p. Greenwich LBC* (1989), *The Times*, 17 May.

49 M. Frankel, *A Freedom of Information Act for Britain*, 1991, Campaign for Freedom of Information, pp. 8–9.

50 The Conservative Manifesto of March 1992 did not refer to freedom of information legislation, but spoke of removing restrictions to information, which is not the same thing as FOI. On 24 January 1992, a FOI Bill sponsored by Liberal Democrat MP Archie Kirkwood was 'talked out' of a Second Reading by the Minister for the Civil Service, who spoke glowingly of the encouragement of openness in the Prime Minister's Citizen's Charter (Cm 1599, 1991). The charter has no provision for a FOI Act.

51 These cover advice from the President's personal staff and, in Canada, Cabinet confidences and secrets of the Queen's Privy Council.

52 See *R.* v. *Secretary of State ex p. US Tobacco* [1992] 1 All ER 212 (CA).

53 On the distinctions drawn by US courts, see Birkinshaw, note 37.

54 The point has been made that identifying a civil servant adviser will be invidious because it might highlight a possible difference between the latter and a Minister, thereby increasing the likelihood that a Minister will not want that adviser. We have to be careful to see what we are protecting here. If it is a Minister's reputation, that does not seem a legitimate reason for secrecy. If it is to protect a civil servant, it should be remembered that Ministers are under a conventional duty to take civil servants' advice seriously, whether they agree with it or not. A difference of opinion is, in any event, unlikely not to suffer leaks. Furthermore, the Next Steps initiative is supposed to give civil servants greater freedom in setting policy. The problem is likely to be exacerbated wherever conviction politics, as under Mrs Thatcher, are in the ascendant.

55 The 1989 Official Secrets Act punished unauthorized leaks of six kinds of information where the leaks were damaging as defined – in some cases the leak of information was *ipso facto* damaging. Protected material under the Labour Party's Bill was confined to that which related to defence, international relations or the lawful activities of the security and intelligence service, the unauthorized disclosure of which would be likely to cause serious damage to the interests of the UK. It would also be an offence where information, if disclosed, would be likely to lead to the commission of any indictable offence, create a serious obstacle to the prevention or detection of such an offence, etc., or cause serious danger to the safety or life of any person. Defences of prior publication and disclosure in the public interest were present in the Bill.

56 See Frankel, note 49.

57 P. Birkinshaw, note 37.

58 See Data Protection Registrar Annual Report HC 553 (1990–1) p. 40.

59 Campaign for FOI, *Secrets*, November 1991, p. 1.

3

Rights and Health Care

MARGARET BRAZIER

The National Health Service, former Prime Minister Margaret Thatcher once declared, was 'safe in our hands'. Her successor, John Major, launched the Patient's Charter,[1] entrenching seven well-established 'rights' to health care and introducing 'three important new rights for you from 1992'. The Labour Party counter-attacked, claiming with vehemence and eloquence that the integrity of the NHS could be preserved only by the election of a Labour Government. Amid the brouhaha, had any politician of whatever hue even questioned the right of a sick citizen to health care, he or she might just as well have retired gracefully as contest the 1992 election. Yet it is extremely dubious whether there is in the United Kingdom any legally enforceable right *to* health care on *demand*. And shocking though it may sound, the case for entrenching any individual right to demand health care is nothing like so clear-cut as it might appear.

There can be no doubt that the patient in receipt of health care enjoys a cluster of legally enforceable rights.[2] She has a right to competent, skilled professional care, a right to confidentiality and, to a limited extent, a right to autonomy, to participate in treatment decisions. From November 1991, the Access to Health Records Act 1990 grants a partial right to access to information held by health professionals relating to their patients. Violation of any of these rights confers on an aggrieved patient a conventional legal remedy. She can go to court to enforce her rights and in appropriate cases will be compensated for any consequential injury. Yet even such classic rights, embodied as Patient Rights 5–7 in the Major charter, cannot be regarded as unqualified *patient* rights. The substance of the patient's right is in each case at least in part defined by professional medical practice. The citizen's rights within health care in the United

Kingdom remain subject to a high degree of medical paternalism. Before we briefly examine the acceptability and implications of that paternalism in health care, it is necessary to consider at much greater length whether any citizen has a right to claim health care, to get past first base and demand treatment. For if a citizen cannot obtain treatment any rights enjoyed in the course of treatment are worthless. What I have to say relates primarily to rights to treatment within the National Health Service. The effect of the existence of a private sector on the implementation of such rights is largely beyond the scope of this chapter. I am concerned with the practical questions relating to claims to health care free of charge. I do not attempt any philosophical enquiry as to the nature of health rights and I concentrate on rights to treatment as opposed to a more general conception of health, which necessarily involves much wider issues, such as the promotion of good health and the state of the environment.[3] Nor do I seek to analyse in any detail the implications of the NHS reforms implemented in the National Health Service and Community Care Act 1990, though, as will become apparent, a public service system that differentiates, as the 1990 Act does, between NHS bodies responsible for *purchasing* services and those responsible for *providing* them does affect the nature of patients' rights to care.

DEFINING A RIGHT TO HEALTH CARE

Rhetoric relating to rights to health care is all very well, but what is the reality, where is the substance? The Major charter declared that from 1 April 1992 every British citizen enjoyed three crucial rights: a right to health care on the basis of clinical need; a right to receive emergency medical care at any time; and, the cornerstone of his charter, a right to 'be guaranteed admission for treatment by a specific date no later than two years from the day when your consultant places you on a waiting list'.

The first right is pure rhetoric; the latter duo do at least attempt to address the substance of a right to demand health care. But where lies the aggrieved would-be patient's remedy? You may complain to the Chief Executive of the NHS, who will take administrative action to correct the failure in the service. Such action will be of little recompense to the family whose breadwinner lies dead for lack of an adequate casualty service. The question which must be addressed is whether 'guarantees' and rights to emergency care are or should be fully enforceable by individuals.

The difficulty of giving substance to a right to claim health care should never be underestimated. It is not a problem peculiar to health care but extends to all economic and social rights. Defining human freedoms, 'negative' rights, is always easier than defining 'positive' rights, claims to certain specific services. Article 25 of the Universal Declaration of Human Rights begins: 'Everyone has the right to a standard of living adequate for the health and well-being of himself and his family including food, clothing, and *medical care.*' Interpreting and applying Article 25 can never be a simple task but I would suggest that of the 'positive' rights encapsulated in Article 25 medical care poses the greatest difficulties of definition. Basic human needs for food, clothing and other material necessities are susceptible to some sort of objective assessment and differ relatively little from person to person. My need for clothing may be marginally less costly to satisfy than my husband's because I am 5 feet 1 inch tall and he is over 6 feet. Needs for medical care vary widely. A baby born with severe disabilities at 25 weeks' gestation will probably consume health care resources sufficient for the basic care required for 20–30 normal infants delivered at full term. The cost of a single heart transplant will cover the cost of chiropody services for elderly patients in a health district for a year or more. The older the patient the more, and more expensive, medical care she needs. Where resources for health care are limited the question becomes not one of any absolute right to care, but one of defining to what share of available resources the citizen has a right. Emphasis on individual rights to health care, high-flown rhetoric that each and every citizen has a right to health care, obscures the issue, which is who has or should have the ultimate responsibility for allocating available resources and determining my proper share of, and claim to, those resources?[4]

Nor are the variable needs of the individual the only difficulty inherent in defining a right to medical care. The more developed the society the more complex the question of just what constitutes medical care becomes. Is fertility treatment for couples unable to conceive naturally necessary for that couple's health and well-being? Can lines be drawn in relation to cosmetic surgery? My desire for a perfect nose is 'vanity care', not health care. But what if my obsession with the existing imperfect nose had resulted in clinical depression?

Defining health care requires hard choices about comparative needs. Such choices governments of whatever political colour may prefer to avoid. Giving a little cash to each potential group of claimants may be easier than making unpopular decisions. For example, there are only two fully funded NHS clinics offering the full range of modern assisted conception techniques, totally inadequate to meet demand. Yet stating that fertility treatment should be excluded from the NHS altogether is no doubt seen as politically unacceptable, although it might be a more honest course of action.

Doctors and health care economists debate with ethicists about the optimum means of allocating health care resources. No politician engages in the discourse about the validity or otherwise of the use of Quality Adjusted Life Years (QALYS) to make choices between patients.[5] They prefer to pretend that such choices are unnecessary, that the patient has a right to care protected by whatever their preferred structure for the NHS may be. And each party claims that it alone plans to ensure the NHS has adequate funds, ignoring the reality of the situation that health care is an inexhaustible demand.[6]

A RIGHT TO PRIORITY TREATMENT

Health care demand derives from the individual's perceived need for skilled professional advice or intervention. It is generally a need with a time limit: its satisfaction cannot be indefinitely delayed. The nature of the time limit will vary with the condition. Cardiac resuscitation for the victim of a coronary is no good to him in three weeks' time. Abortion services are no use in nine months' time. Childbirth cannot wait for a place in the queue. But many illnesses and disabling conditions do not require immediate treatment. When publicly financed resources are stretched the fundamental question is often not whether I receive treatment at all but *when* I can expect to obtain that treatment. Have I any right to priority treatment?

Within the United Kingdom at present rights of access to primary health care are undisputed. Everyone has the right to register with a general practitioner and receive primary care free of charge. The regulatory structure provided by Family Health Service Authorities largely offers effective means of enforcing and policing that right to primary care.[7] The citizen's difficulties ensue when he or his general practitioner consider that he needs specialist care, in particular hospital treatment or surgery. How far will the law assist him to enforce his right to that specialist care? The omens are unpromising.

The state's responsibility for health care is to be found in the National Health Service Act 1977. Section 1 imposes on the Secretary of State for Health the duty:

> to continue the promotion in England and Wales of a comprehensive health service designed to secure improvement:
> (a) in the physical and mental health of the people of those countries and
> (b) in the prevention, diagnosis and treatment of illness and for that purpose to provide or secure effective provision of services in accordance with this Act.

Section 3(1) elaborates on the Minister's responsibilities. She is obliged to meet all reasonable requirements for, *inter alia*, medical, dental and nursing services and hospital accommodation. It might seem therefore that should I be denied a hospital bed within a reasonable period of time after my medical advisers consider surgery to be desirable, the Minister has violated my statutory right to health care. She has failed to meet *my* reasonable requirement for hospital accommodation. Duties to meet local requirements are delegated to local health authorities.[8] However, none of these duties as yet, it seems, creates unequivocal *individual* rights.

COLLECTIVE NOT INDIVIDUAL RIGHTS

A trio of judgments from the Court of Appeal in 1979, 1987 and 1988 establishes the principle that the rights to health care derived from the duties to provide health care imposed by sections 1 and 3 of the 1977 Act are primarily *collective* not individual rights. The individual has no legally enforceable right to demand priority treatment and the courts will intervene to protect the individual interest in the collective right only in the most exceptional and restricted circumstances.

In *R.* v. *Secretary of State for Social Services ex p. Hincks*[9] four patients who had languished for years on the waiting list for orthopaedic surgery suffering from acute osteo-arthritis took the Secretary of State to court. They sought damages for breach of statutory duty in compensation for their considerable pain and suffering. And they asked for an order of mandamus directing the Minister to make available the resources necessary to enable their operations to be scheduled promptly. Both parts of their claim failed.

The Court of Appeal held that sections 1 and 3 of the 1977 Act did not give rise to any private rights of action on the part of would-be patients. The duties imposed by the Act were public law duties only. The Minister's responsibility to ensure the provision of adequate health service was owed to the public at large and was primarily enforceable by Parliament. Refusing the application for mandamus, the court found that in exercising his discretion under section 3(1) to determine reasonable requirements for services, the Minister was properly and lawfully constrained by the financial resources made available to him by the Treasury. The courts could intervene by way of judicial review only if it could be shown that the Minister's judgment about *how* to allocate those resources was so entirely unreasonable that no Minister properly advised could have arrived at such a judgment, i.e. the Minister's decision was *Wednesbury* unreasonable.[10] If a Minister had in effect acted not to promote but to frustrate the underlying policy of the 1977 Act then the courts might call him to account.

The door was thus left ajar. Judicial enforcement of government's responsibility to provide health care was not ruled out altogether. But the judgment offered little comfort to the disappointed litigants. In 1987 and 1988 two further attempts were made to enforce rights to health care, on these occasions against a local health authority. The judgments in *R.* v. *Central Birmingham Health Authority ex p. Walker*[11] and *R.* v. *Central Birmingham Health Authority ex p. Collier*[12] both concerned sick babies needing cardiac surgery to repair a 'hole in the heart'. Their parents watched in anguish as time after time operations were scheduled and then postponed because an 'emergency' case had to be dealt with first. They applied for judicial review, asking the court to order the authority to give priority to their children. Both applications failed. The health authority could act only within the budget provided for it by the Department of Health. Decisions about how to manage and allocate those resources were reviewable only if they were so manifestly unreasonable as to fail the *Wednesbury* test. Sir John Donaldson MR declared that it could not be for the judges to substitute their decisions 'for the judgment of those who are responsible for the allocation of resources'.

The cumulative effect of the judgments in *ex p. Hincks, ex p. Walker* and *ex. p. Collier* suggests that effective legal redress to prevent a violation of any individual right to health care is something of a chimera. An application for judicial review of a delay in treatment looks likely to succeed only if it is grounded on evidence of some gross misjudgment, something approaching bad faith or sheer lunacy. Theoretical examples can be found: for example, a health authority giving priority treatment to paid-up members of one political party or refusing to arrange any sort of treatment for patients with liver disease because 'liver problems always result from alcohol abuse'. Such unlikely examples are of little comfort to the many patients suffering while they wait for treatment and finding that their much vaunted 'right to health care' has scant substance. So should the Court of Appeal have adopted a more interventionist stance to safeguard patients' rights?

Consider first the decision in *ex p. Hincks* to deny the applicants a right of action for breach of statutory duty. Had the claim been allowed, Mr Hincks and his fellows would have received compensation for their very real suffering. Presumably in subsequent cases a patient who had undergone private treatment because of the Department of Health's breach of section 3(1) might well have claimed the cost of that private treatment as an appropriate measure of damages. The money to meet such claims would have to come from the very same resources which had proved inadequate to ensure that NHS treatment was available to the litigants. As a result of the 'benefit' conferred on patient A denied treatment in breach of section 3(1), patients B and C are likely to suffer an inevitable detriment. The cost of litigation itself was a factor in the forefront of judicial concern in all three cases. In *ex p. Collier*, Stephen Brown LJ expressed concern that litigation might mean the courts were 'using up National Health Service resources by requiring the authority to stop doing the work for which they were appointed and meet the complaints of their patients'.

Once any private right of action was ruled inadmissible under the 1977 Act, the judges found themselves inevitably confronting a stark invitation to review the Minister's and local health authorities' priorities. Consider what the Court of Appeal in *ex p. Walker* and *ex p. Collier* was actually asked to do. Central Birmingham Health Authority could not attract enough specially trained nurses to staff its intensive care paediatric unit. It was not simply a question of lack of cash to engage sufficient nurses; too few nurses nationally were coming forward to seek the necessary specialist training. The Court of Appeal could not wave a magic wand and procure more nurses. The core problem was the inadequate pay and career structure in nursing, something beyond the control of the authority; what the judges then were asked to do was decide that Baby Walker and Baby Collier be treated in priority to Baby X and Baby Y, who were regarded by the paediatricians in Birmingham as in greater need of immediate surgery. In the absence of evidence that that judgment was manifestly wrong, the judges were largely helpless. They were impaled on the horns of the health care dilemma; defending A's right to treatment may itself be a violation of B's concurrent right.

Of course, all that I have said is subject to one huge *caveat*, an assumption that resources are limited and A and B cannot both receive effective treatment. It might be argued, as Conservative politicians have, that the problem is not lack of resources but inefficient use of resources. Were that so then the theoretical case for judicial intervention might be strengthened. Damages awarded to aggrieved patients and judicial directions to carry out surgery on X would act as an incentive to efficient management and a deterrent to bad practice. I remain to be convinced that this is in fact the case and, even if it were, that Her Majesty's judges have the expertise to judge such matters.

The unpromising history of resort to law to vindicate a right to health care has not deterred subsequent attempts to use the law. A woman with renal failure who was refused dialysis facilities obtained legal aid for an application for judicial review. An extra £250,000 was made available to local renal units.[13] At the time of writing a father alleging that his son, who suffers from cerebral palsy, was offered totally inadequate physiotherapy is taking his health authority to court.[14] The moral claim to health care exerts a potent influence on the media and legal action focuses that moral claim. Yet the cost remains. Publicity results in priority treatment for a sick child. Less media-friendly patients are the losers.

Can anything be done to introduce objective, quantifiable criteria to weigh my claims to priority treatment against yours? The Major charter made two proposals, the two-year 'guarantee' and an apparently absolute right to emergency care. Could any such 'guarantee' usefully be given legal force? I doubt it. 'Guarantees' add to the rhetoric not the reality of rights to health care. The patient is entitled to non-emergency treatment within two years of a consultant's judgment that he or she should be placed on the waiting list. A medical *imprimatur* is required to qualify for eligibility for guaranteed treatment. Questions of what kinds of treatment the publicly funded system should provide are ceded to the doctors. Health providers seeking to ensure compliance with the guarantee can adopt, and may be forced to do so, at least two avoidance strategies: limit the number of patients who ever get on the waiting list, and prioritize existing waiting lists so that regardless of clinical or social need those approaching the deadline are treated first.[15] An elderly woman with painful disabling arthritis must take her place in the queue behind a younger patient with a fairly minor orthopaedic complaint because the latter, so to speak, staked out her claim first.

RIGHTS TO EMERGENCY TREATMENT

If there is any substance in a citizen's right to health care, surely it must embrace legal redress for a failure to provide emergency treatment? Certainly there are powerful arguments to suggest that a right to emergency care might be regarded as an individual and legally enforceable right in England. The European Convention on Human Rights, while silent on any right to health care as such, does establish in Article 2 a right to life itself. Failure to provide life-saving treatment might be argued to be a violation of Article 2.

Does English law actually recognize a right to life-saving treatment? The common law has traditionally rejected any legal obligation to be a Good Samaritan. No English doctor is required to respond to the call for 'a doctor in the house' any more than I am obliged to rescue a drowning child. The failure to impose in any form even the most limited Samaritan duty is out of line with most of Britain's European partners. Civil law jurisdictions do impose a general duty to assist fellow citizens in peril. The French doctor crossing the road to avoid rendering first aid to a road accident victim could be held civilly and criminally liable for his failure to act.[16] The absence of any form of Samaritan duty within English law could be and has been argued to be a breach of Article 2 of the European Convention. In *Hughes* v. *United Kingdom*[17] a widow complained to the European Commission of Human Rights after the dismissal of an action for negligence arising out of the circumstances of her husband's death. He had collapsed at the school where he worked. Fellow employees who discovered him, including teachers with first-aid training, believed him to be dead and summoned the police rather than an ambulance. The substance of the complaint to the Commission was that the absence of any duty imposed by English law to summon medical aid violated Mr Hughes's right to life. The Commission dismissed the case on its facts. Even on the assumption that the defect in the law could constitute such a breach of Article 2, help if summoned would have been of no avail. An ambulance could not have arrived in time to resuscitate the applicant's husband.

In the context of NHS services, however, it may be the case that despite the absence of any generally applicable Samaritan duty the common law would impose on certain health providers a specific duty to maintain an emergency service. A hospital that operates an accident and emergency unit is clearly liable in negligence if a patient is admitted to the unit and then not afforded adequate treatment.[18] He crosses the Rubicon when he is checked in as a patient. But what if the unit is closed on the night the patient suffers his coronary? A notice at the door indicates that staff shortages have required that the unit be closed that night and directs patients to a hospital five miles to the south. The delay in access to treatment may prove fatal. In *ex p. Collier* counsel for the baby whose operation had been delayed on so many occasions argued before the Court of Appeal that the infant's life was imperilled by the delay. Stephen Brown LJ responded that even if there were immediate danger to health, this would not affect the Court's decision to refuse leave to apply for judicial review, in the absence once again of evidence that the decision to delay treatment was *Wednesbury* unreasonable.

The judge's *dictum* does not end the matter. For should a patient be denied emergency treatment at hospital X and it could be proved that his death resulted from that delay,[19] his family's redress would be to invoke the tort of negligence. They would argue that the hospital, by providing an emergency service on which the local community has come to rely, has undertaken a duty to that community. In *Barnes* v. *Crabtree*[20] counsel for the defendant conceded that the obligations undertaken by a general practitioner in his contract with what was then the Family Practitioner Committee to provide emergency care in his practice area to all-comers gave rise to a duty in tort to patients in need of that treatment. And in a number of US jurisdictions a limited Samaritan duty to treat 'unmistakable emergencies' has been imposed even on private hospitals.[21]

Once the issue of means of redress moves from the field of public law remedies to the tort of negligence the rules of the game undergo something of a change even beyond the context of accident and emergency treatment. Analyse *ex p. Walker* and *ex p. Collier* on the assumption that neither baby was ever operated on[22] and medical evidence proved that failure to operate caused the infants' deaths. Both babies were actually already patients of the health authority receiving care from the paediatric team. They were owed duties of care; if the failure to operate could have been shown to be negligent, damages would be recoverable on ordinary negligence principles. Presumably any patient on a waiting list who can prove damage resulting from delay arguably has a case in negligence.

Does the crux of the question become whether the plaintiff is established as a patient to whom the hospital owes an existing duty of care? Once within the hospital gates, albeit only for an outpatient visit, do you establish a duty relationship with the hospital? Drawing a line between acts and omissions at this point has substantial dangers. Hospital managers will, in order to cover the hospital's potential liability, seek to limit entry to waiting lists. Three more difficulties bedevil the use of the tort of negligence to enforce a right to care retrospectively.

First, there is the question of the respective responsibilities of 'purchasers' and 'providers' within any NHS system, such as that provided by the National Health Service and Community Care Act 1990, which separates out the two functions. It might persuasively be argued that my local health authority, as a purchasing authority, has a duty to me and to all local residents to take reasonable steps to arrange such hospital and other treatment as my general practitioner considers clinically desirable. It is no answer that for reasons beyond their control neither the local trust hospital nor any directly managed unit of that authority can afford me sufficiently prompt treatment. They are now after all free to buy my treatment where they will, which brings us to the *second* problem in using negligence to vindicate rights *to* care. How will breach of duty be established?

The definition of breach of duty in an action for negligence alleging unreasonable delay will be equally problematic whether an action lies against a purchasing or a providing authority. The courts will be obliged to do what in applications for judicial review they have declined to do: assess whether in giving X priority over the plaintiff the authority acted unreasonably. Did the authority act properly in determining that X's claim to priority care was greater than the plaintiff's?

Third, what would be the impact of such litigation? Effective 'immunity' for non-treatment indubitably has adverse results. For example, if there is no legal redress for not providing emergency treatment at all, then the prudent health service manager is subject to a powerful incentive to close his accident and emergency unit rather than risk liability for a negligent error on the part of staff struggling to do their best in the face of inadequate resources.[23] And similarly with all other units in the hospital, it may be perceived as better to shut wards, take operating theatres out of commission and delay operations if staff shortages pose a risk of triggering treatment accidents. The law if it operates any sort of rigid distinction between acts and omissions may be promoting defensive health service practice. A judgment that unequivocally recognized that negligent delay in treatment is as much actionable as negligent treatment and even more a judgment imposing a limited Samaritan duty would have a beneficial impact for rights *to* health care. Manager and clinicians would be forced to ensure the best possible practice in managing services and determining priorities. They would be forced to justify closure or suspension of services to the individual suffering from the absence of sufficiently prompt treatment. But there could be a knock-on effect on medical litigation as a whole. Delay claims would inevitably involve a judgment about what was reasonable in the light of current resources. Would that issue then permeate all negligence claims, allowing an authority sued for a negligent error to claim that its negligence must be judged in the context of its limited resources? A junior surgeon makes an error in an operation which he should not have been performing unsupervised. The health authority contends that it could not afford to pay sufficient consultant surgeons. The NHS health authority's duty becomes diluted to what is practicable rather than what is optimum practice.[24] The cost of an effective remedy for the patient denied treatment could prove to be a diminution in the rights of the patient in receipt of treatment.

There is one final further snag with any formulation of a right that will inevitably be perceived as an absolute right to life-saving treatment. Do we as a matter of policy want to prioritize *all* life-saving procedures over all other health care needs? Should a heart and lung transplant be performed at the cost of diminished standards of care for psychiatric patients? The equation will not always be as simple as whether we ensure that a 22-year-old road accident victim receives the immediate care she needs to survive as against some delay for patients awaiting, say, hernia operations. How far can parents of a very sick, very premature baby *demand* that all measures possible be taken to maximize his prospects of survival? When, if at all, is it permissible to decide not to resuscitate elderly sick patients should they suffer a respiratory collapse? Once the exercise of defining a right to health care is embarked upon, neither judges nor politicians will be able any longer to avoid the questions of moral and social policy that health care professionals and ethicists have agonized over for decades.

EQUALITY OF ACCESS

If definition of the substance of a right to health care is awkward because defining admissible health care needs in any objective manner is nigh on impossible, I have suggested that the right to health care is perhaps best described as a right to a fair share of what is available. I ought to have equality of opportunity with all rival claimants. Equality of opportunity has two aspects. First, does my need – my condition – get a fair deal? Second, do I personally have an equal chance of treatment as against other would-be patients with similar clinical needs?

The residual role reserved to the courts in *ex p. Hincks, ex p. Walker* and *ex p. Collier* is designed to meet both issues of equality of access to some rather limited extent. The 1977 Act demands that the Ministers and all other health providers give proper consideration to how to divide resources among competing health care needs. A complete failure to offer a basic service in its entirety, for example to make no provision for prostate surgery, would fall foul of the *Wednesbury* test. In more realistic examples, defining how far absence of, or drastic reduction in, a service constitutes *Wednesbury* unreasonableness would bring the courts back into social policy and often to moral controversy. For example, is limiting the availability of abortions to a number of cases the authority knows full well is insufficient to meet demand a sufficiently 'unreasonable' division of resources? The courts are likely to continue to be wary of intervention in overall allocation of resources among competing groups of patients.

At the second stage of equality of access, judicial redress may be more forthcoming. Once resources are spread thinly across the various medical disciplines, the underfunded areas will find themselves with more patients with similar clinical needs than they can treat. This was until relatively recently very much the case for patients with renal failure. There were insufficient renal dialysis facilities to treat all those patients who needed dialysis to survive. Diabetics and patients over 65 had little hope of treatment. Now the provision of dialysis facilities has improved but kidneys for transplant remain rationed and erythroprotein, a drug to combat the chronic anaemia prevalent in dialysis patients, is in short supply. NHS facilities for in-vitro fertilization (IVF) and other advanced techniques are totally inadequate to meet the demand from patients who clinicians judge might benefit from those techniques. Doctors choosing between patients have to resort to criteria other than clinical need, to have regard to non-medical, social criteria. Should a mother of three young children have priority for a kidney transplant? Do you give treatment to patients seeking IVF to those the doctors judge will make the best parents? What makes a good parent?

In practice, in 99 per cent of cases of choice between parents those choices are being made by doctors. But it is clear that they do not enjoy an unfettered discretion to determine treatment priorities once non-medical criteria affect their decision-making process. In *R. v. Ethical Advisory Committee of St Mary's Hospital ex p. Harriott* [25] a patient refused IVF treatment sought an application for judicial review against the hospital. Mrs Harriott first attended the IVF clinic at St Mary's in 1983 and in 1984 a laparoscopy was performed to discover the cause of her infertility. However, by December 1984 consultants decided not to offer Mrs Harriott IVF because investigations of her background had revealed that she had convictions for prostitution offences and that she had been rejected as a potential foster parent by Manchester City Council. The consultants referred her case to the informal advisory committee set up to assist them on ethical questions relating to treatment at the clinic. The committee confirmed the judgment not to treat Mrs Harriott. Mrs Harriott was not given the real reasons for refusing her IVF until September 1985. She sought judicial review on two counts: first that the clinic acted unfairly – she was not offered any hearing before the committee; and second that the grounds for excluding her from treatment were *ultra vires* – they bore no relation to her need for treatment.

Mrs Harriott's claim failed. Schiemann J said there was no obligation to allow her any formal hearing. The committee merely advised the consultants. Nor were the grounds for refusing her IVF *ultra vires*. It was proper and reasonable to take into account her suitability for motherhood. The latter is a judgment with which some might well vehemently disagree. [26] Schiemann J did, however, unequivocally state that treatment choices *were* subject to legal control and constraints. He did not accept that clinical judgment in relation to such questions was immune from review. For while he found that on this occasion St Mary's did not act unfairly he stressed that Mrs Harriott had ultimately been given the reasons for refusal of treatment and that she had a sufficient opportunity to argue her case. Moreover, reviewing the grounds for refusal of treatment he envisaged circumstances where judicial review would lie. Refusal based on racial origin or religion affiliation would be clearly unlawful.

The *Harriott* case concerns a very specific form of treatment where Parliament has now endorsed the application of non-medical criteria to treatment decisions. [27] The availability of judicial review endorsed by *Harriott* to challenge treatment decisions generally when non-medical criteria are invoked could have more profound importance. My suitability as a mother may be argued to be relevant to a claim to fertility treatment, but what if my moral character or social usefulness was used to determine my eligibility for, say, non-urgent abdominal surgery? I would suggest that such considerations in that kind of case fall foul of the *Harriott* test.

RIGHTS IN HEALTH CARE

Exposition of patients' rights become simpler once there is an undisputed duty relationship between both the health authority and the patient, and the individual health care professionals and that patient. The patient's rights against his carers and their employers could be summarized as falling into three main categories: to determine what form treatment takes; to be afforded proper treatment; and to control information relating to himself and his state of health. Patient and professionals become partners in the enterprise of restoring the patient to health. That is alas an ideal as yet unrealized in English law. For in each part of the enterprise the medical professional is designated as the dominant partner. The patient's right to information on the basis of which to participate in treatment decisions is limited to information which it is professional practice to disclose.[28] Actionable negligence is established only on proof that the disputed treatment failed to conform to *any* body of responsible professional opinion.[29] Access to your own medical records may be refused where it is judged that information would be likely to cause serious harm to your physical or mental health.[30]

Again and again the English courts have in effect declared that 'doctor knows best' and declined to scrutinize medical practice in the same manner as they seem ready to call other professions to account.[31] The unhappiness self-evident in the judgments restricting rights to claim health care extends into the arena of enforcing rights in health care. In *Sidaway* v. *Royal Bethlem Hospital*[32] the majority judgments, stifling at birth any doctrine of informed consent in English law by applying the professional practice standard to disclosure of information, reveal a very limited perception of patients' rights and indeed ability to make choices for themselves. Doctors should decide what patients ought to know, Lord Diplock declared, because (a) patients did not want more information, (b) patients would not understand more information, and (c) more information would frighten patients off treatment, leading to 'irrational' treatment refusals. The patient, having decided to seek treatment and agreed in broad terms to his doctor's proposals for the appropriate form of treatment, cedes to the professionals control of his health care.[33]

It is interesting to note too how once the legal issue at stake changes from patients' rights *to* health care to their rights *in* health care, the health providers, the NHS authorities, tend to fade into the background of the picture. The focus is on the patient–doctor relationship. And in many cases tort litigation still proceeds as if within the NHS health care was still delivered on a true one-to-one basis. What the consultant said to the patient is at issue in consent cases. An individual's conduct forms the core of a negligence action. It would be possible for a visiting Martian to read medical law judgments from the Law Reports and have no notion that team care is at the heart of NHS treatment, and to come to believe that most consultations still take place directly and exclusively between the senior clinician and her patient. The reality of complex multiple relationships between patients, doctors, nurses, ancillary staff and health service managers has to be fitted into a private law straitjacket.

Resort to court to define rights and obligations in health care is not a trend now likely to be reversed. Patients have become litigious. Doctors have become litigation conscious. So since 1989 judges have been asked *inter alia* to determine when mentally handicapped women may lawfully be sterilized,[34] to decide whether profoundly handicapped infants must be treated to prolong life in all eventualities[35] and to consider yet again the principles governing consent to treatment and children.[36] In many such cases it is the professionals who seek judicial sanction to authorize their treatment decisions. The outcome is often a judicial rubber-stamp of 'responsible professional opinion'.

AVOIDING SOCIAL POLICY

Refusing the parents leave to apply for judicial review in *ex p. Collier*, Ralph Gibson LJ declared that the High Court had 'no role of general investigator of social policy' in the context of allocation of resources. A desire, understandable enough, to avoid social policy also helps to explain the endorsement time and time again of medical paternalism within health care. It is easier to leave moral and social judgments to doctors under the cover of professional clinical judgment. Politicians use rhetoric about *your* right to health care to avoid harsh decisions about what that right consists of, what is *your* fair share of the health care cake. The courts take refuge in professional opinion. The medical profession is 'left holding the baby'. All too often as a result they, collectively and individually, face charges of paternalism, of disregard for patients' rights. But if society through its elected representatives and the courts ducks the issues, the doctors are forced to set the pace, to make the hard decisions. Then society turns round and criticizes what it does not like. Decisions about rights and health care are going to get harder, not easier. Some mechanism for giving substance to those rights is urgently needed. New forms of expensive treatment will compete with existing demands. Fetal surgery is already possible to correct fetal deformities *in utero*. Clinical genetics offers the prospect for a revolution in pre-conception care. Who will weigh the claims of the unborn citizen against the ever-increasing demands of the growing population of citizens over 90? The government has left it to the Nuffield Foundation to set up a Bioethics Council to review the new choices medical technology and science will confront us with in the next century. It is a pity it did not see its responsibility for health care as extending to active participation in that process.

Defining rights and health care is a process which inevitably requires that decision-makers address the most complex and awkward questions of social policy. No government is likely to be able to provide the financial resources necessary to meet each and every citizen's claim for health care in the manner the citizen desires. Publicly funded health care is rationed. Politicians should confront that reality and address how best each citizen's share of the public health care resources should be determined. While a private sector exists side by side with the NHS inequality is ineradicable. If I can pay, I am free to prescribe my own health care needs and arrange their satisfaction. Prohibition of private medicine altogether is not an option seriously considered today. The state can only fulfil its obligation to meet health care needs by attempting to achieve an equitable balance between the competing demands of its citizens. That would necessarily involve unpopular decisions and the public airing of questions we might all prefer to avoid. The cruellest example is perhaps this: just how much of the NHS purse are we prepared to spend on the very, very young and the very, very old?

There is, however, a glimmer of hope which links the vexed questions of rights to and rights in health care. Perhaps if patients were actually more and more involved in treatment decisions both the quality of those decisions and the strain on NHS resources might be improved. There is increasing evidence that few of us wish our life to be indefinitely prolonged faced with an illness that is inevitably terminal. Yet doctors still find it difficult to accept that their special skills have no further purpose and naturally have human hesitations about telling a patient and her family the 'bad news'. So active treatment often continues, at great expense, beyond the stage that the patient, if fully informed, might have desired. Patient autonomy might in a very real sense save money. And there is one final point I almost hesitate to make. Health care ethicists and lawyers argue that patients should be fully informed about the risks and benefits of proposed treatment and any available alternative therapies. Should they also be fully advised of the cost to the NHS? My right to health care in a system that cannot meet all needs is inevitably in competition with my neighbour's. Do I as a citizen have an obligation to weigh her needs against my own?

POSTSCRIPT

Just two months after submission of the original manuscript for this chapter, a case arose encapsulating very many of the issues raised within it. In *Re J.*[37] the parents of a severely brain-injured infant sought a court order requiring doctors to place their son on a ventilator when he ceased, as he certainly would cease, to be able to breathe for himself. Paediatricians caring for the boy judged it not to be in his interests to prolong his life. The Court of Appeal quashed the trial judge's original grant of such an order. Lord Donaldson MR declared that the English courts would never order a medical practitioner to act in a way contrary to his clinical judgment, provided that that judgment was supported by a responsible professional body of professional opinion. Once again professional judgment is recognized by the courts as the arbiter of the content of rights to health care.

Re J. is notable on another ground too. Lord Donaldson MR offers explicit judicial recognition of the inevitable and inextricable relationship between claims of rights to health care and problems of limited resources. He criticizes the first-instance judgment for failing 'to take account of the sad fact of life that health authorities may on occasion find that they have too few resources, either human or material or both, to treat all the patients whom they would like to treat in the way in which they would like to treat them'.[38]

NOTES AND REFERENCES

1 Designed to implement in the NHS the Government's Citizen's Charter: HPCI published by HMSO, 1991. Note that the manifestos of the Labour and Liberal Democrat Parties also proposed 'guarantees' and rights to emergency care.
2 See generally *Medicine, Patients and the Law* (2nd edn), M. Brazier, Penguin, 1992.

3 For discussion of both the nature of health rights and a wider right to health see J. Montgomery, 'Recognising a right to health', in *Economic, Social and Cultural Rights*, R. Beddard and D. M. Hill (eds), Macmillan, 1992, pp. 184–203; J. Montgomery, 'Rights to health and health care', in A. Coote (ed.) *Citizens' Rights in a Modern Welfare State*, Rivers Oram, pp. 100–30.

4 For a general introduction to the social and ethical dimensions of resource allocation see *Law and Medical Ethics* (3rd edn), J. K. Mason and A. McCall Smith, Butterworths, 1991, Chapter 11.

5 Treatment decisions using QALYS require the following formula to be adopted in making choices between patients. A year of healthy life likely to ensue from treatment scores 1. Any diminished quality of the likely life expectancy scores less than 1 and it is possible to arrive at a minus score. QALYS are totalled up per patient and the winners are those with the highest score. Younger patients therefore have a built-in advantage in the system. On QALYS generally see Mason and McCall Smith, *op. cit.* pp. 266–9. For vigorous criticism of ageist bias in QALYS and of the concept in general see J. M. Harris, 'QALYfying the value of life' (1987), *J. Med. Ethics*, 13, 117.

6 See the report of the Nuffield Institute for health services studies: *The Guardian*, 25 March 1992.

7 Not that the system is perfect: see Brazier, *op. cit.*, Chapter 16.

8 Section 13 of the National Health Services Act 1977 as amended by the National Health Service and Community Care Act 1990.

9 (1979) 123 Sol. Jo 436; discussed fully in J. D. Finch, *Health Services Law*, Sweet and Maxwell, 1981, pp. 38–9.

10 *Associated Provincial Picture Houses* v. *Wednesbury Corporation* [1948] 1 KB 223.

11 *The Times*, 26 November 1987, CA.

12 *The Times*, 6 January 1988, CA.

13 See C. Dyer, 'Going to law to get treatment' (1987), *Brit. Med. J.*, 295, 1554; and for criticism of what they style 'shroud waving', see Mason and McCall Smith, *op. cit*, p. 261.

14 See *The Independent*, 21 March 1992.

15 Statistics issued by the Department of Health itself in March 1992 showed that while the majority of regional health authorities were meeting the two-year deadline, the number of patients waiting up to a year increased by 13 per cent; see *The Guardian*, 26 March 1992.

16 See *International Medical Malpractice Law*, D. Giesen, Kluwer, 1988, para. 723.

17 Application No 11590/85. I am very grateful to my colleague Dr Joseph Jaconelli for bringing this decision of the Commission to my attention.

18 *Barnett* v. *Chelsea and Kensington HMC* [1969] 1 QB 428

19 In practical terms proof of causation might often prove an insuperable hurdle, of course; see *Clerk and Lindsell on Torts* (16th edn), paras 11–25 and 11–26.

20 *The Times*, 1 and 2 November 1985.

21 See L. S. Powers, 'Hospital emergency service and the open door' (1968), *Michigan Law Review*, 662, 1455.

22 In fact both infants were operated on soon after the court hearings and sadly both subsequently died.

23 The disincentive to offer treatment for fear of liability has led in the USA and Canada to the enactment of Good Samaritan Statutes exempting hospitals and health care staff from liability for emergency care; see Powers, 19; but see also Giesen, *op. cit.*, para. 721, who found not one example of hospitals or health care professionals held liable because they chose to render emergency aid. But note *Cattley* v. *St John's Ambulance Brigade* (1988), unreported discussed in M. A. Jones, *Medical Negligence*, Sweet & Maxwell, 1991, p. 24.

24 To some extent this has already happened. See *Knight* v. *Home Office* [1990] 2 All ER 237. Of course, any 'practicability' defence would only avail the defendant authority. The individual doctor would continue to be judged by the standard of the reasonably experienced practitioner, and the authority will be vicariously liable for her negligence, but note the seductive argument in the dissenting judgment of Sir Nicolas Browne-Wilkinson VC in *Wilsher* v. *Essex AHA* [1987] QB 730 CA, that junior doctors should be judged only in the context of their actual skill and experience; see generally M. A. Jones, *op. cit.*, pp. 151–3

25 [1988] 1 FLR 512.

26 Denouncing any form of discrimination against the infertile as unacceptable while the fertile need meet no form of conditions for parenthood.

27 See the Human Fertilisation and Embryology Act, s. 13 (5).

28 *Sidaway* v. *Royal Bethlem Hospital* [1985] AC 871.

29 *Bolam* v. *Friern HMC* [1957] 1 WLR 582.

30 Access to Health Records Act s. 5(1); Data Protection (Subject Access Modification) Order 1987 reg. 4(2).

31 See M. A. Jones, *op. cit.*, pp. 64–71.

32 Note 26.

33 See H. Teff, 'Consent to medical procedures: paternalism, self-determination or therapeutic alliance' (1985) 101 LQR 432; M. Brazier, 'Patient autonomy and consent to treatment: the role of the law' [1987] 7 LS 167.

34 *F.* v. *West Berkshire HA* [1990] AC1; *J.* v. *C.* [1990] 3 All ER 735; *Re M. (a minor) (wardship: sterilisation)* [1988] 2 FLR 497; *Re P. (a minor) (wardship: sterilisation)* [1989] 1 FLR 182.

35 *Re C. (a minor) (wardship: medical treatment)* [1990] Fam. 26; *Re J. (a minor) (wardship: medical treatment)* [1990] 3 All ER 930.

36 *Re R. (a minor) (wardship: medical treatment)* [1991] 4 All ER 177; *Re W. (a minor) (medical treatment)* [1992] 4 All ER 627 CA.

37 *Re J. (a minor) (wardship medical treatment)* [1992] 4 All ER 614 CA.

38 Arp 623; see also *Airedale NHS Trust* v. *Bland* [1993] 1 All ER 821, per Lord Browne-Wilkinson at p. 879.

4

The Right to Vote

ROBERT BLACKBURN

The right of every citizen to vote and take part in the political process of a state is the foundation of its democracy. It is a citizen's right which is of immense symbolic as well as practical importance, for it enshrines the principle of political and civil equality in our law, and thereby underpins most other contemporary rights of citizenship dealt with in this book. That as many as 33,610,399 persons turned out to cast their votes for 651 MPs in the general election on 9 April 1992 represents a very high level of popular participation in the main political event of British parliamentary democracy, and also the enjoyment of one of today's fundamental rights of citizenship that was campaigned for by courageous men and women in the face of harsh resistance, and finally won for each adult citizen as of right, regardless of gender or property ownership, only as recently as 1928. Free elections allow ordinary citizens to control power as well as assert their own individual rights. In terms of political responsibility, the important point about elections is that they place a powerful incentive upon those who govern us to interpret what is in the public interest not upon paternalistic notions of what they think is best for us, but according to what we, the voters, believe is good or bad for us. In 1952 the United Kingdom became signatory to the First Protocol to the European Convention on Human Rights, whereby in international law it is committed 'to hold free elections at reasonable intervals by secret ballot, under conditions which will ensure the free expression of the opinion of the people'.[1] How adequately does British law promote this principle and the quality of a citizen's right to vote and be represented? This chapter seeks to answer the question by considering some current problems and issues in the context of parliamentary elections. It will deal in turn with: the qualifications to vote; whether voting should be a voluntary or compulsory act; the role played by candidates and parties in voting; the intervals at which citizens cast their votes in general elections; and, finally, proportional representation and which method of elections is best in the United Kingdom for translating votes into parliamentary seats.

QUALIFICATIONS TO VOTE

Election law in the United Kingdom is not codified in the same way as in most other countries, and to establish the provisions affecting the franchise, candidature, election timing or constituencies different statutes and parts of the common law must be turned to.[2] The most important statute for establishing who can vote is the Representation of the People Act 1983.[3] This statute provides that any person may vote at a parliamentary election so long as he or she is 18 years old or over on the date of the poll, was resident in the constituency where he or she wishes to vote on a specified date in the preceding year, and is a British, Commonwealth or Irish citizen.[4]

The age for voting was previously 21 years, until the Family Law Reform Act 1969 reduced it to 18 years along with the age of majority in general, and thereby added over four million new voters to the electoral roll. Whether or not the voting age should be lowered still further to 16 years has been discussed in several political quarters over the past few years. There is some degree of support for such a change within the Labour Party, including from the veteran socialist Tony Benn, who included it in his scheme for wholesale reform of the Constitution, published and presented to the House of Commons as the Commonwealth of Britain Bill 1991.[5] It was also an election manifesto commitment of the Liberal Democrats at the April 1992 general election, forming part of their written Constitution proposal published two years previously.[6] The Liberal Democrat MP James Wallace has argued that he and his party members

> hope for greater involvement by young people in decision-
> making. The young have an important stake in the future,
> and what they lack in experience may be more than
> compensated for by the fresh ideas that they can bring
> forward. A number of causes now coming to the fore in
> politics – for example environmental concern – were espoused
> by young people long before they gained political
> respectability.[7]

The argument against any further age reduction in voting rests simply upon grounds that some arbitrary age limit has to be drawn, and that many 16- and 17-year-old persons are unlikely to have gained the necessary maturity to be able to express a considered political judgment. At present there is no support for a reduction in the voting age on the Government and Opposition front benches, so there is negligible prospect of such a change, and little chance either of a parliamentary debate on the issue, unless an MP such as William Wallace or Tony Benn comes near the top of the annual ballot of backbenchers for allocation of time in which Private Member's Bills may be introduced, and chooses to make it the subject of his draft legislation.

The key concept in the modern right to vote is one of residency in the constituency. This is in contrast to the requirements before 1918 of property ownership and payment of rates. Within Great Britain there is no required duration for which the citizen must have lived in the constituency in order to qualify for the vote, simply that he or she was living in the locality on the qualifying date, which is 10 October.[8] In Northern Ireland, however, there must have been three months' residency, and a separate qualifying date exists. This residency is established by forms being sent out to the occupier of each house in the United Kingdom from the electoral registration officer for each constituency several weeks before the qualifying date, and the householder filling in on the form the names of all persons aged 16 or over on the following 10 October who are living there, and returning the form promptly. Several ambiguities regularly arise in the minds of recipients of these forms, concerning, for example, persons temporarily away, children who are university students, hostels or residential homes, and persons who own two or more houses. The general rule is that those who normally live in the household but are temporarily away, such as persons on holiday or students, must be included, as must all residents, lodgers and guests apart from short-stay visitors. Persons away on work must be included unless their absence totals more than six months, and special voting arrangements are made for members of the armed forces or civil servants overseas, including diplomats. The results of this annual national exercise are published in lists known as electoral registers in each constituency, a draft being prepared for public inspection between 28 November and 16 December, then formalized on the following 16 February and operative for any election thereafter in the next 12 months.

Only persons whose names appear on the electoral register may vote, so clearly the quality of and efficiency with which each register is compiled is crucial to a citizen's right to vote. This represents a large and difficult administrative task, which is too often forgotten or not fully appreciated as being of fundamental importance to voting and our democracy. Since it is an annual exercise, and with constant population changes, for example from deaths or moving house, perfect accuracy is impracticable. Some commentators, including Dr David

Butler and Professor Bryan Keith-Lucas, believe an error level as high as 3–4 per cent to be 'acceptable', being the margin of error estimated to exist in surveys conducted by the Office of Population Censuses and Surveys in both 1951 and 1966.[9] However, in 1982 the OPCS published a report entitled 'Electoral registration in 1981', which disclosed an astonishingly high level of inaccuracy, calculating that 6.5 per cent of those eligible to vote were not included in the 1981 electoral register at their qualifying address on 10 October 1980, and by the time the register came into force on 16 February 1981 the level had risen to 9 per cent, rightly described as 'an alarming degree of inexactitude'.[10] This meant that out of the total electorate, over three million citizens were effectively disenfranchised from their right to vote.

Following an inquiry into the matter by the Home Affairs Select Committee of the House of Commons in 1983, there is a large measure of agreement among politicians and registration officers about the principles for improvements in the efficiency of compiling the electoral register. But the real question remains one of whether registration officers are to be given the resources to meet them. The first aim must be to secure the return of the annual forms for completion sent to householders. Advertising now used in the weeks preceding preparation of the draft register is still largely confined to billboards, and more extensive press and television campaigns should be undertaken. Greater energy should be devoted to publicity in different languages, and registration officers must identify sizeable ethnic minorities within their constituencies and make arrangements for information leaflets and media advertisements in appropriate languages. The authority to make house to house inquiries under section 10 of the 1983 Act should extend to a greater use of personal canvassing than at present, not only to remind non-respondents of the forms sent out, but also to verify improbable answers. This is particularly so if the address in question is known to be in multiple occupation, or where it is common knowledge that negligent omissions frequently occur, for example in old people's homes where residents are least likely to check the accuracy of the draft register. Such enquiries should check with the registrar of deaths, and weed out obviously erroneous entries; the London Borough of Richmond was not an isolated example of producing an electoral register for the 1992 election with the names of two babies and a dog on it.[11]

The public and the Government must now confront the problem of providing the finances, personnel and other resources to match the civil importance of the work. Some countries, notably the USA, leave the chasing of voter registration to the political parties, in whose interests it is that supporters are able to vote in the forthcoming election. This has never been the tradition in Britain and in any event our parties, particularly those on the left, have had negligible financial resources (especially if compared with the huge amounts of political finance involved in American electioneering) with which to perform their more basic tasks of formulating public policy, encouraging public awareness and participation in politics, publicizing their work and campaigning for office. At present it is reckoned that the Government spends only 1.2 pence per elector on the national promotion of voter registration.[12] In 1988 the Home Office provided £569,000 for its entire domestic electoral registration publicity and advertising campaign for that year. By contrast, it might be noted that it devoted £750,000 towards the one-off campaign to publicize the new voting rights of the relatively far smaller number of overseas voters.[13] But of more fundamental importance, it seems right that there should be a radical overhaul of administrative responsibility for voter registration. Particularly now that 95 per cent of electoral registration offices are installed with computers, a citizen's right to vote should be founded upon the date upon which he files his claim in a particular constituency, not upon an arbitrary annual anniversary. In other words, electoral registration should become a 'rolling' exercise, being constantly updated, with the annual issue and return of forms to householders being just one method of verification and accuracy of the register. Extra resources for voter registration must be centrally derived out of money expressly provided by Parliament, and there needs to be created a national agency with a more interventionist role in coordinating and supervising the practices of electoral registration officers. Central responsibility for this task might be passed to an Electoral Commission, a new body created by statute, with other responsibilities in the field of electoral law, such as the review of constituency boundaries and the regulation of political campaigning and finance.[14]

The Representation of the People Act 1983 confers the right to vote upon not only British citizens but in addition Commonwealth citizens and citizens of the Republic of Ireland. Even before statute controlled the nationality qualifications in 1914, persons born within the British Empire and Dominions were at common law regarded as British subjects and therefore entitled to vote, subject to satisfying the property and other qualifications at that time. The 1914 British Nationality and Status of Aliens Act codified that common law rule, which was then refined by the 1948 British Nationality Act to replace the notion of common nationality with a system of reciprocal citizenship. It also provided a system whereby persons from countries such as India and the African republics were still to be regarded for nationality purposes and the right to vote as 'British subjects', even though they no longer owed allegiance to the Crown but retained their position within the Commonwealth, with the British monarch being recognized as Head of the Commonwealth. There are about one and a half million citizens from other parts of the Commonwealth resident here today and in possession of the right to vote. There are also about 400,000 Irish citizens resident in the United Kingdom who may vote in British elections.[15] This arrangement was provided as part of the settlement in the Ireland Act 1949, and reflects in the worlds of the British Prime Minister at that time, Clement Attlee, 'our propinquity of Eire, the longstanding relations between our peoples and the practical difficulties that flow from any attempt to treat Eire as altogether a foreign country'.[16]

There are no good arguments for excluding these voting rights now enjoyed by Commonwealth and Irish nationals, and indeed it is important that the franchise should now be extended further to European Community state nationals who satisfy a main residency or domicile qualification. This, it might be noted, should supersede the basis of Irish voters here, by virtue of their membership of the European Community. At present there are about 260,000 non-United Kingdom European Community state nationals working and living in the UK.[17] The arguments for extending voting rights to Community nationals is strongest for local authority elections, but it is not possible to draw sensible distinctions between different parts of the democratic process. If a French, German or Italian national from within the European Community is on the one hand being encouraged by the principles of, and mobility offered by, the common market to work and live here, and on the other hand is subject to United Kingdom law, paying taxes and taking part in the life of the community, he or she has a good claim to exercise a vote in local and national community affairs.

Any attempt to restrict voting rights of Commonwealth citizens, and draw some distinction between citizens from the United Kingdom and citizens from Jamaica, Guyana, New Zealand or any other Commonwealth country, would be highly invidious. It would divide families in Britain into voters and non-voters by virtue of the idiosyncrasies of the Nationality Act 1981 and, given the symbolic importance of the right to vote, those persons who had not yet acquired full British nationality would be made to feel second-class citizens. Candidature for public office would presumably also be affected, so not only would Commonwealth state nationals permanently resident here and paying taxes be disenfranchised from voting in the community, but they would be prohibited from playing any active role in the representation and leadership of the community. In constituencies comprising multiracial communities, the insecurities and fears too often already present among ethnic minorities would be aggravated, and attempts being made to construct genuinely representative bodies within those communities and across the country would be seriously impeded. There may be a case for introducing a minimum period of residency within the United Kingdom before eligible non-British nationals, comprising European Community and Commonwealth state nationals, might be allowed to vote. In the case of parliamentary elections, this might be for a period of four continuous years prior to the residency qualifying date for electoral registration, whereas for local council elections a shorter period might be adopted, perhaps for as little as 12 continuous months.

THE DUTY TO VOTE

Should voting be made compulsory in the United Kingdom? This would be consistent with the legal compulsion in the first place to register one's name and address as a voter at the local Town Hall. Several countries have introduced compulsory voting, including Australia and Belgium, and the obvious result is a far higher turnout of the electorate (even if 100 per cent is never in practice attainable) and therefore a more comprehensive expression of public opinion at the polls. The percentage turnout of electors at general elections since 1945 has been as follows:[18]

1945	72.8	1970	72.0
1950	83.9	1974 (Feb)	78.8
1951	82.6	1974 (Oct)	72.8
1955	76.8	1979	76.0
1959	78.7	1983	72.7
1964	77.1	1987	75.3
1966	75.8	1992	77.7

A MORI public opinion poll, commissioned by the Rowntree Reform Trust and published a year before the 1992 general election, rather surprisingly disclosed that a majority of people in the United Kingdom actually favour compulsory voting. The precise response was 49 per cent for, 42 per cent against and 9 per cent don't knows.[19] However, this proposal has never received any substantial degree of support among British politicians. It was one of the issues raised for inquiry by the Home Affairs Select Committee examination of the Representation of the People Acts in 1982–3, but was not dealt with in any depth at all in its discussions, and in its final report was an issue not even mentioned. The general, traditional view on compulsory voting is, first, that it is an infringement of civil liberty: that politics is an essentially voluntary exercise (hence also the lack of public regulation and provision for political parties) and persons should be left alone to decide for themselves how and whether to vote. In other words, a great many British people instinctively feel that there is something rather totalitarian about being forced to vote. Many also feel that it is no bad thing if the country as a whole is relatively depoliticized, and this is simply reflected in a number of citizens not being sufficiently interested in bothering to turn up at the ballot station to vote on polling day. Second, it is often argued that compulsory voting is unnecessary in Britain and as a principle of election law tends to be resorted to only in states with a weak democratic culture or a fragile national identity. Third, it is sometimes said that compulsory voting produces a highly undesirable 'donkey vote'. This was an expression used by the Liberal Party in giving evidence to the Home Affairs Select Committee in 1982,[20] presumably meaning that compulsory voting would produce hoards of politically mindless voters being dragged along to the polling booth. A final reservation has been the alleged impracticality of enforcing such an obligation. This is a factor that has especially troubled those who might be expected to enforce it. A memorandum by Rochdale Borough Council to the Select Committee mentioned that it would result in tens of thousands of prosecutions and clutter up the courts, and, in the view of the Association of District Councils, there would be 'severe enforcement problems, and there would be the problems created by electors who could not vote on account of sickness'.[21]

These arguments when looked at closely are rather weak. There are very few practical problems with compulsory voting in Australia. Easier voting arrangements, such as greater use of postal voting or (as in Australia) centres in each constituency where voters from other constituencies may vote, would alleviate any hardship on voters with physical disability or with travel commitments, and for the ordinary voter a walk to the local ballot station is hardly a very taxing exercise. The 'donkey vote' argument is highly tenuous if it assumes that persons not voting are likely to be any the more stupid in their mental faculties than people who do vote. Neither is any draconian enforcement of compulsory voting any more likely than the prosecutions for failing to respond properly to the electoral registration officer, by completing and returning the annual forms of eligible voters in each household, for which there were just three prosecutions in 1979, one in 1980 and four in 1981.

The real issue is a constitutional one, and whether it is a citizen's duty to vote, as well as a right. It seems to me that unquestionably there is a moral obligation to cast one's vote, and that the arguments of principle against such a duty are no more democratic than those that can be mustered by an anarchist. The 'voluntary' argument,

82

which relies upon a moral right not to vote, or 'optional democracy' as it might be called, is essentially anti-social in nature. There are also good reasons to suppose that a duty to vote would tend towards a better-informed electorate as a whole. Certainly compulsory voting would transform the work of party workers and canvassers away from 'getting out the vote', in other words persuading people to go to the polling station, and allow them to concentrate more on talking with voters about the issues and policies which are represented by their party. At present local party electioneering concentrates almost entirely on canvassers identifying where their party's support is the greatest, so that their colleagues acting as tellers waiting outside ballot stations on polling day can try to calculate which of their supporters have voted or not, and then instruct other party colleagues to call at non-voters' homes to try to persuade them to vote. There is also some reason to suppose that if people know they have to vote, they may be more diligent in taking the trouble to find out more about what the parties and candidates stand for and what their policies are. Generally, therefore, compulsory voting is likely to lead to more discussion and understanding of what the forthcoming election is all about.

Whether or not the moral duty to vote should be consecrated in law confronts traditional British feelings about using the law to encroach upon a citizen's 'right to be left alone'. Legislation which introduced a legal duty upon all our citizens to vote might allow for persons who consciously wished to cast no vote, by providing that all ballot papers should contain a box in addition to the names of the candidates against which the voter could signify an abstention. And if in addition the day of the general election was made a national public holiday, or the election was held on a Sunday, as is the case in many other countries such as France and Germany, then there could be no good reason why those who now possess the fundamental political right to vote should not equally be called upon to cast their opinion on who should represent them in Government and Parliament over the coming four years. This question of compulsory voting, then, raises issues which are of great symbolic and practical political importance. It is a proposal which the next Speaker's Conference on Election Law should consider far more seriously than in the past.

CANDIDATES AND PARTIES

The essential corollary of the citizen's right to vote is that he or she has the right to choose a representative according to his or her own free wishes and feelings. The law which regulates who may or may not stand as a candidate for election to the House of Commons is typically British. It starts with the generality of common law presumption that any British citizen of full age may stand, which then progressively (or in some cases regressively) has been trimmed by miscellaneous *ad hoc* statutory disqualifications over the past three centuries. One might expect such an important aspect of constitutional law to be codified neatly within a single statute, such as the Representation of the People Act 1983, but this is not so. For a full list of disqualifications from membership of the House of Commons, ranging from bankruptcy and mental illness to being a hereditary peer, one must turn to a text on constitutional law written by a law professor, such as Wade and Bradley, or De Smith and Brazier, or else the parliamentary work of reference, *Erskine May's Parliamentary Practice*.[22]

Nationality and age restrictions upon candidature were settled a long time ago. Section 3 of the Act of Settlement in 1700 provided that no one born outside the kingdoms of England, Scotland, Ireland and their dominions is capable of sitting in either the House of Commons or the House of Lords. In this century, section 3 of the Ireland Act 1949 specifically retained Irish candidature upon the independence of that country, and the right of Commonwealth citizens to stand for election is confirmed and provided for in the Nationality Act 1981. Section 7 of the Parliamentary Elections Act 1695 put into statutory form the pre-existing common law rule that candidature was limited to adults, in other words persons over 21 years of age, in order to discourage the practice 'by connivancy' (as Sir Edward Coke put it)[23] of minors actually sitting: even after the Act, a few under-age Members managed to sit in the Commons prior to the 1832 Reform Act, including Charles James Fox and Lord John Russell. Curiously, when the age of majority was reduced to 18 by section 1 of the Family Law Reform Act 1969, and the right to vote was similarly lowered by the Representation of the People Act that same year, neither Ministers nor MPs noticed any inconsistency in failing to reduce the candidature age from 21 years accordingly. There was no parliamentary comment or debate at all on the matter during the passage of the two 1969 Acts.

So currently the situation is that at one end of the political process, namely the exercise of the vote, the age of maturity is set at 18; but at the other, receiving end – candidature – a different level of maturity is prescribed. In practice few persons between 18 and 20 years of age will wish to start a professional political career so young, and it is very rare for a local party association to wish to select someone at that age as their official candidate, especially as there is always stiff competition from experienced party members and campaigners, and former MPs defeated at the last election looking for a new constituency. None the less, it has happened, as with the Conservative MP Sir Richard Body, who had to wait until he was 21 years old to be adopted as a parliamentary candidate.[24] It should also be remembered that some MPs do enter the House of Commons at a young age, including at 23 years both Matthew Taylor and Charles Kennedy (now President of the Liberal Democrats) in 1987. The 21 age restriction upon candidature is anomalous, and should be reduced to 18 years, consistent with the right to vote. After a person has reached adulthood at 18 for virtually all other civil purposes, he or she should be free to offer himself or herself for election to Parliament, and the law should not restrict the choice of local voters to decide for themselves on the suitability of the particular candidate, and whether or not he or she is the best person to be representing them.

Political parties are unknown to British constitutional law, but they are the most important instrument of parliamentary government and the means by which ordinary citizens may participate in the political process. As the former Lord Chancellor, Lord Hailsham, once put it, 'political parties are no part of our constitution, but no part of our constitution can ignore their existence'.[25] They perform the essential democratic functions of providing the basis for electoral choice, representing public opinion and public interests in the community, formulating and reformulating public policy to be pursued by the party in Government or Opposition, and providing the personnel for parliamentary candidates at elections. Whereas the great majority of citizens may have little or no direct interest in politics as such, it is to the respective leading party politicians of the day that the citizen turns to hear an explanation of the major issues of the country, and the differences in social principle and practical policy between the parties, together with the reasons why one party's programme for government policy might be preferred over another's. For those more involved, the opportunity for ordinary citizens to become members of the local and national parties provides the channels for popular participation in policy formulation and the selection of parliamentary candidates and party leaders. But above all, for voting purposes at a general election political parties 'offer a basis for electoral choice by putting what they consider to be the central political issues before the voting public. Clearly, the performance of this function is absolutely vital to modern democracy, for the only way in which the electorate can choose between different policies is to have them structured by political parties presenting alternative programmes for their approval'.[26]

One pressing area into which British law should intervene is with respect to the financial affairs of political parties. At present there is no legal requirement for the parties to account publicly for their sources of income. In other words, the electorate has no legal right to know who is financially underwriting the work of the Conservatives, Labour and the Liberal Democrats, although such associations are clearly not of inconsiderable significance in terms of possible degrees of influence upon decision-making processes and the formulation of policies by the parties. The public disclosure of sources of income would simply be consistent with the principle of MPs declaring financial interests in a Register of Members' Interests required by standing orders in the House of Commons. An exception might be made for small donors of up to £1000 a year, in order to respect their privacy if they do not wish their political opinions or affiliation to be known publicly. The general rule, however, should be that parties prepare and publish annual accounts, in a standard form prescribed by statute, which clearly indicates their income, expenditure and financial status.

Related to this is the question of whether the parties have sufficient resources to perform their functions efficiently. The institutional dependence of the two main parties, the Conservatives upon commercial businesses and Labour upon trade unions, is well known, and in practice the Conservatives are always better off than the other parties. According to the research of Michael Pinto-Duschinsky, during the years of the elections in 1983 and 1987 respectively, the Conservatives received £9.4 million and £15 million, and spent £8.6 million and £11.3 million; Labour received £6.2 million and £10 million, and spent £6.1 million and £11.3 million.[27] The guiding principle in terms of voter choice should be one of a fair rivalry between the parties, but in a free society with voluntary membership and donations to parties, exact parity in financial status is always going to prove unattainable. In effect, the state indirectly funds political parties at election time in a number of ways. Most important is the free use of television and radio time to make party election broadcasts, in 1992 estimated to be worth around £6 million to each of the main parties. Free postage is given to candidates to deliver their election addresses, together with free use of council halls and state school rooms for election meetings. For the party in power, there is also the great advantage of the Whitehall publicity machine promoting government policies over the year or two prior to the election. In July 1991, for example, in the knowledge that an election was imminent, all three main political parties published their policies on citizens' rights; first came the Labour Party's *Citizen's Charter*, then there followed the Liberal Democrat's *Citizens' Britain*, and finally the Prime Minister John Major presented the Conservatives' *The Citizen's Charter*. The obvious difference between the three documents was that the Conservatives' policy statement was a superbly produced, glossy brochure, published officially as a Government White Paper and advertised and promoted nationally, all at the Treasury's expense, estimated at around £8 million.[28]

During the election campaign period most party finance is spent on posters, press advertising and staff costs. Expenditure on such expenses has been tightly controlled at constituency level ever since 1883, and currently under the terms of the Representation of the People Act 1983 no candidate may spend more than £4330 plus 4.9 pence per voter in rural seats or plus 3.7 pence in urban seats. Nationally, however, there is no upper limit on expenditure incurred by each party in promoting and publicizing its policies and leaders, and it is national campaigning which proves most successful in influencing voter behaviour. There is a good case for now imposing a maximum limit upon the amount of money which may be spent on national campaigning, analogous to the limit upon constituency expenses. This would similarly apply during the four-week campaign period between the announcement of a general election and polling day, and also similarly would need to extend to a separate prohibition on persons or companies outside the party spending money with a view to promoting or procuring the election of the party's representatives. The precise limit might initially reflect current practice, being the average amount spent between the two main parties during the 1992 campaign (approximately £8 million), and this might be made subject in the controlling Act of Parliament to amendment by way of statutory instrument laid before the House of Commons. Such a measure would help to ensure that the present tendency towards an ever-growing mass of party propaganda is resisted, which in any event is subject to a diminishing impact, whereas from the point of view of informing the voter the improvements that are crucially needed lie in the arena of quality, rather than quantity. Insofar as one or more parties may be far richer than others, by capping the sum they may spend at a level perfectly adequate for efficient publicity and promotion purposes, they would not be able to enjoy an unacceptably disproportionate advantage based purely upon the wealth of their supporters. Such a limit, plus ensuring that the prohibition on political advertising on television remains in place, should serve to resist any further downward slide into what is generally regarded as the mayhem and excesses of American-style electioneering.

A final improvement would be to introduce a limited form of direct state funding of political parties.[29] What is envisaged here is not huge sums of taxpayers' money, but a modest supplement to the party's own membership subscription fees and fund-raising. The initial annual fund to be distributed between all parties, based upon their level of electoral support at the last general election, might be around £5 million, subject to periodic reviews, and this would simply be an extension of the principle agreed in 1975, whereby opposition parties are now given a small state subsidy for the performance of their parliamentary work.[30] One advantage of such a scheme would be to reduce the excessive degree of institutional dependence of the two main parties, whereby at present the majority of the revenue of the Conservative and Labour parties is derived from companies and trade unions respectively.[31] Perhaps no favours are sought or granted, but for a national popular party aiming to represent the whole country, it is unhealthy for a situation to exist whereby a party is made highly conscious of special sectional interests upon whose financial support it depends for its very survival.

WHEN THE VOTE IS CAST

The principle on democratic voting expressed in the European Convention on Human Rights requires parliamentary elections to be held 'at reasonable intervals'.[32] When does the citizen have the opportunity to exercise his or her right to vote in the UK? The answer, more or less, is whenever the person who is Prime Minister says so. The only law restricting his or her choice is the ancient Septennial Act 1716 as amended by section 7 of the Parliament Act 1911, so that Parliaments automatically terminate five years to the day after the date of their first meeting. Even then, there is no law to require a new Parliament to meet, thus necessitating an election to determine who will be Members of the new House of Commons, except for the even more antiquated Triennial Act 1694, which says that a Parliament should be called within three years. So in legal theory parliamentary elections only need to be held every eight years. In legal practice, however, the Queen controls the calling of elections by virtue of the Crown's common law prerogative, and by political convention she exercises this prerogative upon the request of the Prime Minister. Within each five-year parliamentary term, the Queen issues a Royal Proclamation dissolving Parliament and summoning another, thus requiring the election and causing writs to be sent out to each returning officer in every constituency to start the nomination procedure and ballot arrangements in motion.[33]

The 'reasonable intervals' between elections in the UK have been of a wide diversity. The average length of time between parliamentary elections since 1918 has been three years and eight months, but this tells us nothing about the actual duration of any particular Parliament, nor does it help us to predict with any degree of accuracy when the date of the next occasion for citizens to cast their vote will be. Parliamentary terms have varied widely in practice from less than one year (1922–3, 1924, 1974), to one to two years (1950–1, 1964–6), to two to three years (1929–31), to three to four years (1919–22, 1931–5, 1970–4, 1983–7) to four to five years (1924–9, 1945–50, 1951–5,

1959–64, 1966–70, 1974–9, 1979–83, 1987–92) and during the Second World War even beyond five years through prolongation statutes (1935–45). The 1992 election came four years and ten months after Margaret Thatcher's success on 11 June 1987.

The Prime Minister, John Major, announced the news of a pending poll on Wednesday 11 March, just four weeks before the date of the election on Thursday 9 April. Speaking to a battery of television newscasters and cameras, whose companies had been advised to wait outside 10 Downing Street, Mr Major explained that earlier that morning he had 'asked Her Majesty the Queen to proclaim the dissolution of Parliament' and 'Her Majesty has been graciously pleased to signify that she will comply with this request'. After giving the relevant dates of the following Monday 16 March for dissolution, 9 April for the election and 27 April for the meeting of the new Parliament, Mr Major then gave what was equivalent to a free party political broadcast on why the Conservative Party would win the election and why voters should vote for him.

Thus the citizen does not possess the right to vote at regular intervals prescribed by law, so that the election date is known to all in advance. Instead the right to vote is circumscribed by the political conditions selected by the Prime Minister as being suitable for the occasion. What are the political factors that influence a Prime Minister in his or her choice of date? One purported advantage of the present system is said to be that it allows the Government to consult the opinion of ordinary citizens over an important, single item of policy if the Prime Minister feels a specific mandate is required. Such 'snap' elections, however, would appear to be relatively rare, unpopular and politically unwise. It was the purpose of the second (December) general election in 1910, over the Liberal Government's Parliament Bill to curtail the powers of the House of Lords. Asquith's Liberals were returned to power, with a slightly reduced majority. In 1924, the Conservative premier Stanley Baldwin called an election after only eight months in office, and one year three months after the previous election, to obtain the voters' mandate over the issue of tariff reform: he lost his majority altogether. Much closer in living memory was the débâcle of Edward Heath going to the polls in February 1974 over 'who rules Britain' during the miners' strike. This precedent above all others makes it highly improbable that Mr Major would ever call an election in such circumstances or over any single item of policy, such as Europe and the Maastricht Treaty.

The primary factor in a Prime Minister's choice of timing on when citizens are to vote is simply his or her party's prospects for winning or losing the contest. 'The Prime Minister is likely to have a General Election at the time when he thinks he is most likely to win it', as a former Conservative Party Chairman has put it.[34] Political autobiographies bear evidence to the tactical assessments and strategies made in calculating the best time to win an election.[35] The most immediate indicators, of course, are the results of public opinion polls on voting intentions. By-election results will carry a great deal of significance too. The period of September 1990 to March 1992 was typical of the vacillation and public confusion produced by this British system of a 'floating' election date. At the September 1990 party conference, the then Conservative Chairman Kenneth Baker was dealing with questions on the subject, saying 'my task as Party Chairman is to have the party ready to fight the Election if the Prime Minister decides to have one in 1991'.[36] In the event, the April 1992 election left Mr Major with only a few months' leeway in which he had to call an election, before the five-year term set by the Parliament Act expired on 17 June. Everyone in the country had been half-expecting him to call an election ever since the Gulf War was won in January 1991, which helped boost Conservative ratings in the opinion polls to a four-point lead, following his replacement of Margaret Thatcher as Conservative leader and Prime Minister in November 1990, at which time Labour had been ahead by as much as ten points in the polls. Clearly Mr Major and his new Party Chairman, Chris Patten, were hoping for a safe lead in the opinion polls before chancing an election and, equally clearly, while Mr Major was keen to have his own mandate in office, the prospect of going down in history as the shortest-serving Prime Minister in office since Bonar Law in 1922 prevented him from being too hasty.[37] With the Conservatives and Labour running neck and neck in the opinion polls, alternating narrow leads, for over a year the country had to endure speculation on the election date upon virtually a daily basis in the media, and personal and commercial financial plans had to be kept in a state of abeyance until the composition of the new Government was decided.

Should the governing party be able to dictate the date of a general election and so be in possession of such a strong political advantage over other parties? The explanation for this executive domination over electoral timing is founded simply upon the ancient history of the royal prerogative, that Parliament was the personal creature of each king or queen to be consulted and dismissed as he or she wished; and this legal power still remains with us to be exercised politically by the Prime Minister of the day.[38] Behind the pomp and ceremony of a Royal Proclamation dissolving Parliament and declaring the calling of another, there lie all the political machinations of the Government being able to control the economy and make changes in interest rates or levels of taxation at the right time to gain popularity, while keeping a close eye on public opinion polls and by-election results, with the aim of maximizing the governing party's chances of success at whatever moment its leader chooses as most advantageous to hold an election. Not surprisingly, Government victories at the polls are more frequent than those of the Opposition.[39] Lord Hailsham, the Lord Chancellor throughout Mrs Thatcher's first two terms in office, described this system while he was in opposition to the Labour Government in 1976 as one whereby an 'elective dictatorship has proved more and more powerful, and more and more liable to perpetuate itself'.[40]

The way forward is for all those considering alternative electoral systems for the British Parliament, now including the Labour Party, following its conference decision to set up a working party on elections under Professor (now Lord) Raymond Plant, and the Liberal Democrats, to look not only at systems which are more proportionately representative but at ones which include fixed terms for the timing of citizens' voting. The length of the fixed term should be considered (three, four or five years) and so too should the prescribed circumstances in which an earlier election might be held, for example in the event of a no confidence motion being passed by the House of Commons upon the Government.[41] A system of fixed-term Parliaments must be preferable to that now existing in British constitutional practice, whereby in the words of the late Professor Owen Hood Phillips, 'the Prime Minister and his [or her] fellow conspirators alone' know when the date of the general election will be, so 'they can juggle with direct and indirect taxes and manipulate the economy in such a way as to favour their chances.' He concluded, 'this squalid practice of the Leaders of both main parties as it has developed is the least creditable aspect of the British constitution'.[42]

PROPORTIONAL REPRESENTATION

Proportional representation is not a system for elections in itself, but rather a criterion upon which to evaluate the working of any one of the range of electoral systems which can be used for voting purposes. It is a principle or yardstick by which to test the degree of representative proportionality between citizens' votes and successful party candidates. More precisely, what is looked for is the percentage equivalents between the total national votes cast for the respective parties' candidates, and the respective number of seats won in the House of Commons. No one in British politics is advocating a scheme of electoral reform that is purely proportionately representative in this way (which would require what is called a 'national party list' system) and no country in North America and Europe possesses such a method of voting.[43]

It is well known that applying this yardstick to the present British electoral system of simple plurality voting, or 'first past the post' as it is popularly called, in each of the 651 constituencies throws up a significant measure of distortion. According to the British system, the result of each constituency election 'shall be ascertained by counting the votes given to each candidate and the candidate to whom the majority of votes have been given shall be declared to have been elected.' In typical English legal tradition, this fundamental rule of the political system is buried away at the back of the Representation of the People Act 1983 in Schedule 1, Rule 18. First-past-the-post voting means that if the candidate for party A gets 10,883 votes, the candidate for party B 13,255, the candidate for party C 14,883, the candidate for party D 3108 and others 851, then the candidate for party C is returned as Member of Parliament. This is so despite his percentage support among voters being only 33.7 per cent, and the fact that 66.3 per cent of the local electorate – two out of every three local citizens – voted against him or her. That was the actual election result in Conwy, won by Sir Wyn Roberts for the Conservatives, and is certainly not unusual: in fact, the majority of constituencies are won on a minority vote. Magnified onto a national scale, on 9 April 1992 the Conservative Party won a 21-seat overall maiority in the House of Commons upon the basis of 41.9 per cent of the votes cast. No Government since 1935 has taken office with the electoral authority of a majority of citizens' votes. The former Prime Minister, Margaret (now Lady) Thatcher, at the height of her political triumph after the 1983 election, with a huge Commons majority of 397 seats to Labour's 209, had the backing of just 42.4 per cent of all votes in the country. Simple plurality is the least proportionately representative of all the electoral methods used for translating votes into parliamentary seats. It is easy to see why, on the face of things, the electoral system therefore might be described as 'in the highest degree unjust, unsatisfactory and dangerous'.[44] The huge number of 'wasted votes' by ordinary citizens – in Conwy, for example, 66.3 per cent or 28,097 voters were left unrepresented in the composition of Parliament – means also that 'it actually disenfranchises a large majority of the electors'.[45]

Just as there is no ideal constitution for use by all countries, so there is no ideal model of electoral system for all representative assemblies. The method to be employed for the House of Commons must match Britain's own indigenous political structure and traditions, and seek to improve the efficiency of its system of parliamentary democracy. There are a number of crucial criteria to be considered in the evaluation of any new electoral system for Britain. A closer relation between the proportion of votes cast for a party and its representation in the House of Commons must certainly be one of its principal features. There is nothing wrong *per se* with elections producing a bias towards one particular party which performs better than others across the country and thereby has the greater claim for political authority, but 'this bias must not be so pronounced that one party may obtain a majority of seats, and more or less unlimited power, on the basis of less than 50 per cent of votes cast' across the electorate as a whole.[46]

Proportional representation is regularly lambasted by opponents for being equivalent to coalition government, which is then portrayed as being essentially weak and unstable. The truth is, however, that the likelihood or otherwise of coalitions is a distraction from the central issues involved, and much of the discussion on this important subject of electoral reform unhelpfully revolves around the meaning of the term 'strong government', antagonists drawing upon whatever comparison abroad best serves the purposes of their argument, from Germany's acknowledged success in its economic management of the country under the additional member system, to Italy's crisis in federal affairs and fragmentation of political parties under a list system with adjusted constituency quotas. In practice, any electoral system can throw up circumstances in which no single party has an overall majority and this certainly includes Britain's 'first past the post' method: it has occurred this century in 1910, 1918, 1923, 1929 and 1974, and tiny majorities of less than ten seats were produced by the elections in 1950 and 1966. It is obvious that politicians prefer to get their own way, but will work with one another if circumstances dictate. At national level it might be recalled that the response of Britain's political system in times of crisis has been precisely to embrace coalition government, as in 1915–22 (because of war), 1931–5 (international monetary crisis) and 1940–5 (war), rather than to reject it for a so-called 'strong government' by one party. The experience of local authorities is useful to observe in this context, for it very often happens today that there are hung councils following local elections. Opponents of proportional representation claim that coalitions mean secret deals between parties in 'smoke-filled rooms', in which the distinctive policies of two or more parties are bargained away. But in practice the necessity for agreement between Labour and Liberal Democrats on hung councils, as in Avon, Cambridgeshire, Hertfordshire and Humberside County Councils, has brought about constructive and public debates about their differences, certainly, but also about securing their common aims. For a great many Labour supporters this is far preferable to not being in government at all.

Nor should it be supposed that other voting systems with a greater representative proportionality than Britain's exclude single-party government. In countries with such systems, such as Sweden, Germany, Portugal, Spain and Ireland, single parties have often achieved their own parliamentary majority. With proportional representation, if there is the necessary level of electoral support, Labour or the Conservatives will certainly be able to govern in their own right. But conversely, no single party should command a false majority in the legislature, and be in a position to enact wholly unacceptable legislation (the best recent instance being the 'poll tax') upon the moral basis of a mandate that is considerably less than 50 per cent of the electorate.

Another fundamental of any new electoral system must be to promote a close link between an MP and his or her constituency. It is essential to retain the political advantages of our system of local representation, with MPs being responsive to local opinion and representing local interests in the Commons, and individual citizens being able to call on his or her services in the field of administrative justice. It is here that lies the problem with adopting the single transferable vote (STV) in Britain. To secure its objective of greater proportional representation, STV operates upon the basis of each constituency returning a number of between three and seven MPs, who together represent a balanced ticket of voting preferences within that constituency. But if a constituency is to return five MPs, this means increasing the electoral size of constituencies from the existing number of about 60,000 voters to 300,000, and reducing the number of constituencies from 651 to 150. Under such circumstances the ordinary citizen's sense of political community or identity with such a huge area and number of people would be seriously impaired. For this reason no country in the world with a population as large as that of the United Kingdom employs the single transferable vote. It is more suitable in Ireland, for example, where a far smaller population allows for the 148-seat Dail to be composed from 42 constituencies, each returning between three and five MPs, but maintaining a constituency voting population of 55,000. Keeping a similar size of constituency in Britain under STV would mean expanding the composition of the House of Commons to the wholly untenable number of about 2000 MPs.

The most suitable method of election for the House of Commons is the additional member system, which retains the virtues of the existing constituency system while adding a greater degree of proportionality into the composition of the Commons. It achieves this by allocating seats partly through single-member constituency elections as at present, and partly through additional seats being awarded to the political parties by reference to the proportion of total votes received by each. Most countries in Western Europe have adopted some variety of this method of parliamentary election, and it represents the simplest way of balancing the various democratic factors involved. The precise number of additional seats, and whether the proportionality should be based upon national or regional basis, are important details which ultimately must be a matter for political judgment. The Institute for Public Policy Research recently supported the additional member system and recommended 50 per cent additional seats upon a regional basis, similar to the system which operates in Germany, drawn from lists of candidates prepared by the parties.[47] The Hansard Society report on the subject, chaired by Lord Blake, also supported the additional member system but recommended 160 additional seats, allocated to the 'best losers' in the constituency elections.[48] Although the additional member system undoubtedly works best where there are equal numbers of constituency and party list MPs, in terms of achieving full proportionality and equal status of both kinds of parliamentary member, there may be a political case for adopting a smaller number of party list members for the initial introduction of this reform, as being a less radical departure from the status quo and therefore more generally acceptable. If one-third of the Commons was to be composed in this way, which currently would amount to 217 MPs, then to keep the same total number of seats in the Commons the electoral quota for each constituency would need only to be increased to around 90,000 voters per constituency. This, then, would not greatly affect the size of constituencies. Even following the last Boundary Commission report in 1983, there are in fact at present several constituencies with over 90,000 parliamentary electors, including John Major's seat in Huntingdon (91,779 at the April 1992 election).

Despite 14 new women MPs being elected in 1992, their overall number in the Commons is still only 60, representing a mere 9 per cent of the House, which is one of the lowest ratios of women to men in the parliamentary systems of representation across Europe. This is not acceptable if Britain aspires to be a modern democracy. The determining factor in preferring a party list system of additional members over one of 'best losers' is the simplicity with which an equal and fair representation of women, and also ethnic minorities, can be achieved, so long as the parties themselves are allowed to prepare the lists of candidates for the additional seats in the Commons.

CONCLUSION

In this chapter I have sought to explain a number of ways in which the quality of voting law and practice might be improved in this country. The object of reform must be to create a legal framework and political climate in which fair, free elections and electioneering can flourish. Clearly the concepts today of democracy and citizenship are two sides of the same coin, and what is fundamental to both is the principle of equality between citizens, and the equal right of each individual to political power regardless of property, rank, sex, race or creed. It was written over two thousand years ago that 'The law declares equality to mean that the poor are to count no more than the rich: neither is to be sovereign, and both are to be on a level. . . . A constitution of this kind is bound to be a democracy, for the people are the majority, and the will of the majority is sovereign'.[49] But the right to vote, and to be chosen for political office, is of itself no guarantee of our other basic rights and freedoms. In particular, the operation of democracy depends heavily upon the quality of freedom of expression, and the collective right of the electorate to an informed choice at elections delivered through a fair and balanced media. It depends upon constitutional guarantees against the abuse of political power, such as judicial impartiality and independence, and respect for toleration and minority rights in the parliamentary process. And ultimately, political equality is never real unless it is accompanied by other basic rights affecting social and economic power. A principal object of citizens' voting today is to determine the public policy of the country, administered by the party politicians we elect to office, on how best to regulate economic power and ensure that our citizens enjoy equal rights and opportunities in the quality of their lives, respecting other fundamental rights of a social nature, especially with regard to housing, employment, health and education.

NOTES AND REFERENCES

1 *Convention for the Protection of Human Rights and Fundamental Freedoms* (Council of Europe, 1991).
2 On British electoral law generally, see H. F. Rawlings, *Law and the Electoral Process* (1988), R. J. Clayton (ed.), *Parker's Conduct of Parliamentary Elections* (1992), A. J. Little (ed.), *Schofield's Election Law* (1992).
3 1983, c. 2.
4 s. 1.
5 HC Bill [1990–1] 161.
6 *We the People: Towards a Written Constitution* (1990).
7 HC Deb., Vol. 70, Col. 787.
8 Representation of the People Act 1983, s. 1(1)(a) and ss. 4 and 5.
9 Report of the House of Commons Home Affairs Select Committee on the Representation of the People Acts [1982–3] 32, Vol. 2, pp. 203 *ff.*
10 *Ibid.*, Vol. 1, p. vi.
11 *Richmond Borough Herald*, 15 April 1992. Ballot papers were sent out to them to vote at the general election on 9 April.

12 From Hansard Society, *Agenda for Change* (1991), p. 84.
13 *Ibid.*, p. 61.
14 See Hansard Society, *Agenda for Change* (1991), Chapter 8.
15 See Home Office Memorandum submitted to the Home Affairs Select Committee on the Representation of the People Acts, *op. cit.*, Vol. 2, pp. 1 *ff.*
16 Quoted *ibid.*, p. 2.
17 Excluding Irish citizens and minors.
18 Figures from F. W. S. Craig, *British Electoral Facts 1832–1987* (1989), p. 66, and House of Commons Information Office.
19 State of the Nation poll, 1991.
20 p. 106.
21 p. 244.
22 E. C. S. Wade and A. W. Bradley, *Constitutional and Administrative Law* (10th edn 1985), Stanley de Smith and Rodney Brazier, *Constitutional and Administrative Law* (6th edn 1989), Clifford Boulton (ed.), *Erskine May's Parliamentary Practice* (21st edn 1989).
23 CJ (1547–1628) 681.
24 See Philip Norton, 'The qualifying age for candidature in British elections', *Public Law* (1980), 55.
25 *The Dilemma of Democracy* (1978), p. 37.
26 Hansard Society, *Paying for Politics* (1981), p. 13. See also Report of the Committee of Financial Aid to Political Parties ('Houghton Report'), Cmd 6601 (1976), p. 53.
27 'Trends in British party Funding, 1983–87', *Parliamentary Affairs* (1989), p. 197.
28 *The Independent*, 24 July 1991.
29 The principle of state funding for political parties was recommended by an independent committee of inquiry established by the Labour Government in 1976: see Houghton Report, *op. cit.* See also Keith Ewing, *The Funding of Political Parties in Britain* (1987), and Hansard Society, *Paying for Politics* (1981).
30 This financial allowance is known as 'Short money' after the Leader of the House of Commons, Edward Short, who introduced the scheme in 1975. The current system is regulated by a Commons resolution in 1988, and subject to a maximum of £840,000: see HC Deb., Vol. 135, Cols 1084–6.
31 On sources of income see Michael Pinto-Duschinsky, *op. cit.*, Keith Ewing, *op. cit.*, Houghton Report, *op. cit.*, and Hansard Society, *Paying for Politics* (1981).
32 See above, p. 75.
33 On the summoning and dissolution of Parliament, see Robert Blackburn, *The Meeting of Parliament* (1990), B. S. Markesinis, *The Theory and Practice of Dissolution of Parliament* (1972), and E. A. Forsey, *The Royal Power of Dissolution in the British Commonwealth* (1943).
34 From R. L. Leonard, *Elections in Britain* (1968), p. 5.
35 See, for example, the memoirs of former Prime Ministers: Harold Wilson, *The Labour Government 1964–70* (1971), Sir Anthony Eden, *Full Circle* (1960), Clement Attlee, *As It Happened* (1954).
36 From *The Times*, 25 September 1991.
37 Bonar Law was Prime Minister for seven months. Sir Alec Douglas-Home in similar

circumstances to Mr Major took the Conservative Party to electoral defeat in 1964 after 12 months in office.

38 See Robert Blackburn, 'The constitutional history of the life of Parliament', in R. O. Plender (ed.), *Legal History and Comparative Law* (1990), Chapter 1.

39 Over the past 40 years the party in Government has won seven elections (1955, 1959, 1966, 1974 (October), 1983, 1987, 1992) and the party in opposition has won four elections (1964, 1970, 1974 (February), 1979).

40 *Elective Dictatorship* (1976), p. 9.

41 For one such scheme, see Institute for Public Policy Research, *A Written Constitution for the United Kingdom* (1993), Article 60.

42 *Reform of the Constitution* (1970), p. 52.

43 See Labour Party National Executive Committee Working Party, *Interim Report on Electoral Reform* (The Plant Report) (1991), Hansard Society, *Electoral Reform* (1976), Vernon Bogdanor, *What Is Proportional Representation?* (1984).

44 Ramsay Muir, *How Britain Is Governed* (1930), p. 168.

45 *Ibid.*

46 Hansard Society, *Electoral Reform* (1976), p. 26.

47 Institute for Public Policy Research, *A Written Constitution for the United Kingdom* (Mansell, 1993).

48 Hansard Society, *Electoral Reform* (1976).

49 Aristotle, *Politics* (translated by Ernest Barker, 1948), p. 128.

5

Citizenship and Employment

KEITH EWING

INTRODUCTION

Citizenship is an elusive concept.[1] Dynamic and evolutionary, its
content will vary from community to community, and from time to
time. However, the rights which it embraces are sometimes thought
to be of a political nature, designed to facilitate participation in the
political life of the community. At the present time they may be said
to include above all the right to participate in rule-making institutions, and the right not to be arbitrarily or unfairly treated by those
in positions of authority. The extent to which these rights of citizenship are adequately protected in Britain at the present time is a matter
of some controversy, as is clearly demonstrated by many of the other
chapters in this volume. Yet although the idea of citizenship is well
established in the vocabulary of the public lawyer and the political
activist, it is also important for labour law and for economic affairs.[2]
In the following sections an attempt will be made to explain why and
it will also be shown how, the Citizen's Charter notwithstanding,
these rights of citizenship at work in particular have receded in recent
years, perhaps to an even greater extent than the rights of political
citizenship.

CITIZENSHIP AT WORK

The idea of citizenship at work has a long pedigree, having been
developed by such influential figures as Cole and Laski.[3] Laski's
starting point is his assertion that the state exists 'in order that [its]
citizens may realise in their lives the best of which they are capable'.
From this it is argued clearly and without equivocation that 'the

citizen has a right to work'.[4] The citizen 'is born into a world where, if rationally organised, he can live only by the sweat of his brow. Society owes him the occasion to perform his function. To leave him without access to the means of existence is to deprive him of that which makes possible the realisation of his personality.' But not only does the citizen have a right *to* work; he or she also has rights *in* work. For Laski these rights were of two kinds. The first were what we may refer to as rights of a material kind, such as the right to be paid an adequate wage and the right to reasonable hours of labour. The second were rights of a non-material kind, Laski arguing that it is not enough 'to limit the hours of labour and to make the reward of effort adequate to the basic needs of life'. There was also a right 'to be concerned with the government of industry as there is a right to be concerned in the government of politics', Laski contending that 'The citizen as an industrial unit must somehow be given the power to share in the making of those decisions which affect him as a producer if he is to be in a position to maximise his freedom.'

Laski's work is an important acknowledgment of the reality that political citizenship does not operate in an economic vacuum. It is also important for recognizing that rights of citizenship at work fulfil two quite different functions. First, economic security is essential if individual members of a particular community are to play their full part in the life of that community with confidence and dignity.[5] It is this that lies behind what I refer to as Laski's *material* rights in work. The right to an adequate wage is rationalized as being necessary 'to secure a return capable of purchasing the standard of living without which creative citizenship is impossible', while the right to reasonable hours of labour exists to ensure that the citizen 'may have leisure for creative tasks'.[6] But apart from thus being ancillary or subsidiary to notions of political citizenship, rights of citizenship at work are important as ends in themselves. Protection from arbitrary and unfair treatment and the right to participate in rule-making institutions are matters which cannot be left at the factory gate or office door, to be donned again at the end of a shift. The ideals, values and attitudes embraced within the notion of political citizenship, whatever these may be at any particular time, naturally create assumptions about the exercise of power in other fields, which in this case relate particularly to the workplace. It is this which to some extent lies behind what I refer to as Laski's *non-material* rights in work: the need to ensure that the ownership of capital does not degenerate into dictatorship, by a system of 'representative government in industry . . . through which, in the necessary toil of life, the personality of the worker may find expression'.

Despite the importance of Laski's work, it may be necessary for it to be refined. Rights of citizenship embrace more than the right to material well-being and the right to participate in the rule-making process. They are now understood as embracing the right to be protected from arbitrary and unfair treatment from those in positions of authority. In public law the first limb of this principle is sustained to some extent by the doctrine of the rule of law.[7] Although there is much debate as to the precise meaning of the doctrine, at the very least it is understood as requiring that citizens should not be subject to arbitrary punishment, but may be punished only in accordance with the law. In the employment context this might translate into a requirement that the disciplinary powers of the employer should be regulated to ensure that they are not exercised arbitrarily but only in accordance with clearly defined rules and procedures. In addition to this right not to be treated arbitrarily, the right not to be treated unfairly would ensure that these clearly defined rules meet basic minimum standards of a procedural and substantive nature. As far as procedural justice is concerned, the right not to be treated unfairly would require the right to a fair trial within a reasonable time by an independent tribunal.[8] In the employment context this would require the employer's disciplinary powers to be regulated to require proper investigations and hearings for employees whom it is proposed to dismiss.[9] As far as substantive justice is concerned, the right not to be treated unfairly would require as a basic minimum the elimination of all unnecessary and irrational discrimination, whether this be based upon considerations of race, sex or any other ground.

In this chapter the notion of citizenship at work will be used in both the ways identified by Laski: citizenship as both a primary goal and a secondary goal, that is to say as an end in itself and as a means of satisfying other goals. For the latter purpose, however, the notion will be identified as embracing two rights, the first being the right to protection from arbitrary and unfair treatment, and the second being the right to participate in decision-making institutions. The principles of citizenship as they have been developed in the political arena thus apply with equal force in the economic sphere. Just as in the political arena there is a need to control the political power of the state, so in the economic sphere there is in Laski's terms a need to mitigate the unlimited power which the ownership of capital has conferred. Ownership of the means of production provides a fragile legitimacy for the exercise of power over people and is a highly inappropriate basis, where the employer exercising the power is a public authority. This said, however, it is equally important to keep a sense of perspective and proportion. Unlike the relationship between the individual and the state, the employment relationship is an instrumental one. Its purpose is to facilitate the production of goods or the delivery of services rather than to provide people with a forum for the exercise of political rights. As Laski himself was quick to point out, 'We must not unduly maximise the power [the citizen as worker] will have. The work of the world has to be done.' Citizenship, if not to be discounted by such considerations, will inevitably be influenced by them to the extent that citizens' rights will inevitably have to accommodate the overall objectives of the enterprise or service in question.

PROTECTION OF RIGHTS OF CITIZENSHIP AT WORK

In the political arena rights of citizenship find formal expression and protection in both international law and constitutional law. In international law there is both UN protection in the shape of the UN Declaration on Human Rights and regional protection, for example in the European Convention on Human Rights.[10] In constitutional law there may be protection in a Bill of Rights or a Charter of Rights and Freedoms, which may empower the courts to challenge domestic political decisions that are inconsistent with the Bill or Charter of Rights. As far as the rights of citizenship at work are concerned, there is also international protection, but, as we shall see, constitutional guarantees are not widespread. Foremost among the international bodies is the International Labour Organisation (ILO), a UN agency based in Geneva.[11] The ILO was created in 1919 in the aftermath of the First World War with the aims of alleviating misery and maintaining peace, reflecting the view that there could be no lasting peace without social justice. The original conception was thus largely of citizenship at work as a means to an end – the need to elevate material conditions so that workers could be better political citizens. Early international labour conventions reflect this, with the first, on hours of work, seeking to impose a maximum working week of 48 hours. More recent conventions recognize broader notions of citizenship at work, particularly those dealing with termination of employment[12] and equal pay[13] on the one hand and the right to organize[14] and collective bargaining on the other.[15]

Important regional instruments protecting rights of citizenship at work include the Council of Europe's European Social Charter, which directly complements the European Convention on Human Rights.[16] Also important is the EC Charter of the Fundamental Social Rights of Workers, which is dealt with in some detail below. The Council of Europe's Charter, signed in 1961 and coming into force in 1965, purports to guarantee: the right to work (article 1); the right to just conditions of work (article 2); the right to safe and healthy working conditions (article 3); the right to a fair remuneration (article 4); and the right of employed women to maternity and other forms of protection (article 8). Although the Charter also seeks to guarantee both the right to organize and the right to bargain collectively, the contracting states appear to be committed to these goals as means of improving the material conditions of workers rather than as desirable ends in themselves. Article 5 refers to the right to organize as being necessary for the 'economic and social interests' of workers, though article 3 of the additional protocol to the Treaty reflects a vision of participation in decision-making that regards such participation as important for its own sake rather than as a means to material advancement.[17] But whatever the philosophy underlying these measures, they are welcome features of international labour law, even if, as in the case of ILO Conventions, serious problems arise as to their enforcement.

If we turn our attention to domestic legal systems it is commonplace for the rights of political citizenship to be protected by a Bill of Rights enforceable in the courts. So if a government in Canada, for example, were to remove the right to vote, or the right to stand for election, or the right to freedom of expression, it would be possible for its conduct to be challenged by judicial review. Yet although it is not unusual for governments in the Western liberal democratic tradition to elevate the rights of political citizenship to a form of higher law, there has not been the same concern for the rights of citizenship at work (although Germany, Italy and Spain are important exceptions). None of the great liberal constitutional documents of the common law jurisdictions – whether it be the American or Canadian – contains any express reference to rights of citizenship at work, though they have been used by powerful economic interests to prevent any erosion of their political power.[18] It is true that some rights of political citizenship, such as the right to freedom of association in particular, could have been extended to include rights of citizenship in the workplace. But there has been a reluctance on the part of judges to move in this direction, as most recently illustrated by the Supreme Court of Canada's refusal to interpret the constitutional right to freedom of association to include the right of a union to engage in collective bargaining on behalf of its members.[19]

The failure of the courts to build up rights of political citizenship to include rights of citizenship at work is perhaps not very surprising. The courts traditionally have impeded rather than facilitated the development of such rights. This was most marked in the United States in the period before the first Roosevelt presidency, when the Supreme Court on several occasions struck down measures introduced by state legislatures containing rights of the type articulated by Laski.[20] The attitude of the Court reflected a rejection of the ideas of citizenship subsequently developed by Laski in favour of a competing view which accorded priority to the right to freedom of contract, a right, the Court said which 'is as essential to the laborer as to the capitalist, to the poor as to the rich'.[21] Problems of inequality of bargaining power between employer and worker were brushed aside on the ground that 'it is from the nature of things impossible to uphold freedom of contract and the right of private property without at the same time recognizing as legitimate those inequalities of fortune that are the necessary result of the exercise of those rights.'[22] So in the interests of freedom of contract the Court struck down a District of Columbia statute setting minimum wage rates for women[23] and a New York statute setting maximum hours for bakery and other workers.[24] And in the same era the Court also struck down a Kansas statute prohibiting employers from offering employment on the condition that the applicant agreed not to join a trade union.[25] This minimalist protection for union membership rights was the very least that was required to breathe life into what Laski was later to refer to as the right to a representative government in industry.

EROSION OF RIGHTS OF CITIZENSHIP AT WORK

Although it may thus be argued that the principles of citizenship apply equally to the workplace, this invites consideration of how these rights should best be protected in national law in the absence of any clear constitutional guarantee. Just as there are debates about how best to safeguard and protect the rights of citizenship as they apply in the political arena, so there are debates about how best to protect the rights of citizenship as they apply in the workplace. Traditionally it has been accepted that these rights could be protected only by some form of state regulation to protect workers from the naked abuse of employer power,[26] a power sustained and reinforced by the legal concept of the contract of employment, which, paradoxically, is seen by some as the ultimate right of citizenship. State regulation might take several forms: an economic policy designed to encourage full employment; an industrial relations policy designed to promote strong trade unionism to act as a bulwark against the power of an employer; and a labour law policy designed to protect workers from the arbitrary exercise of power by employers.

Traditionally in Britain there has been a reluctance to intervene directly by legislation to lay down minimum standards of employment.[27] This is not to say that there has been no statutory regulation of the employment relationship; but, as we shall see, such regulation has tended to be selective and indirect rather than universal and direct. The preferred method of intervention, at least until the 1970s, was by encouraging the growth and spread of independent trade unionism not only as a means of advancing the material well-being of workers, but also as a means of protecting workers from arbitrary and unfair treatment in the enterprise. This was done in two ways, the first by the statutory removal of common law restrictions on trade union organization and conduct, and the second by intermittent measures directly or indirectly to extend and strengthen trade union presence in the workplace. Perhaps the most significant measure of this latter kind was the movement to establish Whitley Councils in industries throughout the country in the aftermath of the First World War. Bureaucratic rather than legal intervention by the Ministry of Labour at this time led to the introduction and extension of bargaining arrangements in 62 industries, covering no fewer than 2.05 million workers.[28]

A more recent view argues that these rights of citizenship can be best protected by the forces of the market and that the role of the state should be to intervene to remove obstacles to the effective operation of the market. If workers conduct themselves sensibly and accept reasonable terms and conditions of employment, British industry will be competitive and employment prospects will be enhanced for everyone. In this way will be guaranteed the most basic right of all, the right to work, while at the same time employers who treat their employees harshly or unfairly do so at the risk of losing the employee in question, who may take his or her services to a place where they will be more highly valued. Since 1979 British economic, industrial relations and labour law strategies have moved gradually in this direction, with the introduction of restrictions on trade union freedoms and the modification of employment protection legislation restoring to a large extent (though by no means fully) the common law rules which historically underpinned the employment relationship.[29] This policy shows no indication of increasing citizenship rights at work.[30] Indeed the reverse appears to be the case, with the retreat of the state coinciding with uncomfortably high levels of unemployment, an increase in the unregulated and unrestrained power of employers, and an apparent reduction in the scope for worker participation in management decisions. It is also an approach which runs counter to the spirit of developments in Europe, with the EC Social Charter being inspired by a vision which anticipates state intervention in the social field to protect workers from the full rigours of the market.

Apart from being seen by some as a more efficient way of protecting at least some features of citizenship at work, the removal of regulatory legislation is seen by others as a means of restoring the most fundamental right of citizenship, the right to freedom of contract.[31] It is this fundamental right which strongly influenced the US Supreme Court in the pre-Roosevelt era cases referred to in the previous section.

So the statutory regulation of working hours was struck down on the ground that the legislation 'necessarily interferes with the right of contract between the employer and employees', the Court concluding that the 'general right to make a contract in relation to his business is part of the liberty of the individual protected by the [Constitution]'.[32] Similarly, the statutory minimum wage for women was struck down as 'an arbitrary payment for a purpose and upon a basis having no causal connection with his business, or the contract, or the work the employee engages to do'.[33] In the view of the Court the 'moral requirement, implicit in every contract of employment, viz. that the amount to be paid and the service to be rendered shall bear to each other some relation of just equivalence, is completely ignored'.[34] But as we have seen, it was not only the statutory regulation of minimum terms and conditions that fell foul of the doctrine of freedom of contract. The same fate awaited the legislation designed to promote trade union security,[35] so necessary for the purposes of collective bargaining, necessary in turn to mitigate the economic power of the employer, particularly if the states were not to be permitted to do this by regulatory legislation. It is in such circumstances in particular that 'only the existence of strong trade unions will ensure to the average worker just terms in his contract of service'.[36]

MINIMUM TERMS AND CONDITIONS OF EMPLOYMENT

As already pointed out there is little statutory regulation in Britain of the first right of citizenship at work – the right to what Laski referred to as 'reasonable' terms of employment with regard, for example, to rates of pay and hours of work. This is not to say that these matters have never been regulated by law. An example of statutory regulation of pay (and other working conditions) is the wages councils, first introduced as trade boards in 1909.[37] Based on the practice in the Australian State of Victoria, the trade boards were conceived originally to deal with problems of 'sweated labour' in four trades in particular.[38] The concept was expanded by legislation in 1918, 1945 and 1975, with the law in force at the time of Mrs Thatcher's first general election victory being found in the Wages Councils Act 1979.[39] This legislation enabled the Secretary of State to establish a wages council in an industry where there was no adequate machinery for effectively regulating the remuneration of the workers concerned. The purpose of the wages councils, tripartite bodies appointed by the Secretary of State, was to fix the levels of remuneration, holiday entitlement and other terms and conditions of the workers within their jurisdiction. In 1988 there were a number of councils covering industries as diverse as clothing, toy making and catering.

Just as there has been no comprehensive legislation setting wage rates for workers throughout the UK, so there has been no comprehensive legislation laying down a maximum number of hours each day or each week for which workers were permitted to be engaged. This is despite the fact that the first ILO Convention, the Hours of Work Convention of 1919, laid down a maximum working day of eight hours and a maximum working week of 48 hours, and despite Laski's subsequent claim that in a complex world 'the eight-hour day has become the maximum a man may dare work at manual labour and still hope to understand the life about him'.[40] But it does not follow from the lack of general legislation that there was no selective regulation of working hours. It has to be said, however, that although there was in fact a significant body of such legislation, it is unlikely that its purpose was to enable individuals to participate more fully and effectively in the political life of the nation. The Hours of Employment (Conventions) Act 1936 prohibited women from being employed in industrial undertakings at night, while the Factories Act 1961 laid down a maximum nine-hour day and 48-hour week for women employed in factories. It also specified the maximum periods that women could work without a break, and sought to regulate the conditions governing overtime working by women.[41]

The commitment of the Conservative Governments since 1979 to free-market principles and to the principle of freedom of contract as a means of implementing this commitment has inevitably meant that even these limited forms of regulation of terms and conditions of employment have been either reviewed or removed. The wages councils were abolished by the Trade Union Reform and Employment Rights Act 1993, having been seriously weakened by the Wages Act 1986[42]. The 1986 Act had removed the power of the Secretary of State to create new wages councils, even though fresh areas of need might have arisen in the future. The only industries which could be regulated by wages councils were those which were already covered in 1986. But not only was there clearly no room for expansion, those wages councils which continued to exist lost their powers to regulate anything other than the minimum hourly rate of remuneration for workers in the industries in question, though even here the power no longer applied in respect of anyone under 21. The abolition of the wages councils was the next logical step of a Government that had not only denounced ILO Convention 26 on Minimum Wage-Fixing Machinery,[43] but had also already revoked or secured the repeal of other wage-fixing machinery, such as the Fair Wages Resolution of 1946, which required government contractors to pay fair wages to their employees.[44]

The same commitment to the market and to employment flexibility has led to the removal of the many statutory restrictions on hours of work. The restrictions on night work by women were repealed, ironically, by the Sex Discrimination Act 1986, as were the 48-hour week and the other protections in the Factories Act 1961. Similar provisions in the Mines and Quarries Act 1954 have gone, as have other miscellaneous measures, such as the Baking Industry (Hours of Work) Act 1954, which in restricting night work was said to be one of only a few examples of direct regulation of the working hours of male employees in the UK.[45] The removal of statutory restrictions on working hours is, however, a matter of some difficulty for the Government in view of the draft EC Directive concerning certain aspects of the organization of working time. As proposed at the time of writing this would require member states to adopt measures to ensure 11 hours' consecutive rest in every 24-hour period, a weekly day of rest, annual paid holidays, the regulation of overtime working and the regulation of shift working.[46] These measures would apply to both men and women, so that the Government will need not only to retrace its steps but to retreat much further down the path of regulation. Although derogations would be permitted, this would be only in highly controlled circumstances, one of which – by collective agreements – would give the Government little cause for comfort as it would enable employers to buy flexibility on hours only at the cost of recognizing trade unions.

PROTECTION FROM ARBITRARY OR UNFAIR TREATMENT

As was suggested above, a second principle of citizenship is the right to be protected from arbitrary or unfair treatment. Traditionally, however, there has been little recognition of this principle extending to the enterprise. Through the contract of employment the common law recognizes and reinforces the hierarchy and power that exist in the employment relationship.[47] An employer is generally free to contract on whatever terms he or she thinks fit. It is true that the relationship between employer and employee must then be conducted in accordance with these terms, and to this extent it might be said that the rule of law extends to the enterprise. It is to be pointed out, however, that the employer is free at any time to terminate the contract by giving notice if the agreement is no longer suitable, and even where the employer has acted unlawfully under the contract there is precious little the employee can do in the absence of an adequate and effective remedy. Quite apart from the rather diluted nature of the rule of law in this context, there is no recognition, at least at common law, of any idea that workers as citizens should be entitled to minimum standards of procedural or substantive justice. An employer may be free at common law to dismiss without complying with any procedural requirements and there are no restrictions at common law on the employer's power to discriminate on any grounds whatsoever.

In the post-war period the rigours of the common law have been gradually modified by legislation so that we are able to point to the emergence of a code recognizing the rights of citizenship in the workplace. As far as the three requirements of citizenship identified above are concerned, we can say that measures to strengthen the protection from arbitrary treatment are to be found in the law of unfair dismissal, which was introduced for the first time in 1971.[48] Employees who are covered by the legislation may be dismissed only for one of the five (admittedly wide) grounds permitted by what is now the Employment Protection (Consolidation) Act 1978, regardless of what their contracts may say to the contrary.[49] The law of unfair dismissal has also played an important part in extending primitive concepts of procedural justice to the workplace.[50] A dismissal for a permitted reason may still be unfair if it is executed without complying with procedural obligations laid down in the contract of employment[51] or with the procedural obligations laid down in the jurisprudence of the courts and tribunals. The law of unfair dismissal also plays a part in developing notions of substantive justice, though to the extent that this is something concerned primarily with notions of equal treatment the principal measures relevant here are to be found in the legislation prohibiting discrimination on grounds of race or sex and in requiring equal pay for men and women.

Although these measures are an important step in the direction of extending principles of citizenship to the workplace, they are greatly enfeebled by their inadequate content and by the absence of any effective enforcement machinery. There is little effective protection for workers against arbitrary conduct short of dismissal. In such cases the only practical remedy provided by the law is to permit the worker to leave the employment and to claim that he or she has been constructively dismissed, which is little short of providing no remedy at all. By the same token, there is no effective way of enforcing the standards of procedural justice. There is no realistic way of insisting on compliance with these standards in disciplinary situations other than dismissal,[52] while even in the case of dismissal the best that a worker is likely to secure is compensation rather than reinstatement in his or her job.[53] The requirements of substantive justice are equally inadequately met. There is of course the problem of scope, there being no protection from discrimination on grounds other than sex or race. Disability stands out as the area most transparently in need of reform. But even in those areas where law has been introduced questions remain to be answered about the effect and utility of legislation and jurisprudence in which too many punches are pulled. It remains the case, for example, that despite the enactment of the Equal Pay Act 1970, and its strengthening in 1983 by the introduction of the principle of equal pay for work of equal value, in 1989 average full-time female earnings were only 72 per cent (manual) and 61 per cent (non-manual) of average male earnings.[54]

The failure of the employment protection and equal opportunities legislation of the 1970s more fully to develop and recognize the claims of citizenship at work makes all the more surprising the measures introduced in the 1980s to reverse some of these modest advances of the previous decade. Perhaps the most significant of these was the reduction in the numbers protected by the law of unfair dismissal. This was done principally by providing that only workers with at least two years' service could bring a claim. This measure, phased in gradually, replaced the requirement of six months' service which was in force in 1979 when the Conservatives assumed office. The effect of the change, perhaps one of the most important of the decade, is that for the first two years of employment with a new employer the only protection that workers have against arbitrary treatment is that provided by their contracts of employment. For practical purposes this means none at all. This retreat of the legislation was accompanied by an important jurisprudential development, which also contrived to limit the scope of the statutory protection and restore the application of common law contractual principles. The legislation applies only to 'employees', that is to say people who work under a contract of service rather than a contract for services. In an important decision in 1983, the Court of Appeal effectively denied statutory protection to many already vulnerable casual workers by introducing the new requirement that there should be a mutuality of obligation between the parties before a contract of service can be said to exist.[55] In the same case the Court of Appeal also held that the question of whether someone is engaged under a contract of service or a contract for services is largely a question of fact, thereby excluding the worker's right to appeal against an industrial tribunal decision on this fundamentally important threshold question.[56]

PARTICIPATION IN RULE-MAKING INSTITUTIONS

A third right of citizenship identified earlier in this chapter is the right of citizens to participate in the process of rule-making, that is to say in the process of making and administering the rules by which a community is to be governed. In a political community this usually starts with elections based on universal suffrage, whereby the people choose the representatives who will exercise this rule-making function, these representatives being accountable to the people for the way in which they perform this duty. As already explained, the workplace is different in the sense that while the purpose of government is to serve the interests of the governed, the workplace or enterprise does not exist only to serve the interests of the workforce. There can be no process whereby workers elect those who are to make management decisions, with these managers accountable to the electors for the decisions which have been made on their behalf. The enterprise is a place in which workers' legitimate claims of citizenship have to be accommodated within an institution where there are at least competing and arguably overriding claims derived from the fact of ownership and the responsibility of management.

On this basis, citizenship rights of participation in the workplace can take several forms, though each falls far short of the direct election of those with the ultimate decision-making authority. The weakest form of participation is by a process of consultation whereby management solicits the views of workers or their representatives but reserves the right to make the final decision unilaterally. The second form of participation is by a process of negotiation whereby management is required to bargain with workers or their representatives and may only proceed if an agreement has been reached. In the case of deadlock or failure to agree it may be necessary to provide some third-party machinery to help resolve the differences. The third form of participation is perhaps the strongest, that is where workers or their representatives assume a managerial position, say where workers' representatives become members of the board of directors of a company, or where workers or their representatives acquire part of the ownership of a company through the purchase of a substantial shareholding.[57] These different forms of participation may be exercised in different ways. Consultation and negotiation may be conducted through bodies such as staff associations, works councils or enterprise committees, which may represent the workforce as a whole. Alternatively, consultation and negotiation may be conducted by collective bargaining with a trade union or trade unions representing only the members of the organization, though in practice the agreements concluded by this process will be applied equally to everyone.

As in other areas discussed in this chapter the rights of citizenship at work have receded in recent years. Before 1979 the state had intervened in a number of ways to encourage the growth of joint rule-making machinery through the process of collective bargaining between employers and the representatives of independent trade unions. The Employment Protection Act 1975 gave unions the right to refer to ACAS a complaint about an employer's failure to recognize it for the purposes of collective bargaining.[58] This was reinforced by measures which provided unions with a right to the disclosure of information necessary for bargaining purposes as well as the right to paid time off work to enable lay officials to perform their industrial relations duties. Since 1979, however, public policy has changed quite radically, with trade unions already considerably weakened by the high levels of unemployment in the 1980s. The statutory right to recognition was repealed in 1980, so that Britain stands virtually alone among the major North American and European democracies in failing to provide any legal machinery compelling employers to negotiate or consult with workers or their representatives.[59] In the USA and in Canada employers are under a duty to bargain with unions representing a majority of the labour force, while in Germany employers can be required to establish a works council representing employees. Some indication of the depth of the resistance to the idea that workers should be given a say in decision-making in the enterprise is provided by the British Government's vetoing of an EC draft directive which would require domestic legislation providing for the creation of works councils in companies with substantial numbers of employees in more than one European country.

Despite the absence of any formal guarantees for worker participation in rule-making, the Government can nevertheless point to one important area where rights of citizenship have been extended. Trade union members are now guaranteed by law a greater say in the management and administration of their unions, while at the same time union membership can no longer be made an enforceable condition of employment.[60] The extension of members' rights has been pursued along three routes: first, by requiring executive committees and senior officials to be elected in a secret postal ballot of the members every five years;[61] second, by requiring ballots of the members to be held before industrial action can be taken[62] or before political objects can be continued;[63] third, by allowing members to opt out of certain collective decisions – such as the decision to take industrial action – without the fear of reprisal.[64] Although controversial, these measures are clearly very important in helping to ensure that trade unions genuinely represent and are properly accountable to their members. This is not to say that all these initiatives can be justified on these grounds, with the restrictions on the right of unions to discipline strike-breakers being particularly hard to swallow, especially in view of the fact that the measure applies equally to action which is properly supported by a ballot and to action which is not.[65] Nevertheless, as far as the other measures are concerned, there is something to be said for legislation promoting rights of participation within trade unions if trade unions are in fact the main vehicle for the exercise by workers of their rights of citizenship at work.[66] The paradox, which will not be lost on readers, is that these measures opening up the channels of participation within trade unions have been introduced at the same time as collective bargaining and channels for participation within the workplace (the main justification for such measures) are in retreat.[67]

THE RIGHT TO STRIKE

An additional matter to be dealt with is the right to strike. For Laski too this was a matter of some importance. In this words, 'to limit the right to strike is a form of industrial servitude. It means, ultimately, that the worker must labour on the employer's terms.'[68] Perhaps unsurprisingly, Laski could see 'no justice in such denial of freedom'.[69] In fact the right to strike may be said to perform two functions. The first is its role in enhancing rights of citizenship at work, and in particular the right to participate in rule-making machinery. It was Lord Wright who pointed out in a famous dictum in 1942 that 'the right of workmen to strike is an essential element in the principle of collective bargaining'.[70] Denied the power to strike, workers would be bargaining with their hands tied behind their backs; they could offer no credible or realistic resistance to the power of the employer.[71] But apart from thus reinforcing an important right of citizenship in the workplace, the right to strike may also be seen as a right of political citizenship. Laski for one had little doubt that the strike could be a legitimate method of bringing organized pressure to bear on an elected government. He claimed not to be greatly moved by the argument that it involves coercion of the government. There were, in his view, occasions when that coercion is necessary, even essential. It is a way of restraining a government from taking unpopular and inappropriate action.[72]

In considering how the law protects the right to strike it is necessary to distinguish between sanctions taken against the trade union and its officials on the one hand and those taken against the individual workers engaged in the strike on the other. Traditionally the former issue has received most attention in English law. At common law it is tortious for a trade union or its officials to organize industrial action.[73] Both the union and its officials can be restrained by injunction and damages may be recovered from the union.[74] Since 1906 statutory immunities have operated to protect the union and its officials from liability in tort.[75] The immunities were fairly widely drawn, with no requirement to ballot and no restriction on secondary or sympathy action. However, industrial action was protected only to the extent that any tortious acts were done in contemplation or furtherance of a trade dispute, a term which was defined to exclude disputes between trade unions and the Government.[76] The right to strike in English law was thus most clearly defined as a necessary incident of the rights of citizenship at work only. There was no recognition of the strike as a right of political citizenship, so that any trade union action designed to coerce the duly elected government or indeed to protest against government policies (even ones vitally affecting the rights of trade unions) was liable to be restrained by an injunction at the suit of an employer whose business would be directly disrupted by the action.[77]

Perhaps because of the important role which these immunities played in reinforcing primary rights of citizenship at work, they were strongly attacked by free-market economists. Hayek in particular was very critical of what he referred to as the exceptional privileges which trade unions had acquired, proposing their removal, paradoxically in order to retrieve the rule of law.[78] Conservative administrations of the 1980s appeared befuddled by these views and although they did not completely restore common law liability they have gone a long way in this direction by a series of gradual restrictions, the cumulative effect of which after 14 years is quite profound.[79] The legislation has restricted the purposes for which industrial action may be taken, so that disputes concerned with privatization may no longer be protected by the immunities.[80] The legislation has also restricted the methods that trade unions may employ to make their action more effective, so that both secondary and sympathy action are now excluded.[81] Finally, new formalities were introduced before industrial action could be called, these taking the form of mandatory strike ballots imposing requirements of such detail that trade unionists have been heard to complain that it is almost impossible to organize industrial action within the limits of the new law.[82] Failure to do so invites injunctions at the suit of affected employers and also damages against the union, with statutory protection for union funds having been lifted in 1982.[83]

As already pointed out in consideration of the restrictions on the right to strike, it is necessary to examine not only the legal liability of the union and its officials but also the legal liabilities of the individuals who take part in the strike. This is not an issue that has been satisfactorily dealt with in English law, even before the change of policy introduced and implemented in the 1980s.[84] Participation in a strike is regarded as a breach of contract which would authorize the summary dismissal of the employees in question.[85] When the unfair dismissal regime was introduced an opportunity was available to regulate this power of the employer. However, only a very minimalist protection was in fact provided, with employers being potentially liable in unfair dismissal only if they selectively dismissed anyone engaged in a strike or other industrial action. But they were given an immunity from unfair dismissal liability provided that they dismissed everyone who was or who had been on strike. Admittedly the dismissal of strikers in this way was 'extremely rare in practice',[86] though as the Grunwick dispute[87] showed in 1977 and as Wapping was later to confirm,[88] it was not unknown. Notwithstanding this wide power of employers the Government saw fit to increase it by extending the employer's immunity from unfair dismissal in the event of strike or industrial action dismissals. The Employment Act 1990, for example, permits an employer selectively to dismiss anyone engaged in an unofficial strike which has been repudiated by the union, regardless of the cause of the strike.[89]

PROSPECTS FOR THE FUTURE – THE EUROPEAN DIMENSION

We have seen that rights of citizenship at work have been in retreat since 1979. There was some prospect that this development might have been arrested by the election of a Labour Government at the general election of 1992. One of the ways by which Labour proposed to re-assert citizenship rights at work was by committing a Labour Government more fully to Europe.[90] The Government of Mrs Thatcher, alone of all EC member states, refused to adopt the Social Charter in 1989, referring to it as a socialist charter and fearing that it would lead to at least a partial reversal of the labour law strategy of the 1980s. Labour, on the other hand, had indicated that it would sign up to the Charter as soon as it took office. This in itself would not mean much in principle, given that the Social Charter had no binding legal force or status.[91] But it would have been of great symbolic importance and might have facilitated the speedier implementation of the Action Programme, which was published in 1990 with the aim of making the Charter a practical reality. Labour was also committed in its 1992 general election manifesto to endorsing the so-called social chapter, which had been vetoed by Mr Major at the Maastricht summit of heads of government in 1991. This would have involved an amendment to the Treaty of Rome enabling Community law dealing with a greater range of employment and social measures to be introduced with the approval of a qualified majority of the Council of Ministers, rather than unanimously as is largely the case at the time of writing.

The Social Charter is inspired partly by a belief that 'the completion of the internal market must offer improvements in the social field for workers of the European Community, especially in terms of freedom of movement, living and working conditions, health and safety at work, social protection, education and training'.[92] As such it may be said to be inspired partly by a vision to extend rights of citizenship at work along both of the tracks identified in this chapter. As far as the material rights of workers is concerned, this is a theme that may be said to underlie the commitment to a fair and equitable wage (article 3); to the improvement of living and working conditions (with reference particularly to the needs of atypical workers, who are often denied social protection) (articles 7–9); and to the development of equal opportunities for men and women (article 16). The Action Programme, which was published after the Charter, contained proposals for a number of initiatives to be implemented speedily. These included: a directive on contracts of employment (laying down at Community level minimum requirements concerning working conditions which would have to be complied with in contracts of employment in all the countries of the Community); a directive on working time (laying down minimum standards on the length of the working week, holidays, rest periods and night work); a directive on the introduction of a form to serve as proof of an employment contract (to impose a duty on employers to provide a means of proving the existence of an employment contract, thereby ensuring greater transparency in the respective rights and obligations of workers and employers); and a directive on the protection of pregnant women at work (laying down minimum standards, particularly on health and safety issues, to deal with matters such as exposure to carcinogens and the use of visual display units).

As far as the non-material rights of workers are concerned, these too find expression in the Social Charter. Particularly important in this respect is article 12, which recognizes the right of both trade unions and employers to negotiate and conclude collective agreements under the conditions laid down in national law and practice. But apart from thus recognizing the legitimacy of trade unionism and collective bargaining the Social Charter separately provides in articles 17 and 18 that procedures for information, consultation and participation of workers must be developed along appropriate lines. These procedures would apply especially in the case of companies which operate in several Community states, and particularly in relation to matters such as technological change, company restructuring and collective redundancies. It is perhaps a matter of some regret that the Action Programme deals only with this latter matter in any detail. Collective bargaining rights in Britain have been particularly vulnerable to erosion and might have benefited from a Community-based initiative. Yet on this critical question the Action Programme has almost nothing to say and certainly nothing concrete to offer in terms of proposed legislative instruments. There is, however, a strong commitment to the introduction of a directive to implement the information, consultation and participation provisions of the Social Charter. This found early expression in the issuing by the Commission of a draft Directive for the creation of European works councils in certain companies located in more than one member state. In view of the fact that this measure will need the unanimous approval of the Council, it remains to be seen whether it will ever be implemented in the light of opposition from the Conservative Government in Britain.

There are in fact a number of draft directives that have been issued by the Commission to implement the Action Programme. These are at different stages of the European legislative process, though it has to be said that the chances of any significant advances being made in relation to either of the themes of citizenship identified in this chapter will be hard-won. The Government is likely to frustrate any significant Europe-wide initiatives on citizenship at work, initiatives which are all the more necessary in Britain on account of the policies pursued by successive Conservative administrations. The only circumstance whereby directives can be introduced without the unanimous approval of the Council is under Article 118A, which permits the Council by a qualified majority to adopt directives to promote the objective of 'encouraging improvements, especially in the working environment, as regards the health and safety of workers'. It is otherwise made clear in Articles 100 and 100A that any Commission proposal dealing with the rights and interests of employed persons requires unanimity. So Britain effectively has the power to veto social and economic legislation and it has not been reluctant to use it in order to prevent the introduction of measures that might require Conservative administrations to reverse, however modestly, policies which have involved the deregulation of employment protection legislation and the deconstruction of collective bargaining arrangements in the interests of labour market flexibility. At the time of writing only one Directive affecting employees (other than those relating to health and safety) had been adopted.[93]

CONCLUSION

The concept of citizenship is one that properly embraces the idea of citizenship at work, for two reasons: first, because economic well-being is essential to meaningful participation in the political process; second, because the ideas of political citizenship are as relevant in the economic as in the political arena. Just as in some respects rights of political citizenship may have retreated in the 1980s, the same is true, probably to a greater extent, of the rights of citizenship in the workplace, at least to the extent that these matters are regulated by law. Statutory protection of workers' material rights has receded; the right to protection from arbitrary and unfair treatment has been restricted; and the right to participate in rule-making in the enterprise has been removed, and further undermined by restrictions on the right to strike. As far as this last issue is concerned, the removal of the recognition legislation is merely an early symbol of an attitude that is reflected in the withdrawal of trade union membership at GCHQ and the ending of collective bargaining arrangements for schoolteachers.[94] Although we owe much to Laski for his penetrating insights about the role and importance of citizenship at work, these developments tend to undermine his assertion that rights of citizenship afforded to men and women in the modern state are, at least in Western civilization, 'at all points more ample and more adequate than . . . at any previous time'.[95]

A different outcome at the general election in 1992 might have gone some way to arrest this trend, with the Labour Party committed to a number of initiatives which would have extended the material rights of workers (including its controversial proposals for a statutory minimum wage), restored the protection against arbitrary or unfair treatment, and introduced new rights of participation in the process of rule-making. The election of the Conservatives, however, has ensured that citizenship rights are likely to retreat still further, a paradoxical reality in view of the rhetorical claims by the Government about the introduction of its Citizen's Charter. The Government signalled at an early stage its intention to impose further restrictions on trade unions, an intention realized by the Trade Union Reform and Employment Rights Act 1993. Although these new restrictions relate mainly to the exercise by unions of the freedom to strike, they are nevertheless important in affecting the capacity of workers through their unions to be effective participants in joint rule-making machinery. The new measures require not only that all strike ballots be held by post rather than at the workplace, but also that seven days' notice be given of the intention to take industrial action. Perhaps more controversially, it is also enacted that customers or consumers should be permitted to take legal action to restrain or recover any loss suffered as a result of unlawful industrial action.[96] The rights of the citizen as consumer are given clear priority over the rights of the citizen as producer or as worker. Yet it remains the case that adequate protection of the rights of citizenship at work is a necessary precondition to the effective exercise of the citizen's rights as a consumer in the same way that it is a necessary precondition to the effective exercise of the individual's rights of political citizenship.

NOTES AND REFERENCES

1 For a recent account of citizenship, see D. Oliver, *Government in the United Kingdom* (1992).

2 For a discussion of citizenship and employment, see also P. Davies and M. Freedland, *Labour Legislation and Public Policy* (1993). The idea is equally important in the area of social welfare. See D. S. King and J. Waldron, 'Citizenship, social citizenship and the defence of welfare provision' (1988), *British Journal of Political Science*, 18, 415. See also T. H. Marshall, 'Citizenship and social class', in *Class, Citizenship and Social Development* (1964).

3 H. J. Laski, *A Grammar of Politics* (4th edn 1938). The following account is drawn from Chapter 3.

4 Cf. B. Hepple, 'The right to work' (1981) 10 ILJ 65.

5 See also King and Waldron, *op. cit.*: 'The concept of a citizen is that of a person who can hold her or his head high and participate fully and with dignity in the life of her or his society.'

6 For a possibly more radical approach to the value of material rights, see King and Waldron, *op. cit.*

7 J Raz, 'The rule of law and its virtue' (1977) 93 LQR 195.

8 European Convention on Human Rights, article 6.

9 See *ILEA* v. *Gravett* [1988] IRLR 497.

10 On the international protection of human rights generally see P. Sieghart, *The Lawful Rights of Mankind* (1985). For an account of the role of the ECHR in labour law, see M. Forde, 'The European Convention on Human Rights and Labor Law' (1983), *American Journal of Comparative Law*, 31, 301.

11 For an account of the origins and work of the ILO, see P. O'Higgins, 'International standards and British labour law', in R. Lewis (ed.), *Labour Law in Britain* (1986).

12 See B. W. Napier, 'Dismissals: the new ILO standards' (1983), 12 ILJ 17.

13 ILO Convention 100 (Equal Remuneration).

14 ILO Convention 87 (Freedom of Association and Protection of the Right to Organise).

15 ILO Convention 98 (Right to Organise and Collective Bargaining).

16 For an account of the Social Charter, see P. O'Higgins, 'International standards and British labour law' in R. Lewis (ed.), *Labour Law in Britain* (1986). See also O. Kahn-Freund, 'European Social Charter', in F. G. Jacobs (ed.), *European Law and the Individual* (1976).

17 See V. Shrubsall, 'The additional protocol to the European Social Charter – Employment Rights' (1989) 18 ILJ 39.

18 See, for example, *Buckley* v. *Valeo*, 424 US 1 (1976), and *First National Bank of Boston* v. *Bellotti*, 435 US 765 (1978).

19 *Reference re Public Service Employee Relations Act, Labour Relations Act and Police Officers' Collective Bargaining Act* (1987) 38 DLR (4th) 161. See also *Collymore* v. *AG for Trinidad and Tobago* [1970] AC 538. For an account of the Charter of Rights and Labour Law in Canada, see T. J. Christian and K. D. Ewing, 'Labouring under the Canadian Constitution' (1988) 17 ILJ 73. For a fuller account

of the limits and dangers of constitutional law, see K. Ewing, *A Bill of Rights for Britain?* (Institute of Employment Rights, 1990).

20 For a fascinating account of the early struggles between the courts and the labour movement in the US, see W. E. Forbath, *Law and the Shaping of the American Labor Movement* (1991).

21 *Coppage* v. *Kansas* 236 US 1 (1914), p. 14.

22 *Ibid.*, p. 17.

23 *Adkins* v. *Children's Hospital* 261 US 525 (1923).

24 *Lockner* v. *New York* 198 US 45 (1904).

25 *Coppage* v. *Kansas* 236 US 1 (1914).

26 Cf. H. Laski, *A Grammar of Politics*, pp. 105–15.

27 The classic analysis of British labour law in the period before 1971 is O. Kahn-Freund, 'Legal framework', in A. Flanders and H. Clegg (eds), *The System of Industrial Relations in Great Britain* (1954); and 'Labour law', in M. Ginsberg (ed.) *Law and Opinion in England in the 20th Century* (1959).

28 See K. D. Ewing 'Trade unions and the constitution: the impact of the New Conservatives', in C. Graham and T. Prosser, *Waiving the Rules: The Constitution under Thatcherism* (1988).

29 For an account of labour law developments since 1979, see K. D. Ewing, 'Economics and labour law in Britain: Thatcher's radical experiment' (1990) 28 Alta LR 632. For an account sympathetic to the government, see C. G. Hanson, *Taming the Trade Unions* (1991). An influential figure was Hayek. See in particular his *Constitution of Liberty* (1960). See also Lord Wedderburn of Charlton, 'Freedom of association and philosophies of labour law' (1989) 18 ILJ 1. Cf. S. Auerbach, *Legislating for Conflict* (1990).

30 For a critique, see S. Evans, K. D. Ewing and P. Nolan, 'Industrial relations and the British economy in the 1990s: Mrs Thatcher's legacy' (1992), *Journal of Management Studies*, 29, 571.

31 See, for example, R. Epstein, 'In defense of contract at will' (1984) 51 U of Ch LR 947.

32 *Lockner* v. *New York* 198 US 45 (1904), p. 53.

33 *Adkins* v. *Children's Hospital* 261 US 525 (1923), p. 558.

34 *Ibid.*

35 *Coppage* v. *Kansas* 236 US I (1914).

36 H. J. Laski, *Liberty in the Modern State* (Penguin, 1937), p. 126.

37 Trade Boards Act 1909.

38 For background, see F. J. Bayliss, *Wages Councils* (1962).

39 This was a consolidation measure bringing together changes introduced in the Employment Protection Act 1975 which, apart from extending the jurisdiction of wages councils, also sought to hasten their demise by providing for the creation of joint industrial councils, which were intended to be a halfway house between a wages council and a voluntary collective bargaining arrangement.

40 H. J. Laski, *A Grammar of Politics*, p. 111.

41 See also Mines and Quarries Act 1954, s. 125.

42 For background to the changing of the law on wages councils, see Department of Employment, Consultative Paper on Wages Councils (1985).

43 On the denunciation of ILO Conventions, see K. Widdows, 'The denunciation of

international labour conventions' (1984) 33 ICLQ 1052.

44 On the fair wages resolution, see B. Bercusson, *Fair Wages Resolutions* (1978).

45 See S. Fredman, Sex Discrimination Act 1986, *Current Law Statutes 1986*. For a brief account see D. Brodie, 'Deregulation continued' (1987) 16 ILJ 50. See further S. Deakin, 'Equality under a market order: the Employment Act 1989' (1990) 19 ILJ 1.

46 See B. W. Napier, 'Working time and the law' (1991) 141 NLJ 1667.

47 The classic account of the law relating to the contract of employment is M. R. Freedland, *The Contract of Employment* (1976). For a good example recently of the employers's inherent contractual powers over employees, see *Cresswell* v. *Inland Revenue* [1984] IRLR 190. Cf. Factories Act 1961, s. 97 (4) and (5).

48 For a recent study of the law of unfair dismissal see H. Collins, *Justice in Dismissal* (1992).

49 Some potential grounds for dismissal are expressly forbidden, for example trade union membership or activities, pregnancy, and race or sex discrimination.

50 Also important in this respect is the Employment Protection (Consolidation) Act 1978, s. 1, which requires employers to issue employees with a written statement of principal terms and conditions of employment which should include a note of applicable disciplinary procedures. This was amended by the Employment Act 1989 so that such a note need not be included in the statement issued by employers of less than 20 employees. See further the Trade Union Reform and Employment Rights Act 1993.

51 See *West Midlands Co-operative Society Ltd* v *Tipton* [1986] AC 536.

52 There is the possibility that declarations and injunctions may be available, but these are atypical cases for, a number of reasons. See H. Carty, 'Dismissed employees: the search for a more effective range of remedies' (1989) 52 MLR 44.

53 For an account of the unfair dismissal legislation in operation see L. Dickens, *Dismissed* (1985).

54 Equal Opportunities Commission, *Women and Men in Britain* (1989), pp. 24–5.

55 *O'Kelly* v. *Trusthouse Forte* [1983] ICR 728.

56 For an account of the difficulties faced by atypical workers see L. Dickens, *Whose Flexibility?* (Institute of Employment Rights, 1992). See also S. Deakin and F. Wilkinson, *The Economics of Employment Rights* (Institute of Employment Rights, 1991).

57 See B. Bercusson, 'Workers, corporate enterprise and the law', in R. Lewis (ed.) *Labour Law in Britain* (1986). See also P. Davies and Lord Wedderburn, 'The land of industrial democracy' (1977) 16 ILJ 197.

58 On the 1975 Act, see L. Dickens and G. S.Bain, 'A duty to bargain? Union recognition and information disclosure', in R. Lewis (ed.), *Labour Law in Britain* (1986).

59 For an assessment of the law on trade union recognition, see B. Simpson, *Trade Union Recognition and the Law* (Institute of Employment Rights, 1991).

60 See E. McKendrick, 'The rights of trade union members – Part I of the Employment Act 1988' (1988) 17 ILJ 141.

61 Trade Union Act 1984, part 1. See R. Kidner, 'Trade union democracy: election of trade union officers' (1984) 13 ILJ 193. See now Trade Union and Labour Relations (Consolidation) Act 1992, ss. 46 – 61.

62 Trade Union Act 1984, part 2. See J. Hutton, 'Solving the strike problem: Part 2 of the Trade Union Act 1984' (1984) 13 ILJ 212. See now Trade Union and Labour Relations (Consolidation) Act 1992, ss. 226–235.

63 Trade Union Act 1984, part 3. See K. D. Ewing, 'Trade union political funds: the 1913 Act revised' (1984) 13 ILJ 227. See now Trade Union and Labour Relations (Consolidation) Act 1992, ss. 71–96.

64 Employment Act 1988, s. 3. Now Trade Union and Labour Relations (Consolidation) Act 1992, ss. 64–67. See E. McKendrick, 'The rights of trade union members – Part I of the Employment Act 1988' (1988) 17 ILJ 141. See also S. Leader, 'The European Convention on Human Rights, the Employment Act of 1988 and the right to refuse to strike' (1991) 20 ILJ 39.

65 This measure was condemned by the ILO Committee of Experts as violating ILO Convention 87 on the right to organize. See K. Ewing, *Britain and the ILO* (Institute of Employment Rights, 1989).

66 See P. Elias and K. Ewing, *Trade Union Democracy, Members' Rights and the Law* (1988).

67 Trade union membership fell from a peak of 13.3 million in 1979 to 9.9 million in 1990. This can be explained partly by the rising levels of unemployment in the 1980s, which appeared to hit the unionized sectors of the economy particularly harshly. The decline may also be explained by the significant withdrawal of state support for trade unionism in general and collective bargaining in particular as a strategy for promoting the rights of citizenship at work. The movement towards the break-up of national bargaining arrangements which is encouraged by the privatization of state enterprises and the creation of health service trusts may also serve to speed up the atrophy in the coverage of collective agreements as unions find difficulty in sustaining effective local arrangements.

68 Laski, *Liberty in the Modern State*, p. 129.

69 *Ibid.*

70 *Crofter Hand Woven Harris Tweed* v. *Veitch* [1942] AC 435, p. 463.

71 B. Hepple and O. Kahn-Freund, *Laws against Strikes* (Fabian Research Series, 1972).

72 Laski, *Liberty in the Modern State*, gives the example of the declaration of war: 'A government which knew that its declaration of war was, where it intended aggressive action, likely to involve a general strike, would be far less likely to think in belligerent terms' (pp. 129–30). For further treatment of this issue see K. W. Wedderburn in B. Aaron and K. W. Wedderburn (eds) *Industrial Conflict* (1972); and D. Brodie, 'Political strikes', in W. Finnie, C. Himsworth and N. Walker (eds), *Edinburgh Essays in Public Law* (1991), p. 215.

73 For an account of common law liabilities, see Lord Wedderburn of Charlton, *The Worker and the Law* (1986), Chapters 7 and 8.

74 *Amalgamated Society of Railway Servants* v. *Taff Vale Railway Co.* [1901] AC 426.

75 For an account, see O. *Kahn-Freund's Labour and the Law* (3rd ed, by P. L. Davies and M. R. Freedland 1983).

76 Trade Union and Labour Relations Act 1974, s. 29. See now Trade Union and Labour Relations (Consolidation) Act 1992, s. 244.

77 See *ANG* v. *Flynn* (1971) 10 KIR 17 and *Beaverbrook Newspapers Ltd* v. *Keys* [1980] IRLR 247.

78 F. A. Hayek, *The Constitution of Liberty* (1960), pp. 267–78.

79 For an account of the restrictions on the right to strike introduced since 1979, see R. Welch, *The Right to Strike* (Institute of Employment Rights, 1991). See also J. Hendy, *The Conservative Employment Laws* (Institute of Employment Rights, 2nd edn 1991).

80 *Mercury Communications Ltd* v. *Scott Garner* [1984] Ch 37.

81 See K. Ewing, *The Employment Act 1990: A European Perspective* (Institute of Employment Rights, 1991).

82 See J. Hutton, 'Solving the strike problem: Part 2 of the Trade Union Act 1984' (1984) 13 ILJ 212.

83 See K. D. Ewing, 'Industrial Action: another step in the "right" direction' (1982) 11 ILJ 209. See now Trade Union and Labour Relations (Consolidation) Act 1992, ss. 20–22.

84 For a full account, see K. D. Ewing, *The Right to Strike* (1991).

85 *Simmons* v. *Hoover Ltd* [1977] ICR 61.

86 *Report of a Court of Inquiry under the Rt Hon. Lord Justice Scarman, OBE, into a dispute between Grunwick Processing Laboratories Limited and members of the Association of Professional, Executive, Clerical and Computer Staff* (Cmnd 6922, 1977).

87 For an account of the Grunwick dispute, see P. Elias, B. Napier, and P. Wallington, *Labour Law Cases and Materials* (1980), pp. 29–59.

88 See K. D. Ewing and B. W. Napier, 'The Wapping dispute and labour law' [1986] CLJ 285.

89 Now Trade Union and Labour Relations (Consolidation) Act 1992, s. 237. See H. Carty, 'The Employment Act 1990: still fighting the industrial cold war' (1991) 20 ILJ 1.

90 For a full account of the so far limited influence of EC labour law, see B. A. Hepple, 'European Communities' in R. Blanpain (ed.), *Comparative Labour Law and Industrial Relations* (4th edn 1990). See also B. A. Hepple and A. Byre, 'EEC labour law in the United Kingdom – a new approach' (1989) 18 ILJ 129.

91 See B. Hepple, 'The implementation of the Community Charter of Fundamental Social Rights' (1990) 53 MLR 643.

92 For an analysis, see Lord Wedderburn, *The Social Charter, European Company and Employment Rights* (Institute of Employment Rights, 1990).

93 See J. Clark and M. Hall, 'The Cinderella Directive? Employee rights to information about conditions applicable to their contract or employment relationship' (1992) 21 ILJ 106. Others, dealing with redundancy consultation and the rights of pregnant women, have been adopted since.

94 For an account of both of these developments see S. Fredman and G. Morris, *The State as Employer* (1989).

95 Laski, *A Grammar of Politics, op. cit.*

96 For an interesting critique, see M Ford, 'Citizenship and democracy in industrial relations: the agenda for the 1990s?' (1992) 55 MLR 241.

6

Citizenship and Housing

MARTIN PARTINGTON

INTRODUCTION

The purpose of this chapter is to consider the extent to which employment of the concept of 'citizenship' can illuminate discussion of questions of housing policy and the legal framework needed to implement that policy. In making this argument, I start with the definitions of citizenship that will be used in the discussion. Second, I consider the nature of the housing market and current modes of regulation of that market. Then I turn to the question of how far bringing questions of 'citizenship' into the discussion might open up new approaches to regulation of the housing market. Finally, brief conclusions are drawn.

DEFINITIONS OF CITIZENSHIP

Use of the concept of 'citizenship' in the context of debates on political issues in general and social policy issues in particular is not new.[1] And there has been a considerable revival of interest in the notion in recent months;[2] indeed this volume reflects the development of this interest. The very concept of 'citizenship' is, however, extremely difficult. It is not capable of simple or straightforward definition; rather it incorporates a wide range of meaning from the technical (e.g. the use of the concept in the context of discussions about nationality) to the aspirational ('citizens of the world unite').[3] For the purpose of this chapter, which focuses on a specific aspect of social policy, i.e. housing policy, two specific but nevertheless sharply contrasted views of 'citizenship' will be employed: the first is what may be described as the 'idealistic', the second is the 'consumerist'.

The 'idealistic' notion of citizenship suggests that, in questions of social policy, certain standards of service provision must be reached (whether by means of cash payments, the provision of education or housing) in order that every member of the community can play a part as a fully integrated citizen in that community. Such a view of citizenship will lead to proposals that every person should have a basic right, or entitlement, to income, education or housing. This is an 'idealistic' view in the sense that, given the fact that income, educational opportunities and access to housing are currently distributed on a rather unequal basis, the achievement of such basic rights will require major changes to current patterns of resource distribution, and will only be achieved on the back of fundamental political change.

The 'consumerist' view of citizenship has been used in recent discussions of concepts such as the Citizen's Charter, namely that those who provide services, primarily but not necessarily exclusively in the public sector, should do so to a level of service which should be expected by every citizen in the community. This *may* imply the need for redistributive policies, but does not necessarily do so. Rather the 'consumerist' approach may be more concerned with the operation of the market, and in particular the injection of service standards into the 'social market' in a context where other market mechanisms, particularly competition, do not seem to be relevant or effective.

This chapter will discuss the possible application of both concepts of citizenship that have been identified in the specific context of the provision of housing and the operation of the housing market. The opportunity will be taken to make some suggestions as to the way in which housing law, and the legal regulation of the housing market, might move forward if the social objectives implicit in the notion of 'citizenship' are to be achieved. This discussion will, however, be preceded by a brief analysis of the distinctive features of the housing market within which housing policy has to operate.

THE NATURE OF THE HOUSING MARKET[4]

Many areas of social policy are dominated by *direct* provision by the state: education, health, social security and social services are all provided predominantly by agencies of government, whether central or local. Other areas of social policy are delivered indirectly, with the state using legislation and other forms of regulation to establish basic quality standards; examples include the provision of food, protection of the environment, regulation of the employment relationship and transport policy. A consequence of the recent policies of privatization has been to shift the provision of a number of services from the first category into the second: telecommunications, water, gas and electricity are all examples of this.

The housing market is rather more difficult to classify in these terms. At the turn of the century housing, in common with all other areas of what we now regard as social provision (save, perhaps, defence), was provided almost exclusively by the private sector, with a limited input from charities. During the first half of the twentieth century the private rented sector became increasingly regulated, and a public rented sector was created. At the same time levels of owner-occupation, which historically were very low, began to increase. Unlike those industries that were completely nationalized at the end of the Second World War, direct public provision of housing for rent remained a minority feature of the housing market, taken as a whole. There were further sharp increases in private house ownership.

During the 1970s and 1980s there were further shifts of emphasis and an increasingly complex market fragmentation. First, increasing encouragement was given to the creation of a 'third force' in rented housing provision – the 'quasi-public' sector of the housing association movement. Housing associations are not quite part of the public sector because, while they receive public funds and cater for sectors of the housing market traditionally supported by the public sector, they are not public bodies in the ways central or local government departments are; but neither are they private sector bodies. They are not subjected to the normal private market forces. Second, as part of the increasing emphasis on owner-occupation, the role of local housing authorities was changed: sales of council houses have privatized large parts of this segment of the market,[5] while financial controls have prevented local authorities from building new housing stock.

The primary feature of the housing market, therefore, is its complexity and lack of homogeneity. Partly it is directly provided by the state, but predominantly it is provided by private or quasi-public bodies subject to a wide variety of legislative measures.

There are other features of the housing market that should be borne in mind. First, there is little doubt that, for many people, housing has a very important psychological and social significance. It is the place from which they create the basis for their social lives and their working lives. Housing relates to broader questions of individual identity and the place of individuals in society. Second, housing is, by definition, a less flexible commodity than other social goods. Once a dwelling is built there is an expectation that it will remain in being, in that location, for a relatively substantial period of time. This may not coincide with changes in employment patterns, the rise and fall of particular sectors in the labour market or the restructuring of industry. As a result, it is the case that in the context of housing, the problem of achieving a balance of the supply of housing with the demand for housing is going to be rendered more complex by the fact that there may be a lack of fit between areas where there is an over-supply and those where there is an under-supply of housing provision. Third, housing is a costly commodity to produce. Most housing provision has to be financed by loans, which have to be serviced over a considerable period of time. Investment in housing – particularly private investment – will, therefore, occur only if potential investors perceive that the legislative context within which housing is produced is secure enough to enable a reasonable return on capital to be achieved.

HOUSING POLICY AND THE HOUSING MARKET

Housing policy is not, in fact, a single policy, but rather a compendium of policies designed to achieve broadly defined objectives: that everyone should have access to housing, of decent quality, at a price each person can afford, located where people want or wish to live.

Even at this level of generality, there will be marked differences of view between those who argue that such policy objectives will only be achieved when everyone reaches a high standard of provision (e.g. that everyone has a centrally heated house with a garden) and those who will be satisfied with more modest – some might say, more realistic – levels of provision (e.g. that everyone should have a roof over his or her head, and the price paid should represent value for money).

Even if agreement over the goals of housing policy can be reached, there still remain very substantial problems of implementation because the housing market itself is so highly fragmented. We have already noted, in passing, the basic division between those who own their houses and those who rent. But within the owner-occupied sector there is a marked contrast between those who own outright and those who own but only with the provision of a loan guaranteed by a mortgage. And also included in this sector of the market are those who, technically at law, are tenants, but who are regarded in practical terms as owner-occupiers, i.e. those holding their accommodation on a long lease.

The rented sector is even more fragmented, between those renting from local authorities, from housing associations and from private landlords. A careful analysis of each of these three groups would also reveal widely varying patterns of provision and organization. For example, landlords in the private landlord sector are highly differentiated;[6] so too are housing associations, which provide housing for very contrasting target groups in a wide variety of legal frameworks, offering a variety of tenures (e.g. housing for co-ownership, cooperative housing, housing for rental or for purchase).

127

Within both the owner-occupied and the rented sectors there will also be significant regional variations. Thus any attempt to argue for a new framework for housing policy and housing law must take into account this high degree of fragmentation.

CURRENT MODES OF REGULATION

It is impossible in this brief essay to give a detailed summary of all the policy and law that seeks to regulate the housing market. A few examples can, however, be provided.

The Owner-Occupied Sector

In the owner-occupied sector, the most significant feature of housing policy is the indirect financial support that is given towards the cost of purchase through the tax relief on mortgage interest payments.[7] For those who get into difficulties with repayments, protective legislation seeks to ensure that occupiers are not evicted without a court's being convinced that this is the only realistic and reasonable option.[8]

In the more specialized leasehold sector of the owner-occupied market, leaseholders of houses have, for some years, had rights to enfranchise themselves, i.e. to purchase the reversionary interest from the landlord.[9] More recently, attention has been given to the problems of long leaseholders of blocks of flats, with increased rights to information, control of service charges and, in some cases, the ability to purchase the landlord's interest.[10] More recent proposals from the Law Commission on Commonhold[11] will, if enacted, take these legislative developments a stage further.

The Rented Sector

Regulation of the private rented sector of the housing market has a long history.[12] The potential for private landlords to exploit inequalities in the marketplace arising from an imbalance between supply and demand has resulted in a variety of measures designed to curb rent levels, to give tenants security of tenure and to prevent their being evicted without due process. A particular feature of this area of the law is that layers of legislative complexity have been piled on layers of legislative complexity. Since governments are, quite properly, reluctant to alter accrued substantive legal entitlements, old regulatory structures operate alongside new ones, making it extremely difficult to give succinct accounts of the current position.[13] These changes of policy do, of course, reflect starkly different political views as to how the private rented sector should best be regulated. But they do not make life easy for landlords, tenants or their advisers.

The public rented sector has been less subject to direct regulatory law; it used to be assumed that local authorities would be 'model landlords' who would, without direct intervention, operate efficient and just housing policies. However, over the past 15 years there has been increasing central government regulation of local authority discretion: first, though the homeless persons legislation[14] (which effectively imposes priorities for allocation policies); second, through the enactment in 1980 of the so-called 'tenant's charter'; third, indirectly through housing subsidy legislation, which impacts on the freedom of local authorities to determine rent levels.[16]

Changes to the housing benefit scheme have resulted in substantially increased subsidies of housing costs for individuals, but these have been more than balanced by sharply reduced subsidy for the building of new public sector dwellings, save in the housing association sector.

Housing Conditions and Housing Standards

In addition to the regulation of the fundamental legal terms on which legal accommodation is held, there is also a substantial body of law relating to the regulation of housing conditions. Building regulations now seek to ensure the basic quality of new house building; the Housing Acts and Environmental Protection Act (formerly Public Health Acts) seek to regulate existing dwellings that have become either 'unfit for human habitation' or a 'statutory nuisance'; and there are special regulatory regimes applicable to houses in multiple occupation.

Harassment and Unlawful Eviction

Those to whom bodies of regulatory law apply in theory but who might be tempted to ignore such law have been subject to an increasingly detailed set of provisions in both the criminal and the civil law relating to acts of harassment and unlawful eviction. The financial impact of the new statutory cause of action created by the Housing Act 1988 s. 27 – which gives tenants who have been unlawfully evicted a statutory entitlement to damages reflecting the difference in value of a dwelling with vacant possession and the value of the same dwelling with those tenants still in occupation – is a very significant addition to tenants' rights.

In short, there is already on the statute book a very substantial body of regulatory law. The mere existence of such measures does not, of course, mean that those measures are successful. While a majority of occupiers of housing live in more or less comfortable accommodation, costing more or less what they can afford, there is no doubt that a significant minority of people live in accommodation that is seriously sub-standard in quality terms, and/or is substantially overpriced. There is an even more desperate minority who are actually or practically homeless.

In addition to these obvious measures of the failure of housing policy, there are less obvious issues which tend not to be addressed in discussions of housing policy; for example, the availability of housing in rural areas for local people (as opposed to people with better incomes from the towns and cities), or the relationship between housing design and personal security. And fundamental problems remain about the good sense, or otherwise, of present policies relating to the subsidization of housing costs.[17] It is certainly the case that many influential commentators and lobbyists still argue for significant changes to present housing policy.[18] The issue to be discussed here is the extent to which such arguments might be assisted by being considered in the context of a discussion of citizenship.

HOUSING AND CITIZENSHIP

The 'Idealistic' Model

The 'idealistic' approach to citizenship implies, in this context, an argument for the enactment of a basic legal right to housing for everyone. Superficially this may be a very attractive idea. Interestingly, in the United Kingdom an attempt to create such a generalized legal right was made in the 1970s. The circumstances surrounding that attempt are instructive.

The history of the enactment of the Housing (Homeless Persons) Act 1977 (now Housing Act 1985, Part III) is now relatively familiar. Mr Stephen Ross, then Liberal MP for the Isle of Wight, introduced the original Homeless Persons Bill into Parliament – as a Private Member's Bill – in 1976. As originally drafted it did contain, in clause 3, a statement which – if enacted – would have gone a long way to creating a generalized legal entitlement to housing.[19] The implications of this, for local housing authorities, were too awful to contemplate, so they lobbied hard and strong to get this approach modified. In this, they were successful. Mr Ross was, in effect, given an ultimatum. If he persisted with his original Bill, the Labour Government of the day would ensure it made no further progress; if, however, he utilized an alternative draft Bill, prepared within the Department of the Environment, progress would be made.

Thus there came to be introduced the Bill in, broadly, the form in which we now have it. Entitlement to housing (not, be it noted, a new council house) was to be limited to specified categories of applicant in 'priority need';[20] they were not to have become homeless intentionally[21] if they were to receive permanent housing under the Act. Furthermore, even in some situations where there was entitlement to housing, a local authority could avoid responsibility for provision by demonstrating that the applicant had a 'local connection'[22] elsewhere in Great Britain, and did not have a local connection in the area of the authority applied to.[23]

It has to be remembered, of course, that a *crucial* aspect of the Private Member's Bill procedure is that such bills cannot involve an increase in public expenditure. As many argued at the time, and have continued to argue subsequently, enacting specific legal entitlements without providing resources can seem a hollow political gesture. Thus, instead of the general right to housing initially envisaged, there was created a much more limited 'contingent'[24] set of entitlements. Indeed it can be seen as, in many ways, a rather modest measure designed to bring some greater uniformity to housing allocation proceedings, as had been suggested a few years before by the Council Housing Advisory Committee.[25]

It is certainly the case that there are examples on the statute book of what may be described as 'aspirational legislation' – legislation that flags up a desirable objective but is recognized as being only a contribution to the achievement of that objective. Anti-discrimination legislation is often referred to in such a way.[26]

In the case of housing, my own view is that use of the concept of 'citizenship' in the sense defined for this part of the discussion is much more appropriate in the political, rather than the legal context. Since delivering a general, 'right to housing' will, if nothing else, cost a very substantial amount of money, decisions to provide that finance will be *political* not legal. There is a danger that any legal enactment of a general right to housing could, indeed, be counter-productive by creating expectations that are, simply, not achievable. It is political will, not legal will, that is needed to satisfy the call for 'rights to housing' associated with the idealistic view of citizenship.

The 'Consumerist' Model

Although less radical in its implications than the 'idealistic' view of citizenship, the 'consumerist' view of citizenship might nevertheless prove to be the basis for a useful short- to medium-term programme of reform for housing policy and the consequent legal framework.

The major problems that currently affect the housing market would seem to be:

1 A lack of suitable dwellings for particular groups, particularly the young and single, who are to be found sleeping rough in

Britain's cities; and those recognized as legally homeless, but
required to stay in bed and breakfast accommodation.

2 A great deal of poor-quality housing, particularly in the
rented sectors.

3 An imbalance between what people may have to pay for their
housing and the quality of what they are provided with.

4 Discrimination in patterns of allocation of housing and access
to housing.

It is instructive to compare the housing sector of the economy with
other sectors. In relation to the sale and production of manufactured
goods, or the provision of a whole range of services – particularly
financial services – the consumer movement has lobbied effectively
for measures dealing with trade descriptions, trading standards, unfair
contractual terms, the regulation of credit terms and the like. These
legislative measures are supported by a range of official bodies, from
the Office of Fair Trading to local authority trading standards departments. There are special court procedures to deal with small consumer
claims. More broadly, there is a strong European interest in the effectiveness of the consumer movement, as an adjunct to the operation of
the market. Furthermore, many of the major players in the service and
manufacturing sectors of the economy have themselves established
their own measures of consumer protection – if only to forestall further government intervention.

By contrast, housing has not formerly been perceived in this way.
To be sure, there are housing industry guarantees of quality for new
house building; many local authorities do employ tenancy relations
officers; rent officers play a role in the fixing of fair rents under the
Rent Acts, or setting limits to rents payable under the housing benefit
scheme for assured tenancies created under the Housing Act 1988.
Local authority tenants were granted a 'tenants' charter' under the
Housing Act 1980. But these are piecemeal measures, not part of what
could be described as a coherent package of measures to protect
those – whether owner-occupiers or tenants – who 'consume' housing
services. The proposal for 'citizen's charters' will move us some way in
that direction, but not very far, as their focus is essentially on public
sector rented accommodation only.

There are still extraordinary gaps. For example, 'there is no law
against letting a tumble-down house'[27] – a similar proposition in relation to a motor-car or other consumer goods would not be regarded as
acceptable. Estate agents have begun to improve their customer care
and customer service policies, but they remain far less regulated
(either by statute or voluntarily) than other service providers, such as
insurance companies or banks. The law on consumer credit does not

apply to most credit transactions applicable in the housing context; while this may not normally matter, there are some operators in the secondary mortgage market who surely ought to be brought under control.

A 'consumerist' perspective on housing would encourage the bringing together of the provisions that currently exist and their expansion with a view to ensuring that all citizens are guaranteed proper standards of housing service. Such a view, in the housing context, would involve a re-analysis of the roles of the three main actors in the housing market: the Government, the consumers of housing services and the providers of those services.

The Government

It would be essential for the Government to take the lead in developing the 'citizenship' approach. The first step that would need to be taken would be the creation of an office that could act as the coordinator and focus for the new policy context. A possible title – building on analogies in other parts of the economy – would be Director-General of Fair Housing (DGFH).

The appointee would run an Office of Fair Housing (OFH). In some respects this is a role already undertaken by the Housing Corporation, particularly since the Housing Act 1988 came into force. Its work in developing model standards and contractual terms could be extended into other sectors of the housing market. Not only would the terms and conditions under which tenancies were held come within its scope; the conditions attaching to mortgage agreements, which can cause problems in practice, could also be examined again.

It would not, of course, be essential for the DGFH and the OFH to do all the work themselves. They might sensibly work with the bodies that represent the interests of mortgage lenders and landlords, who would be encouraged, in effect, to generate 'industry' standards (analogous to the work of, say, the Association of British Travel Agents), which would then be evaluated by the DGFH and the OFH to ensure that a reasonable balance was struck between the interests of the consumers of housing services and those who provide them.

One major advantage of this approach might well be that it could encourage the drawing together of the currently very fragmented market of providers into a more coherent structure. And the representative bodies that do currently exist, which currently spend the bulk of their time in parliamentary lobbying, could be given extra responsibility for setting a framework of good practice for their own members.

There would need to be a carefully structured relationship between the terms and conditions set down or approved by the DGFH and other forms of legislative intervention. To take the example of rent levels, the present position is that private sector tenancies created before 15 January 1989 remain 'protected tenancies' under the Rent Acts, subject – where relevant – to a fair rent imposed by the Rent Officer. The wide-scale objection to fair renting is that it distorts market rents and thus prevents landlords who have invested in the provision of housing from getting as good a return on their investment as in other sectors of the economy. Private sector tenancies created after 15 January 1989 are assured tenancies. In relation to these there is little or no rent control. This generates the criticism that it allows landlords to exploit market conditions by charging tenants excessive rents; and, for government, it creates the problem that the housing benefit scheme might be used, by landlords of the poorest tenants, to subsidize exploitative rents that do not reflect any reasonable test of 'value for money'. An industry-driven, but DGFH-approved, formula could be used as the basis for establishing the compromise that is essential, between ensuring that tenants are not exploited and giving landlords a reasonable return on their investment, but that is currently missing. Failure to adhere to the industry standard would lead to government intervention. Such a compromise might also be more politically neutral (in the party political sense) than existing policies, and thus help to establish the longer-term stability in the housing market that is essential with investment that produces a product that can last for a hundred years.

One advantage of this approach might be that much better links could be established between the physical condition of a dwelling and the price payable for it. To some extent this is reflected in both the fair rent and market rent approaches. But these tend to operate rather inflexibly. It is widely recognized that there must be more investment in the existing housing stock to prevent poor-quality accommodation being unfit for human habitation; but those who might make such an investment will not do so if they fear they will not be able to achieve a fair return on that investment. An industry-driven formula – regulated by the DGFH – might provide a more effective way forward.

A similar approach could be adopted for security of tenure and eviction, whether of tenants or of mortgagers. Industry-wide codes of practice and conduct could be established, designed to ensure that consumers of housing services who get into difficulties, e.g. over rent, are subject to procedures that give them appropriate opportunities to get out of those difficulties. At the same time, occupiers of dwellings clearly abusing their situation could be dealt with more swiftly. While it would be desirable for final decisions on eviction to remain with the courts, the judges could be provided with a better-defined factual basis for making their decisions.

The 'consumerist' approach could also offer alternative approaches to resolving problems about estate contracts and gazumping which explode from time to time, particularly in the press. The concept of 'cooling-off periods' is now well established in other contexts; it might, with advantage, be brought into the housing market as well. In the longer term, it might lead to a more fundamental re-appraisal of the legal basis of residential conveyancing. More generally, the DGFH would be able to approve codes of practice and conduct relating to the operation of estate agents and those who provide conveyancing services.

The new perspective could also be used to develop special codes of practice in relation to the use of residential accommodation on a short-term basis. One of the scandals of the present operation of the housing market is the existence of units of accommodation – in both the public and private sectors – which, for a variety of reasons, are not made available for occupation. There may be a variety of good or bad reasons for this. But the DGFH could help to establish acceptable standards on void accommodation. At the same time, insofar as accommodation was held vacant, e.g. pending redevelopment, procedures could be developed for ensuring that accommodation was available when needed for such purposes. In short, new approaches to management of the housing stock would be developed.

By creating the DGFH and the OFH, the Government would provide a focus for a restructuring of the housing market which would help to eliminate areas where abuse currently occurs, and at the same time encourage a stronger 'consumer' perspective.

The Government should also be encouraged to take three further steps. The first is that support should be given to the provision of a network of independent housing advice centres. A 'citizenship' approach must ensure that intended beneficiaries of protective legislation are able to take advantage of it. At present this does not happen. Second, the Government should ensure that the structure and content of housing legislation is simplified. The 'consumerist' perspective outlined above could offer the basis for a simpler legal structure. There is no doubt that the present level of complexity is quite self-defeating. Neither the intended beneficiaries of the law nor those potentially regulated by it take sufficient notice of the law, because of its complexity. The current situation could, indeed, be argued to be a denial of citizenship. Third, although the recent Civil Justice Review rejected the idea of establishing a specialist housing court, this concept should be reconsidered. The present work of rent assessment committees,[28] housing benefit review boards,[29] district judges and the Divisional Court – which currently have an incoherent and fragmented set of jurisdictions over a wide variety of housing matters – could be brought together into a single *housing tribunal*, able to dispose of the bulk of housing disputes.[30]

The Consumers of Housing Services

The new institutional framework sketched above – driven by government – is designed to ensure more effective protection for the consumers of housing services, i.e. mortgagers and tenants, but also including potential consumers, such as the homeless. At present, there is an extensive and complex regulatory framework in place that does not work effectively. The proposed restructuring of the institutional framework within which housing services are provided would, it is envisaged, lead to a range of practices that would ensure that consumers of housing, who themselves acted fairly and responsibly, were dealt with fairly by the providers of housing services.

This new framework could, indeed, lead to the development of a rather stronger consumer interest in housing matters. A novel focus could be given to the work of tenants' associations and residents' associations (as occurs in other sectors of the service and manufacturing economy). In addition to ensuring greater compliance with existing standards, a stronger consumer perspective could also help in discussions about improvement in standards relating to housing.

The Providers of Housing Services

The organizations involved in the supply of housing provision would inevitably respond, were the new institutional framework sketched out above to be put in place. Existing representative organizations would acquire new responsibilities and authority, but they would always have to balance their own interests with those of their customers and be subject to the overall approval of the DGFH.

All those who provide housing services would need to be considered in the development of this consumer perspective; the builders, the agents, the providers of housing finance, the conveyancers, and the sellers and renters of residential accommodation. New standards of honesty and openness in dealings with housing matters could be established.

CONCLUSION

A majority of the citizens of Britain live in good-quality accommodation for which they pay a price they can afford. But a significant minority live in poor-quality housing, or housing for which they pay much too much. And some have nowhere to live at all. The general objective of housing policy must be to ensure that all have a decent home in which to live, if they are to play their part as full members of British society. But calling for a generalized 'right to housing' as part of a campaign for full 'citizenship' rights is, it is argued here, more appropriate for the political arena than the legal.

It is clear, however, that there are current problems with the operation of the housing market, and that many of the current regulatory measures that are on the statute book do not work. The adoption of a 'citizenship' approach that focuses on the consumer of housing services does, it is suggested, offer the basis for the development of a new institutional framework within which housing rights could be set, and the development of a new partnership between consumers and suppliers, regulated and approved by an agency charged with the task of balancing the interests of those two groups; and could lead to the simplification and utilization of an area of law which should be accessible to all British citizens, but which, currently, is not.

NOTES AND REFERENCES

1 See, e.g., T. H. Marshall, *Citizenship and Social Class* (1950); T. H. Marshall and T. Bottomore, *Citizenship and Social Class* (1992).

2 R. Lister, *The Exclusive Society: Citizenship and the Poor* (1992); Commission on Citizenship, *Report, Encouraging Citizenship* (1990).

3 These layers of meaning are discussed above, Chapter 1. See also the Commission on Citizenship, *op. cit*, section 1.

4 See, e.g., P. Malpass and A. Murie, *Housing Policy and Practice* (4th edn 1990).

5 See Ray Forrest and Alan Murie, *Selling the Welfare State: The Privatisation of Council Housing* (new revised edn 1992).

6 See John Allen and Linda McDowell, *Landlords and Property* (1989).

7 See, e.g., A. E. Holmans, *Housing Policy in Britain* (1987); H. Aughton, with P. Malpass, *Housing Finance* (3rd edn 1990).

8 See Administration of Justice Act 1970, ss. 36–38 and Administration of Justice Act 1973, s. 8.

9 Leasehold Reform Act 1967.

10 *Report of the Committee of Inquiry on the Management of Privately Owned Blocks of Flats*, E. G. Nugee (Chair) (1989); Landlord and Tenant Act 1987.

11 The Law Commission, *Commonhold: Freehold Flats and Freehold Ownership of other Interdependent Buildings* (Cm 199, 1987). See too the Housing and Urban Development Act 1993.

12 See, e.g., P. N. Balchin, *Housing Policy* (2nd edn 1989) Chapter 5.

13 At present the private sector regime consolidated in the Rent Act 1977 (but traceable back to the Increase of Rent and Mortgage Interest (War Restrictions) Act 1915) and amended by the Housing Act 1980 runs in parallel with the 'assured tenancy' regime created by the Housing Act 1988, which became operative on 15 January 1989. The position in relation to Housing Association Tenancies is equally complex.

14 See, e.g., P. Q. Watchman and P. Robson, *Homelessness and the Law in Britain* (2nd edn 1989).

15 Kay, Legg and Foot, *The 1980 Tenants' Right in Practice* (1983); C. Brennan, The Illusion of the Gap: A Case Study of the Implementation of the Consultation Provisions of the Tenant's Charter (unpublished PhD thesis, Brunel University, 1989).

16 See, e.g., Malpass and Murie, *op. cit.*, Chapter 7.

17 See Aughton and Malpass, *op. cit*; also R. Forrest, A. Murie and P. Williams, *Home Ownership: Differentiation and Fragmentation*, Chapter 5 (1990).

18 See, e.g., Institute of Housing, *Housing for All* (1991).

19 Clause 3 of the original Bill proposed, simply, that those who proved that they were homeless and had a 'special need' were to be granted accommodation; those who could not prove special need would get 'appropriate advice and assistance'.

20 See definition of law in Housing Act 1985, s. 59.

21 See now Housing Act 1985, s. 60. There were many speeches from MPs about the need for this provision to prevent the Act becoming a character for 'scroungers and scrimshankers': per Mr W. R. Rees-Davies.

22 See now Housing Act 1985, s. 61.

23 This was to prevent places regarded as 'magnets' for potential residents from becoming swamped; some interesting, though implausible, locations were identified as such in the parliamentary debates.

24 To adopt the terminology of G. Mackenzie, who wrote a detailed (unpublished) DPhil thesis at Oxford University on the history of the legislation.

25 Central Housing Advisory Committee, Housing Management Sub-Committee, *Council Housing: Purposes Procedures and Priorities* (1969).

26 See also use of the concepts of 'statutory objectives' and 'general principles' in the Courts and Legal Services Act, 1990.

27 Criticized many years ago by J. M. Reynolds, 'Statutory covenants of fitness and repair: social legislation and the judges' (1974) 37 *Mod LR* 380.

28 A. Prichard, 'New jurisdictions for rent assessment committees?' (1991) *The Conveyancer & Property Lawyer* 447.

29 R. Sainsbury and T. Eardley, *Housing Benefit Reviews: Final Report* (1991, York University).

30 Excluding disputes following relationship breakdown.

7

The Right to Racial Equality

GEOFFREY BINDMAN

RACE AND CITIZENSHIP

The United Kingdom has never been ethnically homogeneous: there has never been a time when all its citizens identified themselves, and were identified by others, as belonging to the same tribe, race, clan or whatever other label one might use to identify racial similarity or difference.

It is vital to stress that when we refer to questions of race, the issue is perception by oneself or others of an appropriate label. Race is in the eye of the beholder; it exists nowhere else. But the perception or label is enough to produce drastic consequences, as no one needs to be reminded.

In Britain, citizenship is not directly linked with such racial perceptions. A citizen of the United Kingdom may identify with and feel part of one or more different groups. A citizen of West Indian descent may feel and be perceived by others as a black person, as of African or Afro-Caribbean race, and, if born and brought up in Cardiff, as Welsh. A Sikh with United Kingdom citizenship living in Southall among other Sikhs may see himself and be seen at the same time as a member of the 'black community', as of Indian national origin and as of Sikh ethnic origin.

Because the concepts of race and ethnicity have no solid scientific validity, the ascription of racial identity is an uncertain and sometimes arbitrary exercise. Even more uncertain – often to the point of absurdity – is the assumption that individuals labelled with membership of a racial group thereby embody particular character traits or mental or physical qualities.

RACE AND INJUSTICE

The above-mentioned assumption, conscious or unconscious, leads to injustice when it is given concrete expression in the form of racial discrimination – when benefits are allocated or withheld on racial grounds. Yet the English common law provided no remedy for racial discrimination, save in a small number of very special cases.[1]

The problem of racial discrimination did not attract much public attention until after the Second World War, although certainly it had long been the common experience of black people in such centres of black settlement as Cardiff and Liverpool, and of Jews in the East End of London.[2] From 1948 onwards, a steady stream of immigrants came to Britain from the Caribbean and the Indian sub-continent, encouraged by the promise of employment. Because they shared a common citizenship with all other members of the Commonwealth, and had been brought up to regard Britain as their mother country, they did not expect the hostility which they frequently encountered from the native population. It seemed that as the British people relinquished the Empire, the racism formerly directed at subjects overseas was turned inwards against those former subjects now enjoying legal equality in Britain.

A LEGAL RIGHT NOT TO SUFFER RACIAL DISCRIMINATION

The notion that one might create an enforceable legal right not to be discriminated against has not been easy to digest. Racial discrimination is often confused with racial prejudice. It is wrongly regarded as a mental attitude, in the realm of thought rather than action, and thus not susceptible to legal regulation; indeed, not *morally* deserving of legal regulation.

This is a complete misunderstanding. An anti-discrimination law is designed to restrain and remedy anti-social and often materially damaging conduct – as is the criminal law and much civil law, such as the law of tort. But the perception that the techniques of law may have a role in the field of race relations is a recent one. It has become widely acknowledged only since the Second World War.

THE DEVELOPMENT OF ANTI-DISCRIMINATION LAW

The eradication of racial discrimination was of course one of the primary objects of those who established the United Nations after the defeat of the Nazi regime. The right not to suffer discrimination was thus enshrined in the Universal Declaration of Human Rights in 1948. But it took many more years to develop international enforcement machinery and even now detailed anti-discrimination laws exist in very few countries of the world.

The United States took the lead. In 1945, President Roosevelt decreed that discrimination on racial grounds should be prohibited in the public service. Complaints were to be investigated and, if upheld, appropriate remedial action was to be taken. Some state legislatures, beginning with those of New York and Massachusetts, created human rights commissions with powers to investigate complaints against private employers. A public hearing could be convened, followed if necessary by enforcement through the ordinary judicial system. In 1964, President Johnson secured the passage of the Civil Rights Act envisaged by the previous President, John F. Kennedy, prohibiting discrimination throughout the United States on grounds of race and sex, not only in the field of employment, but in housing, education and other facilities as well.

It is one thing to state a right not to be subjected to discriminatory treatment; it is another thing to enforce such a right. In the United States, after the Civil War, racial discrimination had been made a criminal offence. But the law soon fell into disuse. There were no prosecutions. If there had been it is unlikely that any jury (whose members would have been white local residents) would have brought in a conviction. The human rights commissions, with power to investigate and seek conciliation, seemed to hold out a better prospect of effective enforcement. The Civil Rights Act adopted the same model.

ANTI-DISCRIMINATION LAW IN BRITIAN

After a false start, when criminal remedies were proposed, the first British anti-discrimination law, the Race Relations Act 1965, followed a similar pattern to that adopted by the state human rights commissions in the United States – a pattern which had also recently been adopted there on the federal level when the Equal Employment Opportunities Commission was established by the Civil Rights Act 1964.

The Race Relations Act 1965 created the Race Relations Board to investigate complaints of discrimination and attempt to resolve them by conciliation. However, the scope of the new law was very limited indeed. It prohibited racial discrimination only in the provision of certain public facilities, such as hotels, restaurants, public houses, public transport and other public institutions. The vital areas of employment and housing, in which there was increasing evidence of widespread and seriously damaging discrimination, were ignored. And the enforcement mechanism was very weak. If the Board failed to achieve conciliation it had no power to take legal proceedings. Only the Attorney-General had this power, and then only if there was evidence that the discrimination was likely to be repeated. Even then, he could only seek an injunction; no redress was available for the victim.

The first annual report of the Race Relations Board, published in 1967, set out the objectives of anti-discrimination legislation, as they were then perceived, as follows:

(1) A law is an unequivocal declaration of public policy;
(2) A law gives support to those who do not wish to discriminate, but who feel compelled to do so by social pressure;
(3) A law gives protection and redress to minority groups;
(4) A law thus provides for the peaceful and orderly adjustment of grievances and release of tensions;
(5) A law reduces prejudice by discouraging the behaviour in which prejudice finds expression.

Because of its limited scope, the 1965 Act achieved little more than a somewhat equivocal declaration of public policy. It did nothing to achieve the remaining four purposes because it did not apply to the main areas in which discrimination was experienced, namely employment and housing.

The first chairman of the Race Relations Board, Mark Bonham-Carter (now Lord Bonham-Carter), had accepted the appointment on the condition that the Board be free to recommend changes in the law, should it find (as he anticipated would be the case) that the scope of the 1965 Act was too narrow to be effective.

The Board initiated two parallel studies. The first, carried out by Political and Economic Planning (PEP), examined the level of racial discrimination occurring in the community at large. The method was to employ three actors to play the parts of job applicants, would-be renters and purchasers of housing accommodation, and seekers of services. Claiming similar qualifications or needs, they recorded the reaction of the employers or providers of accommodation or services. The result was powerful evidence of very widespread discrimination, especially in employment and housing.

The second study was an examination by three lawyers[3] of anti-discrimination laws in other countries, particularly the United States. It recommended extension of the law, both in scope and in enforcement machinery. Consistently with the findings of the PEP report, it recommended that discrimination in employment and housing be brought within the scope of the law. With regard to enforcement, it supported retention of the American model of the administrative agency as already embodied in the Race Relations Board, with the primary function of seeking conciliation between the parties, but with much wider powers. The Board itself was to be able, subject to appeal to the Courts, to make binding awards of compensation and to issue directions for positive steps to remedy any act of discrimination found to have taken place. It was to be given subpoena powers and the power to order discovery and inspection of documents. Contested cases were to be brought by the Board before an independent tribunal composed of lawyers and experts in race relations.

The Government accepted its recommendations in part. The Race Relations Act 1968 extended the scope of the law to employment, housing and the provision of goods, facilities and services; it accepted the recommendation that the Board should be able to bring cases before an independent tribunal, and chose the County Court for this purpose, but providing for two lay experts to sit with the judge.

The Board was not given subpoena powers or the power to determine the remedy once discrimination had been established, as was envisaged by the Street Committee. Those powers were reserved to the County Court, in which the Board could bring proceedings on behalf of the victim, claiming compensation for the injury to his or her feelings, where such had occurred, and for any financial lhss shown to have resulted from the act of discrimination. In limited circumstances the Court could also grant an injunction against the repetition of any discrimination which it found had occurred. Legal proceedings only came at the very end of a long compulsory conciliation process, extended in employment cases by an obligation to refer complaints for resolution by joint union–management negotiating machinery where such existed.

In an evaluation of the 1968 Act in terms of the objectives in the Board's 1967 report, it could certainly be argued that it would provide some support for those who did not wish to discriminate and who could plead in aid the illegality of doing so. But the tortuous process of attempted conciliation which the Act required as a preliminary to any legal proceedings – and the poor record of success in those proceedings that did take place – made the protection given by the law to the victims of discrimination negligible and the prospect of effective redress illusory. For the same reasons the value of the law as an outlet for the peaceful and orderly adjustment of grievances and the release of tensions was slight. Likewise, its impact on the prevalence of racial prejudice and indeed of discrimination must have been small. The best evidence of the insufficient impact of the 1968 Act on the level of discrimination was the second study carried out by Political and Economic Planning in 1973 and 1974,[4] following up and using the same techniques as its 1967 study. This showed that the level of discrimination had not diminished since 1967, notwithstanding the passage of the 1968 Act and other government measures designed to reduce inner-city deprivation. The conclusion was obvious that a law which could be enforced only by pursuing a necessarily limited number of individual cases was never going to make a significant impact on the problem of racial discrimination.

The conciliation process was a major obstacle. Building in a compulsory conciliation process was a novel idea. Its novelty reflects the fact that proceedings under the Race Relations Act were not perceived by Parliament (or indeed by the Street Committee) as concerning only the parties themselves – as is the case with breach of contract and most other tort claims. Conciliation in private law cases is a natural but informal part of the litigation process. Virtually every litigant wants to reach a settlement rather than incur the costs and uncertainties of a trial. Yet the Government, in a misconceived attempt to inject a public interest element into the process, not only insisted on a compulsory attempt at conciliation, but also, where the allegation was of discrimination in the field of employment, shifted conciliation away from the Board and its committees to *ad hoc* arrangements made between the relevant trade union and employers' organization. This added further delay and uncertainty to the process.

Parliament was right to recognize a strong public interest in the elimination of racial discrimination and to provide for the pursuit of that interest in the legislative scheme. Unfortunately, it failed to tackle it in a thorough and effective manner. Instead of promoting that interest, the Board was restricted to investigating and seeking to resolve the individual complaints that were brought before it. It had no means of initiating investigations or of pursuing them beyond the individual complaint. Once the individual grievance was resolved (or abandoned) the Board's role ceased – even though it might have good reason to suspect that the act of discrimination alleged by the complainant was just one example of a wide pattern of discriminatory behaviour.

The Race Relations Board had very limited responsibilities beyond the resolution of individual complaints. A parallel body, the Community Relations Commission (CRC), was responsible for promoting policies within companies and institutions designed to reduce prejudice and discrimination. This was seen as an educational function. The CRC had no law enforcement powers nor even the power to carry out investigations, save with the voluntary cooperation of those concerned.

The realization had already emerged in the United States that discrimination must be seen as the product of practices and systems which could be extremely complex and which might not be attributable to the intentional act of any individual. Reliance on complaints, which are necessarily random, must leave many such situations undiscovered. The assumption underlying the 1968 Act – that the problem of discrimination was a series of deliberate acts of ill-will carried out by racially prejudiced individuals against other individuals – was flawed.

Undoubtedly such cases existed, and some of them had been targeted by the Race Relations Board. But individual prejudices could not explain the widespread disparity in economic achievement and in the opportunities open to black and white people. Nor could individual judicial remedies do more than ripple the surface of institutional practices and patterns that seemed to cause or reinforce that disparity.

Pressure built up in the early 1970s to legislate against discrimination on the ground of sex. Although there are important differences between the politics and practices of sex and racial discrimination, there is little reason to distinguish in the techniques of legal enforcement. The Bill that became the Sex Discrimination Act 1975 radically departed from the precedent of the Race Relations Act 1968 and its novel features were copied in a new Race Relations Bill, which became the Race Relations Act 1976, still in force.

THE RACE RELATIONS ACT 1976

The right not to suffer racial discrimination can be viewed in two ways: as a right not to be subjected to discrimination against oneself; and as a right to live in a society in which racial discrimination is not allowed to persist. The same duality affects all rights in society. They are both individual and collective; they define the citizen as an individual and as a member of the society. But individual discrimination was also too narrowly viewed in the old law. Direct discrimination was prohibited, but not indirect.

The new law extended the definition of discrimination to include indirect as well as direct discrimination. The old law had restricted the notion of discrimination to differential treatment – for example, offering a job to a white applicant and thereby rejecting a better-qualified black applicant. But what of the cases where the same criteria were applied equally to all applicants yet the effect was a major shortfall in the number of succesful ethnic minority applicants? This could easily result from fixing conditions which minorities could less easily satisfy. Borrowing from the United States concept of 'adverse impact' discrimination,[5] indirect discrimination was – to paraphrase the definition – imposing a requirement or condition with which a disproportionately small number of members of the applicant's racial group could comply. Discrimination was thus determined by its effect as well as its intention. A marked disproportion in the representation of different racial groups in a particular workforce, as compared, say, with their representation in the local community, would suggest the possibility of discrimination. It might be found that priority was being given to those who had been long resident in the neighbourhood, or whose parents had worked for the same employer. Either criterion might be regarded as an unjustifiable requirement or condition of recruitment, balanced against its discriminatory impact.

Indirect discrimination causes harm to individuars just as does direct discrimination, so individual redress must be provided for. The 1976 Act simplified and strengthened the litigation process. A direct right of action – without the obligatory and, as it was perceived, paternalistic mediation of a statutory agency – was created for those alleging discrimination, whether direct or indirect. Cases concerning employment are brought in the Industrial Tribunal, others in the County Court.

The most radical development was to provide a mechanism for promoting the elimination of racial discrimination without reliance on individual complaints. The focus df the attack on discrimination was shifted from the individual incident to the policies and practices of institutions, which might, intentionally or not, produce discrimination on a massive scale. The Commission for Racial Equality (CRE), which replaced the Race Relations Board, was given wide investigative powers to order cessation of discriminatory practices. Its role in individual cases was reduced to providing assistance to complainants, instead of pursuing cases on their behalf.

The new strategy embodied in the 1976 Act thus combined three elements. First is the individual complaint – no longer to be pursued directly by the statutory agency, but with the statutory agency in practice the only source of funding. Legal aid is not available in the Industrial Tribunal (save for limited legal advice under the Green Form scheme), and for the small number of cases which go to the County Court legal aid, though theoretically available, has rarely if ever been granted. Thus the control by the CRE of the purse-strings for individual cases gives it considerable power to determine which cases are pursued. Of course it must exercise that power fairly (and undoubtedly does so). Nevertheless, it has the opportunity of developing a litigation strategy which will encourage the best use of limited resources by giving priority to cases of most general importance.

The second element is the widening of the definition of discrimination to embrace indirect discrimination. This immensely extended the scope of the individual's right to redress, because indirect discrimination became a tortious act against each individual affected by it. However, the scope of the individual remedy for *indirect* discrimination was curtailed by restricting the possible award of damages for indirect discrimination to those cases in which the respondent failed to prove that the indirectly discriminatory requirement or condition was not intended to treat the complainant unfavourably on racial grounds.[6] In the vast majority of cases the respondent would be able to prove this.

Third is the power to conduct formal investigations 'for any purpose connected with the carrying out of those duties' (i.e. the duties set out in s. 43(1) of the Act.[7]

HOW THE LAW HAS DEVELOPED

In the years since the 1976 Act came into effect, there has been a substantial amount of case law and the courts have steadily broadened their interpretations of important provisions. By doing so they have made it easier for individuals to prove discrimination and have improved the opportunities for the victims of discrimination to secure redress. Among the aspects of the law that have been strengthened by the courts are the following.

Proving Direct Discrimination

A person directly discriminates by treating another on racial grounds less favourably than he or she would treat a third.[8] Differential treatment is the essential characteristic, but does it have to be intentional? Does its purpose or motive have to be racial discrimination? After many confusing and uncertain decisions, the House of Lords finally in 1990 accepted the simple 'but for' test: it is sufficient to show that the unfavourable treatment would not have occurred 'but for' the perceived ethnic origin of the complainant.[9] This test removes any consideration of motive or racial intention.

The cases have also produced conflicting views about the burden and standard of proof of direct discrimination. There has never been any doubt that the ordinary civil burddn applies, i.e. that the burden rests on the applicant on the balance of probabilities. However, the courts have come to accept that the complainant in a discrimination case has an exceptionally difficult task, especially where the complaint is of discrimination in recruitment or promotion. They recognize that the relevant information necessary to prove discrimination is likely to be in the possession of the employer. Hence they have been willing to order wide disclosure of that information.[10]

Furthermore, it has been held that once the complainant has demonstrated less favourable treatment, it is up to the party complained of to show that the ground of that treatment was something other than race. The courts have tended to discourage the notion that the burden of proof shifts on establishing a *prima facie* case, but in practice it is open to the tribunal or court to draw the inference that the less favourable treatment was on racial grounds unless it is proved to the contrary.

Proving Indirect Discrimination

The definition of indirect discrimination is convoluted and has led to a number of problems. The complainant must prove that the respondent has imposed a 'requirement or condition' equally on persons of different racial groups but with which a considerably smaller proportion of members of a particular racial group can comply. It must also be proved that as a result of the application of such a requirement or condition, the complainant has suffered 'detriment'. The need to identify a 'requirement or condition' led to the rejection of the complaint of a candidate for a legal post in the civil service. The selectors gave preference to candidates with legal experience in the UK (the applicant had practised law very successfully in Sri Lanka), but it was not an essential qualification. Therefore, the Court of Appeal held, it did not amount to a 'requirement or conditions even though it was just as effective to exclude the applicant as if it had been'.[11] This is a bad example of an irrationally literal interpretation which still survives. In earlier cases, the courts refused to acknowledge that the complainant had suffered a detriment unless it was substantial,[12] but now any disadvantage, however slight, is sufficient. In cases alleging refusal of employment or promotion, the loss of the employment or the promotion is itself a sufficient detriment.

In the early history of the legislation there were also difficulties in satisfying the courts that the complainant belonged to a racial group whose members were less capable of *complying* with the 'requirement or condition'. Now it is sufficient to establish that it would be unreasonable to demand compliance for members of the particular group. So it was held that a Sikh schoolboy whose religious observance required him to wear a turban could not comply with a requirement that he replace it with a school cap.[13]

The respondent can escape liability for indirect discrimination by showing that the requirement or condition is justifiable 'irrespective of the colour, race, nationality or ethnic or national origins of the person to whom it is applied'. At first, the courts in several cases allowed the 'justifiability' defence to prevail where the respondent's business did not really need the discriminatory requirement or condition. One example was the condition applied by a confectionery manufacturer forbidding its employees to wear beards. The employer's argument was that a beard was unhygienic and, if it came into contact with the product, could spread infection. But in other factories belonging to the same company, workers were allowed to wear beards as long as they kept them suitably covered. The ban on beards effectively excluded Sikhs, yet the court upheld it. [14]

More recently, however, as a result of decisions of the European Court of Justice affecting equal pay for men and women, a stricter standard has been extended to cases under the Race Relations Act. Now an indirectly discriminatory practice will be found justifiable only if the respondent demonstrates that there is a real need for the requirement or condition, objectively justified. The need must outweigh the discriminatory impact. [15]

Remedies

An Industrial Tribunal, having upheld a complaint of racial discrimination, must then consider remedies, as must a County Court if the complaint concerns a matter other than employment. The most common remedy is compensation or damages, but an industrial tribunal may recommend action by the discriminator to repair the damage (e.g. to offer the victim a job) and may be ordered to pay more compensation if the recommendation is not carried out. The total award of damages may not, however, exceed the maximum jurisdiction of the industrial tribunal in unfair dismissal cases, i.e. about £18,000. The County Court may grant injunctions as well as damages. It had exclusive jurisdiction under the Race Relations Act 1968 and was much criticized for awarding miserably small amounts. In an attempt to increase awards to realistic levels it was provided explicitly in the 1976 Act that compensation or damages could be awarded for injury to feelings. [16]

Unfortunately, awards continued to be small under the 1976 Act, doubtless reflecting an inadequate appreciation by Tribunal members and County Court judges of the hurt discrimination causes to its victims, as well as the economic loss when employment or housing accommodation is at stake. An award of £50 in one case was increased to £500 by the Court of Appeal. [17] Subsequently the Court of Appeal reduced an award of £5000 for injury to feelings to £3000, though at that time the maximum total award was £7500. [18] If these figures are compared with awards by juries in libel actions for damage to reputation, the amounts seem ludicrously small. They neither compensate the victim nor deter the discriminator. The recent increases helpfully encouraged by the courts can only be brought up to realistic levels by statutory amendment.

The overall result of judicial interpretation of the rights of individuals to secure redress for racially discriminatory treatment is that they have been slightly strengthened since the 1976 Act came into force, but the poor prospect of a worthwhile outcome provides little encouragement for the victim to pursue a legal claim. At best, a modest sum of money can be expected. In rare cases the threat of legal action may produce an offer of employment or some other benefit, but the courts and tribunals cannot order such a result. The availability of free advice and legal representation from the CRE is obviously a great advantage. But litigation, even without the financial burden suffered by most litigants, is time-consuming, stressful and not to be undertaken without very good reason.

These disincentives are illustrated by the paucity of recorded cases. In 1990 – the latest year for which figures are available at the time of writing – the CRE received 1381 applications for assistance from individuals. This was a small increase above the figure of 1307 recorded in the previous year. Most of the applicants were recommended to apply by local Community Relations Councils (now called Race Equality Councils) but a significant number came through Citizens' Advice Bureaux, trade unions and other sources. The great majority of the complaints (about three-quarters) related to employment, and of these about two-thirds were complaints of discrimination in treatment at work, including failure to promote and unfair dismissal. Fewer than one-fifth of the employment complaints were about refusal to offer or consider for employment.

Of the complaints dealt with in the year, numbering 1341, only 188 applicants were granted representation in legal proceedings before the Industrial Tribunal or County Court. During the same year only 109 cases were concluded, of which 59 were settled and 50 reached a conclusion in the Industrial Tribunal or County Court. Of the 50 completed cases 26 were successful and 24 were dismissed. Only four of these did not concern employment and were concluded in the County Court.

ENFORCEMENT BY THE COMMISSION

The powers given to the CRE to conduct wide-ranging investigations were intended to promote a sustained attack on patterns and practices of discrimination (especially but not exclusively indirect discrimination), which individual complaints could not tackle. Unfortunately, the procedures imposed on the Commission were complex and time-consuming. They were made even more so by a series of unhelpful judgments of the House of Lords. The fundamental problem was that the CRE itself was given power, following an investigation in which it concluded that unlawful discrimination had taken place, to make an order against the discriminator (called a non-discrimination notice) requiring the discrimination to cease and encouraging changes in practice which would reduce the likelihood of repetition. Because the Commission was given a qkasi-judicial role and power (though extremely limited) to enforce its orders, Parliament introduced a series of safeguards into the Act and the courts added some of their own as well. The virtually unlimited investigative power set out in the Act[19] was removed in cases where the Commission had no evidence supporting the suspicion that a named respondent had discriminated unlawfully. In such a case, the House of Lords held there was no power to investigate.[20] In any event, the Act already included the requirement that before launching an investigation into suspected discrimination, the suspected discriminator had to be given an opportunity to make written or oral representations to the Commission with a view to dissuading it from investigating.[21] In effect, this gives a right to a hearing before the investigation has even started. In several cases companies have spent large sums of money briefing leading and junior counsel in their efforts to avoid investigation. Even where they have not succeeded they have caused delay and tied up the resources of the Commission.

After its investigation, if it is minded to find discrimination, the Commission must allow further representations before reaching a final conclusion.[22] Again, after it finds discrimination, the respondent has a right of appeal to an Industrial Tribunal or County Court in which all factual findings may be challenged.[23] It is hardly surprising in the face of these roadblocks[24] that the Commission has in recent years largely confined itself to general investigations in which it carefully avoids making accusations of unlawful discrimination. Such investigations may have value in exposing areas of potential discrimination and certainly the cooperation of those investigated is more easily obtained when there is no threat of legal sanctions. However, such investigations do not properly form part of the law enforcement strategy envisaged by Parliament in the scheme of the legislation, whatever may be their persuasive force.

THE IMPACT OF THE RACE RELATIONS ACT

It is obviously difficult to evaluate the extent to which the Act has affected the extent of discrimination and the relative share of members of ethnic minorities in the economic benefits of society. In 1984 and 1985 a further study of the level of discrimination was carried out by the Policy Studies Institute (the successor to Political and Economic Planning) and it showed that there had been little change since the studies of the mid-1970s and of 1967. Strictly, this is not evidence that the Race Relations Act has had a neutral or negative impact. If it had not been passed discrimination might be greater. But there is no doubt that it has failed to make a dramatic impact on public opinion and a serious problem remains.

In 1991 the Policy Studies Institute published its own evaluation of the enforcement of the 1976 Act in the field of employment.[25] It concluded that none of the three main elements of the 1976 strategy had worked as intended and that the aims of the Act had been realized only to a limited extent.

The expansion of the definition of discrimination to include indirect discrimination was intended to tackle the wider field of institutional discrimination arising out of traditional patterns and practices that are not necessarily intended to disadvantage ethnic minorities. It was found that the vast majority of the cases coming before industrial tribunals concerned allegations of direct discrimination, as did most of the formal investigations. The potential scope of indirect discrimination has never been fully explored in the courts.[26]

Partly as a result of the legal morass described earlier, the aim of making formal investigations, followed by non-discrimination notices, the spearhead of the law enforcement strategy, has not been achieved either. Investigations were a priority until 1983, but the Prestige case [27] changed all that. Very few non-discrimination notices have been issued since then and the major law enforcement effort has continued to be pursued through individual cases. This again departs from the original strategy of the 1976 Act, by which it was intended that the statutory commission would be freed from the burden of individual cases so as to concentrate on formal investigations and collective or group enforcement. The power to assist individuals was given to the CRE because no legal aid is available in the Industrial Tribunals and some help had to be offered to those seeking redress. But it was expected that other sources of help would be built up and this has not happened. Indeed, on the contrary, the CRE has become so effective in the presentation of cases that litigants with CRE assistance have a distinct advantage over all others.

WHAT CAN BE DONE

There are a number of changes that would help to improve the effectiveness of the Race Relations Act, both in providing redress for individuals and in tackling the wider problem of institutional discrimination. The CRE has submitted detailed reports to the Government on two occasions, in 1985 and 1991, recommending the precise changes that would be required.

In relation to individual complaints, the main requirement is an increase in the level of damages and wider powers of redress, e.g. the power to order an employer to recruit or promote a worker denied these benefits by discrimination. To restore the central role of the formal investigation more dramatic changes are required. The Commission should lose the power to make its own non-discrimination notices. Rather, an independent tribunal, preferably a specialist and upgraded version of the industrial tribunal, should have the power to make a range of orders, including laying down a detailed programme which an employer or other respondent should be obliged to carry out once found to have discriminated, in order to provide redress for all those affected and to ensure that discrimination will not occur in the future. The CRE's present Code of Practice should be given binding effect, at least on the direction of the tribunal to any particular employer, including the provision of an effective equal opportunity policy and ethnic monitoring. The CRE, as well as having investigation powers untrammelled by the unnecessary statutory restrictions and those introduced by the courts, should have the right to bring a case before the tribunal at any time where it considers that there is evidence justifying a finding of unlawful discrimination.

Curiously, many of the improvements sought by the CRE have already been included in the Fair Employment (Northern Ireland) Act 1989, for the purpose of providing remedies against religious discrimination there. A specialized tribunal, the Fair Employment Tribunal, hears complaints brought before it either by individuals or by the Fair Employment Commission. It has the powers which the CRE seeks under the Race Relations Act, including the power to award compensation up to £30,000. On 3 March 1992, in its very first case, it awarded £25,000 for injury to feelings to a Catholic laundry worker rejected for employment in favour of a less well qualified Protestant applicant.[29] Employers must register with the Commission and review their practices periodically. They must monitor the religious composition of their workforces. Where imbalances are apparent, they must take affirmative action to redress them. The Commission itself may specify goals and timetables for the equalization of the workforce as between the religious groups. Extension of the Race Relations Act on similar lines would do much to improve its effectiveness. Given the Northern Ireland precedent it is not unreasonable to expect the Government to introduce a new Race Relations Bill on the lines of the Northern Ireland statute.

NOTES AND REFERENCES

1 See Anthony Lester and Geoffrey Bindman, *Race and Law* (Longman and Penguin, 1972) Chapter 2.

2 For the black experience, see Peter Fryer, *Staying Power* (Pluto Press 1984); for the Jewish experience, see John A. Garrard, *The English and Immigration* (Oxford University Press, 1971).

3 Professor Harry Street, Geoffrey Howe QC and Geoffrey Bindman.

4 See N. McIntosh and D. J. Smith, *The Extent of Racial Discrimination*, PEP Broadsheet No 547 (London: PEP, 1974).

5 First acknowledged in *Griggs* v. *Duke Power Company* [1971] 401 US 424), in which the Supreme Court declared that the rejection of employment applications from those not in possession of a high school diploma discriminated unlawfully against black applicants who, as a result of past discrimination, had been denied access to high school education. The Court held that a high school education was not relevant to the tasks which needed to be performed.

6 RRA 1976 s. 57(3).

7 RRA 1976 s. 48(1). The duties set out in s. 43 (1) are as follows:'(a) to work towards the elimination of discrimination; (b) to promote equality of opportunity, and good relations, between persons of different racial groups generally; and (c) to keep under review the working of the Act and, when they are so required by the Secretary of State or otherwise think it necessary, draw up and submit to the Secretary of State proposals for amending it.'

8 RRA 1976 s. 1(1) (a).

9 *James* v. *Eastleigh Borough Council* [1990] IRLR 288. See especially the speech of Lord Goff.

10 *Nasse* v. *Science Research Council* and *Vyas* v. *Leyland Cars* [1979] IRLR 465 HL; *West Midlands Passenger Transport Executive* v. *Singh* [1988] IRLR 186 CA.

11 *Perera* v. *Civil Service Commission* [1983] IRLR 166 CA.

12 E.g. *Peake* v. *Automotive Products* [1978] QB 233, in which Lord Denning held (applying the rule *de minimis non curat lex*) that there was no detriment to men in being required to stay at work 5 minutes longer than women, who were allowed to leave early to avoid the crowd.

13 *Mandla* v. *Dowell-Lee* [1983] IRLR 209 HL.

14 *Singh* v. *Rowntree Mackintosh* [1979] ICR 554.

15 *Hampson* v. *Department of Education and Science* [1989] IRLR 69 CA.

16 RRA 1976 s. 57(4).

17 *Alexadder* v. *Home Office* [1988] IRLR 398 CA.

18 *Noone* v. *North West Thames Regional Health Authority*.

19 RRA 1976 s. 43(1).

20 *In re Prestige Group plc* [1984] IRLR 166 HL.

21 RRA 1976 s. 49(4).

22 RRA 1976 s. 58(5).

23 *CRE* v. *Amari Plastics Ltd* [1982] IRLR 252 CA.

24 Lord Denning described the CRE's predicament trenchantly in *CRE* v. *Amari Plastics Ltd* (see note 22) as follows: 'The machinery is so elaborate and so cumber-

some that it is in danger of grinding to a halt. I am very sorry for the Commission, but they have been caught up in spider's web spun by Parliament, from which there is little hope of them escaping.'

25 Racial Justice at Work (Policy Studies Institute, 100 Park Village East, London NW1 3SR, 1991).

26 For one example, see Geoffrey Bindman, *Is the System of Judicial Appointments Illegal?* (Law Society's Gazette, 27 February 1991, p. 24).

27 See note 20.

28 'Review of the Race Relations Act 1976' and 'Second review of the Race Relations Act 1976' (Commission for Racial Equality, 10–12 Allington St, London SW1E 5EH).

29 *Equal Opportunities Review Discrimination Law Digest*, No 11, Spring 1992, p. 11.

8

Administrative Justice

JOHN McELDOWNEY

At different times in the history of this country it has been necessary to adjust this relationship [between the individual and authority] and to seek a new balance between private rights and public advantage, between fair play for the individual and efficiency of administration. The balance found has varied with different governmental systems and different social patterns. Since the war the British electorate has chosen Governments which accepted general responsibilities for the provision of extended social services and for the broad management of the economy. It has consequently become desirable to consider afresh the procedures by which the rights of individual citizens can be harmonised with wider public interests.

Report of the Committee on Administrative Tribunals and Inquiries
Cmnd 218 July 1957 (Chairman Lord Franks)

INTRODUCTION

Thirty-five years ago the Franks Committee[1] considered 'the procedures by which the rights[2] of individual citizens can be harmonised with wider public interests'. The findings of the Franks Committee led to the Tribunals and Inquiries Act 1958 and the Council on Tribunals. Since Franks the redress of citizens' grievances, involving the administrative process, may be made through a wide range of institutions and procedures from courts and tribunals to inquiries and ombudsmen. As a result, the underlying assumption which informed the discussion of much of administrative law was that in the 1960s and 1970s administrative discretion and any potential for its abuse was mainly to be found in an obdurate official such as a civil servant or a minister. Grievances were identified as arising from the growth in the role of the state[3] in its development as both a regulator and a service provider. Since the mid-nineteenth century and commensurate with the growth in administrative activities, the franchise was broadened and the system of party government became more fully established. The role of the state as a regulator was recognized in the development of public health and in the commercial regulation of the economy through the development of competition policy and the regulation of banking and insurance. As a provider of services, the state delivered a wide range of activities, the railways, the public utilities, education and the system of welfare provision. The scale and size of the machinery of government encouraged the increase in the use of law to regulate activities which were in the public ownership of the state.[4] Nationalization policy in the 1940s was concerned with the transfer of private to state ownership with monopoly powers through legislation.

Privatization in the 1980s has significantly affected the role of the state.[5] This shift of public ownership to Company Act companies has created a new range of regulatory agencies entrusted with a wide variety of legal powers. The vast array of statutory power is supplemented by a bewildering assortment of administrative rules, such as licences, codes of practice, guidelines, regulations and contractual conditions. Administrative discretion and the potential for its abuse[6] is no longer the sole preserve of civil servants and minister, but may be found in the exercise of administrative powers by various regulators and agencies and in the activities of Company Act companies.

The changing nature of administrative powers and their impact on the citizen requires a fresh look at how administrative justice may be achieved. This chapter sets out to review the new regulatory structures and their impact on the citizen in setting new opportunities for developing fair administrative procedures.[7] While the focus is on the impact of privatization, existing arrangements such as the use of the courts will be reviewed in terms of developing administrative procedures.[8]

JUDICIAL REVIEW OF ADMINISTRATIVE ACTION

Recent Development in Judicial Review

Franks succeeded in making tribunals part of the machinery of adjudication rather than part of the administration. The role of the courts was left to develop on a case-by-case basis. Lord Diplock explained the achievements of the courts in developing judicial review in *CCSU* v. *Minister for Civil Service* (1984)[9] when he suggested that 'the English law relating to judicial control of administrative action has been developed upon a case to case basis which has virtually transformed it over the last three decades'. Discussing the grounds for judicial review, Lord Diplock referred to three 'heads' upon which administrative law is subject to control. These are as follows: 'illegality', meaning the decision-maker must understand the law and give effect to it;[10] 'irrationality', by which a decision which is unreasonable or so outrageous in its defiance of logic or of accepted moral standards that 'no sensible person who applied his mind to the question to be decided could have arrived at it'; and 'procedural impropriety', by which there is a failure to observe basic rules of natural justice or failure to act with procedural fairness towards the person who will be affected by the decision. A further possibility, that of proportionality, was also mentioned. Here the courts have to balance the appropriateness of the various objectives set out in law, the adverse effects which its decision may have on the rights, the liberties or interests of the persons and purposes it pursues. Proportionality, while recognized fully in French, German and EC law, has only become understood in its 'application in English Administrative law in recent years', although it is a concept which has historical roots in much earlier cases. The above developments must be understood in the context of the absence of any codified system of administrative law.

Despite demands from the Law Commission[11] in 1969 for a Royal Commission on administrative law, all that was achieved was a study of the existing law of remedies for the judicial control of administrative action. No review of the whole system of administrative law was undertaken. Following the Law Commission's[12] recommendation on the law of remedies it was left to the Rules Committee of the Supreme Court to implement modest proposals for reforms in the application for judicial review under Order 53 of the Rules of the Supreme Court.[13] This reform received statutory modification in section 31 of the Supreme Court Act 1981.

Order 53 streamlined the procedures for obtaining remedies by permitting an applicant to seek any one or more of the five remedies, which include mandamus, certiorari, prohibition declaration or injunction. At the same time, interlocutory procedures, such as discovery and interrogations, are theoretically available. In addition the court may award damages if claimed by the applicant and if they could have been awarded in an action at the same time.[14]

A first step in the application for judicial review is obtaining the leave of the court based on whether there is an arguable case. The aggrieved citizen has to overcome this hurdle in order to pursue his claim. Normally this first stage is heard by a single judge on affidavit evidence.[15] Applications must be made without 'undue delay' and this falls under s. 31(7) of the 1981 Act as subject to a three-month time limit.

An additional requirement is based on the 'exclusive nature of the application for judicial review'. In the House of Lords in *O'Reilly* v. *Mackman* (1983), the distinction between public and private law was drawn and rigidly imposed. The exact nature of this distinction is problematic and perhaps leaves the need for law reform as greater than in 1969, when the Royal Commission was proposed but rejected.

In 1988 an unofficial Royal Commission, namely the Justice/All Souls Review Committee,[16] reported after a ten-year study of administrative law. The report did not have the status of an official inquiry and its findings focus on setting out principles of good administration. The main criticism of the work of the Justice Review is that it failed to take account of the changing nature of the administrative process and to address fundamental questions about the desirability of the use of judicial review as a means of redressing grievances or developing a systematic administrative system. With regard to the former, the Review considers the development of judicial review without considering the constitutional implications of the role of judges responding, for example, to the need of pressure groups or engaging in adjudication between central and local government. With regard to the latter the exact means to achieve good administration through the work of the courts, tribunals or ombudsman system is left unclear.[17] The Review did make out the case for the introduction of principles of good administration, which sets new challenges for the courts.

Establishing administrative efficiency and securing objectives of good administration is not easily accomplished by the courts. Judicial review is pragmatic and unsystematic. Its focus is primarily on the issues before the court rather than the broader policy objectives. Courts offer *ex post facto* rather than *a priori* review and this is limited to remedies for wrongful actions rather than a prescription for the future conduct of administration.

Despite such shortcomings, in recent years there have been important developments in the availability of judicial review. In *R. v. Panel on Take-overs and Mergers*[18] the Court of Appeal held that the self-regulatory City Take-Overs Panel was subject to judicial review, despite the fact that the Take-Overs Panel was not set up by statute or under any of the prerogative powers. A point which found favour with the court was that if such a body had not been set up on a voluntary and informal basis then the likelihood is that Parliament would have intervened with statutory powers. This raises the possibility that a wide range of domestic bodies or tribunals might fall under the review powers of the court. In deciding whether or not to extend the scope of judicial reviews there is a lack of consistency in the approach adopted by the courts. In this area clear principles are hard to determine. The question is decided on a case-by-case basis. The nature of the body must be considered alongside the activities the body performs. In the case of Walsh, employed by the East Berkshire Health Authority, even though the regulations of his employment were statutory, he was refused leave to challenge his dismissal through judicial review. The Court of Appeal in *R. v. East Berkshire Health Authority, ex p. Walsh*[19] decided that mere employment by a public authority does not make the matter one of public law and therefore justiciable by judicial review. However, if the employment is based on the office or status of a prison officer, then the application for judicial review is available (*ex p. Benwell* [1985] 1 QB 152).

In deciding where to draw the line between public and private law the House of Lords in *O'Reilly* v. *Mackman*[20] suggested a number of exceptions to the exclusivity rule, namely that only questions of public law may be decided under the application for judicial review. The exceptions would permit public law matters to be raised under the ordinary writ procedure. The first is where there is a 'collateral issue'. This might be where the public law issue is only subsidiary or incidental to the private law claim; then a writ or action might apply. A second exception is where the parties might agree that the writ procedure is acceptable. A third possibility is on a case-by-case basis where there are good grounds for so allowing. This permits a court to consider if the case is suitable or not *(Air Canada* v. *Secretary of State for Trade* [1983] 2 AC 394) or where it might be inconvenient or inappropriate for judicial review to apply.

It is noticeable, however, that there are areas where the courts seem unwilling to offer review. In *ex p. Puhlofer*[21] the House of Lords restricted access to judicial review to cases under the Housing (Homeless Persons) Act 1977. Similarly, following *ex p. Swati*[22] the discretion to refuse leave is operated when there are alternative remedies. For example, appeals in immigration cases may fall to be adjudicated by the Immigration Appeal Tribunal.

The citizen's grievance may occasionally find favour with a pressure group, or groups of citizens may wish to combine to litigate on a matter which is perceived to be in the public interest. Public interest litigation raises major issues as to the constitutional role of the courts. David Feldman has argued that 'it is both constitutionally and democratically legitimate to use any legal means, including litigation, to ensure that the representative legislative has adequate opportunity to consider public interest matters'.

Since the House of Lords decision in *Inland Commissioner ex p. National Federation of Self-Employed and Small Businesses Ltd*[23] there has been a noticeable 'change in policy', in the words of Lord Roskill, 'to relax the rules of standing which has given rise to a higher expectation that leave for judicial review might be given'. In suitable cases it is thought appropriate that the Attorney-General could serve on behalf of the public to prevent public wrongs, as in the *Gouriet* case in 1978.[24] However, where the Attorney-General is reluctant to act or where complaints fall on deaf ministerial ears, the citizen may seek his or her own redress.

Mr Justice Schieman in *R. v. Secretary of State ex p. Rose Theatre Co.*[25] rejected the application for judicial review made by the Rose Theatre Company, which was formed for the purpose of campaigning to save the site where it was believed that the Rose Theatre first performed the plays of Marlowe and in which two of Shakespeare's plays received their first performance. According to Schieman J's view not every citizen came within the sufficient interest necessary for standing in the case. Asserting an interest does not give an interest. Neither financial nor legal, a specific interest is always required. He concluded: 'the decision not to schedule [the Rose Theatre site as a protected site] is one of those governmental decisions in respect of which the ordinary citizen does not have a sufficient interest to entitle him to obtain leave to move for judicial review'. This case underlines the difficulty of knowing or being able to predict how judicial discretion may be exercised. Even when procedural breaches of the law have occurred the court may decline to intervene. The Court of Appeal in *R. v. Monopolies and Mergers Commission ex p. Argyll Group PLC*[26] noted that the Monopolies and Mergers Commission, rather than its chairman, should have decided whether to proceed with a reference made to it by the Secretary of State in the case of a take-over bid. The fact that the delegation of power to the chairman was *ultra vires* did not prevent the court from refusing to quash the chairman's decision.

In the *Datafin* case[27] mentioned above, the Court of Appeal declined relief even though it had the powers to review the Take-Overs Panel. In the *GCHQ*[28] case procedural mistakes in not giving the unions any consultation on the decision to ban union membership at GCHQ were a breach of a legitimate expectation to be consulted, and were amenable to judicial review. 'However, considerations of national security outweighed such legitimate expectations and the courts declined relief.

Success in obtaining judicial review does not necessarily lead to the ultimate goal of securing the reversal of a decision or winning the outcome. In *Padfield*[29] mandamus was granted in favour of milk producers who had complained that the differential element in the price fixed for their milk by the Milk Marketing Board was too low. The Minister was compelled under the Agricultural Marketing Act 1958 to set up an inquiry in the form of a committee of investigation. This was duly convened and reported in favour of the complainants but the Minister's ultimate discretion allowed him to take no action.

It is difficult to gauge the effect of judicial review on administration. In recent years within government departments a pamphlet prepared by the Treasury solicitors was circulated entitled 'The judge over your shoulder', with the clear implication that potential judicial intervention might be considered as part of the decision-making process. Judicial review features as an element in the training of civil servants. It may well be that the threat of review has a greater significance than the reality, where its use is confined to specific areas of litigation and it is not uniformly applied. The effectiveness of judicial review requires further research and analysis.

Policy-making and the Role of the Courts

Traditionally in the area of central government, policy-making is often outside the remit of the courts' review powers. Ministerial responsibility provides the courts with an alternative to exercising their own powers of review. For example, in *In re. Findlay*[30] the courts were not prepared to review parole policy. In *Bushell* v. *Secretary of State for the Environment*[31] public inquiries into highway policy are excluded. In *Notts. CC* v. *Secretary of State for the Environment*[32] Lord Scarman refused to review the rate-capping powers of the Secretary of State, pointing out that such powers required parliamentary approval, which provided an acceptable substitute for judicial review as a means of scrutiny over the powers of the Secretary of State.

In contrast, when reviewing local government powers the courts have been more willing to extend review to that of policy considerations, even where there is a political dimension. Relations between central and local government have raised important issues regarding the value of judicial review as a means of requiring local government to conform to central government policies. The fact that local government is elected and represents a second tier of government decision-making adds to the complexity of the problems facing the courts. The absence of any principle of ministerial responsibility in local government appears to allow the courts greater discretion. The courts may seem to act as a legal regulator of local authority discretion.

In *Bromley*[33] the House of Lords was asked to consider the 'fair fares' policy of the Greater London Council (GLC; now abolished). 'Ordinary business principles' were applied to the reduction of fares and as the policy did not operate on those principles the proposed reduction in fares was *ultra vires*. Although the GLC had powers to make grants 'for any purpose' to the London Transport Executive (LTE) the grant, which involved a supplementary rate, was quashed because the purposes for which it was intended were *ultra vires*. There was 'a fiduciary duty' on the GLC as a local authority, and the fares policy failed to live up to that standard which was owed to rate-payers. The courts had to balance the GLC's duty owed to rate-payers against its wider power to provide reasonable transport facilities to transport users. The fact that a 'fair fares' policy had been a manifesto condition in the election of the ruling party in the GLC was not relevant to the courts' powers of review, as such a condition was 'not binding' on the local authority. In *R.* v. *Waltham Forest LBC ex p. Waltham Forest Ratepayers Action Group*[34] the courts struck down a decision of Waltham Forest councillors which was based on instructions from a pressure group known as the Local Government Group.

The courts have developed considerable techniques to intervene whenever necessary. The well-known dicta in *Wednesbury*[35] of 'unreasonableness' might permit the courts to review the policy or motive behind a decision taken by a local authority. In the early case of *Roberts* v. *Hopwood*[36] the House of Lords held that the Council acted unlawfully when it attempted to introduce a minimum wage. The district auditor surcharged the councillors for payments which were contrary to law. The courts upheld the surcharge and rejected the policy arguments advanced by the Council. The role of the courts may also be seen as a means of achieving enforcement powers for the Audit Commission established in 1982 to oversee local authority financial arrangements. A new power was given to the Auditor under the Local Government Act 1988, whereby the Auditor may take action through a prohibition order if he has reason to believe that the body or one of its officers whose accounts he is charged with auditing is about to make or has made a decision which would involve the body incurring unlawful expenditure or engage in an action which would be unlawful or is about to enter an item of account the entry of which is unlawful.[37]

The courts may be invited by the Audit Commission to exercise their powers of review. The Audit Commission has responsibility for the general financial overview of local authority activities and may carry out value for money audit. The latter does not involve the political merits of decisions but looks to the practices and procedures as well as an evaluation of the efficiency and effectiveness of implementing decisions. In *Hazell* v. *Hammersmith*,[38] in proceedings initiated by the district auditor, the House of Lords held that Hammersmith's swap transactions were *ultra vires* for a local authority. Swap transactions were a means for a local authority to engage in the speculative market of debt management as a way of financing local government as a response to the continued pressure on local authority finance by central government legal and financial controls. The effect of the Lords' decisions led to complex unravelling of swaps transactions. Obligations created by such transactions are unenforceable and various default clauses in contracts are rendered ineffective.[39]

The Audit Commission gave advice to local authorities on the impact of the decision.[40] In order to clarify the legal position of various banks the Commercial Court assisted in selecting six lead cases to establish the legal position of the parties. As Loughlin has pointed out, '12 banks had issued 69 writs against 32 local authorities over swaps transactions and many more were threatened'. The outcome of the House of Lords decision exemplifies many of the characteristics of judicial review recognized in the Widdicombe report on local authority business in 1986.[41]

The Widdicombe inquiry[42] made important recommendations on the relationship between members of local authorities and the officers of the authorities. It sought to strengthen the opportunities for judicial review of citizens' grievances over local authority activities. It recommended that the Auditor's role should include powers for an injunction to restrain a local authority from incurring unlawful expenditure or a mandamus to compel an authority to take action where there might be financial loss. The substance of these recommendations appears in the Local Government Act 1988.

Loughlin questions whether the courts in giving reasons for their review of complex technical and financial issues have sufficient 'cognitive, conceptual and material resources' to enable them to perform the functions expected.[43] This is an important issue, as the growth in directive legislation affecting local government provides greater challenges to the role of the courts than hitherto. Such legislation, with precise legal requirements, is intended to provide a comprehensive legislative regulation over local authority activities. This is an contrast to the wider, more open-textured discretion that is a hallmark of the earlier Victorian legislation, which was the foundation of many local authority powers. Very often the permissive legislation of the nineteenth century has been overridden by legislation reflecting a heavy political bias in favour of greater managerial control over local authorities. As we shall see, the challenges posed by such local government legislation have a common theme in terms of the regulatory structures of the major utilities post-privatization.

While doubts may exist as to the quality of the court review powers it is noticeable that modest but important changes were made by the judges in order to accommodate the new challenges in complex public law litigation. In *Hazell* v. *Hammersmith* nearly 130 local authorities were affected by the swaps market. Loughlin noted the use of a 'provisional ruling' by the Lords to the parties concerned, alerting them to the outcome that they were likely to find all swaps transactions *ultra vires*. The Divisional Court set aside a day to enable the judge to read all the documentary evidence. The use of the Divisional Court expedited the hearing of early written arguments. Finally, 'the Divisional Court and Court of Appeal judgments in the Hammersmith case were delivered either before the opening or after the closing of city financial markets in order to minimise any disruptive impact which they might occasion'. In follow-up litigation after the House of Lords decision, the Commercial Court, by grouping the various actions started in order to clarify the implications of the House of Lords decision into a single unity, has limited the potential for the courts to be overridden by hundreds of separate legal actions.[44]

The Availability of Judicial Review

Sunkin,[45] in his research, has kept under review the case-load of applications for judicial review. His research findings underline the breadth, diversity and range of issues which come before the courts. Significantly, he notes that 'there were very few applications brought explicitly by interest or pressure groups; only 19 applications were known to have fallen within this category and eight of these were applications instituted during 1989 by the Friends of the Earth challenging water authorities over pollution control'.

The statistical evidence also shows the occasional use of judicial review by local authorities against central government. A major proportion of judicial review cases came from litigation involving prisoners, housing disputes including homeless persons, planning and licensing disputes. Immigration cases tend to be over refusal of entry or the challenging of asylum decisions.[46]

Many of the conclusions to be drawn from Sunkin's study underline the variables present in determining whether to seek judicial review. Variables include matters such as the availability of legal aid, the existence of alternative remedies, and the ability of complainants to identify legal problems and of lawyers to decide promptly and within the three-month time limit to seek an application for judicial review. The availability of evidence, its preparation and the willingness to litigate are all hidden factors in the availability of judical review.

An additional question in using the courts is whether the adversarial nature of the English judicial system provides an adequate basis to lay down normative principles for the solution of administrative mistakes and inefficiencies or even to provide a grievance resolution for citizens. There is also the issue of how far formal legal rules may not only constrain officials but also condition or determine their behaviour. For example, recent studies on police reactions to critical scrutiny of their behaviour show that much of police behaviour may be made to fit within legal rules because the rules are sufficiently flexible to facilitate the situations where the police need to find a rule to cover their activities. Judicial review of administrative action seldom questions how legal rules are understood or applied by administrative decision-makers. There is a danger that the apparent observance of court-orientated rules may hide or obscure bad decision-making.

REGULATORY STRUCTURES AND ADMINISTRATION

Regulatory Agencies

Many of the shortcomings in judicial review also highlight the complexity of the administrative process itself. McCrudden and Baldwin explain how regulation by agency has developed in importance and offers numerous advantages over the use of the courts.

> The advantages agencies are said to have over traditional courts are numerous. The sheer volume of decisions may call for a separate structure. Economy, speed in decision making, ability to adapt quickly to changing conditions, and freedom from technicality in procedures are other commonly cited advantages. Agencies are also thought to be able to relax the formal rules of evidence when appropriate, to avoid an over-reliance on adversarial techniques, and to avoid strict adherence to their own precedents. Administrative agencies are thought not to be as restricted to formulating policy on a case-by-case basis as are the courts.[47]

The plethora of agencies, ranging from the Gaming Board, Civil Aviation Authority, Health and Safety at Work to the Office of Fair Trading and the Monopolies and Mergers Commission, indicates the diversity, scale and size of regulatory agencies in their work and activities. An additional development has been brought about by the privatization process, with the creation of regulatory agencies for the main utilities, water, gas, electricity and telecommunications.[48]

This form of regulation and the implications for administrative justice may now be considered. Some preliminary considerations may be raised which highlight the complexity of the problems that new regulatory structures pose to our understanding of administrative processes. The decision to privatize carried strong political judgment, with little detailed public discussion concerning the regulatory issues. Each privatization presented its own specialist problems. Pragmatism in deciding which form the privatized industry was to take resulted in little clarity in setting objectives and goals in each privatization sale. Competing objectives are a wider share ownership, the reduction in government expenditure in the industry as part of the public sector borrowing requirement, increased competition and consumer choice. The final form of the regulatory structure in many cases left unresolved priorities[49] and competing objectives have been left for future consideration. Invariably legislative intervention will be a recurring theme in this area. Legal adjustments will be required to take account of changes in government policy, European Community law and perceptions of changes in market policy in the area of competition. Such factors add to the complexity of the subject of administrative regulation.

Graham and Prosser have identified a number of distinctive characteristics in the regulatory structure of the utilities introduced after privatization. First, in the case of telecommunications, gas and electricity, some market liberalization took place before the industry was privatized. Telecommunications had been separated from the Post Office by the creation of British Telecom and the government progressed slowly to identify key elements, such as competition between British Telecom and Mercury. This duopoly has been criticized and is currently under review. In the case of gas, the Oil and Gas (Enterprise) Act 1982 theoretically opened up British Gas's pipelines to competing suppliers for larger customers (not domestic). In the case of electricity, the Energy Act 1983 in theory was intended to promote private electricity generators as competitors to the Central Electricity Generating Board. Water privatization was distinctive because of problems relating to ownership of the water companies, which required specific attention before privatization.[50]

Second, the Government determined the precise economic environment for the future success of the privatized industries. Gas and telecommunications were privatized without any *legal* restructuring of the industries. In the case of electricity the industry was restructured into three component parts. The generating companies, a transmission company (the National Grid) and the distribution companies (the 12 area boards) were all part of an attempt to find a more satisfactory solution to competition than hitherto. It remains to be seen how successful these arrangements will be in promoting competition, fostering efficiency in the industry and reconciling these objectives with consumer protection.[51]

Third, new regulatory institutions introduced for the major utilities commonly adopt similar regulatory techniques and devices to ensure. adequate regulation. It is the multi-dimensional nature of regulation which makes shaping the future of administrative decision-making complex and technical.[52]

The various Directors-General[53] may act as advisers to the Secretary of State, act under a duty to provide information, must be consulted before granting licences and generally give advice to the Secretary of State. The power to amend licences is usually left to the Directors once the licence has been issued. The general enforcement of licences and their conditions is also left to the Director. In addition there are variations in the specific powers enjoyed by each Director.[54] For example, the Director-General of Electricity has a general power to promote competition whereas the Director-General of Gas is confined to promoting competition in the market of large gas users – the contract market only. Accompanying the Directors-General in their consumer protection role there is a large variey of consumers' councils and a committee to oversee the work of consumer protection.[55]

A common theme is the use of some price control formula related to the retail price index (RPI). This provides a 'cap' on fuel costs which can be reasonably passed on to the consumer.[56] Dieter Helm[57] has observed that the formula of RPI – X leaves discretion with the regulator to choose the options to apply.[58]

The question of how best to regulate the newly privatized industry involves a number of different agencies. In terms of competition policy this includes the Monopolies and Mergers Commission (MMC), the Office of Fair Trading (OFT), the Secretary of State for Trade and Industry, the Restrictive Practices Court and the various regulatory bodies, such as the Director relevant to each industry.[59] References to the MMC involve the powers of the Director-General of Fair Trading as to whether a monopoly situation exists and whether the operation of such a situation operates against the public interest. The MMC reports to the Secretary of State, who may then make an order seeking to remedy any defect discovered.[60]

There are such a wide variety of legal powers open to the MMC that its reports first seek compliance by the industry concerned rather than using its enforcement powers. For example, in the case of British Gas the MMC published a report in 1985, with further consideration given by the OFT to the question of how British Gas could be encouraged to promote competition within the industry.[61] The MMC reference was made by the Director-General of Gas (OFGAS) in the first instance. A further MMC report followed in 1988 and concluded a long list of recommendations relating to the pricing and tendency of gas, access to the gas transmission system and transparency in the system of gas schedule. Agreement was tentatively reached with the OFT in July 1991, with the publication of the results of this finding in October 1991.[61] Negotiations with British Gas and OFGAS have continued and currently there is a further reference to the MMC should British Gas not make firm commitments with the OFT. It is likely that British Gas will 'hive off' its pipeline and storage system as an arm's length company. It is assumed that British Gas would reduce its share of the industrial gas market to 40 from 80 per cent. This might be achieved by releasing British Gas from its existing contracts with North Sea suppliers.

The mixture of regulatory supervision by OFGAS and overview by the OFT and MMC combines wide legal power with oversight by the Secretary of State for Trade and Industry.[63] This provides a complex combination of independent regulator and political oversight through ministerial responsibility. An additional overview is provided by the courts.

Judicial review has both a limited[64] and a potentially far-reaching role. The limits of judicial review were acknowleged by Lord Justice Watkins in *R. v. Secretary of State for Trade and Industry ex p. Lonrho*[65] when he suggested that the courts would not take on the responsibility of making 'executive or administrative decisions'. But the far-reaching potential of judicial review may be seen in *Lonrho v. Tebbit*.[66] Sir Nicolas Browne-Wilkinson accepted that the Secretary of State could be sued for negligence in his exercise of statutory powers. The case arose out of the long-running dispute involving Lonrho and its frustrated attempts to acquire a majority shareholding in the House of Fraser. It is also an example of a public law issue being raised as part of a collateral matter in an ordinary action – one of the excepted categories from the principles laid down in *O'Reilly v. Mackman*.[67] The question, which was answered in the negative, was 'whether the courts would not be going beyond their proper role if they sought to attach private liabilities to the discharge of such public functions'. The case is on appeal but recognizes a remarkable extension of judicial supervision over ministers.

The courts have insisted that regulators should apply the rules of natural justice when their investigative powers are use. In *R. v. Director-General of Gas Supply and another ex p. Smith and another*[68] Mr Justice Pill applied the rules of natural justice when OFGAS investigated the use of disconnection powers by British Gas in a case where a meter offence had been committed.

The courts have also considered a related number of diverse regulatory issues. The focus is on the role of the courts in securing different evaluations of the decision-making process.[69] The fairness of procedures or the reasonableness of the decision are common grounds for seeking redress. For example, in *R. v. Independent TV Commission ex p. TSW Broadcasting Ltd*[70] one of the television companies, TSW, applied for judicial review of the Independent Television Commission in seeking to grant licences for TV service. Although the application for judicial review was unsuccessful, the Court of Appeal considered the fair procedures applicable to the award of TV licences under the Broadcasting Act 1990.

Another example of the diversity of judicial review is *R. v. Secretary of State of the Environment and another ex p. British Telecommunication*.[71] Mr Justice Auld dismissed British Telecom's application for judicial review of the 1989 Order setting the rateable values of BT's hereditants. However, the Divisional Court considered the policy and objects of the enabling legislation in order to consider the legality of the 1989 Telecommunications Industry (Rateable Values) Order (S1 No. 24787).

The system of overview of administrative regulation[72] is further complicated by the fact that the regulators are themselves subject to audit by the National Audit Office (NAO) under the direction of the Comptroller and Auditor General.[73] This is an entirely new area which poses new challenges for the scrutiny of regulatory functions by the NAO.[74] The performance of regulations in terms of value for money audit is also part of the remit of the NAO security.

The characteristics of administrative decision-making range from the judicial scrutiny of determinations by regulators to the widest policy questions shared between Secretary of State and regulator. Issues of policy are intertwined with statutory duties and powers. The overview of the administrative process requires careful adjustment of the wide variety of agencies and techniques available.[75]

The Citizen's Charter

The setting of standards and promotion of good administration may be accomplished through a wide variety of techniques. The Citizen's Charter seeks to provide the citizen with standards, more effective complaints procedures, published performance targets and therefore greater consumer choice.[76] The Charter has the far-reaching aim of seeking to make all public services, such as government departments, agencies, nationalized industries, local authorities, the courts, police and emergency services, conform to a standard of quality and service. In addition, the private sector public utilities (as explained above) are expected to conform to the norms of the Charter standards.[77]

The Charter seeks to use contract compliance as a means to achieve quality control across a wide range of services and activities. There is a major question as to how quality might be enforced and how it might be ascertained. Kieron Walsh argues that

> as the contracting, market-based approach begins to be
> extended to more complicated professional services, such as
> medicare, law, finance or social services, it will be necessary to
> develop more sophisticated approaches to quality
> specification. The problem is not simply one of complexity,
> but of coping with the fact that public services involve value
> choices.[78]

The Citizen's Charter has attempted to provide a coherent approach to such problems but the mechanisms for improving the administration process are vague and largely based on political objectives rather than clear-sighted administrative improvements.[79] A potential for change in the role of the regulators is recognized in the Competition and Service (Utilities) Act 1992. Additional powers in the Act envisage that the Director-General of Telecommunications will set standards to be achieved in individual cases, determine compensation where standards are not met and set overall standards of performance.[80] Similarly, the Director-General of Gas Supply is granted additional powers to determine compensation and set standards.[81] Additional powers apply to the Water Services Director-General to collect and publish information and set standards in individual cases.[82] Comparable powers already exist with the Electricity Director-General, but these are supplemented by additional powers.[83]

The difficulty of establishing standards involves questions of privatizing and setting sufficiently clear indications to establish the financial implications of any new quality standards. In a period where the public sector borrowing requirement has grown in deficit, the volume of public expenditure which may be allocated to such objectives is limited. Consistent with the Citizen's Charter have been various efficiency strategies set by central government to achieve a reduction in waste, greater efficiency in management and value for money. These strategies will have an effect on administrative decision-making but the precise outcome is difficult to predict. As Metcalfe and Richard explain, improving public management is frontier territory – an area of genuine innovation where civil servants will have to develop and apply new concepts to fit the tasks and political constraints of government.[84] This is a challenge that awaits a solution.

Principles of Good Administration

The Justice/All Souls Review of administrative law recommended in 1988 the adoption of principles of good administration.[85] The objective is to examine decision-taking from the perspective of setting principles for good administration rather than depending on remedies for bad administration. Good administration principles includes both substantive and procedural rights set out in a code, which on a non-statutory basis are intended to encourage all administrators to undertake decision-taking in accordance with principles of fairness. The publication and formulation of such principles is recommended to be part of the work of the parliamentary ombudsman.

The approach of the Justice Review[86] has common themes with the work of the Committee of Ministers of the Council of Europe, the Recommendations of the Administrative Conference of the United States[87] and work undertaken by the Canadian Law Reform

Commission[88] and the Administrative Review Council in Australia.[89] However, the point that has been broadly acknowledged by the consultation paper 'Towards a modern federal administrative law' (Law Reform Commission of Canada)[90] is that good administration may be achieved through the work of a number of participants with a whole range of techniques.

> Control of Administrative action is a function that can be shared among money institutions or types of decision-makers. Law and bodies entrusted with law application and creation are primary candidates for organising control. However, a plurality of interdependent modes, bodies and procedural regimes that reflect the diverse nature of the control function is called for.

This view acknowledges the importance of internal as well as external controls, non-legal as well as legal, which goes beyond the prospectus chosen by the Justice Review. It is the combination of internal and external controls which may ultimately assist in establishing improvements leading to good administration.

There is a further difficulty with the Justice Review in suggesting that principles of good administration may be effective. However laudable such principles may be, there is a danger that, far from constraining bad administration, the rules themselves may condition or determine behaviour and so provide a veneer of legality to what is otherwise objectionable behaviour.[91] The rules or principles of good administration may still permit undesirable practices but make it insulated from scrutiny and therefore outside the sanctions which should apply. It is therefore suggested that reforms favouring good administration are more difficult to implement than the Justice Review considered. The instrumental effect of rules has to be studied in the context of the expected behaviour of the main administrative decision-makers.

CONCLUSION

Harry Arthurs raised the question: 'What are our concerns about administrative law today? We want to be assured that the vast machinery of administration which is characteristic of all modern government is performing its appointed tasks effectively.'[92] At another point in his discourse he argues that 'one of the important criticisms of modern administrative law has been that the promise of effectiveness has not been kept'. The argument is that regulatory agencies which are intended to control powerful interests might be captured by them and used to impose the views of powerful interests.

An important conclusion is that achieving administrative justice sets complex objectives across a great variety of agencies, institutions, tribunals, ombudsmen and courts. Invariably most regulatory agencies are set up by Act of Parliament. This may combine some form of political accountability through ministerial responsibility with policy objectives. But this only highlights the diffuse nature of our regulatory agencies. Techniques of accountability may be both external and internal, legal and non-legal. The privatized industries are particularly good examples of new challenges to existing techniques. Recent developments, such as the Citizen's Charter, may lead to a new agenda setting economic as well as legal appraisal indicators. There is also an important element of fine tuning, i.e. establishing the necessary expertise to fit the requirements of the activity to be regulated.

Privatized industries[93] have also broadened horizons regarding the nature of regulatory structures. Competition policy, consumer choice, share ownership, environmental efficiency, European Community law, market share and profitability have to be considered together. Carefully balanced judgments have to be taken within a complex legal formulation of the legal powers and duties of regulators. The background political agenda, the use of select committees and parliamentary debate and the policy of the government of the day are all relevant considerations in setting out to assess administrative justice. One suggestion, of setting up a Select Committee on Regulated Industries to replace the defunct Select Committee on Nationalised Industries, might help to coordinate the parliamentary oversight of regulatory agencies.

The question of how judicial review may contribute to the development of administrative justice is also related to the diverse nature of the various agencies and regulating bodies. Doubts exist as to the appropriateness of the adversarial system of courts; the *ex post facto* nature of the proceedings and the narrow issues often confronting the courts may suggest that courts are not ideally suited to providing the formulation of administrative justice. In *R. v. Civil Service Appeal Board*[94] Lord Donaldson suggested how a partnership between regulators and courts might be formed:

we had now reached the position in the development of judicial review at which public law bodies and the courts should be regarded as being in partnership in a common endeavour to maintain the highest standards of public administration, including, I would add the administration of justice.

173

This aspirational view of the role of the courts is a departure from the grievance- or remedy-orientated approach that has historically been influential in this area. However, this raises the question of whether the courts, as Loughlin has asked, 'possess the cognitive, conceptual and material resources to enable them to perform the functions expected'.[95] While doubts may exist as to the technical or conceptual techniques that are available to the courts, it is essential that these issues are addressed as the new challenge facing administrative lawyers in the 1990s. As the Canadian Law Reform Commission concluded:

> Overall contentious procedure in judicial review has many gaps. For example, the multiplicity of remedial avenues and the absence of distinctions between public law and private law are sources of confusion, frustration and inequity. We must explore new solutions, especially the unification of crucial remedies and the clarification of their fields of application in administrative law.[96]

Administrative justice requires that reform of administrative law should take account of the changing nature of Britain's administrative state. Approaches to administrative law must combine the practical with the theoretical, the legal with the multi-disciplinary, the external with the internal rules of good administration.

NOTES AND REFERENCES

1 Report of the Committee on Administrative Tribunals and Enquiries (The Franks Report) (HMSO, Cmnd 218, July 1957).

2 See *Towards a Modern Federal Administrative Law:* Consultation Paper Law Reform Commission, Canada, 1987. *A British Bill of Rights* (IPPR, 1991) Constitution Paper No 1.

3 JUSTICE *The Citizen and the Administration* (1961); also see JUSTICE *The Citizen and His Council – Ombudsman for Local Government* (1969). The British Nationality Act 1981, for example, confers British citizenship and recognizes a legal right to live in and to come and go into and from the United Kingdom by Right. This is one of the very few 'rights' linked with citizenship.

4 David Marsh, 'Privatization under Mrs Thatcher: a review of the literature', *Public Administration*, Vol. 69, Winter 1991, 459–80.

5 John F. McEldowney, 'Law and regulation: Current issues and future direction', in Bishop, Kay, Mayer and Thompson, *Privatisation and Regulation*, 2nd edition, Oxford University Press, 1992.

6 Carol Harlow, 'The Justice/All Souls Review: Don Quixote to the rescue', *Oxford*

Journal of Legal Studies, Vol. 10, No. 1, 85–93. Also see T. Prosser, 'Towards a critical theory of public law 1982', *British Journal of Law and Society*, 1.

7 *Policy implemention, compliance and administrative law*. Law Reform Commission of Canada Working Paper No. 51 (1986).

8 *Towards a modern federal administrative law. A consultation paper*, 1987. In particular see pages 2–3: 'We should approach the study of administrative law mindful of the functions of the state's administrative apparatus.' Legal regimes do not exist in isolation from society, legal structures and rules have profound economic and sociological effects which must be studied; as well, criteria must be developed for assessing the the desirability of proposed alternatives in administrative law. The analytic tools of related disciplines such as political science, enconomics, sociology and public administration can be used to improve our understanding of administrative law.

9 [1984] 3 All ER 935, p. 949.

10 See J. Jowell and D. Oliver, *New Directives in Administrative Law* (Oxford, 1988).

11 The Law Commission No. 20 (1969) Cmnd 4059; also see Law Commission Working Paper No. 13, July 1967. Appendix A to Law Commission No. 20.

12 The Law Commission No. 73, Report on Remedies in Administration Law Cmnd 6407 (March, 1976). Also see a report by Justice, 'Administration under law' (Keith Goodfellow, QC Chairman), London, 1971.

13 See R. Baldwin and J. Houghton, 'Circular arguments: the status and legitimacy of administrative rules', 1986 *Public Law*, 239–84; J.A.G. Griffith, 'Judicial decision making in public law', 1985 *Public Law*, 564–82.

14 *Ex p. Phillips*, *The Times*, November 1986.

15 See S. Sedley, 'Now you see it', now you don't: judicial discretion and judicial review', *Warwick Law Working Papers*, August 1987, Vol. 8. No. 4.

16 *Administrative Justice: Some Necessary Reforms* (Oxford University Press, 1988). Hereinafter, the Justice Review.

17 *Ibid*. See David Feldman, 'Public interest litigation and constitution theory in comparative perspective' (1992) MLR 44–72. For a survey of administrative law see R. Rawlings, *The Complaints Industry*, ESRC, 1986.

18 [1987] QB 815.

19 [1985] QB 152. Also see *R. v. Lord Chancellor's Dept. ex p. Nangla* [1991] 1 RLR 343, *Roy v. Kensington and Chelsea and Westminister Family Practitioner Committee*, *The Independent* 11 Feb. 1992. Lord Bridge allowed private law rights exercised through the writ procedure to raise public law issue incidentally. Lord Lowry regarded the litigant as having a 'bundle of rights', which permitted the case to be heard.

20 [1983] 2 AC 237.

21 [1986] 1 AC 484, *ex p. Benwell* [1985] 1 QB 152. See *ex p. Dew* [1987] 1 WLR 881.

22 [1986] 1 All ER 717.

23 [1982] AC 617.

24 [1977] QB 729 [1978] AC 435. Also *Gillick* [1986] AC 112.

25 [1990] 1 All ER 754.

26 [1986] 1 WLR 763.

27 [1987] 1 QB 815.

28 *Council of Civil Service Unions* v. *Minister for the Civil Service* [1985] AC 374.

29 [1968] AC 997.

30 [1985] AC 318.

31 [1981] AC 75.

32 [1986] AC 240.

33 [1983] AC 768.

34 [1987] 3 All ER 671.

35 *Associated Picture Houses Ltd* v. *Wednesbury Corporation* [1948] 1 KB 223.

36 [1925] AC 579 also *Pickwell* v. *Camden LBC* [1983] QB 962.

37 M. Radford, 'Auditing for change: local government and the Audit Commission', (1991) MLR 912–32.

38 [1990] 2 WLR 17.

39 M. Loughlin, 'Innovative financing in local government: the limits of legal instrumentalism – Part 1 [1990] PL 372.

40 M. Loughlin, Part II [1991] PL 568.

41 *Report: The Conduct of Local Authority Business* HMSO, 1986 Cmnd 9797. Chairman David Widdicombe.

42 *Ibid.*, Chapter 9.

43 Loughlin, *op. cit.* fn. 40, pp. 595–7.

44 *Hazell* v. *Hammersmith and Fulham LBC* [1991] 1 All ER 545.

45 M. Sunkin, 'The judicial review case-load 1987–1989', 1991 *Public Law* 490–9. Also see M. Sunkin, 'What is happening to applications for judicial review?' (1987) 50 MLR 432.

46 Sunkin, 1991 *Public Law*, p. 497.

47 C. McCrudden and R. Baldwin, *Regulation and Public Law*, London (1987), p. 5.

48 C. Graham and T. Prosser, *Privatising Public Enterprises* (Oxford, 1991).

49 Graham and Prosser pp. 191–200.

50 Graham and Prosser pp. 141–2, 163–4, 175.

51 See J. F. McEldowney, *Electricity Handbook: Law and Practice* (Chichester, 1992), Chapter 1.

52 *Ibid.*

53 s. 47(4) Telecommunications Act 1984, s. 34(4) Gas Act 1986, s. 47(3) Electricity Act 1989, s. 26(4) Water Act 1989.

54 Compare ss. 29–42 Electricity Act 1989, ss. 36, 68 Water Act 1989, ss. 26 and 35(4) Water Act 1989, s. 47(3) Telecommunications Act 1984 and s. 39 (2) Gas Act 1986. Now see Competition and Service (Utilities) Act 1992.

55 Graham and Prosser, *loc. cit.* fn. 49 pp. 185–7.

56 *Ibid.*

57 D. Helm, 'A regulatory rule: "RPI minus X"', in C. Whitehead (ed.), *Reshaping the Nationalised Industries* (Oxford, 1988).

58 *Ibid.* The $RPI - X$ formula means that the price is based on the Retail Price Index minus some factor X, to be calculated according to the regulator's discretion.

59 Graham and Prosser, *loc. cit.* fn. 49, pp. 197–214.

60 *Ibid.*

61 See McEldowney, *loc. cit.* fn. 5.

62 *The Monopolies and Mergers Commission*, Cm 5000 (HMSO, 1988).

63 *The Independent*, 8 February 1992.

64 *Ex p. Benwell* [1985] 1 QB 152. Also see Carol Harlow, 'Public and private law: definition without distinction' (1980) 43 WLR 241.

65 [1989] 1 WLR 525.

66 *The Independent*, 26 September 1991.

67 [1983] 2 AC 237, see *ex p.* Lovelle [1983] 1 WLR 23.

68 Co. 1398/88. See John F. McEldowney, 'Theft and meter tampering and the gas and electricity utilities' [1991] Vol. 2, No. 3 *Utilities Law Review*, 121–4.

69 P. Craig, *Administrative Law* (2nd edition) (1989) pp. 147–64.

70 *The Independent*, 6 February 1992. Also see *Luby* v. *Newcastle under Lyme Corporation* (1964) 2 QB 64. Lord Justice Diplock explained, 'it is not for the court to substitute its own view of what is a desirable policy in relation to the subject-matter of the discretion so conferred. It is only if it is exercised in a manner which no reasonable man could consider justifiable that the court is entitled to interfere.'

71 *The Independent*, 5 September 1991.

72 See J. Vickers and G. Yarrow, 'Regulation of privatised firms in Britain', in J. Richardson (ed.), *Privatisation and Deregulation in Britain and Canada* (1990), pp. 221–8.

73 J. F. McEldowney, 'The National Audit Office and privatisation', 1991 MLR 933–55.

74 *Ibid.*

75 *Ibid.*

76 *The Citizen's Charter*, HMSO Cm 1599 (July 1991).

77 *Ibid.*

78 Kieron Walsh, 'Quality and public services', 1991 *Public Administration*, Vol. 69, no. 4, 503–14.

79 *Ibid.*

80 Competition and Service (Utilities) Act 1992, ss. 1–10.

81 Sections 11–19.

82 Sections 25–28.

83 Sections 20–24.

84 L. Metcalfe and S. Richards, *Improving Public Management* (Sage, 1990).

85 Justice/All Souls Review, *op. cit.*, fn. 16.

86 *Ibid.*

87 Also see Patrick McAuslan, 'Administrative law, collective consumption and judicial policy', 1983 MLR 1. J. F. McEldowney, Current privatisation and regulation issues in the UK: a case study of the proposed electricity privatisation. Admin. Law, Law Reform Commission of Canada, Ottawa, 1988.

88 *Canadian Law Reform Commission WP 51*: Policy implementation, compliance and administrative law 1986.

89 M. Partington, 'The reform of public law in Britain', in P. McAuslan and J. McEldowney (eds), *Law, Legitimacy and the Constitution* (1985), pp. 191–211.

90 *Loc. cit.*, fn. 2, Law Reform Commission of Canada, p. 23.

91 This point is admirably made by McConville *et al. The Case for the Prosecution* (Routledge, 1981). Generally see P.S. Atiyah, *Pragmatism and Theory in English Law* (Stevens, 1987), pp. 181–3. Also Lord Goff, 'The search for principle ' (1983) 69, *Proc. Br. Acad.* 169.

92 H. Arthurs, *Without the Law* (1985), p. 196. Also *Regulatory Agencies in the United Kingdom:, Constitutional Reform Centre* (1991).

93 See McEldowney, *loc. cit.* fn. 73. Also see Lord Scarman, *The Shifting State: Public Administration in a Time of Change.* Keynote Address, 14 September 1984. RIPA Conference, University of Aston. Author's own copy. I am grateful to Lord Scarman for sending me his keynote address. J. F. McEldowney, 'British public law and legal history', Universidad de Málaga 1992. Also M. Loughlin, 'Tinkering with the Constitution' [1988] 51 MLR 531.

94 [1991] 4 ALL ER 310 at p. 315.

95 Loughlin, *op. cit.* fn. 40.

96 Canadian Law Reform Commission. Towards a Modern Federal Administrative Law, p. 24. Also see Sir Harry Woolf, 'Public law–private law: why the divide? A personal view' [1986] *Public Law* 220. T. R. S. Allan, 'Pragmatism and theory in public law' (1988) LQR 422, p. 446. Also see proposal for reform in Constitutional Reform Centre, Politics Briefing No.–11 *Regulatory Agencies in the United Kingdom* (1991). Also see The Law Commission, *Administrative Law: Judicial Review and Statutory Appeals.* Consultation Paper No. 126. It is hoped that the Law Commission might also consider the wider context for the application of judicial review and statutory appeals, especially the question of the effects of judicial review on administrators.

9

The Disabled Citizen

TREVOR BUCK

INTRODUCTION

The intention of this chapter is to explore the extent to which disabled persons share in 'citizenship rights' with the rest of the community. To this end the chapter explains some of the difficulties inherent both in the definition of disability and the identification of the disabled and in the implications of this for policy formulation. An indication is given of the extent of disability in the UK drawn from the most recent findings of the Office of Population Censuses and Surveys (OPCS). Next, an outline of formal legal protection of disabled persons from the Poor Law to the present day is offered to give perspective to the current debate concerning the level of citizenship rights that disabled persons ought to enjoy. This latter debate is then explored in the light of recent developments in relevant social movements and a discussion of the politics of disablement is opened up. A concluding section attempts to identify a coherent development in legal protection regarding the disabled and points the way to future directions in this area.

DISABILITY AND THE IDEA OF CITIZENSHIP

It is undoubtedly the case that the disability movement has pursued the goals not only of autonomy and integration but also of the achievement of 'rights'. Sometimes this pursuit has been more rhetorical than real; it has been argued that there has never really been a clear conceptual analysis of 'rights' in this area. Hudson[1] argues that one should distinguish between 'claim rights' and 'moral rights'. The former are associated with areas of 'routine discrimination', e.g.

employment, accommodation, access to leisure and other facilities. The latter are associated with 'fundamental discrimination'; for example, excluding persons with mental handicap from basic human rights, such as rights to life, procreation and parenting. Perhaps this is no more than a distinction between the more familiar terms of 'economic and social' and 'human' rights. Whatever the particular hierarchy of rights, welfare advocacy has pursued the goal of 'rights', often because of their contradistinction to 'discretion', rather than a clear analysis of how such rights might positively enhance citizenship status. Such a goal has often been perceived as an antidote to stigmatized, passive forms of receiving statutory services. Such rights might not only actually achieve calculable material gains but could also contribute to the empowerment and newly found confidence and self-definition that the disabled and other new social movement groups have discovered.

The new discourse on citizens' rights is 'essentially concerned with the nature of social participation of persons within the community as fully recognised legal members'.[2] While academic research is replete with work concerning the impact of, for example, gender and race on the idea of citizenship, there has been less attention given to the disabled citizen. This has been the result of a public perception of the disabled as largely the *objects* of public administration laws and agencies rather than a category of persons presenting any significant challenges to the polity of the nation. Indeed, a traditional view of the disabled as a class was that public policy programmes provided *preferential* treatment and exemptions from the usual obligations of the citizen, hardly a case for the creation of significant citizenship rights. What was lacking was any analysis of the processes by which disabled people were defined and socially constructed in such a way as to become disengaged from the mainstream community, and the myriad ways in which the obstacles to full participation in society would create disadvantage requiring remedial action. However, once this analysis had been initiated (forcefully in the United States),[3] a combination of economic circumstances and the growth of a new Anglo-American social movement – the disability movement – were bound to exert pressure for the inclusion of the disabled in the discourse on citizenship.

T. H. Marshall's work,[4] the *locus classicus* of citizenship rights, outlines the development of civil, political and social rights over the past few centuries, but this analysis, whatever its explanatory power in other areas, has not provided a suitable account of the disabled citizen. While it might be argued that the eighteenth and nineteenth centuries generally saw an improvement in civil and political rights, legal measures relating to the disabled hardly support this thesis. For example, the Mental Deficiency Act 1913 gave local authorities power to place mental defectives in institutions on the written authority of two doctors. This Act has been referred to as 'the nadir of the civil rights of people with learning difficulties'.[5] Marshall's identification of the twentieth century as the origin of 'social' rights does not fit easily with the experience of the disabled. English Poor Law had for long recognized the claims of the 'impotent poor'. Indeed, eligibility for poor relief was exchanged for the surrender of significant civil and/or political rights. The claim of disabled and elderly paupers was undisputed, but the badge of such pauperism could be disenfranchisement. In practice, much modern analysis[6] of disability draws heavily upon the way in which the bureaucracy and professionals administering large public (and voluntary sector) programmes of assistance for the disabled force the disabled to conform with certain stereotypical expectations of the wider community: docility, limited capacity, gratitude.

The identification of the disabled citizen upsets the potential of other groups to achieve full citizenship. For example, some commentators have noted that the prevalence of unpaid female carers prevents women's full participation as citizens. Finch, for example, bases her advocacy of enhanced residential care on such a ground.[7] But research evidence on the alternatives to family-based care (traditionally, institutionalization) shows fairly clearly that the disabled person's autonomy and integration in the community are often adversely affected. It is of course the case that in some sense the claims of one group in society to maximize their potential are inherently in competition with the demands of other groups. This is especially so with regard to social rights, which are formulated in such a way as to depend heavily on the nation's economic growth performance. The claims of the disabled can also be regarded as in competition with claims from the 'poverty lobby' generally, where it is recognized that there is an added complexity.[8]

The notion of citizenship in the context of the disabled has tended to refer to specific areas where legal *protection* has been thought appropriate, e.g. income maintenance, access, employment and the provision of services. A more detailed look at some of these areas follows below. First, it is necessary to look at some definitional problems and an outline of the growth of the disability movement and more recent policy developments, in order to understand the nature of the potential claim that might arise from the disabled for readjustments of their citizen status.

DEFINING DISABILITY AND IDENTIFYING THE DISABLED

The OPCS undertook two large surveys of the disabled in Great Britain in 1968-9 and 1988-9 respectively. The 1971 Report[9] found that there were about three million persons who could be defined as disabled. The report initiated a three-fold distinction between impairment, disability and handicap, which was eventually accepted by the World Health Organization (WHO) as the basis for its classification.[10] 'Disability' is seen as a continuum ranging from the very severe to the very slight (e.g. the difficulty many middle-aged persons have with reading small print). It is defined by WHO as 'any restriction or lack (resulting from an impairment) of ability to perform an activity in the manner or within the range considered normal for a human being'.[11] 'Impairment' refers to the cause of disability, for example the loss of a limb or chronic bronchitis. 'Handicap', on the other hand, 'reflects the social consequences of disability';[12] for example, arthritis may cause severe handicap to one employee while the same level of impairment or disability would not be such a handicap to another.

The OPCS work of the late 1980s revealed much larger numbers of disabled.[13] Over six million adults had one or more disability in Great Britain and around 7 per cent of these lived in some kind of communal establishment. A new feature of this survey work was the construction of a severity scale from 1 (least severe) to 10 (most severe).[14] The survey found that 200,000 persons were in the most severe category while one million were ascribed to the least severe category.[15] Clearly, the survey design was such that a low threshold for 'disability' was set in order to undertake the intended comprehensive survey. However, the problem with identifying a large disabled constituency is that policy-makers may resist improving welfare provision precisely because of the increased numbers potentially involved.

The problem of definition in welfare enactments is often acute and frequently dominated by considerations of resources. In the realm of social security measures, for example, there are broadly two main types of disability benefit: income-replacement benefits and benefits for specific needs. The first group take 'incapacity for work' as their core concept. This must result from 'some specific disease or bodily or mental disablement',[16] a question of fact to be determined by reference to medical opinion. The second relies on the claimant establishing a particular kind of disability, such as the inability (or virtual inability) to walk (Mobility Allowance), or the need for frequent attention to bodily functions and/or continual supervision to avoid substantial danger to himself or herself or others (Attendance Allowance).[17] Definitions of disability in this context, then, represent a much more precise set of criteria, usually involving the use of medical adjudication in a gate-keeping role.[18] However, policy-makers may wish to retain even more flexibility because of fears of potential demand that might otherwise be made on public programmes or the possibility of fraud, or a combination of both. Thus, a fierce debate over relevant definitions of disability raged during the passage of the Chronically Sick and Disabled Persons Act 1970.[19] Some favoured the definition contained in the National Assistance Act 1948,[20] others would have preferred that adopted in the Disabled Persons (Employment) Act 1944.[21] The problem was resolved by conferring power on the Secretary of State to make regulations under the 1970 Act giving definition to the phrases 'disabled' and 'disability' where he thought necessary.[22]

Some commentators have noted,[23] for example, that it was precisely because of the increasing identification of the disabled that the Government took a very restrictive view of the interpretation of section 1 of the 1970 Act. This section placed, for the first time, a duty on local authorities 'to inform themselves of the number of persons to whom that section applies within their area and of the need for the making . . . of arrangements under [National Assistance Act 1948 s. 29] for such persons'. Alf Morris, and the *ad hoc* committee responsible for guiding the Bill through Parliament, had clearly intended that this section would compel local authorities not only to ascertain the number but also to provide a detailed identification of the individual needs of disabled in a local authority area in order that the authority could consider how to fulfil the duty contained in section 2 to provide an appropriate range of services.[24] However, government circulars quickly laid to rest the hopes that the new law would result in such a detailed household survey of needs.[25] They also made it clear that an authority might rely merely on sample surveys to fulfil its duty under the Act. Even where an authority chose the house-to-house type of enquiry, research evidence revealed that this was not satisfactory either.[26] It was perhaps unsurprising that the optimism over the merits of local authority registration would fade away,[27] especially when the more rigorous analyses of the OPCS and other research[28] had shown that the disabled population was a much more dynamic constituency than it was thought to be; the survey work demonstrated that the circumstances of disabled people were constantly changing, even over short periods of time.

LEGAL PROTECTION OF THE DISABLED

Introduction

Before the latter part of the nineteenth century there was no distinct legal protection offered to the disabled. In the absence of family support such persons would be reliant on charitable help or would have to rely on Poor Law assistance. The disabled were classed as 'impotent poor' and provided for on occasion in infirmaries and alms houses generated by that most well-known Poor Law institution, the workhouse. Later, such patronage, frequently mixed with piety, seemed an oppressive and stigmatized approach, precluding disabled persons from participating properly in the community. The great administrative system of the Poor Law, criticized as it must be, nevertheless spawned the foundations of health care, the personal social services and universal education. The fragmentation of various groups within a 'deserving–undeserving' hierarchy of Poor Law clientele was part of that process. Indeed, it is interesting that perhaps the first distinct legal measure aimed to protect the disabled forms part of a wider nineteenth-century concern with child welfare. The Elementary Education (Blind and Deaf Children) Act 1893 took up the recommendations of a Royal Commission Report in 1889[29] that the state should require local education authorities to provide compulsory education for five- to sixteen-year-old blind and/or deaf children, with a permissive power to provide education for mentally handicapped children. More substantial provision for this latter group was delayed until 1899 after the results of another Departmental Committee Report[30] intended to distinguish between the educable and ineducable mentally handicapped child.[31] Mandatory powers to provide education for this group were introduced by the Education Act 1918.

After the First World War, attention shifted to the needs of disabled ex-servicemen. Centres for the war disabled were established for retraining and employers were given limited incentives to recruit a proportion of their workforce from war veterans. Such provision was extended in 1920[32] to include blind civilians. However, partly because of the inter-war Depression, no significant advances were made in state provision for the disabled until the passing of the Disabled Persons (Employment) Act 1944. The 1944 Act was prompted by a serious shortage of labour in 1941 due to the level of conscription of the able-bodied for the war effort. It established a variety of services for the disabled, the assessment of a disabled person's earning potential, provision of training courses and rehabilitation centres, and the formulation of a quota system of employment alongside a formal system of registration. Employers of more than twenty persons were required to obtain at least 3 per cent of their staff from disabled persons on the register. The system was subject to severe difficulties in its operation from the outset. Employers frequently persuaded existing employees who had some lesser disability to register. By the end of the 1950s registration was falling off and becoming increasingly regarded as stigmatized by the disabled themselves.[33] This of course meant that there were never sufficient persons registered to form 3 per cent of the workforce in aggregate, so in practice the system became, and remains, unenforceable against the employer.[34] The Department of Employment reviewed[35] the system in 1972 and recommended the abandonment of the scheme, including the registration of certain occupations[36] as reserved exclusively for registered disabled persons.

Income

In addition to some, albeit flawed, provision for rehabilitation, the post-war period also saw the creation of distinct social security benefits designed to deal with the needs of the disabled and/or to maintain the income of disabled persons. The Beveridge Plan[37] had left large gaps in provision for the disabled, especially for those disabled at birth, and not able to obtain work and thereby accrue National Insurance contributions necessary for entitlement to a range of non-means tested benefits. This omission prompted in the 1960s and 1970s a stick and plaster policy whereby specific needs-related benefits were tacked on to the general social security scheme; e.g. Attendance Allowance[38] and Mobility Allowance.[39] Non-contributory invalidity pension (NCIP) and housewives' NCIP were particularly aimed at those not able to earn sufficient contributions under the general provision. (H)NCIP had to be hurriedly abandoned by the Government because it was clearly sex discriminatory under EC law, although its replacement, Severe Disablement Allowance (SDA), has also been criticized as being indirectly discriminatory.[40] SDA contains some features of the industrial injuries benefits system, such as a percentage rating for a range of specified function failures.

Recently there has been some consolidation of the benefit structure in the form of the Disabled Living Allowance (DLA) and the Disabled Working Allowance (DWA).[41] DLA will eventually encompass the attendance and mobility elements of the former benefits, while DWA represents an innovation, the provision of benefit to disabled persons on low income. DWA is modelled on the Family Credit structure. Despite some demands from the Social Security Advisory Committee[42] for more cohesion in designing an appropriate benefit structure for the disabled, it would appear that, at least for the foreseeable future, an *ad hoc* approach to benefits for the disabled continues. However, although the benefit reforms of the 1960s and 1970s do not reflect any real coherence in strategy, the more recent reforms do at least touch upon a new public mood of concern and consciousness of the needs of the disabled.[43] The income of disabled persons has for many years been the object of an influential lobby group, e.g. the Disablement Income Group (DIG) and the Disability Alliance.[44]

Services

One important landmark measure in relation to legal protection for the disabled was undoubtedly the Chronically Sick and Disabled Persons Act 1970. It is perhaps of note that this Private Member's Bill, skilfully guided through Parliament by Alf Morris MP, was never accompanied by a public statement relying on justifications from any principle of economic rationality,[45] as earlier measures had been. By the late 1960s it was assumed that the state had a continuing role to support and assist disabled persons. It is also significant as a reflection of the developing mood that the 1970 Act finds focus in its emphasis on giving support to the disabled person at home rather than in institutions.

For the first time, the 1970 Act placed a duty on local authorities to identify the number of disabled persons in their areas and to provide a range of services to meet their needs. Of course, the Act provoked difficulties, not least the lack of any definition of needs and the absence of any definition of 'disability'. However, some particular services were specified, for example the provision of aids and adaptations in the home, and for the first time there was established a legal foundation to protect disabled persons' access to public buildings.

There has been some attempt to strengthen the provisions of the 1970 Act in the Disabled Persons (Services, Consultation and Representation) Act 1986, but this Act is only partially in force. The 1986 Act, another Private Member's Bill (Tom Clarke MP), was generally thought to have emasculated the spirit of the original Bill.[46] The intention of the Act, according to one commentator, was 'to improve services for the disabled through better assessment of their needs'.[47] Section 1 (not in force) provides for the appointment by or on behalf of disabled persons of authorized representatives for the purposes of the Act. 'Disabled people' are defined by reference to the definition in the National Assistance Act 1948.[48] Section 3, a key provision (and not yet in force), allows representations to be made to the local authority before any assessment of a disabled person is undertaken. The authority is placed under a duty to make a written statement of the disabled person's needs. Other parts of the 1986 Act have come into force.[49] Section 4 strengthens the duty to assess needs with a view to provide services (under section 2 of the 1970 Act). Sections 5 and 6 require local authorities to identify disabled school-leavers and assess their needs for social services. Other sections have effectively been superseded by community care legislation or the Children Act 1989.[50]

Access to Built Environment

The increasing awareness of handicap as a function of barriers inherent in the built environment has inevitably led to campaigning initiatives designed to secure better access to public buildings. Section 4 of the 1970 Act requires those undertaking the provision of 'any building or premises' to which the public are to be admitted (by payment or otherwise) to make 'provision, in so far as it is in the circumstances both practicable and reasonable'[51] for the needs of disabled members of the public, 'in the means of access both to and within the building or premises, and in the parking facilities and sanitary conveniences . . . available (if any)'. Section 8 sets out a duty to provide means of access in educational establishments and a new section 8A in the 1970 Act[52] contains a similar provision (to section 4) relating to means of access to office, shop, railway and certain factory premises. Finally, section 8B places a duty on the Secretary of State to make annual reports to Parliament on 'his proposals for ensuring or facilitating the improvement of means of access for disabled persons' in relation to premises (in sections 4, 8 and 8A) and public sanitary conveniences, including those provided in places normally used (or used on occasion) for the holding of any entertainment, exhibition or sporting event to which the public are admitted, or places normally used for the sale of food or drink, or betting offices.

These provisions in the 1970 Act have to be read together with the Building Regulations 1985,[53] as amended, made under the Buildings Act 1984. Under these regulations premises are defined to include offices, shops, certain factories, educational establishments and any premises to which the public are admitted (on payment or otherwise) 'as is (or are) on the storey of the building concerned which contains the principal entrance to that building'.[54] Part M of the Regulations merely states that 'reasonable provision' shall be made to enable disabled people to obtain access to the relevant premises. An 'approved document' issued[55] under the Buildings Act 1984, sections 6 and 7, will give practical guidance as to the ways in which the requirements of the new part M of the Regulations can be met. In the original 1985 Regulations some of these details were spelt out. For example, in the case of a sports stadium 20 seats or 0.5 per cent of the total number of seats (whichever is the greater) should be wheelchair spaces. In the case of other audience or spectator seating six seats or

1 per cent of the total number (whichever is the greater) was the required standard.[56] The focus of these regulations on disabled access only in single-storey buildings or only on the storey containing the principal entrance to the building is an obvious limitation, although it has been the government's stated intention to widen the scope of these regulations.[57] Undoubtedly this type of provision will be extended in the future but at present there is little opportunity for legal challenge by the individual disabled citizen unable to reach the second floor of an art gallery or museum, for example.[58] Finally, the activities of the Access Committee for England, set up by the Minister of the Disabled in 1983, should be mentioned. The establishment of this committee followed on the report of the Committee on Restrictions against Disabled People. It is funded mainly by the Department of Health and its role is to increase awareness about access problems and to offer advice to government and non-government organizations on practical implementation of better access for the disabled.

Perhaps a common characteristic of the legislation of this period is the high expectation for such measures, frequently followed by a period of disillusion among the lobby groups.[59] A similar process of euphoria followed by greater circumspection awaited the implementation of the Education Act 1981, which enshrined some of the well-considered recommendations of the Warnock Report[60] on special education. For example, the central concept of a 'learning difficulty' at once underlined the wide continuum of conditions and behaviours that disabled people experience and focused attention on the task of this particular legislation to identify obstacles to the education of the disabled. The concept is also intended to break down the hardened categories of disabilities that had accrued over time.[61] Such dynamic legal concepts, while having a positive educative effect, are difficult to translate into practical terms when the basic restriction of resources still applies to educational provision. The assessment and statementing procedures under the Education Act 1981 offered formal rights to parents to participate in this process, but ultimately, even where needs have been clearly identified, it remains almost impossible to compel local authorities to make adequate educational provision at least in cases where there has not been a wholesale breakdown in provision.[62]

The outline account given above of some of the developments in the law and policy relating to the disabled raises several points. First, it is clear that early legislative measures were frequently based on straightforward principles of economic rationality. The disabled child, the war veteran, the disabled worker, must be educated, trained and rehabilitated into the workforce. The Disabled Persons (Employment) Act 1944 represents a clear economic response to labour shortage in wartime Britain. However, the 1970 Act and subsequent measures have relied on a different rationale. These measures do, albeit in limited ways, address the 'right' of disabled persons to participate in society. That is not to say that principles of economic rationality are not also operative, but they are no longer predominant. For example, the principle of 'integration' in the Education Act 1981 can be seen as a cheaper means to provide special education and the provision of aids and adaptations under the 1970 Act can be viewed as a tactic to preclude the higher alternative costs of admission into residential care. Indeed, the same thing could be said generally about the recent initiatives for 'community care'.

The new public mood, reflecting a much more positive image of what it means to be disabled, contains two interrelated themes: first, the development of a new social movement, the disability movement; second, the development of a particular ideology, a 'politics of disablement', to lend intellectual coherence and direction to the movement.

THE DISABILITY MOVEMENT

One might agree with Oliver that there must be some kind of 'social basis for new forms of transformative political action or change.'[63] It is equally clear that the past 20 years have seen significant developments in the social basis underpinning the changes in the legal protection for the disabled. Of course, there have been enormous numbers of organizations *for* the disabled certainly since the early nineteenth century, but a useful broad distinction can be made between such charitable organizations and the more recent occurrence of organizations *of* the disabled.[64]

Oliver's useful five-fold typology of organizations for (and of) the disabled[65] has the advantage of providing a convenient classification as well as providing a historical analysis of their development. First, he identifies 'partnership/patronage' organizations. Frequently these are charitable bodies providing services, often in conjunction with statutory services; they may also serve professional agencies in an advisory or consultative capacity (e.g. the RNIB). Second are 'economic/parliamentarian' organizations involved in lobbying and research, frequently single-issue bodies (e.g. the Disablement Income Group). Third are 'consumerist/self-help' groups, providing services to meet self-defined needs (e.g. the Spinal Injuries Association). Fourth are 'populist/activist' groups. Frequently hostile to the partnership approach, these organizations emphasize empowerment of the disabled individual, collective action and consciousness-raising (e.g. the Union of the Physically Impaired Against Segregation). Finally, the latest development has been the emergence of 'umbrella/coordinating' organizations, collective groups comprising consumerist and/or populist groups. These reject divisions of the disabled population on the grounds of age, clinical conditions or functional limitations; their focus is overtly political, with the stress on empowerment of the disabled (e.g. the British Council of Disabled People and the Disabled People's Internationale).

Oliver and others argue that the difference between organizations *for* and organizations *of* the disabled is that the former operate according to a medical rather than a social model of disability.[66] In other words, organizations for the disabled assume that the condition of being disabled presents a pathological, individual problem; how are such disabled people to be assisted in order for the 'normal' functioning of the able-bodied society to continue? The social model however, the basis for organizations of the disabled, assumes that the dis-abling elements to the disabled status are mainly to be found in the physical, emotional and psychological barriers erected by society to exclude the disabled from participation.

Disability groups involved in consciousness raising present a more critical evaluation of statutory (and some large non-statutory) providers locked into a partnership relationship with the state. 'A major thrust of this criticism of organisations run by non-disabled people is that they operate within a framework which assumes that disabled people cannot take control of their own lives and therefore, require the "charitable" assistance of well-meaning professionals, voluntary workers or politician.'[67]

Of course there are other influences that have shaped both the development and the style of the disability movement: the rise of similar social movements addressing sexism and racism (and, in the United States, ageism). The disability movement also received a boost from the International Year of the Disabled, 1981.[68] Such developments helped to generate groups such as the British Council of Organisations of Disabled Persons and the Disabled Persons' Internationale. More overt political action by the disabled in the UK could be seen, for example, in protests at the passing of the Social Security Act 1986 (which made certain adjustments in relation to disabled persons' income entitlements). It seems clear that the tactic of conspicuous, direct-action campaigning is something that the disability movement will increasingly adopt in proportion to the increasing frustration felt with the potential of 'welfare enactments' and the traditional disabled persons' organizations' inability to deliver full citizenship.

It is tempting to draw parallels between the New Right philosophy of disintegration and the alleged culture of dependency, and the disability movement's desires for autonomy and integration. However, some commentators condemn such similarities as merely 'superficial'.[69] In fact it can be argued that the Thatcherite emphasis on the new partnership between the state and the voluntary sector has done little to serve the rights of the disabled. Glendinning argues that recent attempts to 'protect' the disabled within a redefined welfare state structure have been ineffective and increased the scrutiny and control exercised by professionals.[70]

INDIVIDUAL RIGHTS AND THE DISABLED – NEW DIRECTIONS

UK legal protection for the disabled has been based largely on a public administration model. The legislation referred to above is directed at focusing attention and improving procedures to provide services or disburse benefits to the disabled. It would be logical for the disability movement to seek a different public response. Legal measures such as the Chronically Sick and Disabled Persons Act 1970 and the Education Act 1981 now have a familiar tendency to expose resource issues as the key element in assessing their effectiveness. In the face of this overriding concern the individual disabled person has been largely powerless. Individual remedies of enforcement have been inaccessible and inadequate. However, several recent Private Member's Bills proposing anti-discrimination legislation in this field reflect a new direction attracting increasing support. Indeed, in 1990 a report of the House of Commons Select Employment Committee recommended that 'the government should explore urgently the possibility of equal opportunity legislation for the employment of people with disabilities and report to Parliament on its potential effects and costs in the labour market.'[71]

Alf Morris's recent Disabled Persons (Civil Rights) Bill 1992[72] epitomizes the more proactive approach consistent with the style of the disability movement and the view that legal measures presented as human rights issues are less vulnerable to dilution by policy-makers appealing to resource arguments. The Bill defined disability as '(a) a physical or mental impairment that substantially limits one or more of the major life activities of that person; or (b) a history of having had such an impairment; or (c) a reputation as a person who has or had such an impairment.' This definition appears to be similar to the definition of 'handicapped individual' in the American Rehabilitation Act 1973.

The Bill contained the familiar prohibition against direct and indirect discrimination,[73] but in the context of employment it contained a useful expansion of the meaning of 'discriminate',[74] which would have included, *inter alia*, 'failing to make reasonable accommodation for the known physical or mental limitations of a qualified person with a disability who is an applicant for employment or an employee, unless the employer can demonstrate that the accommodation would unduly prejudice the operation of the employer's business'.[75] A 'qualified person with a disability' in the employment context was defined to mean 'a person with a disability who, with or without any reasonable accommodation, can perform the essential functions of the employment position that he holds or desires.'[76] Further, 'make reasonable accommodation' would include

(a) making existing facilities used by employees readily accessible to and usable by persons with disabilities; and
(b) job restructuring, instituting part-time or modified work schedules, reassignment to a vacant position, acquisition or modifications of equipment or devices, appropriate adjustment or modification of examinations, training materials or policies, provision of qualified readers or interpreters, and making any other similar accommodation for a person with a disability.[77]

The Bill contained further guidance, again based upon the American model, of factors which ought to be considered in determining whether the employer would be unduly prejudiced by making an 'accommodation' for the needs of disabled persons. They included the 'overall financial resources of the employer, the overall size of the business of the employer including the number of employees, and the number, type and location of its workplaces, and the availability of public funds to defray expenses.'[78] Part III of the Bill provided for prohibition of discrimination in relation to the provision of goods, facilities and services. However, the prohibition would not apply 'where compliance with it . . . would be impracticable or unsafe and could not be made practicable and safe by reasonable modification to rules, policies or practices, removal of architectural, communication or transport barriers or provision of auxiliary aids or services.'[79] In determining the reasonableness of any such modifications, regard would be had to whether the actions could be undertaken 'without undue hardship'.[80] Codes of Practices (to be issued by a new 'Disability Commission') would have given guidance on what was permitted or prohibited in the employment and goods, facilities and services sectors.[81] Regulation-making powers were conferred on the Secretary of State to make exemptions to the Bill's provisions for a period up to five years from the coming into force of the Bill.[82] Curiously, the enforcement provision[83] would have only conferred a right of action in the County Court (in England and Wales and Northern Ireland). The more obvious arrangement would have been to allocate employment discrimination cases to the Industrial Tribunals and part III discrimination cases to the courts.[84] The Disability Commission would have contained up to 15 Commissioners, appointed by the Secretary of State, three-quarters of whom would have to have been disabled (or appointed as a representative of a disabled person under the Disabled Persons (Services, Consultation and Representation) Act 1986). Their duties and mode of investigation are outlined in the Schedule to the Bill and are based on the models provided by the EOC and CRE under sex and race discrimination legislation. However, it is of note that Bynoe et al.,[85] in making out a case for anti-discrimination law for the disabled, are of the view that there may be a need for a new institution to deal with refusal of access; consequently they propose the establishment of a specialized Architectural and Transportation Access Tribunal.[86] The Bill reached a Second Reading but was then talked out. There have been many similar Private Member's Bills over the past decade.[87] However, the 1992 Bill, which was quickly followed by the introduction of a similar measure in the House of Lords,[88] is a much more detailed and professional piece of legislative drafting and undoubtedly benefits from the incorporation of legal concepts taken from the American legislation.

Clearly, the relevant legislation in the United States is likely to have a particularly compelling influence on UK discrimination law. In 1990, Congress passed the Americans with Disabilities Act,[89] making detailed provision for individual rights in employment, public services, private sector services, transport and housing. The Act builds on the success of the Rehabilitation Act 1973, which prohibits discrimination by federally funded schemes against 'otherwise qualified handicapped persons'.[90] The case law under this legislation (and numerous state laws that have followed and expanded the federal provisions) has been much more an engine of development than in the UK. For example, *South Eastern Community College* v. *Davis*[91] concerned a deaf student seeking a place on a nurses' training programme. On the facts of the case it was decided that the student's disability was so severe that it constituted an 'insurmountable barrier' which was not reasonable for the college to remove. The principle was established that if accommodation to a particular type of disability imposed undue financial and administrative burdens or required 'fundamental alteration in the nature of the program' then it would not be necessary to 'accommodate' such disability. Obviously, this somewhat begs the question of the precise extent of the financial burden required before the principle of accommodation can be safely ignored, but, as the court stated, 'We do not suggest that the line between a lawful refusal to extend affirmative action and illegal discrimination against handicapped persons always will be clear.'[92] At least in such litigation these issues are directly addressed.

Case law under the Rehabilitation Act 1973 has also produced significant success regarding transportation systems. 'As a result of individual suits in the US the Washington metro system has been overhauled: lift buttons are marked with raised printing and braille; lights on platforms warn deaf people of approaching trains and discounted fares help those who need a travelling companion.'[93] However, the 1990 Act also reaches into the private sector. It comes into force in 1992 and follows many of the principles regarding discrimination in housing and property in the Fair Housing (Amendments) Act 1988.[94] As with section 504 of the Rehabilitation Act 1973, employers must make 'reasonable accommodation' of the needs of the disabled employee. The 1990 Act gives assistance as to what this might mean.[95] As well as the familiar concepts of direct and indirect discrimination, an employer[96] will discriminate if she or he fails to make reasonable accommodation unless the employer can show that 'the accommodation would impose an undue hardship on the operation of the business'[97] or would cause a 'direct threat' to other employees or a health risk to the public. The Attorney-General is given a key role in the implementation of the Act. Obviously it is too early to come to a definitive view as to its success.[98]

The arguments against such laws in the UK are usually based on objections to the potential cost or on the perceived failures of sex and race discrimination law. The disability movement rebuts both objections. The first is highly debatable if one takes into account the benefits of assisting disabled persons to independent living and working. The second often misses a primary positive point in favour of such laws: they have (literally) incalculable effects on the community in terms of the formulation of attitudes towards the disabled.

Perhaps a more immediate source of development in the UK of laws capable of enhancing the status of the disabled citizen would be the European Community. As with many other social policy areas there have been 'soft law' initiatives, such as 'social action programmes' in relation to the disabled, and a Recommendation was agreed in 1986.[99] However, it is likely that the European Community Charter of Fundamental Social Rights for Workers[100] will provide the most fruitful material from which to develop disabled persons' rights. In February 1991 a Draft Directive was issued.[101] This would facilitate safe travel of workers with reduced mobility to gain access to employment. The Draft Directive was made under article 118a, which relates to the protection of the health and safety of workers. This has the advantage that only a 'qualified majority' will be required to ensure its passage. However, the development of an EC jurisprudence on disabled rights will be hampered by the need for unanimous agreement in relation to other articles in the Treaty.

The strong twin influences from the United States and the European Community would suggest the likelihood of some extension of the human rights model of discrimination law to disabled persons. A unique dimension of such discrimination is what has been referred to as 'unequal burdens' discrimination,[102] by which is meant the failure of, for example, employers to 'accommodate' disabled workers by modifying premises, methods of working and so on. The American legislation attempts to deal with this (as does the model suggested in the recent UK Private Member's Bill). At the very least, it is time for more powerful legal measures to attempt to strike a sensible balance between a duty to 'accommodate' the needs of the disabled and the reasonable needs of employers and others in order to enable the disabled citizen to achieve the fullest possible participation and integration in society. Disability, it must be remembered, is also a status which can be acquired and lost during a lifetime. The claims from disabled persons to have a proper place in the range of citizenship rights have been neglected for too long.

NOTES AND REFERENCES

1 See Hudson, R., 'Do people with mental handicap have rights?' (1988), 3(3), *Disability, Handicap and Society*, pp. 227–37.

2 Turner, B., *Citizenship and Capitalism*, Allen & Unwin, 1986, at p. 134.

3 See, e.g., Stone, D. A., *The Disabled State*, Macmillan, 1984.

4 Marshall, T. H., 'Citizenship and social class', in Marshall, T. H. (ed.), *Sociology at the Crossroads and Other Essays*, Heinemann, 1963.

5 Walmsley, J., 'Talking to top people: some issues relating to the citizenship of people with learning difficulties', (1991), 6(3), *Disability, Handicap and Society*, pp. 219–31 at p. 222.

6 See, generally, Oliver, M., *The Politics of Disablement*, Macmillan, 1990.

7 Finch, J., 'Community care: developing non-sexist alternatives', (1984), 9(4), *Critical Social Policy*, pp. 6–18.

8 See Lister, R., *The Exclusive Society: Citizenship and the Poor*, CPAG, 1990, at p. 68, where she states that 'Poverty spells exclusion from the full rights of citizenship in each of these spheres and undermines people's ability to fulfil the private and public obligations of citizenship. For people with disabilities this exclusion is often compounded.'

9 Harris, A., *Handicapped and Impaired in Great Britain*, HMSO, 1971. See also Buckle, J., *Work and Housing of Impaired Persons in Great Britain*, HMSO, 1971.

10 Wood, P., *International Classifications of Impairments, Disabilities and Handicaps*, WHO, Geneva, 1981.

11 *Ibid.*

12 As explained in the government's White Paper, *The Way Ahead: Benefits for the Disabled*, Cm 917, 1990, para. 2.2.

13 Martin, J., Meltzer, H and Elliot, D., *The Prevalence of Disability amongst Adults*, London, HMSO, 1988. See also Martin, J. and White, A., *OPCS Surveys of Disability in Great Britain: The Financial Circumstances of Disabled Adults Living in Private Households*, HMSO, 1988.

14 The overall severity score was devised from combining scores from thirteen different broad types of disability: locomotion, reaching/stretching, dexterity, seeing, hearing, personal care, continence, communication, behaviour, intellectual functioning, consciousness (e.g. liability to fits), eating/drinking/digestion, disfigurement/deformity.

15 A brief synopsis of the main findings of these reports can be found in Buck, T. G., (1990) *Industrial Law Journal*, 125–32.

16 Social Security Act 1975, s. 7(1)(a)(ii).

17 It should of course be noted that these two benefits are going through the first stage of a 'merger' by means of the new structure of disability benefits contained in the Disability Living Allowance and Disability Working Allowance Act 1991, which will come fully into force toward the end of 1992.

18 See Stone, D. A., *The Disabled State*, Macmillan, 1984, for a stimulating account of the 'gatekeeping' role of the medical profession in this area.

19 For a highly readable and stimulating account of the passage of the 1970 Act, see Topliss, E. and Gould, B., *Charter for the Disabled*, Blackwell, 1981.

20 'Persons who are blind, deaf or dumb, or who suffer from mental disorder of any description and other persons who are substantially and permanently handicapped by illness, injury or congenital deformity or such other disabilities as may be prescribed by the minister' (National Assistance Act 1948, s. 29).

21 Disabled Persons (Employment) Act 1944, s. 1: 'a person who, on account of injury, disease, or congenital deformity, is substantially handicapped in obtaining or keeping employment, or in undertaking work on his own account, of a kind which apart from that injury, disease or deformity would be suited to his age, experience and qualifications.'

22 Chronically Sick and Disabled Persons Act 1970, s. 8. No regulations have ever been made under this section.

23 E.g. Topliss, E. and Gould, B., *Charter for the Disabled*, Blackwell, 1981.

24 It should be noted that these services were usefully particularized: e.g. aids and adaptations, telephone, etc.

25 DHSS Circulars 12/70 (August 1970); 45/71 (September 1971).

26 Report by Department of Social Administration, Birmingham University, 1976.

27 E.g. Topliss, E. and Gould, B., *Charter for the Disabled*, Blackwell, 1981, conclude that 'the registration of disabled persons under the Act has contributed little to the welfare of the disabled.'

28 E.g. Warren, M. D., Knight, R. and Warren, J., 'Changing capabilities and needs of people with handicaps', Health Services Research Unit Report No 39, University of Kent, Canterbury, 1979.

29 *Report of the Royal Commission on the Blind, the Deaf and Dumb of the UK*, (1889), C.5781. 'It is in the interests of the state to educate them, so as to dry up as far as possible the minor streams which ultimately swell the great torrent of

pauperism.' The report continues: 'the blind, deaf and dumb, and the educable class of imbeciles form a distinct group, which, if left uneducated become not only a burden to themselves, but a weighty burden to the state' (vol. xix).

30 *Report of the Departmental Committee on Defective and Epileptic Children*, (1898), C.8746 (vol. xxvi).

31 The distinction was not dropped until the passing of the Education (Handicapped Children) Act 1970.

32 Blind Persons Act 1920. This Act also made old age pensions available to blind persons aged fifty and above (s. 1), and gave local authorities powers to 'promote the welfare' of the blind (s. 2).

33 There has been a steady decline in registration since the peak year of 1950.

34 There have only been ten prosecutions ever under the Act, and these resulted in seven fines, averaging £62, the last in 1975: see evidence of Mencap to the House of Commons Select Committee on Employment, First Report, *Disability and Employment*, 1990–1, HCP 35, (9 December 1990).

35 DE, *The Quota Scheme for Disabled People*, Consultation Paper, 1973.

36 The only occupations so prescribed by order have been car park and lift attendants; see section 12(1) and the Disabled Persons (Designated Employments) Order 1946, SR & O 1946/1257.

37 *Social Insurance and Allied Services*, Cmd 6404 (1942).

38 Entitlement depends on the claimant establishing that he or she needs attention with regard to his or her bodily functions or supervision because of the risk of harm to the claimant or to others.

39 Entitlement is shown by establishing an inability or virtual inability to walk.

40 See Luckhaus, L. (1986) *Journal of Social Welfare Law*, pp. 153–69.

41 Disabled Living Allowance and the Disabled Working Allowance Act 1991. See Wikeley, N. (1992) *Legal Action*, pp. 16–18 (Jan.), 16–18 (Feb.), 16–19 (March) for an account of these benefits and the adjudication procedures.

42 SSAC, *Benefits for the Disabled People: A Strategy for Change*, HMSO, 1988.

43 See *The Way Ahead: Benefits for the Disabled*, Cm 917, 1990, which acknowledges these developments. Para. 8.2 states that 'Perhaps the most dramatic evidence of the determination of a significant number of people with severe disabilities to take control of their own lives is to be found in the independent living movement.'

44 *Ibid.*, paras 3.11, 3.12 where their proposals for the reform of the disability benefit structure are discussed in this White Paper.

45 See Topliss, E., *Provision for the Disabled* (2nd edn), 1979.

46 See Carson, D. (1986) *Journal of Social Welfare Law*, pp. 362–7.

47 Griffiths, A., Grimes, R. and Roberts, G., *The Law and Elderly People*, Routledge, 1990, p. 124.

48 See note 20.

49 At the time of writing, s. 4 (except para. (b)), s. 8(1), ss. 9–13, ss. 16–18.

50 Children Act 1989, schedule 2, para. 2, for example, requires local authorities to keep a register of children with disabilities. See also Department of Health, *The Children Act 1989 Guidance and Regulations*, (vol. 6) 'Children with disabilities', HMSO, 1991.

51 This phrase has been substituted by the phrase 'appropriate provision', by the

Disabled Persons Act 1981, s. 6(1)(2), but at the time of writing no commencement order has been made bringing this into effect. The new provision will define 'appropriate provision' as equivalent to that contained in the Code of Practice on Access for the Disabled to Buildings contained in British Standards Institution code of practice, 5810: 1979. But note that the Secretary of State will have the power to prescribe different bodies and different procedures for different classes of building/premises with the effect that these will be exempt from the duty on the ground that it is not reasonable or practicable to comply.

52 Inserted by the Chronically Sick and Disabled Persons (Amendment) Act 1976, s. 2.

53 SI 1985/1065, as amended by the Buildings (Disabled People) Regulations 1987, SI 1987/1445.

54 See SI 1985/1065, as amended, schedule 1, part N – disabled people.

55 No regulations have yet been made under section 6.

56 See SI 1985/1065, schedule 2, paras 1(4)&(5).

57 See *The Way Ahead: Benefits for the Disabled*, Cm 917, 1990, para. 8.39.

58 See, however, ICOM, *Museums without Barriers*, Fondation de France, 1991, for developments in France relating to disabled access to the arts.

59 See, e.g., Gould, B. and Topliss, E., *Charter for the Disabled*, Chapter 10, Basil Blackwell and Martin Robertson, 1981.

60 Warnock Report 1978.

61 See Tomlinson, S., *A Sociology of Special Education*, Routledge & Kegan Paul, 1981, which, *inter alia*, outlines the various categories of disabled child, including those defined as 'delicate', 'feeble', and 'disruptive'.

62 See Milman, D., 'The Education Act 1981 in the courts' (1987), *Journal of Social Welfare Law*, pp. 208–15. He concludes that 'parents of children with special educational needs can have obtained little comfort from recent developments of the courts in this area. This must be especially galling when one considers that the Education Act 1981 was regarded as a parents' charter. The prospects of a parent successfully challenging the educational provision offered by an LEA are bleak' (pp. 214–5).

63 Oliver, M., *The Politics of Disablement*, Macmillan, 1990, at p. 113.

64 Oliver defines an organization *of* the disabled as one where at least 50 per cent of the management committee or controlling body are themselves disabled. *Ibid.*, p. 113.

65 *Ibid.*, p. 117.

66 Oliver, M., 'The social model of disability: current reflections', *Social Work and Social Welfare Yearbook*, 1988, pp. 190–203.

67 Oliver, M., *The Politics of Disablement*, Macmillan, 1990, p. 115.

68 It should be noted that this was originally labelled as the International Year for the Disabled!

69 Glendinning, C., 'Losing ground: social policy and disabled persons in Great Britain 1980–1990' (1991), 6(1), *Disability, Handicap and Society*, pp. 3–19.

70 *Ibid.*, p. 16.

71 First Report, *Disability and Employment*, 1990, HCP 35, para. 35, para. 23. p. ix.

72 Bill 24: First Reading, 12 December 1991; Second Reading, 31 January 1992.

73 Clause 1(2).

74 Clause 3(2).

75 Clause 3(2)(e).

76 Clause 1(1).

77 See the almost identical wording of the American Disabilities Act 1990, s. 101(9)(A)&(B).

78 Clause 3(5).

79 Clause 6(3).

80 Clause 7.

81 Clauses 5 and 8.

82 Clause 9.

83 Clause 10.

84 This is also suggested by Bynoe, I., Oliver, M. and Barnes, C., *Equal Rights for Disabled People: The Case for a New Law*, Institute for Public Policy Research, London, 1991, p. 69.

85 Bynoe, I., Oliver, M. and Barnes, C., *Equal Rights for Disabled People: The Case for a New Law*, Institute for Public Policy Research, London, 1991.

86 *Ibid.*, p. 69.

87 E.g. Jack Ashley MP, the Disablement (Prohibition of Unjustifiable Discrimination) Bill 1982.

88 See Civil Rights (Disabled Persons) (No. 2) Bill, 1992, [HL]: First Reading 2 February 1992; Second Reading 21 February 1992, proposed by Baroness Lockwood.

89 104 Stat. 27, Pub. L. No. 101–336.

90 'No otherwise qualified handicapped individual in the United States, as defined in section 706(6), shall solely by reason of his handicap, be excluded from the participation in, be denied any benefit of, or be subjected to discrimination under any programme or activity receiving federal financial assistance' (section 504).

91 442 US, 397 (1979) US Sup. Ct. Rep. 60 L. Ed. 2d, p. 980.

92 442 US, 397, p. 412.

93 Coote, A. and Bynoe, I., 'Equal to the law', *The Guardian*, 21 September 1991.

94 102 Stat. 1619 (1988) Pub. L. No. 100–430. This statute remains in force alongside the provisions of the 1990 Act.

95 s. 101(9)A & B: making existing facilities used by employees readily accessible to and usable by individuals with disabilities; and job restructuring, part-time or modified work schedules, re-assignment to a vacant position, acquisition or modification of equipment or devices, appropriate adjustment or modifications of examinations, training materials or policies, the provision of qualified readers and interpreters, and other similar accommodations for individuals with disabilities.

96 Those with 25 or more from 1992 and 15 or more from 1994.

97 s. 102(b)(5)(A).

98 'So long as the necessary resources are available in public and private sectors to afford changes needed without "undue financial burdens" the legislation promises to help individuals with disabilities enter the mainstream of US life.' See Bynoe, I., Oliver, M. and Barnes, C., *Equal Rights for Disabled People: The Case for a New Law*, Institute for Public Policy Research, London, 1991, p. 37.

99 See EC Commission Recommendation 86/379/EEC, OJ No. L225/43.

100 Commission of the EC, Brussels, May 1990. At Point 26, Title 1 the Charter states, 'All disabled persons whatever the origin and nature of their disablement must be entitled to additional concrete measures aimed at improving their social and professional integration.'
101 Com(90) 588 Final-SYN 327, Brussels, 28 February 1991.
102 See Bynoe, I., Oliver, M. and Barnes, C., *Equal Rights for Disabled People: The Case for a New Law*, Institute for Public Policy Research, London, 1991.

10

Personal Liberty

ANDREW ASHWORTH

The focus of this chapter is upon the extent to which the criminal law imposes prohibitions on the use of physical force against or by citizens. First, however, it is necessary to consider the notion of 'personal liberty' adopted here, and the way in which it relates to rights of citizenship.

DEFINING PERSONAL LIBERTY

Most issues concerning the ambit of the law can be reduced to a question of liberty: to what extent should the law, through its various criminal, civil and regulatory provisions, seek to restrict the freedom to do as one wants? The idea of personal liberty is therefore wide enough to embrace a range of political rights, such as freedom of expression and freedom of association.[1] However, the present discussion is confined to forms of personal liberty which may be regarded as more fundamental than, and practically anterior to, those wider rights. Thus the primary concern is with the physical integrity of individual citizens. This includes the citizen's freedom of movement, not in the largest sense but in the form of a right not to be subjected to detention, which may be seen as a minimal requirement of personal liberty.

Three components of this concept of personal liberty may be distinguished. First, a right to physical integrity might be interpreted as a right to be free from the use of force and from detention. This is what has been termed a 'negative liberty', since its content depends on the duties of other citizens not to engage in conduct that violates the physical integrity of others. Personal liberty in this sense arises from the negative duties of other citizens.[2] We shall see that in English law they are subject to several exceptions, the justifications for which must be scrutinized. Second, a right to physical integrity should also include a right to use force in certain circumstances – a positive liberty, which may be exercised in limited circumstances as a means of preserving physical integrity. Third, a right to physical integrity might find expression in certain 'claim rights' or 'rights of positive content',[3] in the form of rights to receive protection or assistance from others. Relatively little is heard of these, but it will be argued that they are important to a proper concept of citizenship.

PERSONAL LIBERTY, RIGHTS AND CITIZENSHIP

Probably the most basic of the three types of 'right' just described is the first, the freedom from violence. Hart has argued that the legal rules which prohibit violence form part of the 'minimum content of natural law', fundamental to any legal order because of the physical make-up of human beings:

> The most important [rules] for social life are those that
> restrict the use of violence in killing or inflicting bodily harm.
> The basic character of such rules may be brought out in a
> question: if there were not these rules, what point could
> there be for beings such as ourselves in having rules of any
> other kind? The force of this rhetorical question rests on the
> fact that men are both occasionally prone to, and normally
> vulnerable to, bodily attack.[4]

The need to secure personal liberty in the sense of freedom from violence stems from our vulnerability: it might be otherwise if we had carapaces. It also stems from the truism that our continued existence is a precondition of the exercise of any other rights, which is surely sufficient to install the right to life as the most basic right. The term 'freedom from violence' is somewhat broad and unspecific: at one level, injuries and serious injuries can have such devastating physical and psychological effects as to prevent the citizen from participating fully in social life, whereas some minor assaults may be far less significant. This is hardly the place to attempt a distinction between the degrees of physical harm, but it can surely be accepted that freedom from injury ranks as a basic liberty in modern society. Feinberg, for example, argues that life and physical security are clearly within his most fundamental category of 'welfare interests', since they are the interests which need to be satisfied in order to have any significant capacity to choose or order one's way of living.[5] Von Hirsch and Jareborg go further by attempting to develop a framework for assessing the degree to which violations affect the living standards of citizens.[6] Loss of life clearly goes into the fundamental category of 'subsistence', but injuries would presumably be distributed between that category and the next one, 'minimal well-being', according to their seriousness.

One reason for developing this abstract argument is that English domestic law, without a written constitution, provides no explicit guarantee of personal liberty, let alone any recognition of the fundamental nature of the right to life. The European Convention on Human Rights does include such a declaration. Article 2 declares the right to life and then goes on to enumerate various exceptions. It reads as follows:

1 Everyone's right to life shall be protected by law . . .
2 Deprivation of life shall not be regarded as inflicted in contravention of this Article when it results from the use of force which is no more than absolutely necessary:
    (a) in defence of any person from unlawful violence;
    (b) in order to effect a lawful arrest or to prevent the escape of a person lawfully detained;
    (c) in action lawfully taken for the purpose of quelling a riot or insurrection.

Article 5(1) declares that 'everyone has the right to liberty and security of person', and among the exceptions which it then lists are 'the lawful detention of a person after conviction by a competent court' and 'the lawful arrest or detention of a person effected for the purpose of bringing him before the competent legal authority on reasonable suspicion of having committed an offence'.

The justifications for the exceptions are discussed below, but their very existence moves the analysis on to a different plane. There is a temptation to discuss personal liberty solely in terms of the rights of the private citizen, without reference to the social context in which he or she must live. Recluses aside, citizens need interpersonal contacts, relationships and mutual support, and the modern state may assist in promoting various collective goals which provide the conditions in which individuals can exercise their wider liberties and choices.[7] The preservation of good order through law enforcement is one of those collective goals. In order to achieve this, Kelsen argued, the state through its law must have a 'monopoly of force',[8] not only prohibiting the use of force by citizens but also reserving its use for criminal sanctions (by which he means not sentences involving physical chastisement but coercive sanctions, including custody). One would wish to add, as adumbrated by the European Convention, that there must also be clear limits to state powers if the liberty of the individual citizen is to be adequately protected. It is no less wrong for the citizen to be open to violations of personal liberty from law enforcement agents than for the citizen to be open to attack by fellow citizens.

It is a truism that the rights of citizenship concern the position of individuals in society. But this social dimension suggests that it is also necessary to consider possible duties of citizenship. Duties to abstain from violence and to pay taxes may require little argument, but it is open to discussion whether the right to life and the right to personal liberty can also be linked, in a social context, to duties to protect and assist others.

One final preliminary point is that a discussion of rights might tend to focus on the rhetoric of the law without reference to practical enforcement. In addition to all the other ambiguities inherent in references to rights, the question 'Do I have a right to x?' may be answered at a philosophical level, at the level of positive law and at the level of everyday availability and enforcement. The last answer is likely to be of greatest interest to the citizen.

FREEDOM FROM THE USE OF FORCE

Recognition of the Right

Statistically, citizens are far more likely to lose their life or to suffer injury through events defined as accidents than through events defined as crimes. But, as far as the criminal law is concerned, its focus has traditionally been upon offences against the person, running from murder to common assault, and the sexual offences.[9] Most of these penalize the intentional or reckless violation of another person's physical integrity. A fuller picture of the criminal law's approach would encompass the various motoring offences, including dangerous driving and causing death by dangerous driving,[10] and the various 'safety' offences, including safety in workplaces, in sports grounds and in consumer goods.[11] However, the enforcement of these 'modern' offences is generally not as vigorous as the enforcement of the traditional offences. This is particularly so in relation to industrial safety, where enforcement is in the hands of the Health and Safety Executive and various other inspectorates. While there are undoubtedly pressures to negotiate with employers rather than to pursue an inflexible insistence which might lead to the closure of a plant or site and consequent redundancies,[12] the system of regulation should in theory enable inspectors to spot potential hazards and thereby avoid deaths and injuries, upholding personal liberty in a far more direct way than can be expected of the police. In practice, however, the restrictive funding of regulatory agencies (compared with the police) and the pressures to negotiate reduce the protection for the citizen.

Let us suppose, then, that we have a system of criminal law which penalizes the use of force and the creation of risks of injury, to the extent that it can be said to respect the citizen's freedom from physical violation. What exceptions is it fair to recognize? The European Convention shows that even the right to life can be subordinated to other interests in certain circumstances. A genuine commitment to the right to life, as the very foundation of citizenship, should mean that the exceptions are closely circumscribed and strongly related to social or public policies that cannot be achieved in any other way. The greater good of the greatest number should not be accepted as a reason for taking away life, nor even for inflicting injury or deprivation of liberty. This is not to overlook the practical possibility of conflicts between the right to life of one person and that of another, nor to retreat from the proposition that rights should be seen in their social context. But the more fundamental the right, the more attractive becomes Dworkin's view that a right should only be overridden, if at all, in a situation of 'vivid danger'.[13]

Arrest and Law Enforcement

One group of exceptions arises from the task of law enforcement, as articles 2(2)(b) and 5(1)(c) recognize. The Police and Criminal Evidence Act 1984 confers on the police powers to stop and search citizens reasonably suspected of carrying stolen or prohibited items (section 3), certain powers of arrest on reasonable suspicion (sections 24 and 25), and powers to detain suspects for up to 24 hours, or 36 hours for serious arrestable offences (sections 41 and 42).[14] These exceptions concern freedom from detention rather than the right to life. Some such powers must be accepted as part of a fair system of criminal justice since, in their absence, it would be difficult for the police to do the job that is expected of them.

On the other hand, a system which allowed the police unfettered powers to take people off the streets and from their homes for unlimited questioning would be unacceptable. The difference between that kind of system and the present English system (and article 5(1)(c) of the European Convention) lies in open-textured terms such as 'reasonable suspicion'. What if a citizen is taken by the police on a flimsy pretext and kept at a police station for some hours before being released? Personal liberty has been violated, but no crime has been committed.[15] An action in tort is possible,[16] although it has to be pursued by the citizen because there is no public authority charged with the task of policing the police. There is a statutory procedure for making complaints against the police,[17] but despite changes in the system it still commands less than complete confidence as an impartial guarantor of citizens' rights.[18]

Decisions of the Courts

A second group of exceptions concerns deprivations of liberty resulting from court decisions. The most obvious of these, recognized by
article 5(1)(a) of the European Convention, is where a sentence which
involves custody is imposed on an offender. However, such an exception should not be accepted without more. Any notion of the rights
of citizenship would surely be emasculated if it were conceded that a
court might impose any length of custodial sentence for any type of
offence. It is arguable that there should, in general, be some correspondence between the enormity of the offence, the decision to
imprison and the decision on the length of incarceration. A citizen
should not forfeit the right to liberty merely by committing a relatively minor offence. The arguments in favour of proportionality as
the primary determinant of sentencing, respecting the autonomy of
the individual citizen, have been set out elsewhere.[19] Most sentencing systems that adopt this approach do compromise it to some extent,
for example by making provision for longer sentences based on 'public
protection' from 'dangerous' offenders, and it is provisions of this kind
that raise most acutely the question of whether a citizen should have
a right not to be punished more than is proportionate to the offence
committed.[20]

The latest English legislation seeks to install proportionality as the
chief criterion in sentencing. Section 1(2)(a) of the Criminal Justice
Act 1991 provides that a custodial sentence should not be imposed
unless the offence is so serious that only custody can be justified, and
section 2(2)(a) adds that the length of sentence must be 'commensurate with the seriousness of the offence'. The Act makes limited provision for longer sentences for 'public protection' from certain violent
or sexual offenders, without some of the procedural safeguards which
ought to be provided when individuals are liable to be sentenced
beyond their desert.[21] However, most cases will turn on the proportionality requirement. Whether this means that there will be more or
fewer custodial sentences is hard to predict.[22] There has been much
emphasis in recent years upon the futility of imprisonment, and even
the Government's 1990 White Paper referred to it as 'an expensive way
of making bad people worse' in cases where it cannot be justified on
grounds of public protection.[23] The resort to deprivation of liberty
for young offenders has been spectacularly reduced in recent years: in
1980 some 7500 young offenders aged under 17 were sentenced to
custody, whereas in 1990 the number was only 1500. The Government has proclaimed a 'twin-track' policy, whereby fewer custodial
sentences should be imposed on those whose offences are not serious
but longer sentences should be imposed on those convicted of offences

involving sex, violence and drugs. It remains the case, of course, that the UK has one of the highest rates of custodial sentencing in Europe. Proportionality tends to be a culturally bound concept: what is thought proportionate in the UK might be thought draconian in some other European countries, and yet considered the height of leniency in the United States. Thus the practical content of any right not to be disproportionately deprived of one's liberty cannot be determined in any internationally objective way, save at the extremes.

Sentencing is not the only context in which a court can deprive a person of liberty. There is also the power to remand offenders in custody pending trial, recognized in article 5(1)(c) and 5(3) of the European Convention.[24] The ostensible thrust of the Bail Act 1976 is that all defendants have a right to bail, which a court is only justified in taking away if it has substantial grounds for believing that the defendant, if released on bail, would fail to return for the trial, commit an offence or interfere with witnesses. In practice, it is known that rates of custodial remand vary considerably from court to court, even taking account of the different offences charged; and that around one-half of those remanded to custody before trial at a magistrates' court are given a non-custodial sentence on conviction.[25] Of course the latter figure might be explained on the basis that the court in its sentence is taking account of the deprivation of liberty already suffered by the offender before trial. But no one knows in what proportion of cases this is true. The contrast with the restrictive provisions on custodial sentences, just considered, is obvious. This is not to suggest that there should be an absolute right to bail: clearly there may, at the very least, be justifications for protecting other potential victims from harm. The difficulty is that in practice the juxtaposition between the declared right and its exceptions seems to be imperfectly regulated, and subject to local policies. Moreover, once a defendant is remanded into custody, there is the question of waiting time before trial. Although the position is much worse in some other European countries, average waiting times in England and Wales have almost doubled, from one month to two, in the past decade. Over a quarter of those held in prison are awaiting trial. Should the 'right to liberty' proclaimed in article 5 of the European Convention be so diluted in practice by this exception?

Forfeiting Physical Security

Article 2(2)(a) of the European Convention provides that a person's right to life may be lost as a result of the use of no more force than is absolutely necessary to defend a person from unlawful violence. The European Convention does not appear to require that the force should be proportionate to the danger apprehended by that person: it might therefore 'justify every weak lad whose hair was about to be pulled by a stronger one, in shooting the bully if he could not otherwise prevent the assault'.[26] Nor does the European Convention provide expressly that the right of 'security of person', articulated in article 5, might be lost in a case of self-defence. It might, however, be inferred that, since the right to life might be lost in extreme circumstances, the right to physical security might be forfeited in less extreme circumstances.

English law obliquely recognizes a number of situations in which a person may, in effect, forfeit these basic rights. However, the idea that a citizen may lose the right to life without any fault on his or her part has been strenuously resisted by the criminal courts. In *Howe* (1987)[27] the House of Lords held that, if D is threatened with death unless he kills another, there should be no defence of duress if he succumbs to the threat and kills the other. Lord Hailsham held that he could not 'regard a law as either "just or humane" which withdraws the protection of the criminal law from the innocent victim and casts the cloak of its protection upon the coward and the poltroon in the name of a "concession to human frailty".' This seems to uphold the right to life of the innocent third party who is the intended victim of the duressed killing, on the basis that no citizen can ever be justified in taking another life in order to save his or her own. There are criticisms of this approach in the context of criminal law,[28] and it certainly fails to cater for situations in which a net saving of lives might be in prospect. After the capsize of the ferry *Herald of Free Enterprise* many passengers were trying to gain access to the upper deck by means of a rope ladder. On the ladder was a young man, petrified through fear and unable to move up or down. People were shouting at him, but he did not move. Eventually it was suggested that he should be pushed off the ladder, and this was done. He fell into the water and was never seen again, whereupon several passengers used the ladder to reach safety.[29] Was he justifiably deprived of his right to life? The situation did not come before a criminal court,[30] but it seems doubtful that a court would require several people to accept death 'heroically' rather than causing the death of one person who, through no fault of his own, was in effect denying to the others the opportunity to save their lives.

Cases involving fault are more clear-cut, in principle. A citizen who attacks or threatens to attack another thereby lays himself open to defensive force by the intended victim. The attacker forfeits some of the normal rights. However, this is not to suggest that an attacker should forfeit all rights: someone who does no more than kick another or spray him with water should not forfeit the right to life itself. The English common law recognizes this limitation with its requirement that the use of defensive force be both necessary and reasonable, even if the concept of reasonableness tends to be construed fairly liberally in favour of the intended victim of the initial attack.[31] Other situations in which a citizen may lose some of the normal protection are where he or she is evading apprehension by the police, or is in the process of committing crime. The issues of self-defence and the prevention of crime are discussed further in the next section.

FREEDOM TO USE FORCE

Although the main thrust of the criminal law is to take away the right to use force on others, reserving that to those who are enforcing the law, it is recognized that the state cannot protect its citizens in all situations at all times. The law should therefore provide for the right of self-defence, in circumstances where the individual is attacked or threatened with attack. We have seen that the European Convention recognizes the right of an individual to use such force as is absolutely necessary in self-defence. English law (rightly) stops short of this, allowing the citizen to use only such force as is both necessary and reasonable. However, the broad approach to the question of reasonableness[32] means that in practice there are relatively few restrictions. The 'defensive' action would have to be manifestly disproportionate – the example of shooting someone who threatens to pull one's hair has been given – before a court would convict a citizen whose involvement began only as the innocent victim of an attack.

The liberty to use force in self-defence includes a right of pre-emptive strike: the citizen does not have to wait until the first blow has been struck if an imminent attack is apprehended.[33] The same applies where force is sought to be justified in the prevention of crime, under section 3 of the Criminal Law Act 1967. Most situations may be analysed equally in terms of either self-defence or the prevention of crime, since the attack on the citizen constitutes a crime. In recent years there has been a number of well-publicized shootings by the police in mainland Britain and, whether it is sought to justify them in terms of preventing crime or defending the lives of potential victims, they raise further issues. On the one hand, police officers may be expected to be trained in the use of firearms and in response to stressful situations; the great indulgence shown to hapless citizens who are caught up in life-threatening situations may therefore have less place here.[34] On the other hand, the police would argue that they must shoot to kill in such situations: to try merely to disable is far more difficult, and would not remove the threat if the attacker had a firearm or bomb.[35]

Similar issues have been raised even more vividly as a result of shootings by the Royal Ulster Constabulary and by soldiers in Northern Ireland. Several shootings of people in situations that presented little actual danger led to claims that a 'shoot to kill' policy was being pursued by the security forces.[36] One soldier has been convicted of murder for shooting dead someone who had committed a minor assault,[37] but such other prosecutions as have been brought have failed. The acquittal of one soldier was challenged unsuccessfully by the Attorney-General in a case which went up to the House of Lords.[38] The tendency, in that decision and in others, has been for the courts to exploit the amplitude of the concept of 'reasonableness' and to rely on the established doctrine that the defendant must be judged on the facts as he or she believed them to be. There has been no movement towards applying higher standards to trained members of the security forces than to ordinary citizens, and the abnormal conditions in Northern Ireland would presumably be relied upon to support this. This, however, is a matter which requires careful examination.

The variety of possible situations, both concerning the police or army and for individual citizens, makes it tempting to say that it should always be a question of what was reasonable in the circumstances. The temptation should be resisted. A line must be drawn between defensive force and revenge, for example. Police officers and soldiers should be expected to follow certain procedures[39] and to have respect for the value of each individual life, no matter what the individual may have done in the past. Values such as proportionality of response and maximum certainty in the law should not be allowed to disappear into the maelstrom of 'reasonableness', for with them might disappear both some basic rights and some degree of accountability of public servants.[40]

A RIGHT TO PHYSICAL PROTECTION?

Both the European Convention and, to a considerable extent, English criminal law show respect for the right to life and the right to physical integrity. Generally speaking, using force on other people is not merely a civil wrong but a crime. There are exceptions, but in the main they also stem from a similar respect for life and physical integrity – the right of self-defence, and so on. Should this respect for basic values be taken further? Is there a strong argument for imposing a duty on citizens, in certain circumstances, to assist another citizen who is in danger of death or injury?

The European Convention is silent on this point. So, to a large extent, is English criminal law. The one relationship in which there is a clear duty is parent–child: section 1 of the Children and Young

Persons Act 1933 makes it a criminal offence for a parent to neglect or abandon a child in a manner likely to cause him or her unnecessary suffering or injury to health. This provision, together with the general common law duty of parent towards child, ensures that a parent who watched her or his child drowning in a shallow pool would be liable to conviction for murder for failing to rescue it. The child has a right to receive physical protection, as far as practicable, from his or her parent or guardian.

Apart from that, it remains largely true now, as in Stephen's day, that none of a group of adults who stand watching a young child drown in a shallow pool is liable to conviction in English law.[41] A few scattered duty situations have been recognized – where the defendant has caused a prior dangerous act; where the defendant has undertaken a contractual or other duty; where the defendant is the owner of property; and perhaps where the defendant is a member of the same household[42] – but English law's general approach is that the liberty to go about one's daily business should not be curtailed by the imposition of duties towards complete strangers. This sturdy individualism is not to be found in several other European countries, however. Typical of the provisions is article 63(2) of the French Code Pénal, which penalizes a person who voluntarily neglects to render, to a person in peril, assistance which could be given without personal risk or risk to others. Although many of the appellate decisions on this provision concern somewhat atypical situations,[43] it can be claimed that it has a significant symbolic effect in fostering a culture of citizenship duties. That is, it recognizes that citizenship concerns the relation of individuals to the society in which they live. Furthermore, building on the proposition that the right to life and (to a slightly lesser extent) the right to physical integrity are fundamental to social life, it recognizes that the strongest case in favour of a duty to do a positive act is likely to arise where there is a danger to the fundamental rights of another citizen.

It is no counter-argument to say that this would be to penalize an omission and English law leans against penalizing omissions. This is merely a restatement of the existing position. Nor is it a counter-argument to claim that such a law would require too much of citizens: such offences are rightly limited to what is reasonable in the circumstances, given the defendant's capabilities. As one French commentator put it, 'the law does not require heroism but does condemn indifference'.[44] If English law really does claim to respect the right to life and physical integrity, should it not do more than condone the indifference of the adults standing round the shallow pool?

CONCLUSION

Examination of the idea of rights of citizenship guaranteeing personal liberty brings to the surface several deep conflicts inherent in the regulation of human conduct by law. Some might dismiss the whole discussion as mere rhetoric, irrelevant to the realities of life for those with least power in society. A more persuasive conclusion would be that, vague and malleable as notions such as 'the rule of law' and 'rights of citizenship' might be, they are integral to any transformation of the law into a genuinely egalitarian force in an unequal society. Many other practical steps would also be desirable, in both the social sphere and the legal.

Even though this chapter has been limited to criminal law, and has therefore focused on the grosser invasions of physical integrity and of freedom from detention, difficulties have been apparent. The European Convention on Human Rights contains some strong affirmations, but requires refinement in certain respects. English law is more specific on some issues, and the provisions of the Criminal Justice Act 1991 on sentencing tend to suggest a somewhat greater respect for the value of freedom from detention than has been apparent in the past. On the other hand, the Act's provisions leave it to the courts to set the overall level of punitiveness, and when it comes to pre-trial detention the Bail Act 1976 is a fairly blunt instrument. If there was reliable evidence that high rates of custodial sentences or pre-trial detention were effective in protecting the public, it could be argued that they contributed to the greater liberty of the majority even though they deprived a minority of their liberty. The evidence, such as it is, is no more than equivocal.[45]

English law on self-defence and the associated liberties to use force relies too much on the concept of 'reasonableness', and the greater specificity embodied in the draft Criminal Law Bill proposed by the Law Commission is a welcome advance.[46] Progress must be made towards distinguishing situations of unexpected attack from those in which the citizen has time for consideration, and situations of sudden peril from those in which trained law enforcement officers are involved. It may be suggested that, even where the criminal law is concerned, citizenship is not simply a question of rights. In particular, the state is entitled to expect certain standards of behaviour from its officials. And it was argued above that, if respect for life is one of the most fundamental values, there is a case for imposing citizenship duties in the shape of a criminal offence of failing to assist a citizen in peril when this can be done without personal danger. This would be a symbolically important step towards a fuller concept of citizenship, more cooperative and less individualistic.

NOTES AND REFERENCES

1 For a more general survey, see K. D. Ewing and C. A. Gearty, *Freedom under Thatcher: Civil Liberties in Modern Britain* (1990)

2 For the concept of negative duties, see G. Williams, 'The concept of legal liberty', in R. S. Summers (ed.), *Essays in Legal Philosophy* (1968), p. 129; for discussion of negative liberty as a philosophical concept, see I. Berlin, 'Two concepts of liberty', in A. Quinton (ed.), *Political Philosophy* (1967), p. 141.

3 See Williams, *ibid.*, 129–31.

4 H. L. A. Hart, *The Concept of Law* (1961), p. 190; see also his essay 'Are there any natural rights?', in A. Quinton (ed.), *Political Philosophy* (1967), p. 53, which begins with the proposition that if there are any natural rights, the first one should be 'the right to forbearance on the part of all others from the use of coercion or restraint against him save to hinder coercion or restraint'.

5 J. Feinberg, *Harm to Others* (1984), pp. 37–8.

6 A. von Hirsch and N. Jareborg, 'Gauging criminal harm: a living standard analysis', (1991) 11 Oxford JLS 1.

7 See J. Raz, *The Morality of Freedom* (1987), pp. 206–7; N. Lacey, *State Punishment* (1988), pp. 172–81.

8 H. Kelsen, *The Pure Theory of Law* (1967), p. 36.

9 See, e.g., Offences Against the Person Act 1861, Homicide Act 1957, Sexual Offences Act 1956.

10 Road Traffic Act 1991.

11 E.g. Health and Safety at Work Act 1975, Safety of Sports Grounds Act 1975, Consumer Safety Act 1987.

12 Cf. B. Hutter, *The Reasonable Arm of the Law* (1988).

13 R. M. Dworkin, *Taking Rights Seriously* (1977), Chapter 1.

14 See further Ewing and Gearty, *op. cit.*, pp. 20–34.

15 There is a little-used crime of false imprisonment, which is similar to the tort: see Archbold, *Criminal Pleading, Evidence and Practice* (43rd edn 1991).

16 Article 5(5) of the European Convention requires 'an enforceable right to compensation' in such circumstances. For English law, see R. Clayton and H. Tomlinson, *Civil Actions against the Police* (1987).

17 Police and Criminal Evidence Act 1984.

18 See Ewing and Gearty, *op. cit.*, pp. 46–7.

19 E.g. A. von Hirsch, *Doing Justice* (1976), A. von Hirsch, *Past or Future Crimes* (1985), and much more briefly A. Ashworth, 'Criminal justice and deserved sentences', [1989] CLR 340.

20 See A. E. Bottoms and R. Brownsword, 'Dangerousness and rights', in J. Hinton (ed.), *Dangerousness: Problems of Assessment and Prediction* (1983).

21 For critical appraisal, see A. Ashworth, *Sentencing and Criminal Justice* (1992), Chapter 6.9.

22 For general discussion of the provisions and likely impact the 1991 Act, see Ashworth, *ibid.*, Chapters 4 and 9.

23 Home Office, *Crime, Justice and Protecting the Public*, Cm 965 (1990), para. 2.7.

24 These articles also provide, as does English law, for the detention of a person by

the police pending the first court hearing. For reasons of space this will not be pursued here.

25 For discussion and references, see Editorial [1987] CLR 437 and Letters [1993] CLR 324–7.

26 Royal Commission on the Law Relating to Indictable Offences, C. 2345 (1879), discussed in A. Ashworth, *Principles of Criminal Law* (1991), pp. 112–13.

27 [1987] 1 AC 417; see also the subsequent decision of the House of Lords in *Gotts* [1992] 1 All ER 832.

28 See Ashworth, *Principles of Criminal Law*, pp. 199–200.

29 See the discussion by J. C. Smith, *Justification and Excuse in the Criminal Law* (1989), pp. 73–9.

30 Cf. the well-known case of *Dudley and Stephens* (1884) 14 QBD 273, in which two men who killed and ate a cabin boy, after they had been adrift in an open boat for many days, were convicted of murder.

31 See *Palmer* v. *R.* [1971] AC 814, and Ashworth, *Principles of Criminal Law*, pp. 121–2.

32 See note 26.

33 See *Beckford* v. *R.* [1988] AC 130, p. 144.

34 See J. Horder, 'Cognition, emotion and criminal culpability', (1990) 106 LQR 469.

35 See the arguments of P. A. J. Waddington, 'Overkill or minimum force?', [1990] CLR 695.

36 For discussion, see Ewing and Gearty, *op. cit.*, pp. 230–5.

37 *Thain* [1985] 11 NILR 31.

38 *Attorney-General for Northern Ireland's Reference (No. 1 of 1975)* [1977] AC 105.

39 The 'yellow card' system which operated in Northern Ireland.

40 For fuller discussion of the issues in this section, see Ashworth, *Principles of Criminal Law*, pp. 110–22.

41 J. F. Stephen, *History of Criminal Law* (London, 1883), vol. III, p. 10.

42 For wider discussion, see A. Ashworth, 'The scope of criminal liability for omissions', (1989) 105 LQR 424, pp. 439–47.

43 For explanation and analysis, see A. Ashworth and E. Steiner, 'Criminal omissions and public duties: the French experience', (1990) 10 LS 153.

44 A. Vitu, in R. Merle and A. Vitu, *Traité de Droit Criminel: Droit Pénal Spécial* (1982), p. 1463.

45 For custodial sentences, see S. Brody and R. Tarling, *Taking Offenders out of Circulation*, Home Office Research Study No. 64 (1980); for remands in custody, see P. M. Morgan, *Offending While on Bail*, Home Office Research and Planning Unit Paper 65 (1992).

46 Law Commission Consultation Paper No. 122, *Legislating the Criminal Code: Offences Against the Person and General Principles* (1992), clause 28, following the earlier recommendations of the Law Commission, *A Criminal Code for England and Wales*, Law Com. No. 177 (1989), clause 44.

11

Towards Educational Rights

JULIAN LONBAY

INTRODUCTION

This chapter first attempts to examine the links between citizenship and education. It then examines this link in the French context. France is used in this analysis as the link was overtly recognized in law historically. The chapter then briefly assesses the impact of human rights law, and finally the growing role of the European Community in this area. Its growing role has re-animated the citizenship debate, though at its current stage of development the EC has very unstable political and economic institutions which are likely to be substantially altered and adjusted over the next decade.[1] It also has no discernible ethos. So apart from the legal (jurisdictional) impediments to action in the educational arena one can also imagine that the Community would, at this stage, have only a limited 'message' for transmission to its 'citizens' through the educational forum.

Citizenship and Education

Citizenship implies a relationship between the state and the individual, a two-way allegiance. In relation to education one assumes that the state provision of education might therefore be somehow linked to the citizenship status of the individual receiving it. This could be by means of access being granted only to citizens.

Another method of linking citizenship and education would be if the provision of education itself were designed subtly and/or overtly for the fostering of 'citizenship attributes' among the participants.[2] Drawing, in particular, on the formative French historical experience, this chapter looks at how educational rights became legalized and linked with the idea of *parens patriae* state powers to form citizens.

The creation of a common bond between citizens, or to be more vulgar what was called earlier in this century, in America, the problem of how to 'Americanize the mongrel hordes', has been recognized as a state right. This, in general, is expressed by compulsory education laws, though with explicit exceptions, normally to guarantee religious opinions and freedom of thought.

Having examined the expression of this state interest in the French context, the chapter then briefly assesses the limits imposed on the state's powers by international law in this domain and assesses what might amount to a European citizen's rights in education and the related problems of determination and definition, with reference to the emerging Community law in this area.

Access

A first essential difficulty lies in the fact that citizenship (in the national sense) implies exclusion of non-citizens. Moreover, the formation of citizens, whether overt or implicit in the education process,[3] is strongly culturally linked with national societies, not pan-European entities.[4]

Although the Western state has typically regulated, controlled or financed educational provision, there is commonly no legally overt link between access to education provided and citizenship. It is normally available to all within the jurisdiction.[5] National educational rights in England and Wales are not limited to citizens. In England the law provides statutory duties on the Secretary of State for education to promote the education of the people,[6] on local education authorities, *inter alia*, to ensure an efficient education system[7] (i.e. schools and other facilities[8]) and on parents[9] to ensure that a child receives a 'suitable education'. In circumstances where pupils and students were either of British nationality or had got through the strong British immigration rules,[10] it was hardly necessary to specifically link rights of access to education to citizenship. After all, the only persons having access to national education were those already within the realm, and therefore either citizens or there by the will of the sovereign.

In any event it could certainly be argued that the European Convention on Human Rights (ECHR)[11] and its First Protocol, which attributes rights to all within the jurisdiction of the contracting state parties, has already granted a right of access to educational resources for all individuals within the EC.[12]

Parens Patriae

There is little doubt that educational systems are imbued with the culture in which they are sited, and that this rubs off on those experiencing the education in both the formal and the 'hidden' curriculum. The creation and structure of the educational systems clearly have origins in religious endeavours of the churches and also more recently in the economic needs for a skilled workforce. The general policy interest of the state in an educated citizenry can be expressed in the phrase *parens patriae*.

This was forcefully expressed in France, which is used here as an illustration both of the recognition of the formative power of education, and of the legal crystallization of the link between citizenship and schooling. The following brief (and selective) synopsis of an important and influential period in French history looks at the 'battles' to control and channel education.

A French Excursus

In the religious wars that shook France during the late eighteenth to twentieth centuries the schools were a prime battlefield. The Government of Louis XIV on 13 December 1698 issued a royal edict proclaiming that all the children of heretics (aged over five years old) should be taken from their families, and be brought up in Catholic schools. As these schools did not yet exist, a taxing power was granted to pay for the teachers.[13] This episode indicates an awareness of the formative power of education, and the politico-religious uses to which it might be put. Such legislation was not unique to France.

The experience of the Huguenot schools (they were suppressed) had awakened a realization of the importance of schooling. During the seventeenth century many teaching orders sprang up. In 1611, Pierre de Berulle had founded the Oratorians. In 1612 he received Royal Letters, and in 1613 a Papal Bull of Confirmation. The Oratorians were essentially gallican and national. They introduced history into their curriculum, although they did not go as far as to use the vernacular.

Possibly the most important of the new societies was that founded by Jean-Baptiste de la Salle, canon of the cathedral church of Rheims, in 1684, l'Institut des Frères des Ecoles Chrétiennes, more commonly known as the Christian Brothers (*Ignorantins* being a nickname that was often used in contemporary France). De la Salle is considered the inventor of the 'simultaneous method' of teaching (class teaching), and he used French in teaching; in learning to read and write pupils used 'decent Christian texts'.[14] In 1724 the Christian Brothers received the Bull of Papal confirmation and approbation. By 1785 they were teaching approximately 30,000 pupils. Temporarily dispersed during the Revolution, when reconstituted they were practically left in charge of primary education.[15] In Paris the *maîtres-écrivains* were constantly trying to enforce their teacher-licensing powers granted by their Letters Patent.[16]

The eighteenth century was a century of enlightenment. The ideas of Locke and Comenius on the childishness of children and the importance of early childhood education had started seeping into public awareness, largely through Rousseau's book *Emile*.[17] As the century progressed an increasingly anti-clerical fervour, especially pronounced among the *philosophes*, was evident. In the 1760s many of the *parlements* started attacking and banning the Jesuits, the symbol of dogmatic and ultramontane Christianity. Rolland d'Erceville, President of the Paris *parlement*, presented a scheme for national education to the *parlement* in 1768. The banishing of the Jesuits in 1762[18] had left a large gap in educational provision, hence the spate of plans that appeared around this time.[19]

Although education was increasingly the subject of public debate, and a national or state involvement in education was more and more recognized as necessary, universal education was not generally recognized as a desirable goal. Locke, in many ways the forebear of modern educational thought, considered that, 'of all the men we meet with, nine parts of ten are what they are . . . by their education'.[20] None the less Locke did not believe that all should be educated. Most of the *philosophes*, including Voltaire, considered that state responsibility for education did not entail provision of equal education for everybody, as this would raise the expectations of the masses, who would become dissatisfied with their lot.[21] Even Rousseau wrote:

> Ceux qui sont destinés à vivre dans la simplicité champêtre n'ont pas besoin pour être heureux du développement de leurs facultés et leurs talents enfouis. . . . N'instruisez point l'enfant du villageois car il ne lui convient pas d'être instruit.[22]

One can agree with the conclusions of Chartier *et al*. that 'L'hostilité des élites administratives et politiques à une scolarisation massive de la paysannerie constitue un courant majeur qui traverse le XVIIe et le XVIIIe siècle'.[23]

Jean Debiesse estimated that 'primary education at the end of the eighteenth century was a luxury reserved for less than forty percent of the children in the country'.[24] Professor Gaudemet considered that 'le diffusion de l'enseignement élémentaire et sa qualité étaient d'ailleur très inégales dans la France de 1789'.[25] Secondary education, by contrast,

> étaient très également réparti sur toute la surface du territoire . . . [et était] sous l'ancien régime et sans qu'il coutât presque

rien au trésor, dans un état de prosperité ou il n'est parvenue de nos jours qu'au prix de longs efforts et de grands sacrifices.[26]

The French Revolution was a period rich in educational projects, laws and ideas.[27] Many of the ideas of the *lumières* were declared and legislated upon, but in practice little was actually accomplished. Matthew Arnold asked Guizot (who had been Minister of Education under the July monarchy) what he thought the French Revolution had contributed to popular education. He replied: Un déluge de mots, rien de plus.'[28] One could add that the Revolution had only destructive effects in the short term.

Après avoir jeté bas toutes les fondations de l'ancien régime, constituants, législateurs, et conventionnels entreprennent successivement d'éléver sur ses ruines un monument grandiose, et s'équisent en d'interminables et fastidieux efforts sans y parvenir.[29]

Many of the *Cahiers de Doléances* had included pleas for the establishment of an educational system, though not necessarily a state-run system. 'Quand on parcourt les cahiers presentés par les Etats Généraux, on est frappés de voir combien sont nombreuses les communautés qui demandent la création d'un plan d'éducation nationales.'[30] However, the first acts of the revolutionaries, in educational matters, were to destroy its financial basis.[31] 'La Révolution . . . ne voulut rien conserver du passé';[32] it swept the plate clean, and then was unable to refill it. All educational endowments were confiscated (decree of 8 March 1793). The grip of the Church on education was destroyed. Education was destroyed.

The Revolution legitimized and to some extent gave birth to the idea of state endeavour in the educational realm. Thus were spawned the seeds of future conflict, and the consequent evolution of French conceptions on *la liberté de l'enseignement*. The Declaration of the Rights of Man and of the Citizen, published on 26 August 1789, did not include the right to education in its provisions, although it might be considered an implicit requirement if all men were to help form the law, personally or through their representatives.

Title One of the Constitution of 1791, *alinéa* 11, declared:

Il sera créé et organisé une instruction publique commune à tous les citoyens, gratuite à l'égard des parties d'enseignement indispensables pour tous les hommes et dont les établissements seront distribuée graduellement, dans un rapport combiné avec la division du royaume.[33]

Clearly we have here an overt link of citizenship with education. Education was to help form an equality between citizens. Throughout the Revolutionary period, despite the chaos raging all around, committees of the various assemblies considered the question of public education.

The first report to appear was presented by Talleyrand, ex-bishop of Autun, to the Constituent Assembly on 10, 11 and 19 September 1791, just before it dissolved itself.[34] No action was taken on this report. The Committee of Public Instruction of the Legislative Assembly presented its report on 20–21 April 1792, through the Marquis of Condorcet. It recommended free universal education, but did not advocate a public monopoly of educational provision, because the competition of private schools would keep the state system on its toes, and would ensure the freedom of thought. The state's role in the proposed system would be limited to that of paymaster. Condorcet recognized that education of the people was necessary for a true democracy.

> Les hommes ne sont rassemblés en sociétés que pour obtenir
> la jouissance plus entière, plus paisible et plus assurée de leur
> droits naturels, et . . . on doit y, comprendre celui de veiller
> sur les premières années de ses enfants.[35]

War with Austria was declared as Condorcet was introducing the report. No action was taken by the Assembly on the report, and the king's veto on war legislation in June 1792, and the subsequent *chute du trône*, led to the dissolution of the Legislative Assembly and the creation of the Convention. The trial and execution of Louis XVI and the drafting of the new Constitution did not stop the Convention from decreeing on 12 December 1792 that 'Les écoles primaires formeront le premier degré d'instruction. On y enseignera les connaissances vigoureusement nécessaires à tous les citoyens.'[36] Again we see a strong 'educational' link between the state and its citizens being promulgated.

On 18 December Lathenas, a member of the Committee of Public Instruction, presented a plan that recommended obligatory primary schooling for four years, to be provided by the communes. The discussion got out of hand until Marat observed, 'Vous rassemblez à un général qui s'amuserait à planter, déplanter des arbres pour nourir de leur fruits des soldats qui mourraient de faim.'[37] His plan was reduced to one article, declaring the function of the primary schools, and their teacher's title, *instituteur*.

Two days later Romme presented a report recommending a two-tier system, which was criticized by Leclerk for not making education compulsory. Leclerk considered that all those who might refuse to send their children to state schools were either aristocrats or sacerdotal, and thus should be deprived of their rights. No action was taken on either of these two initiatives. The Girondin–Jacobin conflict was near to bursting into violence as the *Déclaration des droits*, a compromise document, was adopted in May 1793. Article 22 of the Declaration read: 'L'instruction est le besoin de tous. La société doit favoriser de tout son pouvoir les progrès de la raison publique, et mettre l'instruction à la portée de tous les citoyens.'[38]

On 30 May 1793 another decree declared free and obligatory instruction. In June the downfall of the Girondins left the Jacobins in power, and shortly thereafter a new Constitution was adopted, and endorsed by public referendum. 'Le principal mérite de la Constitution de 1793 ne réside pas dans ces possibilités d'application. Il tient surtout dans les principes qu'elles a proclamés pour la premier fois (les droits sociaux).'[39] Among these *droits sociaux* were guaranteed 'à tous les Français une instruction commune' (article 122). Yet again the link between state duties and the formation of citizens is expressly legalized.

A project for a national system of education drafted by Sieyes, Daunow and Lakanal was dismissed by the Jacobins, but a project found among the papers of the 'martyr' Louis-Michel Lepeletier, ex-Marquis de Saint-Fargeau (assassinated by a Royalist after voting for the execution of the King), was read to the Convention by Robespierre on 13 July. Albert Duruy considered that the project was 'un mauvais pastiche, un mélange de rudesse . . . prenez . . . ce travail et pressez-le tant que vous voudrez vous n'en ferez pas sortir une idée juste et raisonnable'.[40] This radical project radiated equality and suggested the creation of *maisons d'égalité*. Children belonged to the nation, not to parents, and thus all should be educated away from home, issued with the same clothes and made to eat the same food. Manual labour was to be a major part of the curriculum. The programme was criticized for the expense that it would entail, and after it was modified to allow for non-boarders, a decree was passed initiating the system of 13 August 1793. Of course, it was never implemented. This was the time of the Reign of Terror, civil war and foreign invasion. 'La période qui suit n'offre à l'histoire qu'une succession de projets incohérents, et de débats aussi pauvres de forme que de fond.'[41] Revolutionary fervour declared that schools were unnecessary. People should learn from real life, membership of political clubs, and national fetes. In fact decrees flew thick and fast, and none of them was ever implemented.[42]

During the Directory the opponents of the Revolution increasingly came into the open and found schools an ideal target for their wrath. On 13 December 1795 the constitutional bishops published rules to re-establish the discipline of the Gallican Church. The last chapter of the rules emphasized the importance of having a school in each parish. On November 17 1797 a law entitled Arrêté pour faire prospérer l'instruction publique' was passed, requiring attendance at a republican school as a prerequisite for unmarried persons who wished to have a job in the governmental administration. All those who were married had to prove that their children attended a republican school. Thus the Directory tried to control the growing numbers of private schools.

Laws were passed to reserve state buildings for use as schools and to allow local rates to be raised to help provide teachers with lodgings. On 5 February 1798, in order to ensure that proper republicanism was taught in the private schools, it decreed that all private schools should be inspected at least once a month (unannounced) by canton authorities. The Government by circulars tried very hard to implement the *arrêté* of 5 February 1798.[43] It wanted 'porter enfin le dernier coup à ces institutions monstreuses ou le royalisme et la superstition s'agitent encore'. But this had little effect in reducing the number of private schools. 'Ces mesures plus vexatoires qu'efficaces ne purent avoir raison d'un esprit religieux encore profond, qui faisait préférer les écoles privées.'[44]

Professor Barnard states that in April 1797 in the *département* of Doubs there were 336 private schools, and only 90 state schools.[45] The Government attacked the freedom of education in the name of the republican state. But the Constitution allowed the *liberté de l'enseignement* (article 300). The Constitution of 25 December 1799, instituting the Consulateship, had no declaration of rights preceding it, and made no mention of *instruction publique*.

On 9 November 1800 the Minister of the Interior, Chaptal, presented a report on education. He strongly deplored the lack of educational facilities and recommended that there should be at least one *école municipale* per commune, financed by the state. The teachers should be chosen by the parents, and their salaries paid half by the commune and half by the *arrondissement*. He further recommended that an *école communale* be set up in every *arrondissement* for secondary education provision. Independent schools should be allowed with minimal state interference, but should take an 'oath of fidelity' and be run by French citizens. This liberal report was not implemented by Napoleon.

Conclusions

The formative powers of education and education as a fundamental human right were both explicitly recognized during the French

Revolutionary period, and were given legal (if ineffective) form. Overt links were made between citizenship and teaching and education. Imparting education was in the state's interest, indeed duty, for the common good (*parens patriae*). Other Western states have similar, if less dramatic, historical experiences. Battles over the control of education of citizens are a familiar and common theme. Indeed, all the member states of the EC now enforce a period of compulsory education on those living within their jurisdictions.

In the United States compulsion to attend school has been accepted,[46] along with the *parens patriae* rationale of state interest.[47] An attempt by Texas to charge fees for the education of children of illegal aliens was struck down in *Doe* v. *Plyler*.[48] The Supreme Court argued that education was such a fundamental interest to the individuals concerned that if the law was enforced it would impose lifetime hardship, illiteracy and stigma and deny those children the ability 'to live within the structure of our civic institutions'. The USA, of course, had an ethos and well-established political and social institutions, the ideas of which it wished to instil among its citizens.

The possible contents of the right to education are now examined in a brief survey of international human rights law. The chapter then evaluates potential rights from an EC perspective.

THE CONTENT OF EDUCATIONAL RIGHTS

Traditionally education has been reserved by states as a matter falling within their 'domestic jurisdiction', and it is often the subject of delicate internal political compromises[49] or policies.[50] Western states have strongly resisted twentieth-century attempts by international organizations to intervene in this area of their jurisdiction.[51]

International Human Rights Law

At the international level, human rights treaties have recognized the role of the state in regulating the right to education in order to 'ensure such minimum educational standards as may be laid down or approved by the State'.[52]

Freedom of education

The right to education is made subject to parental rights to choose non-state schooling and to ensure religious and moral education of their children in conformity with their own convictions, thus forming a limitation on state authority in this field. Both international and European human rights law recognize that individuals have a right to establish independent educational institutions.

Recipients' rights
At the European level, article 2 of the First Protocol (article 2P) to the European Convention on Human Rights outlines the rights of children and parents in relation to the provision of education.[53]

Determination of the Content of the education itself
The *Kjeldsen* case[54] (1976) made it clear that the state had primary responsibility for the educational programme[55], subject to conveying controversial topics 'in an objective critical and pluralistic manner' and respecting the rights of the parents as regards religious and philo-sophical convictions, and the rights of children. The *Campbell and Cosans* case emphasized the rights of the child to receive education, Cosans being granted £3000 in damages for having missed part of his education.[56] We have seen that states have used schooling to 'socialize' their citizens. Does human rights law specify any particular knowledge that should be taught?

There must be a core of education provided to allow socialization of the child to take place. The European Court of Human Rights is well placed to survey and to determine the content of this basic core of knowledge.[57]

In the *Belgian Linguistic* cases, M. Petren in the Commission Report considered that a core would include 'an elementary educa-tion'.[58] In *Kjeldsen* the interest of the child in receiving an accurate knowledge concerning sexual matters was recognized. This amounts to the reverse side of the state's right to ensure a minimum necessary education. Parental objections could not disallow the child from receiving the knowledge that the state, supported by the European Court of Human Rights, thought necessary.

The content of this 'core of knowledge' could also be determined by reference to the recipient of education. In the *Campbell and Cosans* case the court gave a very wide definition of education:

> It is the whole process whereby, in any society, adults
> endeavour to transmit their beliefs, culture and other values
> to the young, whereas teaching or instruction refers in
> particular to the transmission of knowledge and to intellectual
> development.

The court found that

> the use of corporal punishment . . . is an integral part of the
> process whereby a school seeks to achieve the object for which
> it was established, including the development and moulding
> of the character and mental powers of its pupils.[59]

Education so widely defined clearly gives scope for the recipient alongside the state to determine the core content, which must be directed to the aims mentioned. This interpretation is reinforced by the European Social Charter[60] where, although there is no direct endorsement of the right to education, articles 9 and 10 nevertheless support the notion of the individual influence over curriculum. In particular they recognize that the development of the abilities of the recipient and the recipient's rights to seek his or her appropriate career are for the individual to determine and for the state to help implement, even to the extent of giving 'financial assistance'.[61] So we can perhaps say that in determining the contents of schooling the interests of the state, parents and children must all be recognized.

The right to recognition of qualifications

A further concrete element of the right to education under article 2P is the right to have one's qualifications respected. As the European Court of Human Rights held in the *Belgian Linguistics* case,[62]

> For the right to education to be effective it is further
> necessary that, *inter alia*, the individual who is the beneficiary
> should have the possibility of drawing profit from the
> education received, that is to say, the right to obtain, in
> conformity with the rules in force in each State . . . official
> recognition of the studies which he has completed.[63]

In this case the refusal of homologation of school-leaving certificates for schools in violation of the language laws was found not be a violation as alternative means of recognition of qualifications were reasonably easily available.[64] The judgment establishes the principle of recognition of qualifications, but weakly. One must note the subjection of the right 'to the rules in force in each State'.

The recognition of qualifications, as an aspect of the right to education, has considerable potential as a citizen's right for EC nationals. Although under the auspices of the Council of Europe and Unesco several conventions on recognition of qualifications have been adopted,[65] they are weakly formulated and relate primarily to academic recognition. The mobility of the economically active requires at least recognition of qualifications for professional purposes, and this has been recognized by EC institutions, including the European Court of Justice.

THE EUROPEAN COMMUNITY PERSPECTIVE

Jurisdiction

It is clear that the Treaty of Rome, even as amended, does not endow the EC with extensive powers in relation to education[66] even though articles 128 and 235 have been extensively interpreted[67] by the European Court, and article 235 has now been used to establish a European Training Foundation[68] designed to coordinate educational help to Central and Eastern European countries. The Treaty on European Union signed in February 1992 will create a citizenship of the Union.[69] The scope of Community action in the field of education is also much enhanced.[70] Article 126.1 emphasizes the member states' responsibility for the content of teaching as well as their cultural and linguistic diversity. However, article 126.2 does, *inter alia*, recognize that Community action 'shall be aimed at . . . developing the European dimension in education'.

Access Rights

A major factor curtailing individual access to non-national educational provision within the EC is the lack of true free movement of persons within the Community.[71] Without residence rights it would be impossible for individual pupils and students to claim access to cross-border educational provision as a right. The EC has now adopted directive 90/366,[72] which grants students, from June 1992, the necessary rights of movement and residence,[73] and the *Raulin* case decides this issue in any event.[74] Of course some individuals, because of their particular status (e.g. member of a migrant worker's family), have rights of access,[75] and once ensconced in another member state individuals can use article 7 of the Treaty, which prohibits discrimination on grounds of nationality, to good effect.[76] The Social Charter intends that Community citizens should have a right to vocational training.[77]

Content Rights

As we have seen, the Community is unlikely, directly, to create any educational institutions, and is mainly influencing educational curricula indirectly through a mass of funding programmes.[78] The EC, despite its jurisdictional handicaps, has in fact succeeded in influencing the content of education. It has managed this indirectly through the operation of article 57[79] and by funding its educational programmes (most famously the Erasmus programme, which includes the pilot European Credit Transfer Scheme)[80] and also directly, and exceptionally, through the operation of Directive 77/486/EEC on the education of the children of migrant workers.[81]

Teachers' Rights and Establishment Rights

The right of mobility for teachers[82] that Community law grants clearly will have an impact on the content of educational provision, especially if it is widely exercised. This can be considered as helping to break down 'national' education.

International human rights law entrenches the right to establish educational institutions. Community law could enhance this right, by enabling the cross-border establishment of educational institutions by non-national Community citizens.

The difficulties here are to be found in the terms of article 52(2), which explicitly refer to the national treatment standard for those exercising the right to take up and pursue activities as self-employed persons. This, without mandatory mutual recognition of qualifications, could have been a major impediment to such establishment. Moreover, if a member state subsidizes given categories of private school (which is quite common on the Continent) it would also be obliged to support non-national enterprises that fulfil any non-discriminatory conditions[83] it may impose. The Community dimension added here is the implementation of a cross-border element to an existing right. Again the right has the effect of diminishing the scope of a state's ability to maintain 'nationalist' educational policies.

Remedies

One of the prime values of Community law, as compared to traditional international law, is its relative strength when it comes to enforcing EC rights in national courts. This applies for all the rights it grants, but one can single out this feature because the European Court of Justice in the *Heylens* case[84] established particular remedies in an educational context.

M. Heylens was a Belgian national who was prosecuted in France for acting as a football trainer in Lille without the appropriate French certificate (or a recognized foreign certificate). On an article 177 reference the European Court ruled that

> since free access to employment is a fundamental right which
> the Treaty confers individually on each worker in the
> Community, the existence of a remedy of a judicial nature
> against any decision of a national authority refusing the
> benefit of that right is essential in order to secure for the
> individual the effective protection for his right.[85]

It went on to insist that such national decisions must be reasoned to allow for effective judicial review of them.[86] The remedy ordained by the European Court as regards the equivalence of diplomas (though arguably it operates more widely than simply this category) ought to be mentioned in any future Community catalogue of rights that includes rights of recognition of qualifications.

Right to the Recognition of Qualifications

The right to have one's qualifications recognized was posited above as a potential right for the European citizen. The European Court of Human Rights has recognised it explicitly, if weakly, as forming part of the right to education in the *Belgian Linguistics* case.

The EC's quest to harmonize educational courses and programmes directly has diminished, being replaced with a system of comparability and mutual recognition of qualifications. The right to have one's qualifications recognized, it is suggested, could usefully be listed in a future Community Charter of Rights. This is a 'right' that is granted only to EC nationals as regards qualifications received mainly in the Community,[87] to enable them to work wherever they like within the Community, and as such it would seem to be particularly appropriate for it to be recognized.

The right has been made manifest in numerous 'sectoral' Directives.[88] Directive 89/48/EEC, 'on a general system for the recognition of higher education diplomas awarded on completion of professional education and training of at least three years duration',[89] is the most recent and daring example of Community legislation in this field and marks a new approach in this area. No longer are courses of study to be harmonized and then recognized. Instead the competent authorities of the member states must recognize the professional qualifications of Community nationals subject to safeguards where they do not match national qualifications as regards either their duration or content. This Directive, which entered into force on 4 January 1991, has been followed by a second general Directive, which will complement it as regards other qualifications.[90] It is not appropriate here to expand on the difficulties of application that are likely to be experienced in implementing Directive 89/48/EEC.[91] It would seem that the Community already nearly has in place a complete framework[92] to ensure the recognition of the right, coupled with procedural mechanisms to enable the individual to enforce the right.[93]

FINAL OBSERVATIONS AND SUMMARY

This chapter has, it is hoped, demonstrated (using France as the main illustration) that education has a recognized socializing role and that states have utilized this to form citizens. This has been largely implicit in an island nation such as the UK, but overt for France and many Continental states. The chapter has also argued that the European Community's institutional and political structure is currently too unstable for it to be desirable to 'communitize' national education. Although it could not be said that there is currently anything approaching a Community ethos in the same way that one can talk of a national ethos that would justify 'communitizing' education in a 'national' fashion, the Maastricht Treaty on European Union does indeed, in a limited way, provide for this.

The chapter then outlined what might be considered as the existing educational rights recognized by international human rights law, relating to the freedom to establish schools, controls over the content of education and the right to recognition of one's qualifications. It assessed these from the EC's perspective, also evaluating the Community's jurisdiction in this area as well as other contending educational rights, such as teachers' rights. It briefly rehearsed the powerful position of Community-based remedies, which the European Court had adumbrated in the context of the *Heylens* case (which concerned the procedures to be used when assessing the equivalence of qualifications).

That access to the educational provision in the nation states was, normally, *de facto* limited to citizens is more an inevitable result of the existence of nation states with strict geographical boundaries than a matter of national policies. It seems that states were more than happy, even strived, to export their education wherever possible. All the member states of the Community have developed educational infrastructures and all insist that residents must attend schooling. One could talk of a right of access to educational institutions (as did the European Court of Human Rights in the *Belgian Linguistics* case, but equally one could describe individuals as having a duty imposed on them to get educated.

The European Community is clearly neither able nor willing[94] to compete with member states as regards the provision of educational institutions in any major way. Nor is it capable, effectively, of enhancing the rights of parents and children as regards the provision of education to themselves. This is so despite the fact that it seeks to enable cross-border mobility. The European Convention on Human Rights, in article 2P, already grants individuals a right of access to existing educational institutions, as well as guaranteeing them the right to establish alternative schools, and protecting their religious and philosophical opinions in state educational institutions. The Community can nevertheless perform a useful function in this area.

First, the Community could, and intends to, establish true cross-border mobility for individuals.[95] Should it succeed in this aim, then the individual's educational rights under Community and international law could be effectively exercised on non-national territory. This significant enhancement of rights could be classified as an explicit Community right of access to non-national educational provision on equal terms to nationals. This factor will significantly, in the long term, diminish 'nationalist' education in the member states.

Second, the Community has the capacity to enhance particular aspects of educational provision, such as language training or cross-border educational cooperation, either by direct means (e.g. Directive 77/486/EEC) or though funding (e.g. the LINGUA or Erasmus programmes), so that it can positively 'add' a Community dimension to national educational provision. However, it is not so easy to express these contributions in terms of citizens' rights, nor would there appear to be any merit in doing so. The more silently this revolution occurs the less likely it is that negative national reactions will spring up. It is clear from the programmes funded that a more 'European view' will result for those participating in them, thus challenging any 'nationalist' elements in the traditional schooling received.

Third, the Community is already heavily involved in making educational and professional qualifications more transportable and transparent. The case law of the European Court of Justice and Community legislation has now developed to the point that cross-border recognition of educational qualifications could be said to be a right for the Community citizen. It is suggested that the right of recognition of qualifications could be included in a future Community Charter of Human Rights and this would be a signal contribution to such rights, the more so should procedural safeguards also be added.

Overall it is clear that the political nation state's interest in 'moulding' its citizens is now in the early stages of being challenged by a wider vision of a 'European citizenship', and this challenge is being mounted openly through political, financial and legal changes to the educational environment. To the United Kingdom, where the link between citizenship and education was never very fully recognized in law (except in relation to Ireland), this change will have a strong impact and lead to reassessment and questioning of the meaning of 'citizenship'.

NOTES AND REFERENCES

1 The impact of developments in Central and Eastern Europe, as well as purely internal developments taking their toll on the existing order.

2 See Lonbay, J., 'State control of education', in Gardner, J. P. (ed.) *United Kingdom Law in the 1990's* (UKNCCL, 1990) p. 293, especially note 11 and related text.

3 *Report of the Commission on Citizenship* (HMSO, 1990) indicates that it is, at best, 'implicitly' taught.

4 See Lonbay, J., 'Education and law, the Community Context' (1989) 14 ELR 363, p. 365 (where the Irish example is used to illustrate the argument).

5 In Ireland, for example, the state recognizes the parents' educational rights, as parents, not as citizens. The state provides for free education, and guarantees a minimum education to all. In Belgium, article 17(2) of the Constitution makes it clear that education benefits are available to everyone.

6 Education Act 1944, s. 1.

7 Education Act 1944, s. 8.

8 Including adequate sports and recreation facilities, Education Act 1944, s. 53.

9 Education Act 1944, s. 36.

10 See Evans, *Immigration Law* (1983).

11 ETS No. 5; 213 UNTS 221 (includes the first protocol). Article 1 declares: The High Contracting Parties shall secure to everyone within their jurisdiction the rights and freedoms defined in Section I of this Convention.'

12 Lonbay, J., 'Implementing the right to education in England', in Beddard, R. and Hills, D., *Economic Social and Cultural Rights: Progress and Achievement* (Macmillan, 1992). Note that educational rights within the UK are weakly enforceable following *R. v. ILEA ex p. Ali and Murshid* 15 February 1990, *The Independent*.

13 In fact this measure was never actually put into effect, and was re-enacted in 1724.

14 See Zind, P., 'La méthode pédagogique de Jean-Baptiste la Salle au debut du XVIIIe siècle', and Prevot, A., 'Une pédagogique réaliste et adoptée: Jean-Baptiste de la Salle et ses disciples', both in Actes du 95e Congrès National des Sociétés Savantes, *Histoire de l'enseignement de 1610 à nos jours* (BN, Paris, 1974).

15 In 1848 they had 19,414 schools, teaching 1,354,156 children. Especially in the towns, charity schools were established.

16 Chartier, Compère and Julia, *L'éducation en France du XVIe au XVIIIe siècle* (CDU et Sedes, Paris, 1976), pp. 54–7.

17 There were of course many others who spread these ideas. See Axtell, J. L., *The Educational Writings of John Locke* (Cambridge University Press, 1968).

18 In 1762 Louis-René de Caradeuc de la Chalotais, the first to adumbrate the modern lay and national systems of education, wrote the *Compte-rendu des constitutions des jésuites* for the *parlement* of Rennes, an important and influential document, helping to cause the downfall of the Jesuits. Barnard, H. C., *The French Tradition in Education* (Cambridge University Press, 1922) p. 233; also Mallinson, 'Church and state in French education', 1966 *World Yearbook of Education*.

19 Chartier *et al.*, *op. cit.*, p. 208, write that between 1762 and 1765, 35 books on education were published.

20 Locke, 'Some thoughts concerning education', in Axtell, *op. cit.*, p. 114.

21 Trenard, L., 'Les finalités de l'enseignement primaire de 1770 –1900', in Actes du 95e Congrès National des Sociétés Savantes, *op. cit.*, p. 38. 'Les philosophes et les constituants . . . ne croient pas en la vertu d'une instruction generalisée.' La Chalotais also wrote, in 1763, *Essai d'éducation nationale ou plan d'études pour la jeunesse,* in which he emphasized the need for good textbooks, and limited

universal education. He reasoned that: 'Parmi les gens du peuple il n'est presque nécessaire de savoir lire et écrire qu'à ceux qui vivent par ces arts du à ceux que ces arts aident à vivre.' Chalotais, *op. cit.*, quoted by Chartier *et al.*, p. 38.

22 Rousseau, *La nouvelle Héloïse (Oeuvres complètes)*.

23 Chartier *et al.*, *op. cit.*, p. 37.

24 Debiesse, *op. cit.*, p. 15.

25 Gaudemet, J., 'Le droit à l'éducation', tiré a part de *'L'enfant': Recueils de la Société Jean Bodin*, T. 39 (1975), p. 50.

26 Duruy, A., *L'instruction publique et la Révolution* (Hachette, Paris, 1882), pp. 26–7. Dominique Julia, examining the results of a questionnaire sent out to parishes in the diocese of Rheims by the co-adjutor, Alexandre-Angélique de Talleyrand-Périgord, at the end of 1773, found a wide disparity in responses to the two articles containing questions on the state of education. Her conclusions support the contention that what education existed was very unevenly distributed, even in the area of Champagne, which was generally considered to have a high density of educational facilities.

27 Mirabeaux, Talleyrand, Condorcet, Lathenas, Romme, Lepeletier, Daunow, Sieyes and Chaptal all, *inter alia*, either put forward or defended plans for education. It is not intended to go into the details of all these plans here.

28 Arnold, *The Popular Education of France* (Longman, Green, Longman & Roberts, 1861), p. 33.

29 Duruy, *op. cit.*, p. 51.

30 Grimaud, L., *Histoire de la liberté d'enseignement en France; depuis la chute de l'ancien régime jusqu'à nos jours* (Université de Grenoble, 1898), p. 6.

31 This was achieved by abolishing tithes (4 August 1789, 20 April 1790), and confiscating the property of the clergy (2 November 1789). Seigneural dues and the octrois, an indirect tax, were also abolished. The suppression of the teaching orders, and the imposition of the civic oath on the clergy, disastrously reduced the teaching force. From 22 March 1791, the oath was imposed on all teachers. Grimaud, *op. cit.*, p. 22.

32 Duruy, *op. cit.*, p. 55.

33 Godechot, J., *Les Constitutions de la France depuis 1789* (Garnier-Flammarion, Paris, 1970), p. 37.

34 The Report was referred to the Legislative Assembly. It recommended universal compulsory primary education. This was to be free, although in the first stage there would be a generous scholarship system. Pupils for secondary education were to be selected on their merit. A secular morality was to pervade the schools. He did not recommend a state monopoly of schools, 'car c'est du concours et de la vivalité des effort individuels que naîtra toujours le plus grand biens'. He was in favour of *liberté d'enseignement*. Talleyrand, *Archives Parlement* t. XXX (Harper, New York), p. 448.

35 Guillaume, *Procès-verbaux du comité de l'instruction publique sous l'Assemblée législative* (Imprimerie Nationale, Paris, 1889), p. 231.

36 Hippeau C. *L'instruction publique en France pendant la Révolution* (Didier & Cie, Paris, 1883), t.ii, pp. 2–3.

37 Hippeau, *ibid.*, p. 29.

38 Godechot, J., *ibid.*, p. 82.

39 Godechot, J., *ibid.*, p. 76.

40 Duruy, *op. cit.*, pp. 93–4.

41 Duruy, *ibid.*, p. 97.

42 On 21 October 1793 another decree was passed (Romme's), which was little more than a copy of Condorcet's. Education was to have been universal and free at the primary level. Priests and nobles were to be excluded from education. On 19 December 1793 the Bouquier decree declared compulsory schooling. It allowed independent schools to be set up by all certified as having *bonnes moeurs* and *civisme*. This decree 'fut loin d'atteindre le but qu'elle poursuivait, l'instruction universelle'.

43 Grimaud, *op. cit.*, pp. 65–6.

44 Gaudemet, *op. cit.*, pp. 133–4. Gontard, *op. cit.*, 'les resultats sont négligeables'.

45 Barnard, *Education and the French Revolution*.

46 It is nevertheless clear that the liberty interests of parents and guardians to direct the upbringing and education of children under their control was to be respected. So attempts to 'Americanize mongrel hordes' by insisting on attendance at district public schools in Oregon were struck down. *Pierce* v. *Society of the Holy Names of Jesus and Mary, Pierce* v. *Hill Military Academy* 268 US 510, 45 S.Ct 571 (1925).

47 The curriculum to be taught in public schools is a matter for the state legislatures, subject to the overriding principles of the American Constitution. *Epperson* v. *Arkansas* 393 US 97 (1968).

48 *Doe* v. *Plyler* 457 US 202 (1982).

49 The example of Belgium is well known.

50 See Lonbay, J., 'Education and the law: the Community context', (1989) 14 ELR 363 for examples.

51 *Ibid.* 363, pp. 364–7.

52 International Covenant on Economic, Social and Cultural Rights, 1966 (article 13(3)). See United Nations, *A Compilation of International Instruments* (New York, 1988), 7.

53 See Lonbay, J., 'Implementing the right to education in England', in Beddard, R. and Hill, D. (eds) *Economic, Social and Cultural Rights: Progress and Achievement* (Macmillan, 1992).

54 *Kjeldsen, Busk Madsen and Pedersen*, Eur. Court HR (1976), Ser. A, No. 23.

55 The 'setting and planning of the curriculum' fell in principle within the competence of the contracting state: 'This mainly involves questions of expediency on which it is not for the Court to rule and whose solution may legitimately vary according to the country and era.' Ser. A, pp. 26–7 (para. 53).

56 *Campbell and Cosans* (article 50 judgment), para. 26.

57 As it has done, *mutatis mutandis*, in other fields, for example *Tyrer* v. *UK*, Ser. A, No. 26 (1978) and *Dudgeon* v. *UK* Ser. A, No. 45 (1981).

58 Series B, *Belgian Linguistic* cases, Vol. 1, p. 340.

59 Ser. A, No. 48, para. 33.

60 ECTS No. 35 (1961).

61 Cf. the Community charter of fundamental social rights, COM(89) 248 final (30 May 1989).

62 *Case Relating to Certain Aspects of the Laws on the Use of Languages in Education in Belgium*. ECHR Ser. A, No. 6 (23 July 1968).

63 *Ibid.* This aspect of the Court's ruling has been applied restrictively by the Commission. In *X* v. *Belgium* (7010/75) 3 *Decisions and Reports* the holder of a military diploma was refused civil equivalence. The Commission felt that this military certificate was sufficient as he had received it in accordance with Belgian law. On a strict reading this is a permissible interpretation. But the spirit of the Court's ruling was that the certificate should enhance the 'effectiveness' of education received. Effectiveness would be enhanced by equivalence. In fact identical diplomas issued after 1965 were accorded equivalence. In *X* v. *Belgium* (7864/77) 16 *D and R* 82, a Romanian doctor was required to undergo an examination prior to equivalence being granted.

64 Ser. A, No. 6, *op. cit.*, p. 86.

65 For a brief list see Lonbay (1989) 14 ELR, *op. cit.*, p. 366. For brief extracts see NARIC, *Academic Recognition of Higher Education Entrance, Intermediate and Final Qualifications in the European Community*.

66 See generally Lonbay (1989) 14 ELR, *op. cit.*, where this question is extensively analysed.

67 *Ibid.*, p. 363.

68 COM (90) 15 final/3, 5 March 1990. OJ L131/1 (23 May 1990).

69 Articles 8 and 8a–e.

70 See articles 126.1–4 and 127.1–4.

71 See Lonbay, *op. cit.*, 363, pp. 381–383.

72 Directive 90/366/EEC, OJ L180/30. This directive was struck down by the Court.

73 Generally see Lonbay, J., 'Free movement of persons, recognition of qualifications and working conditions' (1992) 41 ICLQ 212 and 714, and C-295/90 *European Parliament* v. *Council of Justice* (9 July 1992) (not yet reported). In this case the European Parliament successfully challenged the legal base of the directive (though not its contents) but its effects were preserved.

74 C-357/89 *Raulin* v. *Ministre néerlandais de l'enseignement et des sciences* (26 February 1992) (unreported).

75 The European Court has extensively interpreted the notions of 'worker' (Lonbay, *op. cit.*, pp. 375–80) and 'vocational training' (*ibid.*, pp. 373–5), thus extending the Community net to cover more individuals and granting them greater rights to partake in non-national education.

76 *Ibid.*, pp. 372–3.

77 *Ibid.*, p. 382 for text.

78 These mostly have splendid acronyms and include the following non-exhaustively listed programmes: EUROTECHNET, ERASMUS, LINGUA, TEMPUS, PETRA, IRIS, FORCE, SCIENCE, BRIDGE, BRITE/EURAM, DELTA.

79 And its offspring on the mutual recognition of qualifications. Lonbay, *op. cit.*, 363, pp. 370–1. Note also the programme coordinated by CEDEFOP on the comparability of vocational training qualifications under Decision 85/368/EEC.

80 *Ibid.*, pp. 384–5.

81 *Ibid.*, p. 384.

82 *Ibid.*, p. 385.

83 The imposition of discriminatory conditions (relating to nationality) would, it is argued, be unlawful following *Matteucci* v. *Communauté française de Belgique* [1989] 1 CMLR 357. See Lonbay, *op. cit.*, 363, p. 373.

84 *UNECTEF* v. *Heylens* [1987] ECR 4097.

85 Para. 14.

86 Para. 15. These rights have now been extensively extended by the *Vlassopoulou* case, 340/89 *Vlassopoulou* v. *Ministerium für Justiz, Bundes- und Euroangelegenheiten Baden-Württemberg* (7 May 1991), *The Times* 3 June 1991. See Lonbay, 'Picking over the bones: rights of establishment reviewed' (1991) 16 ELR 507.

87 The Directive only grants rights to nationals of member states (article 2), and shows a preference for training that has been carried out in the Community (article 1(a)).

88 The impact has been particularly felt in the following areas: medicine, dentistry, veterinary medicine, architecture and pharmacy. See Lonbay, *op. cit.*, pp. 370–1.

89 Directive 89/48/EEC OJ L19/16 (24 January 1989).

90 COM (89) 372 final (8 August 1989).

91 See Lonbay, J. *et al.*, *Training Lawyers in Europe* (The Law Societies of the UK and Ireland, 1990) Chapter 1, where they are briefly alluded to as regards the legal professions. Also Lonbay, J., 'Diplomas directive: recognising legal qualifications in the EC', in (1991) 1 *Lawyers in Europe* 7, pp. 10–13, and 8, pp. 5–10.

92 The European Court certainly went a long way in *Heylens*, *Vlassopoulou* and *Newman* C-104/91 (7 May 1992) (not yet reported) to establish the general principles that should apply in this field.

93 These result from the terms of the Directive itself, in particular article 8(2), as well as from the European Court's jurisprudence, particularly the *Heylens* case dealt with above.

94 See, e.g., COM(89) 236 final (2 June 1989), Communication from the Commission to the Council, 'Education and training in the European Community; guidelines for the medium term'.

95 See Lonbay, J., 'Free movement of persons, recognition of qualifications, and working conditions' (1990) 39 ICLQ 704 and (1992) 41 ICLQ 212 and 714.

96 For a different, but complementary, view of a European dimension in education, see the report of Mr Marcelino Oreja on the problems of education and training in Europe, Council of Europe, Parliamentary Assembly, Doc. 5864 (12 April 1988).

97 The Community has expressly recognized the principle of 'subsidiarity' in relation to education. See, e.g., COM (89) 236 final (2 June 1989), *op. cit.*, pp. 4–5.

12

Lawyers and the Courts

ROBIN WHITE

INTRODUCTION

Citizenship does not appear to be a lawyer's concept, but rather that of the social scientist. Legal literature seldom discusses the concept of citizenship explicitly beyond its technical meaning under nationality law. The literature of social science, however, contains frequent discussions of the concept.[1] For Marshall there were three basic elements to citizenship. The first was the political element: the right to participate in the exercise of political power as a citizen and elector. Second, there was the social element: the right of citizens to enjoy minimum standards of welfare and security with access to institutions designed to deliver these goals. Finally, there was the civil element: the rights necessary for individual freedom, including a right to justice, offering due process of law.

The social science literature identifies two types of mechanism for the delivery of citizenship rights – the participatory and bureaucratic models – although many institutions will display elements of both models. The bureaucratic models tend to stress the ability to offer an efficient and rational distribution of the resources necessary for all citizens to receive appropriate entitlements to their rights. The participatory model tends to have wider terms of reference than the bureaucratic model and encourages a cooperative approach between itself and the consumers of its services. The priorities of the consumer become as important as the institutional goals and objectives set for the system. Citizenship appears to be about the rights and duties of natural persons rather than artificial legal persons, such as associations and companies.

Citizenship involves entitlement to rights. It also assumes some form of participation. Participation assumes knowledge. That may be knowledge of the law, of procedure, of the circumstances in which professional help is appropriate or of the range of help available. The essence of participation is the ability to make free and informed choices about the course of action to be pursued. Once a course of action has been selected, the institutions and services involved in the pursuit of that course of action should be available and accessible to all members of the community.

There may be many barriers to participation: information may not be readily available, or that which is available may not be comprehensible. This is often a problem for the substance of the law. There is a frequently quoted maxim that ignorance of the law is no defence. Yet it is virtually impossible for the ordinary reader to read cases and discover the underlying legal principles from them,[2] nor is it possible for the ordinary citizen, even of above average literacy, to unravel the complexities of statutory texts. The important task here is to know how statute users process legislative texts,[3] which is affected by judicial attitudes to statutory interpretation as well as the arcane techniques of legislative drafting adopted in the United Kingdom. A lengthy quote from the Renton Report will serve to spell out the ideal, but little progress has been made towards achieving it:

> It is of fundamental importance in a free society that the law should be readily ascertainable and reasonably clear. To the extent that the law does not satisfy these conditions, the citizen is deprived of one of his basic rights and the law itself is brought into contempt. [The] user of the statute book who turns to it for information about the way in which the law affects his or her client's interests should be able to find this information without undue trouble. There will of course be certain Acts which are not readily intelligible and it will usually be necessary for the layman to seek the advice of a professional lawyer. It should be possible for the professional adviser to find his way in the statute book without difficulty, and unnecessary obstacles ought not to be placed in his path. He has a right to expect that statutes should be drafted and arranged in a way which makes plain to him the relevance of the law, even of complex provisions, to the problems of his client. [If] lawyers find the law difficult, how can the layman expect to fare?[4]

This chapter examines a number of barriers to participation presented by lawyers and the courts and discusses attempts to reduce those barriers. The objective is not to suggest that a system should be developed in which there is no role for lawyers. No complex society with a complex legal system is able to achieve this. But legal services must be readily available to all sections of the community if the legal system is not to become a vehicle for use by only the privileged in society. Much of the literature on legal services tends to be lawyer-oriented, whereas viewing this area from the perception of the user may produce results which suggest that more radical changes in system design could produce startling results in terms of the user-friendliness of both lawyers and the courts.

LAWYER USE

Patterns of lawyer use by individuals (rather than businesses) show that the incidence of use is low and very selective. Lawyers offer a reactive service[5] and tend to deal only with the individual issue brought to them. Patterns of lawyer use were examined in detail by the Royal Commission on Legal Services[6] in a survey based on interviews with a random sample of nearly 8000 households. The results showed that age, socio-economic group and type of problem presented affected lawyer use. The age group using lawyers most were males aged between 25 and 34. Semi-skilled and manual workers accounted for only 21 per cent of lawyer use, while professionals, employers and managers accounted for 46 per cent of lawyer use. The evidence of the survey showed that the use of lawyers is problem connected. Interestingly, once property matters, which are unsurprisingly linked with social class, are excluded, the Royal Commission conclude: 'The profile of users of lawyers' services by socio-economic group is not greatly different from that of the adult population in general.'[7]

This has led to the development of a number of theories to explain the pattern of lawyer use. The notion that lawyer use and poverty are linked clearly does not account for the significant use of lawyers by poorer members of the community where crime or divorce is involved. Equally, lawyer use does not rise dramatically as income increases. There is, for example, comparatively little lawyer use for advice on employment or consumer problems.

The legal competence theory has many attractions and may be especially helpful in viewing lawyers and the courts from the perspective of citizenship. This theory suggests that low usage of lawyers arises predominantly among the poor because they do not recognize problems as legal or perceive lawyers as a resource available for them, save in very specific areas.[8] When the poor use lawyers, it is argued, they tend to be 'one-shotters' taking action against repeat players and so their participation is surrounded by the fear of the unfamiliar.[9] Mayhew and Reiss[10] have posited the social organization theory, which provides a better explanation of the incidence of lawyer use by rich and poor alike. This theory links particular types of work with networks of social contacts. Thus everyone takes for granted the need for a lawyer if a person is charged with a serious criminal offence, and the accused's circle of contacts is likely to advise consultation with a lawyer. Michael Zander has described this as advice from a knowledgeable and trusted lay person who identifies or confirms the identification of the problem as one that requires the services of a lawyer.[11]

The picture that emerges is of a reactive institution, which responds to individual issues brought to lawyers by clients who are very selective in the problems they present. Once instructed, the lawyer is likely to 'take over' the case and process it for the client. There is little emphasis on empowering the client, but much more on carrying out the instructions of the client.[12]

SUBSIDIZING LAWYER CONSULTATIONS

One way of increasing participation is to provide the citizen with a lawyer subsidized at the public expense. This can assist not only where the community recognizes the existence of the need for lawyers, but may also be used to generate lawyer use. The introduction of advice and assistance in 1973 had its origins in a wish by the Law Society to move beyond a system of subsidized legal services merely for litigation. A simplified means test operates and, subject to this, the client was originally entitled to legal advice on any point of English law[13] up to a specified sum and beyond that if an extension was obtained. More recently the amount of help available has been expressed in time rather than a money figure. The initial standard limit is now two hours of a solicitor's chargeable time at the appropriate legal aid rate, which can be extended on application. Research conducted on behalf of the Lord Chancellor's Department concluded that the scheme was an invaluable point of contact with legal services for the ordinary citizen. The report discovered that more people were helped under this scheme, which accounts for only 20 per cent of legal aid expenditure, than under all other components of the legal aid scheme. Client satisfaction with the help received was also high and the matters brought to solicitors under the scheme were far from trivial.[14] Legal aid for civil and criminal proceedings is well established and clearly valuable. Its focus is, however, on providing a fee indemnity and not on changing the quality of the lawyer–client contact.

Two issues have plagued the legal aid system since its introduction. The first is its litigation bias. The early development of legal aid in England and Wales was closely linked to providing a fee indemnity for those engaged in civil litigation. Litigation itself was naturally tied to the court system, which was largely fashioned in the eighteenth and nineteenth centuries to meet the need for a system of dispute resolution for a country at the heart of a great commercial empire. It developed before the rise of the twentieth-century expectation that access to law is a right for all citizens. The court system is as a result not well suited to the needs of a modern democracy with increased legal regulation of many everyday activities and a mass of rights given by law, whose enforcement may need to be secured by law.

The second issue is the integration of the legal aid system into the system of service delivery offered by the private sector practitioner. The system has been constrained by the need to seek to duplicate for the legally aided client the service provided to the fee-paying client. As a result legal aid has become trapped in the reactive and individualistic approach to problem-solving characterized by the delivery of legal services by lawyers in private practice. To these two long-standing issues must be added a third more modern concern: that of funding. With close to £1 billion being spent annually on legal aid, the Treasury is increasingly telling the Lord Chancellor, who is in turn telling the legal profession, that the country can no longer afford an open-ended budget for subsidizing lawyer use. There seems no doubt that the system of service delivery through the legal aid scheme will change dramatically in the next decade.

THE QUALITY OF LAWYER CONTACTS

It may be just as important to question the extent to which use of lawyers' services involves participation by the client. Lawyers seldom talk of empowering clients to become personally more competent in a society where law touches upon so many areas of activity. Many lawyers simply adopt a 'leave it to me' approach with which clients frequently concur. But the result is loss of control of the matter and an inability to participate as the client might wish in the process. Lawrence, writing of representation before tribunals, criticizes what he labels co-option, where the representative takes over the case and does not involve the client save to take instructions and to give evidence at the hearing.[15] This is contrasted with the joint or cooperative approach, which involves working with the claimant, advising on the legal framework within which the decisions are made, and avoiding the reduction of the claimant to a passive participant in the process, whose only role is to give evidence. The benefits of the cooperative approach are underlined by surveys into claimant satisfaction with tribunal hearings, which have shown that claimants prefer proceedings in which they are involved and participate.[16]

In her book *Hard Bargaining*,[17] Hazel Genn shows that lawyer selection may be crucial to outcome in personal injuries cases, since many lawyers fail to provide an effective service for their clients. The catalogue of risks run by inexperienced lawyers includes a reluctance to go to court and, consequently, too ready a willingness to settle, delays in the collection of evidence with disastrous effects on a case which is contested, and a risk that the client will be advised to settle for too low a figure. Michael Joseph catalogues some examples of legal incompetence in his polemic against lawyers in personal injury work.[18]

Hazel Genn also notes that those lawyers who adopted a confrontational approach to the settlement of personal injury disputes did better for their clients than those who argued that the insurance companies and they were pursuing the same goal of fair compensation for the victim of the accident. Both approaches can involve participation, though this is not necessarily inherent in either approach.

Guidance issued by the Law Society[19] has emphasized the need for lawyers to keep their clients informed. Yet even this modern approach to practice management does not use the language of empowering clients, but rather of proper management of client business:

> Communication between the solicitor and the client is at the heart of a 'client care' approach for solicitors. It is also the subject of the new Rule 15 and revised Written Professional Standard. The purpose of ensuring good communication is threefold:
> - You will have a clear idea of what the client expects.
> - The client will know what you are doing for them and how much it is going to cost.
> - You will get early warning if things are going wrong.[20]

Many complaints about lawyers concern their failure to provide the client with information. The Solicitors Complaints Bureau reports: 'Given the Bureau's determination to give a much higher profile to complaints showing a possibility of an inadequate service it is depressing to note that poor communication continues to be the chief cause of inadequate service.'[21] It is argued that an informed client is more likely to be a participating client and so more likely to be a satisfied client.

ALTERNATIVES TO LAWYER USE

The main alternatives to use of lawyers are the Citizens Advice Bureaux and law centres. Citizens Advice Bureaux[22] are increasingly being seen as an important feature of overall legal advice provision in England and Wales. An explicit feature of service provision by the bureaux is the empowering of the client and considerable emphasis is placed on this aspect of service delivery in the carefully structured training required of all advisers. The effectiveness of Citizens Advice Bureaux caused the Legal Aid Efficiency Scrutiny in 1987 to see them as the first-tier legal advisers in a new system of legal aid, replacing the Green Form scheme. The proposal foundered not simply because of the opposition of the Law Society, which was reluctant to see the loss of this work for its members, but also because the Citizens Advice Bureaux had no confidence that sufficient resources would be made available to them to meet the demands they knew existed for a first-tier legal advice service. Their cheapness to run is the result of the use of volunteer advisers, who work on a part-time basis. Within the service, each bureau retains considerable autonomy subject to meeting minimum standards laid down by the National Association of Citizens Advice Bureaux. There is unsurprisingly a considerable variation in the service provided by around 1000 outlets within the service. By contrast, law firms can offer over 15,000 outlets.[23]

The best bureaux are law centres in all but name; the least developed represent the best traditions of voluntarism in England and Wales and would not pretend to provide a comprehensive service. Indeed, the increasing demands made on the Citizens Advice Bureaux have raised a debate within the service on amateurism versus professionalism.

The philosophy of the Citizens Advice Bureaux is one of informing, advising and supporting members of the public in the handling of their problems. Considerable emphasis is given in training to interpersonal skills, which equip advisers to involve clients in decision-making.

Law centres, with at their peak just over 60 outlets and probably no more than 200 lawyers working in them, have since 1969 made a remarkable contribution to thinking about strategies for the delivery of legal services and about methods for delivering those services. Originally opposed, but later embraced, by the Law Society, the challenge to the traditional method of delivering legal services was apparent in early statements by the Law Society on the new institutions. The Law Society said that the new scheme 'contemplates a radical departure from the concept of legal aid as so far developed in this country and, by introducing a separate and distinct legal service, it would exercise a divisive social influence'.[24]

The philosophy that grew up within law centres, many of which deliberately called themselves neighbourhood or community law centres, is epitomized in the following statement from the 1980 Annual Report of the Harehills and Chapeltown Law Centre:

We are an agency in which there is a strong element of user control. This is not seen by all as a virtue, but we see it as an incontrovertible fact that in areas like Harehills and Chapeltown it is only through bodies identifiable by the community as by them, of them and for them, that any real advancement can take place. This is perhaps just our way of stating the widely accepted doctrine of community self help.

However, community involvement arises most frequently by membership of community leaders on the management committees of law centres. The parallel between meetings of management committees and partners' meetings or executive committee meetings in the large firms is not often made, but seems apposite. Just as the partners shape and control the work of the High Street practice, it is the management committee that shapes the law centre practice.

The enormous flood of work which came to the law centres is a feature of many annual reports of law centres and one response was the development of group work as contrasted with individual case work. The distinction lasted for over a decade and was misunderstood and criticized by the Benson Commission.[25]

Much has been written about law centres and citizenship.[26] A key discussion in the literature concerns the contrasting styles of service delivery of law centres, taking two extreme forms of service delivery as relevant paradigms: the open door or casework-oriented centres and the closed door or groupwork-oriented centres. The former are labelled reactive and the latter proactive. It is recognized that many law centres are not at the extremes of this spectrum but are somewhere in the mid-range, offering both types of work.

Reactive law centres tend to mimic private practice, but adopt a more friendly, less formal atmosphere designed to remove the inhibitions of their perceived client group[27] in engaging in lawyer consultations. They are also located within the neighbourhoods where the client group lives and, because the lawyers are salaried from public or charitable funds, they are liberated from the need to generate fees from their clients. They have undoubtedly been successful. Stephens says: 'Open-door reactive law centres with their shop-front image and sympathetic and friendly staff typically have been inundated with individual clients wherever they have opened.'[28]

In marked contrast to reactive law centres, proactive law centres do not open their doors to all but adopt a variety of strategies for organizing those with common problems into groups which are then encouraged to pursue collective remedies for their grievances. The remedies selected are often said not to be legal, because the first choice of remedy is not litigation or demands backed by the threat of litigation. Stephens says: 'This approach often seeks to combine legal and non-legal strategies and to resist the individualisation of client problems.'[29]

In the proactive law centres the staff act as resources for local community groups and encourage an active participatory relationship between lawyer or adviser and client. It was this kind of work that the Benson Commission felt was inappropriate for law centres. Yet the Benson Commission appears to have failed to realize that the work being done by proactive law centres for community groups was remarkably similar in scope and style to that provided by City solicitors for large corporate clients. Structuring, organizing and negotiating to secure objectives are at the heart of much City work. Such practices seek to attract, and succeed in attracting, some of the brightest new recruits to the profession, who enjoy high status and high rewards. By contrast, working in a law centre remains low-status work for those dedicated to serving the interests of others rather than advancing their own careers and maximizing their earnings.

CHANGING THE LEGAL PROFESSION

There is no doubt that the character of the legal profession is changing. At one time the profession was homogeneous; now it is increasingly stratified. The practitioner in the large City firms has little in common with the sole practitioner in a provincial town. The barrister in commercial chambers in London has little in common with the provincial barrister doing routine criminal work in the local Crown Court. The changes heralded by the Courts and Legal Services Act 1990[30] will result in the type of work a lawyer does being more significant than the title under which that lawyer practises. There will be new legal professionals entering the market place for legal services. The changes present both opportunities and threats. There are opportunities to establish a national legal service consisting of a variety of components, each capable of dealing efficiently and effectively, in both cost and client-care terms, with the needs of all sections of the community. The threat of a system where there is still too much talk of regulation by competition in the marketplace is that legal services provision will not change its style. Work which does not generate fee income could become routinized to the point at which the protection of legal rights becomes purely notional. This is a charge that can be levelled at magistrates' courts, where the volume of work means that few cases can have much attention devoted to them and lawyers are reluctant to challenge prosecution evidence with great vigour.[31]

Lawyers work within an institutional structure, however. To date courts and tribunals have not been considered as service providers but, with the increasing move to do-it-yourself litigation for small matters, the issue of the usability of the courts and the participation of the litigant has become much more significant. So a brief survey of some of the courts and tribunals with which the ordinary citizen may have contact will serve to demonstrate the centrality of the lawyer in the legal system as the mediator between citizen and system.

CRIMINAL COURTS

Magistrates

It might be expected that the magistracy would present citizenship in practice, since lay judges deal with most crime. Indeed the magistracy is intended to be a cross-section of the community. Sir Thomas Skyrme says:

> The collective views of a cross-section of the population, representing different shades of opinion, can be more effective in dispensing justice acceptable to the public than the single individual necessarily drawn from a fairly narrow social class and whose experience of local problems may be limited. . . . The system enables the citizen to see that the law is his law, administered by men and women like himself, and that it is not the esoteric preserve of lawyers.[32]

Yet, although documentation issuing from the Lord Chancellor's Department indicates that magistrates are drawn from all walks of life, the reality is rather different. The middle classes are over-represented and the picture which emerges from those attempts at a social profile of the magistracy is of the comfortably well-off, middle-aged magistrate sitting in judgment on the misdeeds of motorists and of the less well-off working class members of society. Women and ethnic minorities are not well represented.[33]

King and May note that the magistracy presents a dilemma: between populism and professionalism. On the one hand, it seems beneficial to have a system of lay magistrates in touch with society and handing down decisions which are seen by those on the receiving end of them as produced by ordinary citizens. On the other, the workload of magistrates and the need for efficiency in the despatch of heavy case loads means that the ideal of popular justice is not achieved. Indeed there is evidence that decision making in magistrates' courts routinized to the point where individual justice suffers and many defendants are unaware of the processes occurring around them.[34]

Juries

Jury service is the one area of the legal system for which most citizens are eligible. Selected randomly, they will be responsible for the determination of the guilt or innocence of those pleading not guilty in the

Crown Court. There is a very rare chance of being called to serve on a civil jury. The jury is seen as a great strength of the system, despite spasmodic complaints of jury members' gullibility. No research has yet shown that jurors approach their task of decision-making in other than the most responsible and careful manner.

The key feature of jury service is its passivity. The role of the jury is to listen and learn from counsel and the judge before retiring to deliberate in secret. Although a defendant may draw some comfort from the presence of the lay jury, their role does little to ensure a process which is accessible to the defendant. The Crown Court is clearly a professional court heavily circumscribed by rules so arcane that each side usually has at least two lawyers (solicitor and barrister), whose submissions on the law and whose battles about the admissibility of evidence can baffle the most astute observer.

CIVIL COURTS

Since so few major claims (whether debt cases or personal injury cases) are actually tried in court, it is the processes out of court, which have been discussed above in relation to the role of lawyers, that will dominate. There is, however, one part of the civil justice system which has sought to become usable by the citizen without the assistance of a lawyer or an advocate. This is the small claims procedure in the County Courts. Around 50,000 such cases are heard by district judges (formerly registrars) each year. That number should be set against just over 20,000 trials in the County Court.[35]

The new 'plain English' leaflets produced for small claims are a welcome improvement to the complete, but rather forbidding, booklet previously produced. But it is what happens in the courtroom that will be important. The system's ambivalence over adopting a procedure which actively helps and protects litigants is highlighted in the decision of the Court of Appeal in *Chilton* v. *Saga Holidays plc*.[36] The case concerned a small claim for £184 arising out of a holiday provided by Saga Holidays plc for the plaintiffs, Mr and Mrs Chilton. The plaintiffs were unrepresented while Saga Holidays plc was represented by a lawyer. The defendant's solicitor wished to cross-examine Mr Chilton on certain evidence he had put to the registrar, who was sitting as arbitrator. The registrar refused to allow this and insisted that any questions for Mr Chilton be directed through him. The plaintiffs secured judgment against Saga Holidays, which then applied to have the award set aside because of the registrar's ruling on the questioning of Mr Chilton. The judge refused to do so and the matter went on appeal to the Court of Appeal, where the company succeeded. The Master of the Rolls underlined the nature of the small claims proceedings and the sanctity of cross-examination:

> Both courts and arbitrators in this country operate on an adversarial system of achieving justice. It is a system which can be modified by rules of court; it is a system which can be modified by contract between the parties; but in the absence of one or the other, it is basically an adversarial system and it is fundamental to that that the other party shall be entitled to ask questions designed to probe the accuracy or otherwise, or the completeness or otherwise, of the evidence which has been given.[37]

The decision is clearly a bad one for the small claims procedure and has been recognized as such by section 6 of the Courts and Legal Services Act 1990, which amends the County Courts Act 1984 in order to enable rules to be made concerning the procedure and rules of evidence to be followed in small claims cases, including in particular provision concerning the manner of taking and questioning evidence. Rules have been made under this provision which effectively overrule *Chilton* v. *Saga Holidays plc*. Be that as it may, the decision serves to show how unresponsive the courts can be to innovations designed to provide some equality of position between litigants.

A final indication of the resistance of the system to change is the failure to adopt the best features of the independent arbitration schemes which operated for a while in Manchester and London.[38] The schemes claimed to be speedier, cheaper, simpler and more user-friendly than the County Court schemes. The claims to simplicity and a sympathetic approach to litigants in person can certainly be sustained, though more doubt surrounds the claims concerning speed and cheapness. Speed is difficult to judge on a comparative basis since the comparative workloads of the schemes are so different, while costs are disguised because there is a transfer to the system of process costs[39] normally suffered by the litigant.

The High Court has been reserved for the most complex civil claims and for judicial review. The latter is an extremely important and growing remedy which much to contribute to the enforcement of the citizen's rights. This chapter is not the place for detailed consideration of the development of a proper system of administrative law in England and Wales.[40] For the purposes of this chapter it is sufficient to note that judicial review remains surrounded by technical rules and is a process which is only usable by those able to afford the services of lawyers or whose litigation will be supported under the legal aid scheme.

TRIBUNALS

Tribunals are modern alternatives to the courts, established because the legislature wished to create something distinguished from the courts and not tied to their traditions. It should perhaps therefore come as no surprise to see that the bastions of tradition attacked them,[41] though judicial opposition to tribunals has long since evaporated. The contrast between Social Security Appeal Tribunals and Industrial Tribunals provides an interesting case study on the development of these modern forms of court. In summary, the procedures of the Social Security Appeal Tribunals have become a model of flexibility and accommodation to parties appearing before them, though unfortunately the law they have to apply has remained an unnecessarily complex web of primary and secondary statutory material, elaborated by decisions of the Social Security Commissioners, while Industrial Tribunals have become just as adversarial as the County Courts.

Since their establishment out of the discredited Supplementary Benefit Appeal Tribunals and largely respected National Insurance Local Tribunals in 1984, it has been the policy of the first two Presidents of the Social Security Appeal Tribunals[42] to stress the enabling function of the tribunals. This involves recognizing that virtually all those claimants who appeal and appear before the tribunals will do so only once and that for them the experience will be a strange and uncertain one. The objective of the tribunal should be to adopt a procedure which enables them and all others appearing before the tribunal to tell their story and make their arguments as fully and openly as possible. The objective is to secure a formal procedure in an informal atmosphere. In this it seems that the tribunals largely succeed:

> During observations of social security appeal tribunal hearings
> the vast majority of chairs were found to be courteous,
> sensitive and at pains to be helpful to appellants, reflecting,
> presumably, the 'enabling' role that has been stressed under
> the new regime and the belief expressed by all chairs that
> hearings were fundamentally 'inquisitorial'. In this context,
> the term inquisitorial seems to mean that chairs feel they
> have the freedom to investigate cases and elicit the
> information they think they need in order to get to the truth
> of the situation, rather than to choose between competing
> arguments.[43]

Despite such complimentary comments, the research from which the quotation is taken concludes that, though the merits of the formal procedure in the informal atmosphere of Social Security Appeal

Tribunals should be retained, it is wrong to think that they are a substitute for advice and advocacy. Compensating for the absence of representation could be time-consuming and difficult when appellants are confused or inarticulate.

By contrast, two important research studies into the work of Industrial Tribunals describe them as having an 'underlying accusatorial model of hearings and a tendency towards legalism'[44] and as 'totally adversarial' or 'courts of first instance'.[45]

So on the one hand the desire of those establishing the tribunals for a formal procedure in an informal atmosphere has succeeded, and on the other hand it has completely failed. The explanation appears to be that the Industrial Tribunals have been colonized by lawyers, while the Social Security Appeal Tribunals have not. Lawyers have little interest in social security law, but developed some expertise and interest in employment law as employers sought their advice concerning their employment relations with their workforce, which were increasingly subject to statutory intervention.

A new tribunal has been established to deal with disability questions arising under claims for the new disability benefits,[46] whose composition represents an important development in participation. The tribunals are composed of a lawyer chair sitting with a person who has experience of dealing with the needs of disabled people, because he or she is disabled or has experience of caring for disabled people, and with a medical practitioner, most of whom are GPs. All three have an equal say on all issues of law and fact arising before them. There is an embargo on any medical examination being undertaken by the tribunal. The clear intention is to combine the three expertises – those of legal adviser, disability adviser and medical adviser – to produce decisions that are procedurally fair, legally correct and individually just.

THE NATURE OF PROCEDURE

A recurring theme in considering the role of courts and tribunals is that the final outcome is often largely determined by what happens outside the courtroom. It is also clear that the adversarial system adopted throughout the English legal system gives an advantage to those who are represented, even in those proceedings designed to be used without assistance and advocacy.[47]

It may not be simply the adversarial nature of English procedure that results in litigants often playing a small role in the cases in which they are involved. There is no evidence that participation by litigants is higher in inquisitorial systems, which are frequently suggested inappropriately as a panacea for all the perceived ills of English procedures. What few would dispute is the need for courts and tribunals to be easier environments in which litigants can participate in the cases in which they have invested so much. The key to participation is understanding and control. The concept of due process requires that not only the final result but also every preliminary stage leading to final determination be just. Notions of informed choice for litigants and maximizing participation require a change not only in the way the courts work but also in the way in which lawyers advise and represent those litigants. These requirements may well be more important in an adversarial system, where party initiative is at the heart of the process, than in inquisitorial and investigative procedures. Mere simplification of procedure is unlikely to suffice. The access to justice approach must be adopted,[48] involving 'the need to relate and adapt the process to the type of dispute'. This approach requires the implementation of change in order to remove the causes of structural inequities or imbalances in the system. The focus is on the needs of participants in the process.

All this must be achieved within the finite resources available to the legal system. There are certain to be trade-offs between value of the dispute and cost of the process. Equally, there is little reason why the full cost of dispute resolution should not be borne by business users. Indeed, the use of arbitration clauses by business as a substitute for court-based methods of dispute settlement has long been commonplace. More recently, the high costs not only of litigation, but also of arbitration, have resulted in increasing interest in alternative dispute resolution (ADR) despite reservations expressed by members of the judiciary.[49]

Ultimately, it is the lawyers who must do better, by a genuine commitment to improved client care. Increasing specialization and more efficient working methods should enable this to be done without increasing costs.

MAXIMIZING PARTICIPATION

So far most of the blame has been placed with lawyers and institutions of the legal system, but there is a role for increased education in legal matters. Recent years have seen a marked increase in the population's health awareness. The benefits of a healthy diet and the main causes of heart disease are now well known. There has, however, been no corresponding increase in the community's legal knowledge and the profession has shown comparatively little interest in making people more aware of how they can secure their legal 'health'. This a shortsighted view. An informed citizenry is no more likely to attempt to be its own expert lawyer than to attempt surgery. The informed citizen is, however, much more likely to know when it is appropriate to consult the lawyer for advice and assistance and to have realistic expectations about the remedies the legal system has to offer. Most significantly, legal work may change since lawyer use will not be restricted to crisis intervention and property transfer or management, but will extend to a wider range of advice and assistance in managing the business of daily life in a highly regulated society. When litigation becomes necessary, the client will work much more closely in partnership with the lawyer, with the result that cases will be better prepared and better argued and the outcomes more likely to be just to both parties.[50]

NOTES AND REFERENCES

1 See, for example, Nonet, 'Legal action and civic competence', in J. Floud, P. Lewis and R. Stuart (eds), *Proceedings of a Seminar: Problems and Prospects of Socio-legal Research*, 1971; Marshall, 'Citizenship and social class', in T. H. Marshall, *Class, Citizenship and Social Development*, 1976; R. Hadley and S. Hatch, *Social Welfare and the Failure of the State*, 1981; and A. H. Halsey, 'T. H. Marshall: past and present' (1984), *Sociology*, 18(1), pp. 1–18.

2 Davies, 'Reading cases', (1987) 50 MLR 409.

3 See generally F. Bennion, *Bennion on Statute Law* (3rd edn 1990) part I; J. Bell and G. Engle, *Cross on Statutory Interpretation* (2nd edn 1987), Chapter 8; W. Dale, *Legislative Drafting – A New Approach*, 1977; and *The Preparation of Legislation (Report of the Renton Committee)* (cited in this chapter as the Renton Report), Cmnd 6053 (1975).

4 Renton Report, paras 7.4, 7.6.

5 That is, they tend to wait for clients to bring business to them rather than to search out legal problems and offer solutions to them.

6 *Final Report of the Royal Commission on Legal Services*, Cmnd 7648 (1979), Volume 2 (cited in this chapter as the Benson Commission).

7 Benson Commission para. 8.115.

8 Carlin and others, 'Civil justice and the poor – issues for sociological research' (1966) 1 LSR 9.

9 Galanter, 'Why the "haves" come out ahead: speculation on the limits of legal change' (1974) 9 LSR 95.

10 Mayhew and Reiss, 'The social organisation of legal contacts' (1969) 34 ASR 318.

11 M. Zander, *Legal Services for the Community*, 1978, p. 293.

12 This theme is developed below.

13 The scope of the scheme was restricted in 1990 by excluding certain types of enquiry.

14 J. Baldwin and S. Hill, *The Operation of the Green Form Scheme in England and Wales*, 1988.

15 R. Lawrence, *Tribunal Representation*, 1980.
16 Bell and others, 'National Insurance Local Tribunals – a research study' [1974] 3 JSP 289 and [1975] 4 JSP 1; K. Bell, *Research Study on Supplementary Benefit Appeal Tribunals. Review of Main Findings: Conclusions: Recommendations*, 1975.
17 H. Genn, *Hard Bargaining: Out of Court Settlement in Personal Injury Actions*, 1987.
18 M. Joseph, *Lawyers Can Seriously Damage Your Health*, 1984.
19 See, for example, The Law Society, *Civil Litigation: A Guide to Good Practice*, 1990, and *Client Care: A Guide for Solicitors*, 1991.
20 The Law Society, *Quality: A Briefing for Solicitors*, 1991.
21 Solicitors Complaints Bureau, *Annual Report Nineteen Ninety: The New Look Bureau*, p. 9.
22 J. Citron, *Citizens Advice Bureaux: For the Community by the Community*, 1989; J. Richards, *Inform, Advise and Support: The Story of Fifty Years of the CAB*, 1989.
23 The Law Society, *Annual Statistical Report 1992*, para. 3.4.
24 The Law Society, *Legal Advice and Assistance*, 1968, para. 20.
25 See, generally, Stephens, 'Law centres and citizenship: the way forward', in P. Thomas (ed.), *Law in the Balance: Legal Services in the 1980s*, 1982 and *Final Report of the Royal Commission on Legal Services*, Cmnd 7648, and Stephens, 'Law centres, citizenship and participation' (1985) *Law and Policy* 77.
26 See particularly Stephens, 'Law centres and citizenship: the way forward', in P. Thomas (ed.), *op. cit.*, p. 107; Stephens, 'Law centres, citizenship and participation', *op. cit.*; Stephens, *Community Law Centres: A Critical Appraisal*, 1990.
27 The lower socio-economic groups.
28 Stephens,'Law centres, citizenship and participation', *op. cit.*, p. 78.
29 *Ibid.*
30 See R. White, *A Guide to the Courts and Legal Services Act 1990*, 1991, Ch. 1.
31 See J. Vennard, *Contested Trials in Magistrates' Courts*, Home Office Research Study No. 71, 1982.
32 T. Skyrme, *The Changing Image of the Magistracy* (2nd edn 1983), p. 8.
33 See, generally, T. Skyrme, *op. cit.*; M. King and C. May, *Black Magistrates*, 1985; E. Burney, *JP: Magistrate, Court and Community*, 1979.
34 See, generally, R. White, *The Administration of Justice*, 1991, Chapter 5, *passim*.
35 This is certain to increase with the massive transfer of business to the County Courts resulting from the implementation of recommendations of the Civil Justice Review.
36 [1986] 1 All ER 841.
37 *Ibid.*, p. 844.
38 Their work is summarized in R. White, *The Administration of Justice*, pp. 178–180.
39 This refers to court costs, the cost of any legal advice, loss of earnings in attending court and placing a money figure on the stress and anxiety of litigation.
40 The procedure is certain to be the subject of discussion in other chapters in this volume.

41 Lord Hewart, *The New Despotism*, 1929.

42 HH Judge John Byrt, QC and HH Judge Derek Holden.

43 H. Genn and Y. Genn, *The Effectiveness of Representation at Tribunals*, 1989, p. 159. See also J. Baldwin *et al.*, *Judging Social Security: The Adjudication of Claims for Benefit in Britain*, 1992.

44 L. Dickens and others, *Dismissed: A Study of Unfair Dismissal and the Industrial Tribunal System*, 1985, p. 84.

45 H. Genn and Y. Genn, *op. cit.*, p. 198.

46 Disability living allowance and disability working allowance: see ss. 71–76 and 129 of the Social Security Contributions and Benefits Act 1991.

47 In particular, small claims in the County Court and tribunal proceedings.

48 M. Cappelletti (ed.), *Access to Justice*, 6 volumes, 1978.

49 See, for example, comments of Lord Donaldson MR reported in the *Law Society's Gazette*, 3 July 1991, p. 8.

50 The Government issued *The Courts Charter* in July 1991 after this chapter had been written. The commitments in the Charter relate principally to administrative procedures outside the courtroom. Nothing in the Charter relates to the quality of the hearing in court.

13

Nationality and Immigration

ANDREW NICOL

'Citizen's charters' were the vogue of the 1992 election in the UK. The Conservative Party, in particular, promised a series of reforms across the range of public services to provide better rights for 'citizens'. The Conservative Party's use of the term, like its use in the title of this book, is different from the legal concept of citizenship. Indeed it is striking how few rights within the United Kingdom are dependent on citizenship.

It was not always so. The common law divided the world into subjects – those who owed allegiance to the King – and aliens. Aliens could not own or inherit land and a testamentary claim could not be made through an alien. Land holdings were based on feudal ties, which could not continue in wartime. In the Middle Ages war between England and France was so common that it became impractical for a Frenchman to hold English land. This hardened into a rule of law and, as the English were prone to treat the French and foreigners as synonymous, the rule was generalized to all aliens. The fear that foreign-born monarchs, such as William III, might otherwise grant British lands to their foreign friends gave new life to the rule at a time when other feudal anachronisms were being discarded as redundant.[1]

The early common law precluded aliens from owning personal property as well. However, suspicion of foreigners gave way to the economic need to encourage their merchants to trade with England. Edward I gave alien merchants not only the right to sue in debt but also the right to double damages for their wrongs as well. By the seventeenth century, aliens could bring any personal action in the courts.[2] New types of property, such as patents or copyrights, could also be owned by aliens (at least if they were produced or published in the UK or if the alien was resident there).[3] Aliens were equally free to devise their personal property by will. English law never adopted the civil law principle known as *droit d'aubaine* of forfeiting a dead alien's belongings.

Aliens were, however, banned from owning an interest in a British ship. The Navigation Acts of the seventeenth century gave British ships a monopoly of carriage to and from British plantations and colonies and of the coastal trade. Nationalist sentiment has sustained this rule long after the repeal of the Navigation Acts, and it remains the case today that an alien cannot own a British ship.[4]

One reason why this rule survived was that it could be circumvented by the simple expedient of foreigners incorporating a British company to own their ship.[5] Similarly, the ban on aliens owning land continued as long as it did because through a company or a trust for sale the economic end could be achieved while still paying lip service to the formal prohibition.[6] None the less, the inability of individual aliens to own freehold land was irksome and those who bought in ignorance were often shaken to find that their property could be forfeit to the Crown. A Royal Commission in 1869 found evidence that this was a disincentive to foreign capital. Its recommendation that the rule should be scrapped was adopted and since 1870 aliens have had the right to own, transmit and receive almost all types of property.[7]

Because of the First World War the ban on foreign ownership of UK land was revived for a brief time. There were good reasons even then for not reviving it. As well as jeopardizing investment in Britain it would expose land holdings abroad by Britons to reciprocal measures. The sometimes unfathomable issue of whether or not a present or previous owner was an alien or British subject would make land titles unreliable. Besides, the policy was open to avoidance or evasion behind corporate veils and bearer securities.[8] None the less, antipathy to Germans was so strong that these considerations were overborne and until 1922 former enemy aliens were banned from owning UK land.[9]

Anti-German feeling prompted Parliament to ban alien share-holders in British ships.[10] This ban lasted for only a few years, but the same sentiment provoked a panic at the thought of alien infiltration into the crews of British ships. The restrictions then instituted still continue, so that, apart from modifications for EC nationals, aliens cannot hold a pilot's certificate or be the master or one of the senior officers of a British-registered merchant ship or fishing vessel.[11] Ironically, of course, these restrictions have lost most of their practical significance as the bulk of the former British mercantile marine has passed to the laxer control of countries with flags of convenience.

Regulation has since become more sophisticated and where Parliament now prescribes who may not hold property or enjoy similar statutory rights much greater care is taken to deal with corporate ownership and influence. Thus while aliens may hold broadcasting licences they must either be EC nationals or be resident in the UK. Extensive provision is made in an effort to stymie avoidance devices.[12]

As far as personal liberty is concerned the common law (we will look at statutory controls of immigration later) drew no distinction between subjects and aliens, or at least did not discriminate against 'friendly aliens'. The term friendly alien has nothing to do with whether the individual loves or loathes Britain but refers to the relations between Britain and the state of which he or she is a national: if the two countries are at peace, the national is 'friendly'; if they are at war, the alien is an enemy.

Friendly aliens could and can invoke *habeas corpus* to test the legality of their detention. To describe that ancient writ as being concerned with the liberty of the 'subject' is accurate, but only if it is taken as embracing 'alien subjects'. This apparently contradictory term was coined to describe the status of friendly aliens who were present in the jurisdiction. They did not lose their alien status, but while in the UK they owed a temporary or local allegiance to the Crown. Correspondingly, they were entitled to the protection of the courts if they were improperly detained.

The position with enemy aliens remains unclear. The procedural issue of their entitlement to seek *habeas corpus* is easily confused with the issue of substance as to the Crown's power to detain.[13] Iraqi detainees at the time of the Gulf War did apply for *habeas corpus*.[14] No issue was taken as to their standing to do so, but this may have been because in the absence of a formal declaration of war, they did not have the character of enemy aliens. It would be remarkable if a modern court were to hold that even a properly described enemy alien had no standing to seek *habeas corpus*. It would leave him or her powerless to challenge unlawful detention by private persons or confinement by the state in excess of its powers. Even in the nineteenth century the Government seemed reluctant to push this argument, for when it was rumoured that Napoleon would apply for *habeas corpus* special legislation authorizing his detention was hurriedly passed.[15]

From time to time the Crown has asserted a prerogative power to intern and deport enemy aliens. However, since the First World War it has in practice relied on statutory powers. Thus while the Immigration Act 1971 preserves the Crown's prerogative,[16] the Government has ample power to deport those who are not British citizens whether or not they are formally enemy aliens.[17]

Since at least *Entick* v. *Carrington*[18] tortfeasors have not been able to defeat an action by a subject on the grounds that the wrong was commanded by the Government. 'Act of State' was traditionally no defence, because in return for a subject's allegiance the Crown was obliged to respect his or her freedom and property, except to the extent permitted by law.[19] In *Johnstone* v. *Pedlar*[20] the House of Lords applied the same principle to a friendly alien in the jurisdiction. The case was an interesting one. Pedlar sued for money taken from him on his arrest for illegal drilling in County Dublin. He was an American but a republican supporter and admitted having taken part in the Easter Rising of 1916. The Lords rejected the Crown's argument that the seizure was Act of State which a court had no jurisdiction to investigate. Pedlar, they said, was a friendly alien whatever animosity he personally bore the British government. While in Ireland (then part of the King's dominions) he owed a temporary allegiance to the King. In turn, Crown officials could take his property only in accordance with the law. His republican activities might lead to his prosecution or deportation, but they did not relieve the Crown of its duty to protect him as one of its alien subjects. It was ordered to repay his money.

An over-logical approach might suggest that Act of State could be pleaded by the Government to justify state interference with property left behind by absent aliens. Since their allegiance only lasts as long as they are present in the jurisdiction, might it be argued that once they had departed, the Crown's correlative duty to respect their property also ended? However, the principle that the Government must act only within its lawful powers has outgrown its origins and the courts would no doubt follow dicta of Lord Justices Scrutton and Bankes that it must be able to justify to the court all its acts within the jurisdiction, even in relation to absent foreigners.[21]

Apart from immigration control (see below) there are three particular areas concerning matters within the UK where nationality is important: the franchise, eligibility for jury service and government positions. Aliens have long been barred from the vote.[22] In 1949 when election law was codified, Parliament had to deal with the reworking of nationality law that had taken place the year before.

The British Nationality Act 1948 adopted a new concept of nationality. Instead of a semi-feudal idea of 'subjects', defined as those who owed allegiance to the King, it was necessary to create a category acceptable to a commonwealth of independent states, some of whose members were republics. In brief, the new idea was that a person's primary nationality should be that of his or her individual country if that was a self-governing dominion (e.g. Canadian, Indian, Australian) and that by virtue of that nationality he or she would be a British subject. This term was to have the alternative name (again with republican sensibilities in mind) of Commonwealth citizen.

Those whose connection was with the UK or its colonies or whose dominion had not adopted its own nationality law would become 'Citizens of the United Kingdom and Colonies'. They, too, would enjoy the derivative status of British subject (in its new meaning) or commonwealth citizen. Although the self-governing members of the Commonwealth could create their own citizenships, the intention was that they would grant political rights (including the franchise) to each other's citizens.

It was for this reason that the Representation of the People Act 1949 did not limit the franchise to the new category of Citizens of the United Kingdom and Colonies. Instead the potential voter had to be a British subject or Commonwealth citizen. Because voters also had to be resident in their constituencies, relatively few citizens of Commonwealth countries (apart from Britain) were entitled to vote in British elections. None the less, the provision showed that the term 'British subject' was not just an empty rhetorical flourish, but had continuity with the common law concept. The Irish, who by the 1948 Act and the Government of Ireland Act 1949 were neither British nor alien, also retained the right to vote.

Nationality law was revamped again by the British Nationality Act 1981. This scrapped the concept of citizen of the United Kingdom and Colonies (CUKC). Very broadly, CUKCs who were connected with Britain became British citizens; those who were connected with a colony became British Dependent Territories' citizens. The rest were (generally) classed as British overseas citizens. 'Commonwealth citizenship' was retained as a status that derived from citizenship of Britain or some other Commonwealth country, but it was no longer synonymous with 'British subject'. This term was used instead to refer to a relatively small category that did not fit into one of the others.

The drafters of the 1981 Act disavowed any intention to change the consequences of nationality law. As a result the franchise in essence still extends to any Commonwealth or Irish citizen resident in the UK.[23] The goal of reciprocity has not been completely achieved, but there are a significant number of Commonwealth countries in which UK citizens can vote.[24]

Should only British citizens have the right to vote? A House of Commons Select Committee in 1982 decided against recommending this change.[25] It thought that it would undermine the expectations of some who had settled in Britain believing that they could exercise political rights without changing their nationality. It would force some migrants whose states prohibited dual nationality (such as India) into choosing between giving up that citizenship and losing their vote. It would exacerbate the fears of racial minorities, who would view such a change as a further stimulus to racist hostility. In any case the Committee detected no great support for the idea.

Conversely, should the franchise be extended to resident aliens? Should the government not represent all who live in the country and pay its taxes? Sweden and New Zealand use residence rather than nationality as the basis for their franchise and the EC encourages its members to give other Community nationals a vote in at least local and European elections. In practice the impact of such a change would be lessened by the large number of resident aliens who are already (illegally) registered. The 1982 Committee found this all too radical and preferred to examine naturalization procedures to see whether these posed unreasonable obstacles to citizenship and the franchise (it later produced a scorching report on these procedures). The Committee reserved its reforming zeal for Britons abroad. In 1985 the Government responded by allowing overseas residents to retain their vote for five years. This was extended to 20 years in 1989. The facility is, however, limited to British citizens.[26]

The second area where nationality matters inside the UK is eligibility for positions in the legislature or executive. Aliens cannot be Privy Councillors or members of either House of Parliament, or hold any office or place of trust, either civil or military. These restrictions in the Act of Settlement section 3 were intended to prevent the House of Hanover rewarding foreign cronies with British estates or positions of power. The courts interpreted the restrictions broadly and ruled that such lowly positions as constable or church warden were closed to aliens.[27] Clearly civil servants held office under the Crown if their positions were permanent or established. Doubts about whether other public service jobs were included, coupled with the xenophobia of the First World War, led to the Aliens Restriction (Amendment) Act 1919, which comprehensively barred aliens from 'any office or place in the Civil Service of the State'.[28]

The fear of foreign influence in the corridors of power has always had to contend with pragmatic needs arising from shortages of suitable British subjects. Thus the Aliens Employment Act 1955 permits the employment of aliens in the Civil Service overseas if the Minister certifies that there is no suitably qualified British subject or the candidate has exceptional qualifications or experience. Likewise, the army's demands for manpower led to a relaxation of the Act of Settlement. By the Army Act 1881 the government could approve the enlistment of aliens in the regular forces if their proportion did not exceed 1 in 50 and they did not become commissioned officers.[29] Even this provision was qualified so as not to shut off a rich source of cannon fodder, for the section provided that: 'any negro or person of colour, although an alien may voluntarily enlist . . . and when so enlisted shall while serving in Her Majesty's regular forces be deemed to be entitled to all the privileges of a natural born subject.' Broadly similar restrictions apply today,[30] though the explicit racialism has been replaced with blander language: 'persons enlisted outside the UK and serving in prescribed units and officers in such units'. The only units now prescribed are in the Brigade of Gurkhas. Recruitment to the Royal Air Force is governed by an identical provision,[31] but the Royal Navy is still closed to aliens by the Act of Settlement.

Third, nationality is also a condition of eligibility for jury service. In order to qualify as a juror a person must be on the electoral roll.[32] British citizens, British Dependent Territories' citizens, British Overseas citizens, citizens of Commonwealth countries and Irish people resident in the UK are entitled to register to vote. Consequently, they, too, will be liable to be called for jury service.

The current provision is a partial reflection of the common law. Aliens could not be empanelled to try an indictment against an English defendant or a civil case between English parties.[33] However, from an early date legislation gave an alien the right to be tried by a special jury called the *jury de meditate linguae* or the jury of the half tongue. It was composed half of Englishmen and half of aliens and was intended to soothe the fears of foreign merchants who, with some justification, were concerned at the partiality of a jury made up exclusively of Englishmen. Its introduction is impressive evidence of the importance that was placed on attracting foreign merchants to England.

The right was a crude one. Just as the common law grouped all foreign nationalities together in its category of 'alien', so the foreign half of a *jury de meditate* could include aliens from any country, irrespective of whether they shared the same nationality or even the same language as the alien defendant or litigant. There was a practical reason for this: it might not be possible to find jurors of some nationalities. There was also a kind of logic: the purpose of the jury was to mitigate anti-alienism, not to make the alien feel at home. This example of medieval pragmatism proved remarkably resilient. It survived until 1870 and as late as 1825 special provision was included in legislation to ensure that it continued.[34]

It gave defendants an opportunity to make a political point in some trials. Irish republicans would sometimes apply for a *jury de meditate* as a way of demonstrating from the outset of the trial their desire to be aliens and their rejection of the British Crown's dominion over Ireland.[35] Other political defendants made capital out of their refusal to ask for a mixed jury. Simon Bernard, a Frenchman tried in 1848 for complicity in the Orsini conspiracy to assassinate Napoleon III, declared that he would 'put his trust in a jury of Englishmen', whose dislike of foreign-inspired prosecutions he then exploited. He was acquitted to tumultuous applause.[36]

The last straw for the Government was the case of William Nagle, who was another Fenian. He was charged with complicity in a hopeless 'invasion' of Ireland. As an American he was able to claim a *jury de meditate*. The aliens first summoned for jury service failed to attend court. The second panel had militiamen, whom the alleged revolutionary understandably challenged. No other aliens could be found and before a fresh panel could be summoned, American diplomatic pressure secured Nagle's release. To some this demonstrated the folly of retaining an anachronistic institution; others saw it as the Government's come-uppance for moving the trial from Dublin to the far less cosmopolitan town of Sligo in the hope of pushing it out of the public eye.[37] Two years later the half-tongue jury was abolished.[38]

Although the half-tongue jury was a crude device for correcting bias, its technique is not unattractive as a method for dealing with modern problems. In 1975, for instance, the Heilbron Committee recommended that rape charges should be tried by a jury which included at least four members of each sex because of concern at such charges being tried by all-male juries.[39] No action was taken because the abolition of the property qualification (which existed until the Juries Act 1974) was anyway leading to more women jurors. The problem remains acute for black defendants facing an all-white jury. Although some trial judges, recognizing the problem, were willing to direct that the jury panel should be chosen from a particular area or to allow potential jurors to be removed in order to achieve a racially balanced jury, the Court of Appeal has ruled that a judge has no power to engineer the empanelling of a mixed jury.[40]

If nationality is of limited significance within the UK, it is of cardinal importance elsewhere. Claims under international law can generally be pursued by the state of which the individual is a national; with certain limited exceptions that is the only state which can advance such claims. The Foreign Office often used to pose nationality law conundrums for its lawyers in order to decide whether it could intervene on behalf of a particular claimant.

Britain is entitled but not obliged to give assistance to Britons who get into trouble abroad. Where it chooses to help it may seek payment. The Court of Appeal so held in 1932 when it allowed the crown to claim reimbursement of its costs in protecting a trading company from pirates in China. British subjects who went to foreign countries, whether in search of profit or out of 'self-sacrificing devotion to religious vows', must be taken to know of the dangers to which they were exposing themselves and could not expect to be rescued as of right and free of charge.[41] More recently, the Court of Appeal ruled that Ugandan Asians who were citizens of the United Kingdom and Colonies could not compel the UK government to negotiate with Uganda for compensation for their property which was confiscated or destroyed by the regime of Idi Amin. The conduct of international relations was said to be still beyond the judicial pale.[42] If the government does recover compensation as a result of negotiations, the money is not held on trust for the victims,[43] but since 1950 there has been a statutory scheme to regulate its disbursement.[44] It was in the context of this legislation that the House of Lords delivered its seminal administrative law decision that errors by a statutory body in interpreting its own powers were susceptible to judicial review even if the legislation provided that the body's decisions should not be called into question in any court of law.[45]

We saw that within the jurisdiction the Government cannot plead Act of State whether the injured person was alien or subject. Outside the jurisdiction the position is different. If the Crown acknowledges responsibility for causing the loss, but claims that it was done as a matter of policy in its relations with another state or the nationals of another state, an alien cannot challenge its legality in the English courts. Act of State is in these circumstances a plea that prevents the litigation from continuing.[46] The states of which the victims are nationals might seek redress by diplomatic negotiation (the plea is, after all, dependent on the Government's accepting that it caused the loss) but it is open to the Government to argue that its actions were permitted under international law.

Here is another situation in which nationality matters because it is unlikely that Act of State can be raised against a British national even when the act takes place abroad. The opportunity to decide the matter arose in 1969 when the House of Lords considered the case of a British hotelier in Cyprus who claimed compensation for his property, which had been requisitioned by British forces. However, only Lord Reid decided the issue (in favour of the hotelier). The others joined him but on a different basis (the requisitioning did not have the character of Act of State). They expressed only varying degrees of doubt about whether Act of State was available against a British subject. They were troubled at the thought that a single act (say an army explosion) might give a cause of action to expatriate Britons but not their alien neighbours. Yet there are two good reasons for the distinction: first, the Britons, but not their neighbours, owed duties to the British Crown; second, the neighbours, but not the Britons, would have another government to negotiate on their behalf with Her Majesty's Government at a diplomatic level. Besides, even in the absence of the plea of Act of State, the Government would have a range of prerogative and statutory powers under which it might be able to justify its actions. If it could not, there is no good reason why it should not pay compensation to its own citizens.[47]

The duties that Britons abroad continue to owe to the Crown are limited but of symbolic and sometimes practical importance. Most criminal law is local; that is, it applies only to acts done within or which have an effect within the jurisdiction. However, there are exceptions.

Treason can be committed inside the jurisdiction by aliens as well as subjects, since both owe a duty of allegiance within the realm. Abroad, only subjects could commit treason. Unlike aliens, they owe allegiance to the Crown wherever they are. This rule was much more draconian when coupled with the common law concept, which lasted until 1870, that allegiance was indelible and could not be unilaterally renounced by a subject. Dr Story, a Roman Catholic priest, was condemned to death as a traitor in 1571, although he had deliberately left England because of the intolerance of his faith. Aeneas Macdonald was convicted of treason in 1747 for his part in the Jacobite uprising, although he had resided in France since his infancy. Irish republicans particularly resented the refusal of the British Crown to let its people go. Even naturalization by another state had no effect. English emigrants to the USA were press-ganged into the Royal Navy and English-born US citizens were tried for treason if they fought against Britain. This was a hopelessly unrealistic way to conduct international relations in the nineteenth century and the diplomatic crises it provoked led to the introduction of a statutory procedure for renouncing the status of British subject in the Naturalisation Act 1870.[48]

The statement that aliens cannot commit treason abroad has to be qualified by the case of *Joyce* v. *DPP*.[49] Joyce was an American citizen who had grown up in England and Ireland. He was a right-wing fascist and just before the outbreak of the Second World War travelled to Germany, from where he broadcast Nazi propaganda in English. He became widely known by his nickname, Lord Haw-Haw. Captured after the war, he was tried for treason. Although he was not British and none of his activities took place in Britain his conviction was upheld by the House of Lords. Their excuse was that he had travelled on a fraudulently obtained British passport. Their reasoning has been convincingly and comprehensively demolished by many writers[50] and the decision has come to be seen as the product of a post-war climate in which a man who had tricked a passport out of the Government and broadcast enemy propaganda with an upper-class British accent was not going to be allowed to escape punishment.

Like treason, murder abroad can be tried in Britain, but only if the defendant is a British citizen, British Dependant Territories' citizen or British Overseas citizen.[51]

Nationality can close doors. Like Britain, many countries require visitors from certain (sometimes all) foreign countries to have a visa before they arrive and/or to go through screening by immigration officials before entering.

Nationality can also open doors. An increasingly important feature of British nationality is the derivative rights it confers on a person as a national of a member state of the EC. The principles of free movement of persons, capital, and goods and services within the EC are set out in the Treaty of Rome. In some cases these are sufficiently precise to give rights by themselves, which must be recognized and enforced by domestic courts. In most cases the Treaty rights have been worked out in considerably greater detail by regulations and directives emanating from the European Commission and Council of Ministers.

On joining the EC, Britain made a declaration as to who were to be regarded as its nationals for the purpose of these rights.[52] That declaration was amended in 1983 following the British Nationality Act 1981.[53] The present definition covers: British citizens, British subjects (as the term is used in the 1981 Act) with the right of abode in the UK and British Dependent Territories' citizens who acquire that citizenship through their connection with Gibraltar. There remains some doubt as to whether Britain had the right in 1983 to eliminate certain groups from the status of national of a member state and thus deprive them of accrued EC rights, but the issue has yet to be tested in either the British or EC courts.

For the main part these new EC rights are of value only abroad. They are intended to facilitate the three freedoms listed above. Generally speaking an EC national cannot assert the same rights against his or her own state. Thus, for instance, EC law gives a national of a member state the right to work in another member state. To enable workers to take up this right it is supplemented by a right to be joined by a wide range of family members, whether or not those family members are also EC citizens.[54] The provisions are far more liberal than the British immigration rules (or the immigration provisions of many other EC states), which govern immigration by those who do not have EC protected rights. This leads to a highly anomalous situation. It is much easier for a British worker to be joined in Paris by her Pakistani husband than it would be if she remained in Britain. More piquantly, the difficulties she will face in bringing her husband to Britain will not be shared by a French woman working in London who seeks to be joined by *her* Pakistani husband. The European Court of Justice has been confronted with these and similar examples of 'reverse discrimination', but has resolutely refused to apply Community rights against the national's own state unless there has been exercise of European free movement rights.[55]

As intra-Community movement becomes more common, this qualification will increase in significance. Thus the Court has already held that an EC national who becomes professionally qualified in another member state cannot on return to his or her own state be treated differently from other EC nationals with the same qualification.[56] If EC law requires member states to recognize the qualification, they must do so whether it is held by a foreigner or their own national. The Court has applied a similar principle in insisting that a member state admit the spouse of one of its nationals whom the national married while working elsewhere in the Community.[57]

The essential point needs repeating. EC rights of the kind discussed here are available only to the nationals of member states and their families. They cannot be claimed in other member states by an alien, even if settled in Britain, or, for instance, by a Commonwealth citizen who has lived in Britain for the majority of his or her life.

Nationality remains critical in the context of immigration control in the UK. British citizens are immune from deportation.[58] A person who has been settled in the UK for many years is in practice unlikely to be deported, but the possibility remains. An EC national and members of his or her family can only be deported on limited grounds and then only if given proper opportunities to appeal against the decision,[59] but again the possibility of deportation exists unless and until they are naturalized.[60]

For rights of entry into the UK there is not a simple dividing line between British citizens and others. British citizens do have the right to enter the country 'without let or hindrance', subject to the important caveat that they can prove their identity and entitlement.[61] However, they are not alone in this right.

Until 1962 any British subject or Commonwealth citizen had a common law right to enter Britain.[62] However, the Commonwealth Immigrants Acts of 1962 and 1968 severely curtailed those rights. These and the Immigration Act 1971 tried to carve out a sub-category of Commonwealth citizens who 'belonged' to Britain. The debate was infused with racism and it was no coincidence that the belongers were in the main white and those excluded principally black. The 1971 Act used the terms 'patriality' and 'right of abode' to describe the belongers who continued to have the unfettered right to enter Britain. It is important to appreciate that these categories were applied as well to citizens of the United Kingdom and Colonies with the possibility (translated into heartbreaking reality) that Britain would refuse to admit Britons who had no other nationality and no other country where they were entitled to live. It was mostly Asians from East Africa who suffered. Their exclusion was condemned by the European Commission of Human Rights as violating the guarantee in article 3 of the European Convention on Human Rights against inhuman and degrading treatment.[63] The Government's response was to increase the 'special vouchers' for families in this category for entry to the UK, but the numbers are still inadequate and many families have queued for years before being allocated a rationed ticket to enter their own country.

Following the 1981 Nationality Act most of the CUKCs in this category became British overseas citizens, with no greater rights of entry into the UK. Indeed, one of the purposes of that statute was to bring nationality law more into line with immigration control: a case, many thought, of the tail wagging the dog.

Since the 1981 Act the right of abode is confined to British citizens and those Commonwealth citizens who had established patriality before the Act went into effect (1 January 1983).[64] Nationals of other EC states and their families have, as we have seen, rights to enter the UK under EC law. Others seeking to come to the UK must obtain leave to enter from an immigration officer. The immigration rules set out the categories of visitors and immigrants who will be allowed in and the conditions which attach to each class. Some place an intolerable burden on would-be migrants. The most notorious is the 'primary purpose rule', under which a person wishing to come as the spouse of a man or woman settled in the UK must show that the primary purpose of the marriage was not to obtain entry to the UK. This is not synonymous with establishing that the marriage is genuine rather than a bogus union that will fracture as soon as the absent spouse has entered the UK. Even genuine couples carry the burden of showing what the primary purpose of their marriage was not. Proof of motive is never easy; disproving a particular motive is very hard. There is scope for appealing a negative decision to an immigration adjudicator, but in almost all cases the appeal has to be lodged from abroad and the adjudicator has to decide on the motives of a person whom he has not seen and has 'heard' only through documents and the advocacy of his or her representative.

Since nationality is so important in the context of foreign travel and since proof of nationality is customarily achieved by presentation of a passport, it might be thought that British nationals had the right to a British passport.

The great majority of passport applications are, of course, granted. Although no explanation is given for individual refusals, they are said to fall into four categories: criminal suspects; people previously repatriated who have not reimbursed the Government's expenses; children travelling against the wish of their parent or guardian; and 'in very rare cases, a person whose past or proposed activities are so demonstrably undesirable that the grant or continued enjoyment of passport facilities would be contrary to the public interest'.[65] In each of these cases it is not easy to see why the decision should be taken by the executive when it more properly lies with a court. Criminal courts can issue arrest warrants and determine bail conditions; family courts can move swiftly to restrain the removal of children from the jurisdiction. Civil courts (where this is appropriate) can prevent a debtor leaving the jurisdiction[66] and it is difficult to see why the Foreign and Commonwealth Office's debts merit more stringent enforcement. The last category, if it can be justified at all, again ought to be a matter for judicial rather than executive decision.

Passports are granted by the Crown under the prerogative. Traditionally, prerogative powers were considered beyond the scope of judicial review.[67] However, this assumption can no longer stand following the 'GCHQ' decision of the House of Lords in 1984.[68] Passports would not generally be among the rare cases (e.g. treaty-making and the appointment of ministers) that the Lords conceded to be non-justiciable. In *R*. v. *Secretary of State for Foreign and Commonwealth Affairs ex p. Everett*[69] the Court of Appeal accepted that it had power to review passport refusals on the normal principles of judicial review.

EC law may go further and give those who are regarded as British nationals for EC purposes a right to a passport subject to limited exceptions to do with public policy, public security and public health.[70]

NOTES AND REFERENCES

1 Pollock and Maitland, *History of English Law*, Volume 1, p. 444; Salmond, 'Citizenship and allegiance' (1902) 18 LQR 49, 60; Holdsworth, *History of English Law*, Volume 9, pp. 92–6; cf. Report of the Royal Commission on Naturalisation and Allegiance 1869 Cmnd 4109, Appendix, p. 137.

2 Holdsworth, Volume 9, pp. 96–7; Coke, on Littleton 129b.

3 *Chappell* v. *Purday* (1845) 14 M & W 303; *Low* v. *Ward* (1868) LR 6 Eq. 415.

4 Merchant Shipping Act 1988 s. 3(1).

5 *R.* v *Arnaud* (1846) 9 QB 806. Air transport licences are restricted to UK nationals or a company incorporated in the UK but in this case the company must also be controlled by UK nationals – Civil Aviation Act 1982 ss. 165 and 105.

6 *Attorney-General* v. *Duplessis*, Parker 144; *Du Hourmelin* v *Sheldon* (1839) 4 My & Cr. 525.

7 1869 Royal Commission (see above) p. 139; Naturalisation Act 1870 s. 2, and see British Nationality and Status of Aliens Act 1914 s. 17.

8 See the Report of the departmental committee of the Board of Trade, 'General questions of trade relations after the War', 11 January 1916; and the Report of the Committee on Industrial Policy after the War (1919), Public Records Office HO 45/307584; Minutes of the Aliens and Nationality Committee, 4 April and 23 May 1991, PRO HO 45/11843 and HO 45/19966.

9 Aliens Restriction (Amendment) Act 1919, s. 11.

10 Aliens Restriction (Amendment) Act 1919, s. 11(1)(c).

11 Aliens Restriction (Amendment) Act 1919, ss. 4 and 5.

12 See Broadcasting Act 1990, schedule 2, parts I and II.

13 See *Netz* v. *Ede* [1946] 1 Ch. 224; *R.* v. *Superintendant of Vine Street Police Station ex p. Liberman* [1916] 1 KB 268; *R.* v. *Commandant of Knockaloe Camp ex p. Forman* 117 LT 627; *R.* v. *Bottrill ex parte Kuchenmeister* [1947] 1 KB 41.

14 *R.* v. *Secretary of State for the Home Department ex p. Cheblak* [1991] 2 All ER 319 CA.

15 Bellot, 'The detention of Napoleon Buonaparte' (1923) 39 LQR 170.

16 Immigration Act 1971, s. 33(5).

17 See *Cheblak* above.

18 (1765) 19 St. Tr. 1030.

19 Glanville Williams, 'The correlation of allegiance and protection' (1948) 10 CLJ 54.

20 [1921] 2 AC 262.

21 *Commercial Estates Co. of Egypt* v. *Board of Trade* [1925] 1 KB 271, pp. 290, 297.

22 A resolution in 1698 (see *House of Commons Journals*, Vol. 12, 367) prohibited them from voting in elections but even before then they were usually excluded because the franchise was confined to those who owned land of a specified value. Aliens could not own land.

23 Representation of the People Act 1983, s. 1.

24 See House of Commons Home Affairs Committee, first report of 1982–3 Session (HC 32), vol. 2, pp. 1, 4.

25 *Ibid.*

26 Representation of the People Act 1985, s. 1, as amended by Representation of the People Act 1989, s. 1.

27 *R.* v. *de Mierre* (1771) 5 Burr 2787; *Anthony* v. *Seger* (1789) 1 Hagg. Con. 9.

28 Aliens Restriction (Amendment) Act 1919, s. 6.

29 Army Act 1881, s. 95(1).

30 Army Act 1955, s. 21(1).

31 Air Force Act 1955, s. 21.

32 Juries Act 1974, s. 1.

33 Holdsworth, *History of English Law*, Vol. 9, pp. 91–2.

34 The Juries Act 6 Geo 4c. 50, s. 47; see W. E. Davies, *The Law Relating to Aliens* (Stevens 1931), p. 191.

35 See Royal Commission on the Laws of Naturalisation and Alienage (1869) Cmnd 4109, Addenda, p. 80 – the case of John Warren.

36 8 St. Tr. NS 900.

37 *The Times*, 2 and 3 March 1868; Leon O'Brian, *Fenian Fever* (Chatto & Windus 1971), p. 186.

38 Naturalisation Act 1870, s. 5.

39 Cmnd 6352 (1975), para. 188.

40 *R.* v. *Thomas* (1989) 88 Cr.App.R. 370 (CCC) *R.* v. *Bansal* [1985] Crim LR 151; *R.* v. *Chandler (No. 2)* [1964] 2 QB 322; *R.* v. *Frazer* [1987] Crim LR 418 and *R.* v. *Mcalla* [1986] CLR 335; *R.* v. *Ford (Royston)* [1989] 3 WLR 762.

41 *China Navigation* v. *Attorney-General* (1932) 147 LT 22.

42 *R.* v. *Secretary of State for Foreign and Commonwealth Affairs ex p. Pirbhai* (1985) 129 SJ 756 CA.

43 *Rustomjee* v. *The Queen* (1876) LR 2 QBD 69; *Civilian War Claimants' Association* v. *The King* [1932] AC 14.

44 Foreign Compensation Act 1950.

45 *Anisminic Ltd* v. *Foreign Compensation Commission* [1969] 2 AC 147.

46 *Buron* v. *Denman* (1848) 2 Ex 167.

47 Collier, 'Act of State as a defence against a British subject' [1968] CLJ 102.

48 See *Story* 1 St. Tr. 1087; *Macdonald* 18 St. Tr. 858; Report of the Royal Commission on Naturalisation and Allegiance 1869, Cmnd 4109.

49 [1946] AC 347.

50 E.g. Glanville Williams (1948) 10 CLJ 54; Biggs (1947) 7 Univ. of Toronto LJ 182.

51 Offences Against the Person Act 1861, s. 9.

52 (1972) Cmnd 4862, p. 118.

53 (1983) Cmnd 9062.

54 Regulation 1612/68, Article 10.

55 E.g. Case 35,36/82 *Morson* v. *Jhanjan* v. *Netherlands* [1982] ECR 3273.

56 E.g. Case 115/78 *Knoors* v *Secretary of State for Economic Affairs* [1979] ECR 399.

57 *R.* v. *Immigration Appeal Tribunal ex p. Surinder Singh* [1992] 3 CMLR 358.

58 Immigration Act 1971, s. 3(5). Commonwealth citizens who had the right of abode in the UK (see below) before the commencement of the 1981 Act share this immunity from deportation – *ibid.*, s. 2(1)(b).

59 Council Directive 64/221/EEC of 25 February 1964; Council Directive 72/194/EEC of 18 May 1972.

60 Even naturalization is not a complete bar since there are procedures for revoking a naturalization certificate on the grounds, for instance, that it was obtained by fraud: British Nationality Act 1981, s. 40. In some circumstances the fraud will have the effect of rendering the certificate void so that there is no need for the Government even to go through the revocation procedure: *R.* v. *Secretary of State for the Home Department ex parte Parvaz Akhtar* [1981] QB 46.

61 Immigration Act 1971, ss. 1(1), 2(a).

62 *DPP* v. *Bhagwan* [1972] AC 60, 69.

63 *East African Asians* case [1981] 3 EHRR 76.

64 More precisely, the Commonwealth citizen had to have patriality on one of two specific grounds: birth to or adoption by a parent who was a citizen of the UK and Colonies by virtue of birth in the UK; or marriage to a patrial Commonwealth citizen – see Immigration Act 1971, s. 2(2).

65 Hansard HC Debs Vol. 997 col. 234 WA, 22 January 1981.

66 The old writ of *ne exeat regno* has been revived to achieve this; see, e.g., *Felton* v. *Callis* [1969] 1 QB 200; alternatively, the defendant can be ordered by injunction to surrender his passport temporarily: *Bayer AG* v. *Winter* [1986] 1 All ER 733.

67 See, e.g., Foreign Office communication of 1909 in 5 British Digest of International Law 309.
68 *Council of Civil Service Unions* v. *Minister of State for the Civil Service* [1984] 3 All ER 935.
69 [1989] 1 All ER 655 CA.
70 Council Directive 68/360 of 15 October 1968.

14

Citizenship and Freedom of Expression

CONOR GEARTY

INTRODUCTION

'Liberty of thought soon shrivels without freedom of expression',[1] wrote US Supreme Court justice Felix Frankfurter in 1951, and there can be no doubt that few concepts are more immediately or more directly connected with the idea of citizenship than a right of free expression. In this chapter, I will explore the extent to which this freedom is protected in the UK by a judicially enforceable guarantee of free speech. There is no such provision in British domestic law, of course, and because of this it is highly artificial even to pose the question in terms of rights, at least as far as UK domestic law is concerned. There is an indirectly domestic right to free expression, however. It is to be found in article 10 (and to a lesser degree article 11) of the European Convention on Human Rights. This guarantee is indirect because the articles cannot be explicitly relied upon in British courts,[2] but it is nevertheless domestic because litigants who have exhausted local remedies in Britain may take their cases to the supra-national European Commission and European Court of Human Rights, and the latter court's judgments must be acted upon by the defendant government as a matter of international law.

Before analysing the Convention, and as a guide to its jurisprudence, I will explore what is meant by a right to free expression and consider the extent to which the idea is rooted in a particular understanding of what citizenship entails. In doing so, I will draw mainly on case law from the United States Supreme Court, a body which has long experience in dealing with a constitutional imperative to protect free speech. In a sense my enquiry involves a plundering of the well-established American record and a consideration of the much newer Convention jurisdiction in light of the themes to be gleaned from it. The comparison will lead to certain conclusions about the success of articles 10 and 11 as a means of enhancing the rights of the citizen in this vital area.

THEORIES OF FREEDOM OF EXPRESSION

To think is to speak. If freedom of thought is the cornerstone of liberal democratic government, then the individual's entitlement to express those thoughts is a vital emanation of that right. As to why these freedoms matter in quite this particular way, three theories tend together to cover the spectrum of traditional opinion. The first two of these are less obviously concerned with citizenship than is the third. First, there is the market optimism of the United States Supreme Court justice, Oliver Wendell Holmes, nowhere more powerfully expressed than in his opinion in *Abrams* v. *United States*:

> [W]hen men have realized that time has upset many fighting faiths, they may come to believe even more than they believe the very foundations of their own conduct that the ultimate good desired is better reached by free trade in ideas, – that the best test of truth is the power of the thought to get itself accepted in the competition of the market; and that truth is the only ground upon which their wishes safely can be carried out. That, at any rate, is the theory of our Constitution. It is an experiment, as all life is an experiment.[3]

Holmes's views are close to but not identical with those of John Stuart Mill.[4] Both men believed that the prime purpose of freedom of expression was to facilitate the search for truth. This is more a philosophical than a political quest and as such is connected only indirectly with the individual as the citizen of a state. The market approach has been criticized by a powerful UK committee set up to enquire into obscenity and film censorship under the chairman-ship of the philosopher Bernard Williams. Reporting in 1979, the committee considered that the 'faith in *laissez-faire* shown by the nineteenth century and earlier does not altogether meet modern conditions'.[5] It went on:

> If everyone talks at once, truth will not prevail, since no one can be heard and nothing will prevail: and falsehood indeed may prevail, if powerful agencies can gain an undue hold on the market. Even in natural science, which Mill regarded as the paradigm, he neglected the importance of scientific institutions and the filter against cranks which is operated,

and necessarily operated, by expert opinion, excluding from serious consideration what it sees as incompetence. Against the principle that truth is strong and (given the chance) will prevail, must be set Gresham's law, that bad money drives out good, which has some application in matters of culture and which predicts that it will not necessarily be the most interesting ideas or the most valuable works of art that survive in competition – above all, in commercial competition.[6]

The committee proceeded to offer an alternative view as to the most appropriate theoretical justification for freedom of expression:

The . . . idea, to which Mill attached the market-place model, remains a correct and profound idea: that we do not know in advance what social, moral or intellectual developments will turn out to be possible, necessary or desirable for human beings and for their future, and free expression, intellectual and artistic – something which may need to be fostered and protected as well as merely permitted – is essential to human development, as a process which does not merely happen (in some form or other, it will happen anyway), but so far as possible is rationally understood. It is essential to it, moreover, not just as a means to it, but as part of it. Since human beings are not just subject to their history but aspire to be conscious of it, the development of human individuals, of society and of humanity in general, is a process itself properly constituted in part by free expression and the exchange of human communication.[7]

This emphasis on personal fulfilment, which is prominent in the writings of the legal philosopher Ronald Dworkin,[8] and which underpins American case law on artistic freedom,[9] once again stresses broader issues than those that we would normally associate with citizenship, with its connotation of the individual as an active participant in civil society.

This is the sense best captured by the third approach to freedom of expression, which has been more prominent in the jurisprudence of the US Supreme Court than either of the first two. One of its earliest and clearest judicial expressions was in the concurring opinion of Justice Brandeis in the 1927 decision, *Whitney* v. *California*:

Those who won our independence believed that the final end of the state was to make men free to develop their faculties; and that in its government the deliberative forces should prevail over the arbitrary. They valued liberty both as an end and as a means. They believed liberty to be the secret of happiness and courage to be the secret of liberty. They believed that freedom to think as you will and to speak as you think are means indispensable to the discovery and spread of political truth; that without free speech and assembly discussion would be futile; that with them, discussion affords ordinarily adequate protection against the dissemination of noxious doctrine; that the greatest menace to freedom is an inert people; that public discussion is a political duty; and that this should be a fundamental principle of the American government. They recognized the risks to which all human institutions are subject. But they knew that order cannot be secured merely through fear of punishment for its infraction; that it is hazardous to discourage thought, hope and imagination; that fear breeds repression; that repression breeds hate; that hate menaces stable government; that the path of safety lies in the opportunity to discuss freely supposed grievances and proposed remedies; and that the fitting remedy for evil counsels is good ones. Believing in the power of reason as applied through public discussion, they eschewed silence coerced by law – the argument of force in its worst form. Recognizing the occasional tyrannies of governing majorities, they amended the Constitution so that free speech and assembly should be guaranteed.[10]

What is important about this passage is its emphasis on political speech, on expression as facilitative of good government. To describe public discussion as a 'public duty' as Justice Brandeis does here is to talk the language of active citizenship. It is this functional dimension to the freedom that, armed with the clear words of the First Amendment, American judges have returned to time and again. Chief Justice Hughes declared in 1937 that it was 'imperative . . . to preserve inviolate the constitutional rights of free speech, free press and free assembly in order to maintain the opportunity for free political discussion, to the end that government may be responsive to the will of the people and that changes, if desired, may be obtained by peaceful means. Therein lies the security of the Republic, the very foundation of constitutional government.'[11] More recently, in the course of his opinion in the Pentagon Papers case in 1971, Justice Douglas went so far as to maintain that 'Secrecy in government is fundamentally anti-democratic, perpetuating bureaucratic errors', and that 'Open debate and discussion of public issues are vital to our national health.'[12]

These three theories tell us why freedom of expression is important.

They do not necessarily inform us as to how broad the freedom has to be. Even an absolutist like Mill contemplated at least some narrow exceptions and it was Justice Holmes who observed that the 'most stringent protection of free speech would not protect a man in falsely shouting fire in a theatre, and causing a panic'.[13] Given that exceptions are therefore inevitable, it is hardly surprising that they have duly made their appearance in the American case law. Their breadth and range has varied from era to era, but three points may be made about them, in relation to both freedom of expression generally and the US experience in particular. First, much has depended on how a thought is manifested, on the vehicle of expression that is deployed to communicate it. First Amendment law has traditionally drawn a distinction between expressing oneself through conduct alone on the one hand and words or words and conduct on the other. As regards conduct alone, there has been a tendency towards wider restriction, a fact both inevitable and justifiable in view of the greater capacity of conduct for public disturbance and the availability of words as an alternative mode of expression.[14] To add to these problems, there is also the difficulty that protecting conduct as a form of expression may raise difficult questions as to when behaviour is intended to be communicative of some idea and when it is not – a dilemma that does not generally arise with words, or with words used in tandem with conduct. This is not to say that conduct alone is not sometimes a powerful expression of a communal thought – the recognized importance in the USA of freedom of assembly testifies to the fact. But it is the case that such expressions are more likely to be limited than the communication of the equivalent sentiment by means of words alone.[15]

Second, as the dictum from Holmes J clearly recognizes, the use of words alone, whether spoken or written, can be absolutely guaranteed by no theory of freedom of expression that aspires to be coherent. The question will always be a two-fold one: to what extent should a presumption in favour of free speech operate in any given case; and to the extent that it does, how far is it outweighed (if at all) by conflicting public interests? As regards the first of these, much depends on the type of speech that is in issue, and the degree to which it fits within a type contemplated by a relevant theory of free speech as being deserving of protection.[16] The expression of an unpopular political sentiment too has on this ground more claim to our attention than a simple call to kill for cash. Similarly a novel is less likely to be judged obscene than a pornographic magazine produced solely for profit. As regards the second element to the question, it is a reminder that here, as elsewhere in public law, there is an inevitable concern with a balancing of interests. Not even political speech is immune from this process, despite the heavy presumption in its favour. 'Reasonably limited,' said one US supreme court justice in 1925, 'this freedom is an inestimable privilege in a free government' – but he went on to add that 'without such limitation it might become the scourge of the Republic'.[17]

Third, it is important when considering the nature of this balancing of interests and these exceptions to freedom of expression to be aware of a possible shortfall between theory and practice. An impeccable commitment to free speech, rhetorically supported by judges, is worth rather less if it produces few end results in favour of the freedom in hard cases. Once again the United States example is instructive. There could be few more unequivocal guarantees of freedom of expression than the First Amendment's declaration that 'Congress shall make no law . . . abridging the freedom of speech, or of the press'. Yet in 1919 this did not stop the Supreme Court unanimously upholding legislation which had led to the jailing of the socialist leader Eugene Debs for ten years, for obstructing the recruitment of men to fight in the First World War by declaring that he abhorred war and by asserting that the courts, the press and the entire political system were controlled by the rich.[18] Justice Holmes's powerful dictum on the breadth of the First Amendment in *Abrams*,[19] quoted earlier, was a dissenting opinion and did not affect the conviction in that case of the five defendants under the Sedition Act 1918 for doing no more than distributing leaflets attacking American military intervention in Russia. A 1925 case widely hailed as a breakthrough for civil liberties, because in it the court suggested that the First Amendment applied to states' as well as federal law, similarly left unaffected the defendant's conviction for publishing a pamphlet called *The Left-Wing Manifesto*.[20] Two years later Charlotte Whitney's conviction for nothing more subversive than organizing a left-wing political party was also upheld; Justice Brandeis's eloquent defence of free speech, quoted above, was delivered as a concurring judgment.[21]

Nor are these refusals to apply the First Amendment in all its rigour limited to a brief historical moment of high tension. When the Cold War unleashed an anti-communist crusade in the United States, epitomized in its later phase by Senator McCarthy's attacks on all forms of dissent, the court did next to nothing to protect the many individuals whose lives were being routinely destroyed by casual allegations of guilt by association – despite the fact that their culpability (if it existed) lay in their exercise of freedom of thought and of expression. The nadir was reached in 1951 when in *Dennis* v. *US*[22] the court upheld the legislation which underpinned McCarthyism, a decision described by the then director of the

American Civil Liberties Union as 'the worst single blow to civil liberties in all our history'.[23] Justice Frankfurter's dictum, with which this chapter begins, is drawn from his concurring opinion in that case. More recently, the court has denied First Amendment protection to counsellors prevented by federal regulations from advising pregnant women about the availability of abortions.[24] None of this is to say that there are not a large number of American decisions strongly in favour of free speech – but it is to enter the caveat that even unequivocal wording can be vulnerable in times of high political tension, particularly in cases that raise central questions about law and governmental practice.

THE EUROPEAN CONVENTION ON HUMAN RIGHTS

General Principles

The foregoing analysis, derived in the main from the American case law, provides a useful base from which to consider the way in which the European Convention on Human Rights protects freedom of expression. The first point of course is that, in common with the American approach, freedom of expression is guaranteed in the Convention as a matter of positive right. This is in stark contrast to Britain, where expression functions merely as a residual freedom, dependent for its very existence upon the absence of restrictive legislation and hostile judicial decisions. It is this peculiarity which makes it so difficult intelligibly to discuss any connection between the rights of the citizen and freedom of expression in the context of United Kingdom domestic law. Article 10(1) of the Convention in contrast declares that 'Everyone has the right to freedom of expression.' This is even wider than the US formulation, with its emphasis on 'speech'. Indeed, although article 10(1) goes on to specify that this right 'shall include the freedom to hold opinions and to receive and impart information and ideas', it would seem clear that the paragraph is potentially very much broader than this.

Thus in *Müller and others* v. *Switzerland*,[25] the first applicant, a distinguished painter, produced three works for a public exhibition organized by the other nine applicants. The exhibition was part of a cultural celebration, and Müller's paintings generated strong feelings. They were attacked by one visitor and when a girl reacted violently to them her father informed the authorities, who then prosecuted the applicants for obscenity. The national courts considered the emphasis in the work to be on sexuality in its offensive forms – one of the paintings, for example, depicted sexual relations between men and animals – and the applicants were convicted. The court sentenced them to a fine and ordered the confiscation of the paintings, which were not restored to the artist until almost eight years later. As we shall see presently, the applicants were unsuccessful in their application to Strasbourg but for present purposes what is interesting to note is that neither the Court nor the Commission had any difficulty in classifying the case as one falling full-square within article 10. Freedom of expression was said by the Court clearly to embrace the freedom of artistic expression. The words of the article raised no issue about whether or not it was restricted to speech as such.

A dramatic illustration of the potential breadth of article 10(1)'s formulation came in *Autronic AG* v. *Switzerland*.[26] The applicant was a private commercial company specializing in home electronics. It applied to the Swiss authorities for permission to receive, by means of a private dish aerial, uncoded television programmes intended for the general Soviet public from a Soviet telecommunications satellite. The company was not interested in the least in the content of what the Soviets were communicating; its commercial interest lay in demonstrating the virtuosity of its own technical equipment. In the absence of Soviet consent to the proposal (which was not forthcoming), the Swiss refused the application. The matter reached the European Court of Human Rights as an alleged breach of the right to free expression, where the judges held by a majority of sixteen to two that article 10(1) indeed applied:

> In the Court's view, neither Autronic AG's legal status as a limited company nor the fact that its activities were commercial nor the intrinsic nature of freedom of expression can deprive Autronic AG of the protection of Article 10. The Article applies to 'everyone', whether natural or legal persons. The Court has, moreover, already held on three occasions that it is applicable to profit-making corporate bodies. Furthermore, Article 10 applies not only to the content of information but also to the means of transmission or reception since any restriction imposed on the means necessarily interferes with the right to receive and impart information.[27]

In vain did the two dissentients argue that article 10 presupposed 'a minimum of identification between the person who wishes to exercise the right protected by that Article and the "information" which is transmitted or received. However, in the present case the content of the information – purely by chance, Soviet broadcasts in Russian – was perfectly immaterial to the company and to visitors to the fair who were likely to be present during the broadcast.'

Apart from this extremely broad approach to the speech side of expression, article 10(1) would also seem wide enough to encompass many types of conduct within its protective umbrella, but this point has yet to come full-square before the court. A specific type of behaviour is, however, given explicit protection by article 11, the first sentence of which declares unambiguously that 'Everyone has the right to freedom of peaceful assembly.' The two articles together are much wider than their American equivalent, but unlike the First Amendment, both contain explicit exception clauses. This relieves the judges of the task that the US Supreme Court has found so challenging, namely the introduction of exceptions into an apparently absolutist constitutional provision. But the Convention's qualifications are so numerous that the equally difficult task of balancing interests remains and indeed seems remarkably open-ended. Article 10(2) reads:

> The exercise of [freedom of expression], since it carries with it duties and responsibilities, may be subject to such formalities, conditions, restrictions or penalties as are prescribed by law and are necessary in a democratic society, in the interests of national security, territorial integrity or public safety, for the prevention of disorder or crime, for the protection of health or morals, for the protection of the reputation or rights of others, for preventing the disclosure of information received in confidence, or for maintaining the authority and impartiality of the judiciary.

Article 11(2) similarly declares that no restrictions shall be placed on the exercise of the right of freedom of peaceful assembly 'other than such as are prescribed by law and are necessary in a democratic society in the interests of national security or public safety, for the prevention of disorder or crime, for the protection of health or morals or for the protection of the rights and freedoms of others.'

Contrary to the impression that a casual reading of such a lengthy group of savings might indicate, the qualifications do not quite swallow up the freedoms entirely. A common feature of every exception is that it must be 'necessary in a democratic society'. A recent summary of what this means in the context of freedom of expression was provided by the Court in the course of its judgment in the *Spycatcher* case:

> The adjective 'necessary' . . . implies the existence of a 'pressing social need.' The Contracting States have a certain margin of appreciation in assessing whether such a need exists, but it goes hand in hand with a European supervision, embracing both the law and the decisions applying it, even

those given by independent courts. The Court is therefore empowered to give the final ruling on whether a 'restriction' is reconcilable with freedom of expression as protected by Article 10 . . . [W]hat the Court has to do is to look at the interference complained of in the light of the case as a whole and determine whether it was 'proportionate to the legitimate aim pursued' and whether the reasons adduced by the national authorities to justify it are 'relevant and sufficient.'[28]

A curious feature of the European Convention's approach to expression and assembly is that it is the exceptions to the freedoms rather than the freedoms themselves that are justified by reference to being 'necessary in a democratic society'. Perhaps it is implicit in the document that the freedoms are inherently necessary in such a society, in a way that transcends the need for explicitness. But the breadth of article 10(1) indicates, and cases like *Autronic AG* demonstrate, that expression often has little or nothing to do with the needs of democracy. Neither article on its face gives any clear clue as to its underlying rationale. Faced with this uncertainty, the Court has had the task – similar to that of the US Supreme Court – of developing principles to explain why freedom of expression is important. But, unlike their American counterpart, they have had the elaborate exception clauses in articles 10(2) and 11(2) to guide them. It is now appropriate to consider which, if any, of the three theories of free expression discussed earlier has been most often invoked by the European Court.

First, the cases do not reveal a commitment to a Millian or Holmesian view of expression as a facilitator of truth. Nor do they show any clear trend towards developing articles 10 or 11 as vehicles for individual self-fulfilment. In *Müller*, for example, the Court ruled by six votes to one that the convictions of the artist and the exhibition organizers complied with article 10(2) and by five votes to two that the confiscation orders were similarly legitimate. The majority considered that

having inspected the original paintings, [they did] not find unreasonable the view taken by the Swiss courts that those paintings, with their emphasis on sexuality in some of its crudest forms, were 'liable grossly to offend the sense of sexual propriety of persons of ordinary sensitivity'. In the circumstances, having regard to the margin of appreciation left to them under Article 10(2), the Swiss courts were entitled to consider it 'necessary' for the protection of morals to impose a fine on the applicants for publishing obscene material.[29]

The acceptance of artistic freedom as part of article 10(1) did not betoken a commitment to such expression sufficient to outweigh the morality exception in article 10(2), despite the requirement that the restriction be 'necessary in a democratic society'. There could be no clearer indication of the court's reluctance to enter battle against the member states on behalf of aesthetic freedom and cultural licence.

The Convention and Political Expression

There is evidence that the political importance of freedom of expression, which we earlier saw articulated in Brandeis J's judgment in *Whitney*, has been to the fore in the court's decisions in the field of political speech. The leading case is *Lingens* v. *Austria*.[30] Shortly after the Austrian general election in 1975, the well-known 'Nazi hunter' Simon Wiesenthal accused the leader of one of Austria's political parties of having been during the Second World War a member of an SS infantry brigade which had on several occasions massacred civilians behind the German lines in Russia. The man concerned, Friedrich Peter, admitted membership but denied involvement in the killings. At the time, the party he then led was in consultation with the sitting Chancellor Bruno Kreisky about the possibility of cooperating to form a government. Kreisky vigorously supported Peter and referred to Wiesenthal's organization as a 'political mafia' that employed 'mafia methods'. The applicant was the editor of a magazine. He printed two articles critical of the Chancellor. In particular, he accused him of protecting former members of the Nazi SS for political reasons and of facilitating their participation in Austrian politics. Chancellor Kreisky reacted to this by launching a private prosecution for criminal defamation against Lingens. He relied upon a very broad provision of the Austrian criminal code, which said that 'Anyone who in such a way that it may be perceived by a third person accuses another of possessing a contemptible character or attitude or of behaviour contrary to honour or morality and of such a nature as to make him contemptible or otherwise lower him in public esteem shall be liable to imprisonment not exceeding six months or a fine.'[31] After lengthy proceedings in Austria, the applicant was convicted and a fine of 15,000 Schillings was imposed. The Vienna court of appeal found that Kreisky had been criticized in his capacity both as a party leader and as a private individual and that both could give rise to this form of legal action.

When the case reached Strasbourg, both the Commission and the Court were unanimous that the conviction amounted to an infringement of article 10. Since the interference with freedom of expression was obvious, the key issue was whether the conviction could be justified as being 'necessary in a democratic society'. After rehearsing the established law on the subject,[32] the Court went on to develop some important general principles:

> freedom of expression, as secured in paragraph 1 of Article 10, constitutes one of the essential foundations of a democratic society and one of the basic conditions for its progress and for each individual's self-fulfilment. Subject to paragraph 2, it is applicable not only to 'information' or 'ideas' that are favourably received or regarded as inoffensive or as a matter of indifference, but also to those that offend, shock or disturb. Such are the demands of that pluralism, tolerance and broadmindedness without which there is no 'democratic society'. . . . . These principles are of particular importance as far as the press is concerned.[33]

Therefore it was true to say that 'freedom of political debate [was] at the very core of the concept of a democratic society which prevail[ed] throughout the Convention'.[34] The Court went on:

> The limits of acceptable criticism are accordingly wider as regards a politician as such than as regards a private individual. Unlike the latter, the former inevitably and knowingly lays himself open to close scrutiny of his every word and deed by both journalists and the public at large, and he must consequently display a greater degree of tolerance. No doubt Article 10(2) enables the reputation of others – that is to say, of all individuals – to be protected, and this protection extends to politicians too, even when they are not acting in their private capacity; but in such cases the requirements of such protection have to be weighed in relation to the interests of open discussion of political issues.[35]

Applying these principles to the facts before it, the Court pointed out that the articles 'dealt with political issues of public interest in Austria which had given rise to many heated discussions'[36] and that the 'impugned expressions [had] therefore to be seen against the background of a post-election political controversy'.[37]

The European Court in *Lingens* described the applicant's attack on the Chancellor as 'in no way unusual in the hard-fought tussles of politics',[38] and it would certainly surprise many British and American politicians that the Chancellor seemed to have such a thin skin when it came to public criticism. The facts of *Lingens* were unusual, and the extreme nature of Kreisky's action may be demonstrated by the fact that he failed to command a single supporter in either the Commission or the Court. Nevertheless, the principles enunciated in the course of the decision are valuable and have been frequently returned to. In *Oberschlick*,[39] the facts were once again both Austrian and unusual. Mr Walter Grabher-Meyer was the secretary-general of one of the political parties which was then a participant in Austria's ruling coalition. During the spring 1983 parliamentary election campaign, it was reported on television that he had suggested that the family allowances for Austrian women should be increased by 50 per cent in order to obviate their seeking abortions for financial reasons, while those paid to immigrant mothers should be reduced to 50 per cent of their current levels. A month later, the applicant and several other persons laid a criminal information charge against Grabher-Meyer, which the public prosecutor subsequently decided not to proceed with. On the day that it was laid, the applicant published the full text of the criminal information in a magazine which he edited. The substance was that Grabher-Meyer had racist and national socialist tendencies that were contrary to law. In setting aside the applicant's conviction in the Austrian courts for criminal defamation under the same article that Kreisky had used against Lingens, the Court agreed that this method of publishing the material, as a pseudo-report on a criminal matter, certainly would have 'a particularly telling effect on the average reader', but quoting extensively from its *Lingens* judgment, it concluded that 'in view of the importance of the issue at stake . . . [the applicant could not] be said to have exceeded the limits of freedom of expression by choosing this particular form'.[40]

Two further cases demonstrate the application of these principles in the field of freedom of assembly. In *Ezelin* v. *France*,[41] the Court held that the disciplining of a lawyer for having participated in a lawful political demonstration infringed article 11, and declared that 'the freedom to take part in a peaceful assembly . . . [was] of such importance that it [could] not be restricted in any way, even for an *avocat*, so long as the person concerned [did] not himself commit any reprehensible act on such an occasion.'[42] In *Plattform 'Ärzte für das Leben'* v. *Austria*,[43] the applicants were an association of doctors who were campaigning against abortion. In 1980 and 1982, the association held two demonstrations that were disrupted by counter-demonstrators despite the presence of a large contingent of police. The applicants' complaint that insufficiency of police protection amounted to an infringement of article 11 was declared manifestly ill-founded by the Commission and the case reached the Court on a more technical issue relating to whether (as required by article 13) the applicants had even an arguable case that article 11 had been breached.

While ruling unanimously against the association on this point, the Court did make the following general statement of principle:

A demonstration may annoy or give offence to persons opposed to the ideas or claims that it is seeking to promote. The participants must, however, be able to hold the demonstration without having to fear that they will be subjected to physical violence by their opponents; such a fear would be liable to deter associations or other groups supporting common ideas or interests from openly expressing their opinions on highly controversial issues affecting the community. In a democracy the right to counter-demonstrate cannot extend to inhibiting the exercise of the right to demonstrate.

This important gloss on the principles already developed in the article 10 cases is reminiscent of the controversial *Skokie* case in the United States[44] and the equally celebrated United Kingdom decision from the nineteenth century, *Beatty* v. *Gillbanks*.[45] If followed, it may prove to have far-reaching implications for British public order law, which has long justified restriction by reference to the risk of attracting the violent attention of others. These points were not directly before the court in the *Plattform* case – the applicants were doomed to fail on the facts. No high-risk consequences flowed from this statement of high principle.

Restricting Political Speech

These various cases show the European Court in a powerful light, defending expression and assembly in the political arena and demonstrating in doing so a mature grasp of the importance to democracy of a free and open political dialogue, even when it is distastefully or extravagantly conducted. But, remembering that many of the US Supreme Court's most powerful dicta on free speech came from judges who were either in dissent or voting for repression, we need to be alive to the possibility that the rhetoric may not in practice match the reality. This is not true in any of the cases discussed so far, where the Court – usually unanimously or by large majorities – has generally decided in favour of freedom and not just spoken about its importance. But, as their facts make clear, none of these cases raised issues which went very far beyond their own circumstances or compelled a major change in law or in governmental practice. It does not undermine their correctness to recognize that they all originated more or less in 'one-off' incidents of excess. But this does serve to focus attention on the freedom of expression cases before the Court and the Commission that have attempted to go further than this. These are the cases in which success would have involved governments in far-reaching changes of much greater importance to them than reacting to a single episode. Here, although the rhetoric remains the same, it is clear that a rather different and more disturbing trend is in operation.

An early presage of this trend came in what was then only the fifteenth case before the court, and the first to raise squarely a freedom of expression issue, *Engel and others* v. *Netherlands*.[46] The decision was primarily concerned with a procedural challenge to the disciplinary system to which individuals were subject when doing military service in the Netherlands. However, two of the five applicants were the editors of a journal published by the Conscript Servicemen's Association and they were punished for publishing an article in their journal which was said by the authorities to have tended to undermine military discipline. Because of this, they raised article 10 as well as other articles in their application to Strasbourg. When dealing with this point, the Court somewhat surprisingly accepted the contention of the defendant government that the interference with the applicants' freedom of expression had been 'necessary in a democratic society for the prevention of disorder in the armed forces'. The Court took the view that the 'disorder' referred to in article 10(2) was not intended only to refer to disorder generally but could also be defined as limited to the 'confines of a specific social group', in this case the army.[47] Clearly this was a major expansion of this legitimate exception. But the Court was clear that 'the proper functioning of an army [was] hardly imaginable without legal rules designed to prevent servicemen from undermining military discipline, for example by writings'.[48] Furthermore, the applicants had not been deprived of their freedom of expression but only punished for the 'abusive exercise of that freedom'.[49]

Two important decisions in 1986 show even more clearly the limitations of the Convention when difficult and far-reaching issues of free speech are thrown up by the litigation process. Both concerned the Federal Republic of Germany's *Berufsverbote* legislation. In *Glasenapp* v. *Federal Republic of Germany*,[50] the applicant, a German national, was appointed as a secondary school teacher with the status of probationary civil servant. She undertook, as required by law, to uphold the free democratic constitutional system within the meaning of the German basic law, in accordance with legislation enacted in 1972 to control the employment of people holding what were judged by the authorities to be extreme political views. The inquiries into Mrs Glasenapp conducted under this legislation revealed little tangible evidence against her, other than that she

285

had lived for a short period in the same house as persons believed to have been members of a Maoist communist organization, and after a delay her appointment was allowed to go through. However, after she had obtained her position, Mrs Glasenapp wrote a letter to the newspapers in which she indicated that she shared some of the aims of the German Communist Party; particularly in relation to the establishment of an international people's kindergarten in Dortmund. This expression of a political sentiment caused the authorities to revoke her appointment as a teacher; she 'had represented herself as favouring a party which worked against [the] system and whose policy was aimed at overthrowing it in the Federal Republic of Germany by force'.[51]

Her appeal against this dismissal failed at every stage in the German judicial process, and she applied to Strasbourg, where her principal argument was that the *Berufsverbote* legislation had illegitimately infringed her freedom of expression guarantee under article 10. The Commission agreed with her by the narrowest of margins (nine votes to eight), but the Court found for the Government by sixteen votes to one. In a short judgment on the law, the majority preferred to see the case as one in which a right of access to the civil service was being claimed, and since this right 'was deliberately omitted from the Convention', the German practice could not 'be considered incompatible' with it.[52] Article 10 was 'certainly . . . material . . . in the present case'[53] but it was not decisive. Only one of those who concurred in the result, Judge Cremona, considered that the facts clearly disclosed an interference with freedom of expression: 'as in a picture, civil service status provides no more than the general background whereas the dominant feature in the foreground is a prejudice suffered because of the holding and expression of opinions'. Despite these observations, the judge held that the interference fell within article 10(2), though he did not specify which exception applied. It was left to Judge Spielmann alone to argue that the restrictions were 'not necessary in a democratic society for any of the purposes referred to in Article 10(2)',[54] and to end his judgment by rhetorically asking his colleagues whether a solution to the *Glasenapp* case at the national level would not also 'be in the spirit of the European Convention on Human Rights'.[55]

Kosiek v. *Federal Republic of Germany*,[56] decided on the same issue on the same day, is to similar effect, with the applicant this time being denied employment on account of membership of the National Democratic Party of Germany. The decisions are different from *Lingens*, *Oberschlick* and *Ezelin* not only in the result but also in the fact that defeat for the Government would have involved a major liberalization of the system, a reform to which it would have been deeply antipathetic. Both decisions are reminiscent of the United States Supreme Court's acceptance (despite the First Amendment) of the anti-communist witchhunting of the 1950s.[57]

The Commission's narrow support for Glasenapp was exceptional. Even more than the Court, this body has had a vital role in diluting the protection afforded by article 10, through the device of finding applications inadmissible, which decisions may be used to prevent sensitive cases ever reaching the Court. Of course in any system with only one court and thousands of applications annually, some syphoning process is inevitable. It may be this which explains why a reprimand handed out to a senior scientist at a UK defence establishment after he took part in a television programme without permission was found by the Commission not to be in breach of article 10.[58] It may also explain why a political speech claim relating to the presence of the French army in Germany was declared to be 'manifestly ill-founded'[59] and why the United Kingdom's laws on blasphemous libel have also survived challenge.[60] More difficult to comprehend other than as an example of a reluctance to strike too hard at central government was the decision to uphold as in compliance with article 11 the British Government's decision in 1984 to end trade union membership at GCHQ.[61] Equally sensitive to the Irish Government is the media ban operating in Ireland, under which certain political figures and others are banned from all radio and television programmes, even during election campaigns in which they are candidates. Perhaps to the surprise even of the Government itself, an article 10 challenge to this ban in Strasbourg was recently dismissed as being 'manifestly unfounded'.[62] On this basis, the more liberal British media ban on Sinn Fein and other groups and individuals is almost certain to survive challenge, and it may be that the case will not even be taken to Strasbourg.[63] If such bans on political speech by lawful political parties do not even begin to raise an argument under article 10, what value should be placed on all the fine rhetoric in *Lingens*, *Oberschlick* and *Ezelin*?

Spycatcher

The strengths and limitations of the European Court as a protector of freedom of expression are well illustrated by the two *Spycatcher* decisions in November 1991.[64] The facts of this well-known *cause célèbre* need briefly to be recapped. A former member of the UK security service MI5, Peter Wright, produced a book of memoirs (*Spycatcher*) containing a number of grave allegations that the service had in effect been engaged in a series of illegal and treasonous activities. These claims were not new, having already been made both by a journalist with whom Wright had cooperated and by Wright himself in a television interview which had been broadcast in Britain. Despite the fact that he had taken no action on these occasions, the Attorney-General for England and Wales now instituted a series of legal actions to prevent the publication of Wright's memoirs. These actions included an ultimately unsuccessful attempt to restrain publication of the memoirs in Australia (where Wright lived), based on the breach by Wright of his duty of confidentiality to his former employers. While these Australian proceedings were ongoing, *The Observer* and *The Guardian* published reports from the trial and extracts from the controversial manuscript. The Attorney-General secured *ex parte* and then interlocutory injunctions from Millett J in the English High Court restraining any further publication of matter relating to *Spycatcher* or to the Australian proceedings. These temporary injunctions were maintained with variations on two occasions by the Court of Appeal[65] and (13 months after they were first issued) by the House of Lords.[66]

The basis for upholding the injunctions was the need to maintain the efficiency of the civil service by preserving the confidentiality of information gained while working there. By the time the case reached the Law Lords, however, three other British newspapers had printed the substance of Wright's allegations,[67] *The Sunday Times* had actually published the first part of a serialization of the book[68] and, most importantly of all, the book had been published in the United States, where – protected by the First Amendment – it was already promising to be a bestseller. These changes of circumstance persuaded a minority of two of their lordships that, whatever their earlier merits, the injunctions against *The Guardian*, *The Observer* and *The Sunday Times* should now be set aside. For their part, the majority stressed that the injunctions were merely temporary (albeit as regards two of the newspapers already in place for over a year) and that, in light of this, freedom of expression would not be unduly affected if the court orders were to be maintained pending trial of the full action. When this trial duly took place, the injunctions were found to be unwarranted by the High Court, by the Court of Appeal and eventually – two and half years after they were first issued – by the House of Lords.[69]

When the matter reached it, the European Court was accordingly concerned not with any permanent prohibition on publication by the newspapers (none had ever been forthcoming) but rather with the full period during which the temporary injunctions had been in place. This covered the moment from the issuance of Millett J's *ex parte* orders in June 1986 through to the House of Lords' eventual decision finally to lift the injunctions in October 1988. The argument by the three newspapers concerned was, predictably, that the injunctions amounted to a restriction on freedom of expression which was not in any relevant sense 'necessary in a democratic society', as that term had been developed in the Court's own jurisprudence.[70] As regards the period after publication of *Spycatcher* in the United States, both the Court and the Commission were unanimous in agreeing with the newspapers that there had been a breach of article 10. The Court viewed American publication as having been a critical event, 'which changed the situation that had [earlier] obtained. . . . In the first place, the contents of the book ceased to be a matter of speculation and their confidentiality was destroyed . . . [and furthermore], Mr Wright's memoirs were [now] obtainable from abroad by residents of the United Kingdom, the Government having made no attempt to impose a ban on importation.'[71] As regards the period before publication in America, however, the Court held by a majority of fourteen to ten that the injunctions had been justified interferences with freedom of expression, having been necessary in a democratic society both for the protection of national security and for the maintenance of the authority of the judiciary. The injunctions had not erected 'a blanket prohibition' since 'they did not prevent [the newspapers] from pursuing their campaign for an independent inquiry into the operation of' the security service.[72] It was true that these temporary injunctions had been in force for what was 'a long time where the perishable commodity of news is concerned',[73] but the case had been certified as 'fit for a speedy trial' and 'the news in question, relating as it did to events that had occurred several years previously, could not really be classified as urgent'.[74]

Even more serious from the point of view of freedom of expression were two further passages in the judgment of the majority. First, the Court explicitly justified the injunctions pending the trial by reference to 'the central position occupied by Article 6 of the Convention and its guarantee of the right to a fair trial'.[75] This would appear to regard the interlocutory process not as a necessary and limited deviation to one human right but rather as the vindication of another, perhaps superior, one. The Court's reluctance to push article 10 far down the freedom of expression road may be seen in a second passage, when it declared that 'For the avoidance of doubt . . . the Court would only add . . . that Article 10 of the Convention does not in terms prohibit the imposition of prior restraints on publication, as such.'[76] Such a blanket ban on injunctions before publication would have had a major effect on the law of member states, since all courts[77] would from then on have known that every such act of judicial censorship would have automatically left such a court open to successful challenge in Strasbourg. Instead of this clear rule, however, the *Spycatcher* decision is a very narrow 'one-off' determination on an extreme set of facts, much more in the tradition of *Lingens* and *Oberschlick* than it might have been if the papers had triumphed on every point. Even the victory for free expression that it does deliver is almost entirely dependent not on any principle within the Convention itself, but rather on the happy chance of publication of the controversial work in the United States, an event made possible only because of the existence in America of a ban on prior restraint similar to that rejected by the *Spycatcher* court.[78]

CONCLUSION

The protection afforded to freedom of expression in the European Convention is heavily qualified. On the positive side, the Convention contains explicit presumptions in favour of both expression and assembly. On a number of occasions, the Court has interpreted these provisions in a way which has displayed an awareness of the vital importance to a thriving democracy of the freedom of political debate. On the negative side, the many exceptions to these freedoms contained within the Convention itself have given the Court a room for manoeuvre which it has employed to baulk at the difficult challenges that a genuine commitment to free expression would have resolved in favour of speech, no matter how inconvenient to or difficult for the defendant governments concerned. In contriving to avoid tough confrontations on the free speech issue, the Court has been more than ably assisted by the Commission, which has prevented controversial cases, particularly the Irish media ban applications, from even reaching the Court.

Thus our appreciation of the way that the Court has assisted free speech must ultimately be a qualified one. It may validly be observed that at least the Court has acted positively in a number of cases but it is questionable whether this is enough in itself to justify the value of the jurisdiction. For the upholding of governmental or judicial restriction in the sphere of free speech is worse than just losing; such defeats legitimate the restriction that is the subject matter of the application by solemnly declaring it to be in compliance with rather than in contravention of human rights. Repression which complies with judicially defined codes of human rights is not quite so easy to dislodge as that which is at least shamefaced in its awareness of its own wrong. Furthermore, there are ways in which free speech, as interpreted by the courts, can hinder rather than help active citizenship. This has not yet occurred in the European Court, though the emphasis on commercial speech in recent decisions shows how far article 10 has drifted from any rationale which is rooted in the needs of active citizenship.

A couple of cases from the United States serve as a salutary warning against over-reliance on judicial perceptions of freedom. In *Buckley* v. *Valeo*,[79] a legislative effort by Congress to control the spending that candidates or their supporters could incur in their campaigns for public office was struck down by the Supreme Court as an uncon-stitutional restriction on free speech. Professor Barendt has observed that there are 'considerable difficulties in accepting the reasoning' in the case,[80] but that despite this it is 'most unlikely to be over-turned'.[81] It is somewhat paradoxical that freedom of speech should be responsible for the vast increase in funding required to run for office in America, with the inevitable restriction that this entails on the range and political persuasion of the available candidates. Second, in *Miami Herald Co.* v. *Tornillo*,[82] the Supreme Court unanimously struck down as in violation of the First Amendment a right of reply law which required editors to print a reply by a political candidate who had been subject to adverse comment in the paper. After the experience in Britain of newspaper reporting of the 1992 general election, there are few in the centre or to the left of the political spectrum who would not agree that exactly such a law is vitally necessary to help revive Britain's fast-disappearing political culture. The notion that it would be in violation of the human right to free expression would surprise many. *Tornillo* is a reminder of the danger of handing over to the judges responsibility for the protection of vital aspects of our democratic heritage. In the area of freedom of expression, the courts may sometimes be useful but there are costs as well as gains in too powerful a judicial role. In the continuing battle for the rights of the citizen, there will never be any real alternative to politics and continuing democratic vigilance.

NOTES AND REFERENCES

1 *Dennis* v. *United States* 341 US 494, 550 (1951).

2 The Convention may be relevant to the development of the common law and to the resolution of ambiguity in legislation. As to the precise relationship between the Convention and United Kingdom law, see the recent survey by the court of appeal in *Derbyshire County Council* v. *Times Newspapers Limited* [1992] 1 QB 770. Note the different views of the House of Lords in the same case, [1993] 1 All ER 1011.

3 250 US 616, 630 (1919).

4 See E. Barendt, *Freedom of Speech* (Clarendon Press, Oxford, 1987), pp. 8–10. Mill's ideas on this subject are most clearly expressed in *On Liberty*, Chapter II.

5 Report of the Committee on Obscenity and Film Censorship (Cmnd 7772, H*MSO*, 1979), para. 5.19.

6 *Ibid.*

7 *Ibid.*, para. 5.21.

8 See generally R. Dworkin, *Taking Rights Seriously* (London, Duckworth, 1977). For further discussion of this theme, and additional references, see Barendt, *op. cit.*, pp. 14–20.

9 See *Freedman* v. *Maryland* 380 US 51 (1965).

10 274 US 357, 375–6 (1927).

11 *De Jonge* v. *Oregon* 299 US 353, 365 (1937).

12 *New York Times* v. *United States* 403 US 713, 724 (1971).

13 *Schenck* v. *United States* 249 US 47, 52 (1919).

14 See, for recent examples from the United Kingdom, the Public Order Act 1986 and *R.* v. *Gibson and Sylveire* [1990] 2 QB 619. On the distinction in the United States, see Barendt, *op. cit.*, pp. 41–8.

15 For a remarkable example of the constitutional protection of offensive conduct, see the flag-burning case, *Texas* v. *Johnson* 491 US 397 (1989).

16 See J. Gardner, 'Freedom of expression', in G. Chambers and C. McCrudden (eds), *Individual Rights and the Law in Britain* (Oxford University Press, forthcoming).

17 *Gitlow* v. *New York* 268 US 652, 666 (1925). The justice was Sanford J.

18 *Debs* v. *United States* 249 US 211 (1919).

19 *Op. cit.*

20 *Gitlow* v. *New York*, *op. cit.*

21 *Whitney* v. *California*, *op. cit.*

22 341 US 494.

23 Quoted in S. Walker, *In Defence of American Liberties: A History of the ACLU* (Oxford University Press, New York and Oxford, 1990), p. 187.

24 *Rust* v. *Sullivan*, 114 L Ed 2d 233 (1991).

25 (1988) 13 EHRR 212.

26 (1990) 12 EHRR 485.

27 *Ibid.*, para. 47. The three cases referred to in the extract were: *The Sunday Times* v. *United Kingdom* (1978) 2 EHRR 245; *Markt Intern Verlag GmbH* v. *Federal Republic of Germany* (1989) 12 EHRR 161; and *Groppera Radio AG* v. *Switzerland* (1990) 12 EHRR 321.

28 *The Sunday Times* v. *United Kingdom (No. 2)* (1991) 14 EHRR 229, para. 50.

29 *Op. cit.*, para. 36. See also *Handyside* v. *United Kingdom* (1976) 1 EHRR 737.

30 (1986) 8 EHRR 407.

31 Article 111.

32 See *The Sunday Times* v. *United Kingdom*, *op. cit.*

33 *Ibid.*, para. 41.

34 *Ibid.*, para. 42.

35 *Ibid.*

36 *Ibid.*, para. 43.

37 *Ibid.*

38 *Ibid*.
39 Decision of the European Court of Human Rights, 23 May 1991. Article 6 has also been useful in the context of political speech: *Demicoli* v. *Malta* (1991) 14 EHRR 47.
40 *Ibid*., para. 63.
41 (1991) 14 EHRR 362.
42 *Ibid*., para. 53.
43 (1988) 13 EHRR 204.
44 *Skokie* v. *National Socialist Party* 373 NE 2d. 21 (1978).
45 (1882) 9 QBD 308.
46 (1976) 1 EHRR 647.
47 *Ibid*., para. 98.
48 *Ibid*., para. 100.
49 *Ibid*., para. 101.
50 (1986) 9 EHRR 25.
51 *Ibid*., para. 24.
52 *Ibid*., para. 52.
53 *Ibid*., para. 50.
54 Para. 40 of the partly dissenting judgment of Judge Spielmann.
55 *Ibid*., para. 43.
56 (1986) 9 EHRR 328.
57 See in particular *Dennis* v. *United States*, *op. cit*.
58 See *Application 10293/83*, reported at (1986) 9 EHRR 255.
59 *Application 11567/85* and *Application 11568* v. *France* (1989) 11 EHRR 67.
60 *Gay News Limited and Lemon* v. *United Kingdom* (1982) 5 EHRR 123. The United Kingdom's blasphemy laws have survived an article 9 challenge arising out of the Rushdie affair: *Choudhury* v. *United Kingdom* (1991) 12 HRLJ 172 [Decision of the European Commission].
61 *Council of Civil Service Unions* v. *Minister for the Civil Service* [1985] AC 374; *Council of Civil Service Unions* v. *United Kingdom* (1987) 10 EHRR 269.
62 *Purcell* v. *Ireland* (1991) 12 HRLJ 254. For the Irish law, see *The State (Lynch)* v. *Cooney* [1982] IR 337, and more recently *O'Toole* v. *RTE*, unreported decision of the Irish Supreme Court, 30 March 1993.
63 For the proceedings before the British courts, see *R.* v. *Secretary of State for the Home Department, ex p. Brind* [1991] 1 AC 696 (HL).
64 *Observer and Guardian* v. *United Kingdom*, (1991) 14 EHRR 153; *The Sunday Times* v. *United Kingdom*, *op. cit*.
65 On the second occasion because Browne-Wilkinson VC had overturned them on an application by both newspapers, made after they had already been in operation for over a year.
66 *Attorney General* v. *Guardian Newspapers Limited* [1987] 3 All ER 316.
67 For the legal sequel to such journalistic temerity, see *A.G.* v. *Times Newspapers Limited* [1992] 1 AC 191 (HL).
68 The Attorney-General obtained an injunction to prevent further disclosures after this first part of the serialization. *The Sunday Times*'s involvement in the case in Strasbourg resulted from its decision to challenge this injunction under article 10.
69 See *A.G.* v. *Guardian Newspapers Limited (No. 2)* [1990] 1 AC 109.

70 *The Sunday Times* v. *United Kingdom (No. 2)*, *op. cit.*

71 *Observer and Guardian* v. *United Kingdom*, *op. cit.*, para. 66.

72 *Ibid.*, para. 64.

73 *Ibid.*

74 *Ibid.*

75 *Ibid.*, para. 63.

76 *Ibid.*, para. 60.

77 See *Derbyshire County Council* v. *Times Newspapers Limited*, *op. cit.*

78 *New York Times* v. *United States* 403 US 713 (1971).

79 424 US 1 (1976).

80 Barendt, *op. cit.*, p. 52.

81 *Ibid.*

82 418 US 241 (1974).

15

Citizenship and the Honours System

ROBERT BLACKBURN

Shortly after winning the general election in April 1992, the Prime Minister, John Major, let it be known that as part of his drive towards a 'classless' society, he was instituting within Downing Street a review of the honours and titles system.[1] It would be appropriate for any such review to begin by linking the aims and purposes of honours and titles to the concept of citizenship, the terminology of which Mr Major himself has done much to promote in his Citizen's Charter, first published in July 1991, which formed a key part in the Conservatives' election manifesto in 1992.[2] But, whereas Mr Major's Citizen's Charter has laid emphasis on the rights of the ordinary citizen as consumer, any review of his on the honours and titles system might be expected to articulate some set of principles about the responsibilities or virtues of the ordinary citizen. In other words, whom by their efforts should society be recognizing as making a valuable contribution to the life of the nation?

The amazing range and quantity of honours in Britain is unique.[3] No other country in the world has anything remotely similar. The Americans have a genuinely exclusive Presidential Medal of Freedom, awarded to only five recipients including Martin Luther King since the 1960s, and also a Congressional Medal of Honour for civil and military distinction. The French have a not-so-exclusive Legion of Honour, currently held by a third of a million citizens, and the Germans have a very modest system of civilian medals, awards of which are controlled by their parliament, the Bundestag. The British by comparison, it is commonly said, have turned honours and titles into both a science and an art. The highest class of honour is the peerage, grants of which are traditionally hereditary and, ranking in descending order of dignity, include dukes, marquesses, earls, viscounts and barons.[4] Since the Life Peerages Act 1958, to this list should now be added peerages for life, all of which are baronies. All peers are Lords, but there are strict differences in the prefixes by which they are addressed: thus a baron or viscount is a 'Right Honourable Lord', but a Duke is a 'Most Noble Lord' and usually referred to as 'Your Grace'.[5] Then there is the baronetcy, also hereditary, and currently famous for being conferred upon the former Prime Minister Margaret (now Baroness) Thatcher's husband, Sir Denis Thatcher of Scotney Castle, in March 1991, the first time this particular form of title had been granted since 1964. It was created by the early Stuart kings as a 'second-class' peerage, without the right to sit in Parliament, and sold in great abundance by Charles I to raise cash prior to the Civil War.[6] There are still 1400 heirs to these honours, all entitled to be called a 'Sir', to which number in due course Sir Denis and Baroness Thatcher's son, Mark Thatcher, will be added. Then lower in precedence come knighthoods conferred for life, all of whose holders are called 'Sir', including either knights batchelor or knights grand cross of one of a range of orders such as the Most Noble Order of the Garter (recently conferred by the Queen personally upon the former Prime Minister Sir Edward Heath), the Most Ancient and Most Noble Order of the Thistle, the Most Honourable Order of the Bath, and so on. These orders then contain lower awards of honours, conferred as medals, the best known of which belong to the Most Excellent Order of the British Empire, whose ranks contain Commander (CBE), Officer (OBE) and Member (MBE). Finally, there are a host of particular decorations, conferred as badges, which are divided between military honours such as the Victoria Cross and the George Cross, and civilian honours such as the British Empire Medal.

The honours and titles system is all about Britain's past history, stretching back a thousand years, and it is difficult to identify a coherent purpose for its operation today. It represents a curious blend of continuing past ceremony, ritual and tradition, all of which is viewed as very British and gives recipients and foreign tourists and caricaturists pleasure and something to talk about, with an attempt to perform the more serious social function of giving national recognition to individuals who have made some positive contribution to the life of the country. The names of up to about a thousand recipients of honours and titles are published in each of two annual sets of Honours Lists, one at new year, the other in June. Legally the monarch is 'the fount of honours', and Queen Elizabeth personally confers the honours upon recipients at investitures held at Buckingham Palace. The Queen also herself decides on suitable recipients for a small, exclusive number of honours, including the

Orders of the Garter, Thistle, Merit and Royal Victoria. But for all other honours and titles she makes the awards upon the recommendation of the Prime Minister (or foreign and defence secretaries of state in the case of certain decorations within their departments).

The ceremonial officer at 53 Parliament Street, London SW1, is charged with responsibility for receiving nominations for honours, but for top honours the Prime Minister helped by his or her close personal advisers will personally decide the list. There is also a well-known 'formula' within the civil service whereby senior members have a virtual entitlement to certain decorations: for a retiring permanent secretary, a knight commander of the Order of the Bath; for senior career diplomats, the CMG, the KCMG and GCMG; and for a grade 7 principal civil servant, the OBE. To pre-empt the embarrassment of any person selected rejecting the title or decoration offered, letters are sent out in advance from the Prime Minister's office, saying:

> The Prime Minister has asked me to inform you, in strict confidence, that he has it in mind, on the occasion of the forthcoming list of [New Year/Queen's Birthday] honours, to submit your name to the Queen with a recommendation that Her Majesty may be graciously pleased to approve that you be appointed. . . . Before doing so, the Prime Minister would be glad to be assured that this would be agreeable to you. I should be grateful if you would let me know by completing the enclosed form and sending it to me by return of post.[7]

There have been many known, or surmised, instances of refusals of honours. It is reckoned that on average there are 15 to 20 refusals per list, some because it is felt the honour offered is not high enough, and others because of disapproval of the system.[8] The socialist historian R. H. Tawney wrote back abruptly to Ramsay Macdonald in 1933: 'Thank you for your letter. What harm have I ever done the Labour Party?'[9]

The honours system is hardly without its critics.[10] For many, its past associations alone discredit it as a thriving industry today. It is seen as completely embedded in a hierarchical, class-ridden vision of society, with the aristocratic stable of titles of earls and viscounts and barons all contributing to the perpetuation of Britain's upper-class institutions and snobbery. Its historical foundation is of course pure wealth, not just the vast inherited estates of the blue-blooded relatives of the Crown, but the *nouveaux riches* men of commerce and industry who at various times have been able simply to buy their titles for the social cache they bring. Even in the twentieth century, Lloyd George when he was Prime Minister, through his accomplice Maundy Gregory, arranged for the sale of hundreds of honours, the going rate during his premiership between 1916 and 1922 being £20,000 for a knighthood, between £20,000 and £40,000 for a baronetcy, and up to £100,000 for a peerage. Within those six years Lloyd George handed out 25,000 OBEs, 481 knighthoods, 130 baronetcies and 26 peerages. A speech in the House of Lords in 1922 indicated the extent of the corruption:

> The Prime Minister's party, absolutely penniless four years ago, has . . . amassed an enormous parliamentary chest, variously estimated at between one and two million pounds. The strange thing about it is that it has been acquired during a period when there has been more wholesale distribution of honours than ever before, when less care has been taken with regard to the service and character of the recipients than ever before.'[11]

This scandal led to a Royal Commission and the passing by Parliament of the Honours (Prevention of Abuses) Act 1925, making it a misdemeanour to either solicit or offer for sale any honour or title. Under the terms of this Act today,

> s. 1 (1) If any person accepts or agrees to accept or attempts to obtain from any person, for himself or for any other person, or for any purpose, any gift, money or valuable consideration as an inducement or reward for procuring or assisting or endeavouring to procure the grant of a dignity or title or honour to any person, or otherwise in connection with such a grant, he shall be guilty of a misdemeanour.
>
> (2) If any person gives, or agrees or proposes to give, or offers to any person any gift, money or valuable consideration as an inducement to reward for procuring or assisting or endeavouring to procure the grant of a dignity or title or honour to any person, or otherwise in connection with such a grant, he shall be guilty of a misdemeanour.

Additionally, a recommendation of the Commission led to a Political Honours Scrutiny Committee being established. This body comprises three members of the Privy Council, persons not associated with the Government, and may express opinions to the Prime Minister and the Queen on the suitability of all those names put forward for honours for political services by the Prime Minister and those recommended for life peerages.[12]

Then there is the criticism of hereditary honours. It is seen as the greatest anachronism of all that Britain retains a system for granting peerages and baronetcies that descend to the recipient's issue in perpetuity regardless of the individual's merit, and, in the case of peerages, that it allows such persons to sit in the Second Chamber of Parliament and influence the content of national legislation. There are currently 1211 members of the House of Lords (more than double the 591 members in 1900), 777 of whom – almost three-quarters – are hereditary peers by succession.[13] All these persons have a social rank and right to sit in Parliament not through their own efforts but by accident of birth, and it will come as no surprise to learn that such persons are four times more likely to take the whip of the Conservative Party in the Lords than that of any other single party.[14]

The decision of the former Prime Minister, Margaret (now Baroness) Thatcher, to resurrect the institution of the hereditary peerage in 1983 was viewed by many as extraordinary, given her own declared distaste for privilege based on rank or birth. But all of a sudden, after four years in office, she arranged for William Whitelaw, George Thomas and Harold Macmillan to be given hereditary peerages, despite the precedents of 19 years and three Prime Ministers before her who had allowed the power to grant them to fall into disuse. The 1958 Life Peerage Act had provided a new statutory basis for peerages, whereby distinguished persons might be given the title of Lord, and a right to sit in Parliament, for the duration of their own life only. Not surprisingly, many Labour MPs saw the new hereditary creations in 1983 and 1984 as unconstitutional, and several opposition MPs tried unsuccessfully to present legislation in the Commons to terminate the legal power to grant any further ones. Thus a Hereditary Peerages Bill sought 'to end the practice of the creation of hereditary peerages; to make provision for the ending of existing peerages on the demise of the present incumbent; and to end the custom whereby retired Prime Ministers and other senior government and parliamentary office-holders are offered peerages'.[15] Still another extraordinary feature of the 1983 hereditary political honours was for the peerages granted to be blatantly discriminatory in terms of sexual equality: the letters patent conferring the honours restricted the peerages to male heirs only. So Macmillan's son's son now has a peerage, but none of the four daughters of William Whitelaw is thought good enough to succeed to the honour that on his future death would have passed had he a son. Whichever way you look at the granting of hereditary peerages, they are offensive to contemporary values of citizenship.

Or should the whole business of honours not be taken too seriously? Some would argue that they are just a bit of harmless fun. There is evidence that many recipients do not regard their honour with any great degree of importance. The Oxford wit Sir Maurice Bowra remarked frivolously upon accepting his knighthood, 'You should always accept an honour for the pain it brings your enemies.'[16] But if honours are not a serious matter, why has the subject of who may or may not be granted a knighthood or peerage regularly excited such strong views, as over the former Prime Minister Harold (now Lord) Wilson's notorious 'lavender' list in 1976[17] or the Scrutiny Committee's rumoured rejection of Rupert Murdoch for a knighthood and Jeffrey Archer for a peerage in 1990?[18] Why do industrialists place great store upon titles in the boardroom, particularly to impress their overseas clients and financiers? And why has Mr Major conducted a review of the whole honours and titles system at present as part of his drive towards a classless society?

Another heavily criticized feature of the present system is the proliferation and wealth of decorations that go to diplomats and civil servants with the job.[19] Many politicians of all parties have for a long time argued that this practice should end and be replaced by genuinely selective awards based upon individual merit. In 1992 the Conservative MP Richard Shepherd said, 'The automatic assumption that you get knighthoods or gongs is out of date. It almost has the quality of handing out lollipops to the general satisfaction of the recipients.'[20] And Labour's Tony Banks has also recently complained in the House of Commons that

> Honours given to civil servants and senior military officers as a matter of course, accompanying their not insubstantial pay and rations, are not worthy of being described as honours. . . . The entire edifice reeks of snobbery and class division. If the Prime Minister meant what he said about a classless society, he could do a lot worse than start on the honours system and eliminate some of those preposterous awards. We know that there are class divisions galore in the civil service and the armed forces. Routine awarding of honours to those people simply reinforces and reflects that class system.[21]

The final and most serious criticism of the honours system is that Prime Ministers, or those who work for them, may abuse their patronage over political honours to reward both political support for their leadership and financial support for their party. According to this view, the honours system should be divorced from party politics, and should not display unevenness in political balance. But throughout the 1980s many knighthoods were awarded to influential and vociferous political supporters of the party leadership, extending to media proprietors and editors, with hardly any examples of prime ministerial patronage being distributed to anyone known to have voiced opposition or dissent.[22] Mrs Thatcher gave ten times more knighthoods to Tory backbenchers than did the former Conservative leader and Prime Minister, Sir Edward Heath, who himself received a knighthood only after her departure. And despite the work of the Political Honours Scrutiny Committee, now chaired by Lord Shackleton with Lord Grimond and Lord Pym as its other members, there remains an astonishingly close relationship between those who make substantial donations of money to the party in power and those who are awarded knighthoods and peerages. During Baroness Thatcher's first term of office between 1979 and 1983, the ten companies that donated £200,000 or more to Conservative office funds received six peerages and five knighthoods.[23] Between 1979 and 1991, the Conservative Party received twelve million pounds in donations from companies that collectively between them received 75 knighthoods or peerages.[24] Of course this might be pure coincidence, but, as the former Lord Chancellor Lord Haldane remarked during the parliamentary passage of the 1925 Act, our existing safeguards can only stop 'the more flagrant cases' of money changing hands in the pursuit of titles.[25] Many people today simply take it for granted that many titles are in fact effectively bought and sold. A leading article in *The Times* last year was entitled 'Baubles and bribes', and while attacking the honours system as being 'a parody of honour and an insult to those members of the community who truly merit national recognition', it said that among its multifarious purposes, 'Party funds need replenishing other than from taxes, and the *de facto* sale of honours achieves this.'[26] Or as Adam Raphael has put it, since the time of Lloyd George's premiership

> The rates may have changed with inflation, but in essence not much else has. Of course, the award of honours is nowadays conducted with slightly more discretion. But the correlation between those who give large sums of money and those who receive high political honours remains disturbingly close. The whiff of corruption is such that it is now acknowledged at the highest levels in Whitehall that the current procedures are unsatisfactory and will have to be changed.[27]

Sir Winston Churchill once remarked that 'the object in presenting medals, stars and ribbons is to give pride and pleasure to those who deserve them'.[28] Few will wish to spoil the genuine enjoyment and pleasure that the British honours system brings with it, and there is every advantage to the quality of citizenship in retaining an honours system that allows the country at large to express its gratitude to those individuals who have contributed something very special to the life of the community, whether by virtue of acts of heroism or bravery, or selfless dedication in a valued cause or service to others, or by enriching science, the arts or sport. The task ahead is to seek to bury social division and snobbery, as well as political partisanship, in the distribution of those forms of honour we choose to keep.

It is right that the operation of the whole honours system should now be the subject of a comprehensive review, the work of which should not be kept confined behind closed doors in Whitehall and Downing Street, and the results of which should lead to the publication of guidelines for the future. An independent Royal Commission on Citizenship should be established for the purpose, inviting views and comments from across public and political opinion on the honours system, and to this Commission there should be remitted several other important, closely related issues, including the future funding of political parties. The Commission should question whether it is appropriate for hereditary honours of any description to continue to be awarded today, and it should express an opinion about the principles of citizenship and democracy upon which the Second Chamber of Britain's parliamentary legislature should be composed. It should consider whether there is a need to rationalize the enormous number of different types of honours, and whether the present quantity of 2000 or so medals and titles distributed each year is too large. The Commission must confront the 'whiff of corruption' surrounding political finance, and the need to protect the impartiality and integrity of persons working in positions of political influence. One suggestion that might be explored was recently put forward in an Abolition of Political Honours Bill, which was supported by many MPs in the House of Commons: that persons currently working in certain categories of employment should ordinarily only be eligible for honours by way of medals, not the titles of peers or knights, and this might include MPs, senior figures in broadcasting and the press, and members of company boards of directors that donate significant financial sums to any political party.[29] The Commission should also question what functions we expect political parties to play in our modern society, such as encouraging community participation and keeping citizens informed of political developments, especially at election times, and whether they are worth the allocation of some level of state financial subsidy instead of relying entirely on gifts of money from private individuals, or else companies or trade unions.[30] On the machinery responsible for the distribution of honours, the Commission should consider whether the decision-making power over precisely who should be selected as suitable recipients for honours (particularly with respect to knighthoods and the top awards) should now be transferred to a wider and more impartial body, such as an independent commission operating from Buckingham Palace, with a parliamentary select committee entrusted with the task of scrutinizing and keeping under review the future operation of the honours system. Finally, the Commission should clearly lay down the criteria upon which recipients of honours should be selected.

Whatever its recommendations, the Commission should affirm that questions about the role of the individual in society will be of even greater importance to the politics of the twenty-first century, and that whatever honours system we choose to operate should clearly express the qualities of citizenship we most value in a democracy.

POSTSCRIPT

On 4 March 1993, while this book was in press, the Prime Minister, John Major, announced to the House of Commons the conclusions of his review of the honours system.[31] It included a small number of minor changes which were described by one commentator as 'more tinkering than reform'.[32] On the most controversial aspects of the present system, such as the creation of hereditary peerages, political honours, and the machinery for selecting recipients, there were to be no changes at all. Of the minor modifications announced, two particular medals will no longer be awarded (the British Empire Medal and the Imperial Service Order), and instead a greater number of awards of Member of the British Empire and Officer of the British Empire will be conferred. The suggestion from the Opposition leader, John Smith, that the references in these medals to the British Empire was an anachronism and should be replaced was rejected by the Prime Minister.[33] Two other matters, which are improvements, are that in the armed forces non-commissioned ranks will become eligible for crosses or equivalent decorations previously available only to officers, and that information concerning the nomination of persons for honours generally is to be made more widely available.

The only change of political significance was Mr Major's announcement of the termination of automatic honours for top civil servants. He said that he would 'end the recommendation of honours where they are given solely by seniority or on appointment'. He indicated an overall reduction in the total number of honours to be distributed across the civil service, and said that greater importance in future was to be attached to charities and voluntary acts of service to the community. The ending of automatic honours is welcome, and was supported across the political parties, but it now exposes a further problem to be addressed concerning the political impartiality of the public service and the way in which civil servants may perform their work with respect to ministers. Britain's top civil servants will now be wholly dependent upon the goodwill of their political masters for receiving honours that may understandably mean a great deal to them. Interestingly, Mr Major announced that he was exempting High Court judges from the change (they will continue automatically to receive knighthoods), referring to the need to protect their independence from favours in the hands of the Government. Yet a similar concern for protecting the integrity and political independence of senior civil servants in government did not feature in the announcement. The ending of automatic honours in the civil service considerably strengthens the already powerful case for transferring the decision-making power over the award of honours into the hands of a more broadly based and politically neutral body.

The most striking feature of Mr Major's review of the honours system is that it was conducted entirely by him and his personal advisers. There was no consultation in Parliament, no consultation in the country, and negligible consultation across Whitehall. The results of his changes were simply announced to the House of Commons, not submitted for discussion and approval. This is symptomatic of the real problem with the current honours system. It operates upon the antiquated legal basis of the prerogative, which lies within the exclusive political control of the party leader occupying 10 Downing Street. The honours system should not be treated as though it was the personal possession of the Prime Minister – it belongs to us all. A more thorough and radical review of the honours system is still required, and will need to be conducted by a Royal Commission comprising a membership drawn from all sections of the community.[34]

NOTES AND REFERENCES

1 Reported in *The Independent* and *The Guardian* newspapers, 6 June 1992.

2 *The Citizen's Charter* (1991), Cm 1599.

3 On the British honours system generally, see Michael De la Noy, *The Honours System: Who Gets What and Why* (1991), John Walker, *The Queen Has Been Pleased* (1986), J. H. B. Bedells, *The British Honours System* (1974), and Valentine Heywood, *British Titles* (1951).

4 See *Burke's Peerage and Baronetage* (105th edn 1980).

5 See *Debrett's Correct Form: Standard Modes of Address for Everyone from Peers to Presidents* (1990).

6 See Michael De la Noy, *op. cit.*, Chapter 3.

7 *Ibid.*, p. 160.

8 John Walker, *op. cit.*, p. 18.

9 Quoted in Peter Hennessy, 'Standing guard on mercenaries of the class war', *The Independent*, 2 April 1990.

10 Just a few examples are: Tony Banks, MP ('The honours system has always been wholly or partially corrupt') HC Deb., Vol. 190, Col. 172, 30 April 1991; Bernard Crick ('a muddle of snobbery with jobbery'), *The Guardian*, 7 May 1992; a leading article in *The Independent* ('Automatic honours for civil servants and other public figures – the sort which 'come with the rations' – are mildly cringe-making. . . . As for honours granted for political services, they, by their very nature, are inappropriate and lead inevitably to accusations of cronyism or to rumours of rewards for disreputable services rendered.'), 8 July 1991; a leading article in *The Times* ('It is as class ridden as ever, and riddled with . . . gongs for the boys and with automaticity. It remains a parody of honour.'), 13 June 1992; William Hamilton, former MP ('No other country in the world has perfected a more sophisticated package of genteel and cheap corruption and snobbery than the British have with their honours system.'), *My Queen and I* (1975), p. 27; Adam Raphael ('Last week's resignation honours list continues the pattern of rewarding her [the former Prime Minister, Baroness Thatcher's] closest political associates and fawning journalists, as well as businessmen whose companies have contributed to party funds. If after a decade all this has become so familiar that it no longer has the capacity to shock, more is the pity. There is no doubt that abuse of the honours system has contributed to the creeping corruption of our political life.'), *The Observer*, 23 December 1990.

11 See Michael De la Noy, *op. cit.*, Chapter 6; James McMillan (1969), Chapters 13–16; Central Office of Information, *Honours and Titles* (1992), Appendix 6.

12 See John Walker, *op. cit.*, Chapter 1; Stanley de Smith and Rodney Brazier, *Constitutional and Administrative Law* (6th edn 1989), p. 155.

13 House of Lords Information Office, 18 July 1992.

14 The political composition of the Lords is: Conservatives 469, Labour 117, Liberal Democrat 58, with the remainder being bishops, or belonging to other parties, or being politically independent: House of Lords Information Office, 13 July 1992.

15 HC Bill [1983–4] 109, which proceeded no further than a formal First Reading. Formal supporters of the Bill, who are still in the Commons today, included Gordon Brown, Jack Straw, Tom Clarke, Ray Powell, John Maxton and Roger Stott.

16 Quoted in Peter Hennessy, *op. cit.*

17 For a critical account by Harold (now Lord) Wilson's own Press Secretary at the time, see Joe Haines, *The Politics of power* (1977), Chapter 7.

18 Reported in *The Observer*, 23 December 1990. Jeffrey Archer went on to be granted a peerage in 1992.

19 See John Walker, *op. cit.*, Chapter 1, and Michael De la Noy, *op. cit.*, Chapters 7 and 8.

20 Reported in *The Guardian*, 6 May 1992. Dr David Owen is another critic: see Michael De la Noy, *op. cit.*, p. 169.

21 HC Deb., 30 April 1991, Col. 173.

22 For an account and observations on the practice of the 1980s, see Adam Raphael, 'Honours that carry a whiff of corruption', *The Observer*, 23 December 1990; Michael De la Noy, *op. cit.*, Chapter 9; John Walker, *op. cit.*, Chapter 8.

23 From John Walker, *op. cit.*, p. 168.

24 HC Deb., 30 April 1991, Col. 174.

25 HL Deb., 29 June 1925, Col. 822.

26 13 June 1992.

27 'Honours that carry a whiff of corruption', *The Observer*, 23 December 1990.

28 Quoted in Michael De la Noy, *op. cit.*, p. 180.

29 HC Bill [1990–1] 150, introduced by Tony Banks. The Bill received a first reading following a vote in the Commons of 122 MPs in favour, 90 opposed, but proceeded no further.

30 See above, pp. 85–7.

31 HC Deb., 4 March 1993, Col. 453.

32 Leading article in *The Independent*, 5 March 1993.

33 HC Deb., 4 March 1993, Col. 455.

34 See above, p. 302.

16

Public Law, Sovereignty and Citizenship

PAUL CRAIG

INTRODUCTION

Citizenship is very much the word of the moment. This is evident in the plethora of Citizen's Charters that have made their appearance in recent times, as rival political parties sought to capture the 'moral' high ground in the run-up to the 1992 general election. The precise implications thought to follow from the idea of citizenship have, not surprisingly, differed since, as will be argued below, the more particular conceptions of citizenship reflect differing background political theories which posit the relationship between citizen and state in different ways.

The discussion in this chapter will proceed in three stages. First, there will be a methodological section, in which my own understanding of the meaning and relevance of citizenship for public law discourse will be made clear. This is important in order to avoid any misunderstanding or confusion within the substantive analysis.

The second stage will focus on constitutional law and sovereignty, for the following reason. One of the hurdles that is felt to lie in the way of protecting citizenship in the United Kingdom is the sovereignty of Parliament. It is this concept that is felt to render protections of citizens' rights within a Bill of Rights precarious, because, *inter alia*, of the difficulties of entrenching those rights. It will be argued that the concept of sovereignty has been seriously misunderstood. It will be contended that justifications for sovereign power advanced by writers in the eighteenth, nineteenth and twentieth centuries were based upon arguments of principle, in a way that has been forgotten in the more recent academic debate. These earlier writers realized that there had to be a normative justification for the existence of such power, and they constructed principled rationales in order to substantiate this conclusion. Whether those principled justifications were in fact sustainable at the time they were propounded, and whether they remain of relevance in the modern day, are two of the issues that will be considered below. Whatever answer is given to these two questions, the nature of these earlier analyses is of considerable importance. The realization that the *reasons* for sovereign power must be found in arguments which are defensible, if at all, in terms of normative principle opens the way for a modification of traditional ideas on sovereignty if no convincing normative justification can be found in the present day.

The third section of this chapter will examine some of the implications of the reasoning and conclusions reached in the preceding section for public law. Space precludes any detailed analysis of such matters, but some of the consequences can be glimpsed.

CITIZENSHIP: MEANING AND METHODOLOGY

The meaning attributed to the term citizenship may well differ among the different contributors to this volume, and therefore it is appropriate to set out my own understanding of the concept.

The concept of citizenship could be used in three differing ways. It could, first, be used to describe and evaluate the law relating to nationality and immigration, in order to determine who is, and who can become, a citizen of the United Kingdom.[1] This is an important topic, but it will not be the focus of the present discussion. A second meaning of citizenship would be a description of the legal rights and duties which actually operate between citizens and the state. This exercise would require one to decide which rights and obligations presently flow from the relationship of citizen and state. The answer to this question will, as will be seen, depend in part on the theory of adjudication which one adopts, and therefore the exercise will be a mixture of the descriptive and the normative. A third meaning of the concept of citizenship would be concerned with the principles that ought to appertain between citizens and the state. It is an undisguisedly normative study. Thus, for example, while it might be maintained that, at present, citizens do not, on any theory of adjudication, have entrenched rights which are constitutionally protected, they ought as a matter of normative principle to do so. The nature of such normative arguments that apply to this particular issue will be considered below. It is aspects of the second and third senses of citizenship that will be explored in this chapter.

In general terms any assessment of this descriptive and normative relationship requires a background political theory, which will serve as the foundation for an understanding of *what* range of rights and duties do and should exist as between citizen and state, and which will also serve to determine *what* meaning is and should be attached to concepts such as legitimacy. The reasons why one requires a background political theory in order to undertake this normative analysis have been examined elsewhere, and it is not my intention to repeat them in detail here.[2] However, even at an intuitive general level, the sense of this argument can be appreciated. The contentious issues that divide commentators concerning the meaning of citizenship do so precisely because those commentators disagree as to the nature of the rights and duties that do, and should, appertain between citizen and state. This disagreement is simply reflective of the fact that the proponents of these contestable positions adopt differing background political theories concerning the relationship between citizen and state. It has been thus for over two thousand years, or ever since it was meaningful to talk of a concept of citizenship at all. Some brief responses to certain of the comments on this thesis are directly relevant to the present discussion and will, therefore, be made here.

Part of my argument was that in deciding many of the types of cases which can arise in a constitutional jurisprudence, a court would have to make choices between competing aspects of differing political theories. One of the examples proffered was of a putative case which raised the issue of the divide between rights and the worth of rights. It was argued that a judge might decide that the protection of certain rights required also that attention be given to ancillary rights designed to protect the worth of the primary rights. It was argued further that a judge might reach this conclusion by relying on one of a range of background political arguments which lead to it. Brazier has commented that he would find it astonishing if a judge were to reason in this fashion. This comment simply misrepresents the argument made. It was expressly stated that a judge faced with the choice stated above would, *explicitly* or *implicitly*, have to rely on a background theory in reaching the conclusion on this issue.[3] Now if Brazier knows of a way in which it would be possible to resolve this, and many similar issues, without implicitly relying on a prior background theory then it would be very interesting to hear how this could be achieved. A great many of the issues that arise for adjudication at the constitutional or administrative level are not resolvable by any purely empirical analysis, and require a normative frame in order to be resolved at all. Indeed it is common in many areas of academic discourse to see commentators arguing perfectly sensibly that a court has, for example, based its reasoning on a particular conception of fault, causation or contract, and such arguments are not dependent on the fact that a court explicitly based itself on the philosophical literature in issue.

Oliver objects to the approach advocated for differing reasons.[4] She argues that the adoption of any particular background theory would be divisive, that agnosticism might be preferable or that, at the least, some solution of what I have termed a 'mix 'n' match' nature is the best that could be attained. Attempts at more general theorizing are regarded as dangerously alien imports from the United States and Europe. There are three responses to these objections.

The first is that Oliver proffers no effective substantive argument against the type of analysis advanced in any of the the more general theories which have been put forward in the United Kingdom and the United States as explanations for the direction and shape of public law. She appears to believe that those who advocate any such approach would, for some reason, have also to believe that this must be introduced in its totality at some particular time; that it would somehow be inconceivable for an advocate of, for example, republicanism to argue that the development of a republican constitutional discourse could be approached in stages within a society which did not at present conform wholly to those ideals. There is no warrant whatsoever for this assumption in any of the theories discussed. The fact that an end, represented by a particular conception of the relationship between citizen and state, can only be approached in stages is clearly not the same as desiring an end which is itself a 'mix 'n' match' of differing conceptions of citizen–state relationships. Moreover, the fact that there are difficulties with general approaches is conceded by their proponents, but this is not conclusive for the following obvious reason. Public law has to have some normative foundation, which serves to explain the shape, content and direction of the norms contained therein. Those who reject *any* of the general approaches must therefore be in favour of some more 'mixed' solution, which draws on more than one of the theories to provide answers to these foundational enquiries. Any such mixed solution will, however, also have imperfections. Whether such a mixed solution is indeed better than the pursuit of a more general theory can, therefore, only be determined when the nature of the mix and the problems therewith are identified. Only then can any meaningful assessment be made.

The second comment follows from the first. If a commentator does wish to propose such a 'mixed' solution, and to argue that this is the best that can be done, I have no objection to this whatsoever, *provided* that the nature of the mix is plausible and conveyed in some comprehensible fashion, *provided* that the requisite normative justifications are advanced for the differing parts of the mix and *provided* that we are told why this is the best package on offer. In fact what occurs much more often is one of two things. Little is offered by way of normative justification for the different parts of the mix, and/or the mix cannot be properly evaluated in any real sense, since it leaves many of the important issues unresolved. Oliver's own usage of the concept of citizenship, examined below, provides an apt example of both these traits. Or is it being suggested that we are not entitled to demand even this degree of justification for the proposed direction of public law? At times Oliver appears to suppose that a mixed solution is the same as an agnostic one. This is manifestly not so. A mixed solution still represents a choice, the constituent parts of which have normative implications, which must be justified and evaluated. The idea of a regime of public law that is meant to be agnostic is, therefore, quite simply meaningless. Moreover, the assumption that there can be a particular mixed solution, which does not somehow embrace a range of normative choices as to the component parts thereof and a normative view as to the quality of the package as a whole, is dangerous. It serves to stifle debate as to the most efficacious direction for public law on the pretence that contentious normative choices are not being made. Those choices are contentious, and they will not be rendered less so by attempting to argue that a particular mixed option is neutral.

The third point is that the objections advanced by Oliver are beset by a parochialism which manifests itself in three different ways. There is, in the first place, a *temporal* parochialism: we in the United Kingdom simply do not go in for this sort of theorizing. Now this is an instructive proposition, provided that the 'we' ignores Blackstone, Bentham, Dicey, Laski, Barker, Lindsay, Maitland and Cole, to name but a few, who have based their conception of public law on normative assumptions as to the way in which society is organized; and these normative assumptions continue to affect our existing constitutional norms. If I am to await with trepidation the call from the committee on dangerous constitutional discourse, then at the least I can have my fears alleviated by the realization that I will be in some distinguished company. Oliver's argument also reflects a straightforward *geographical* parochialism: we in the United Kingdom do not wish our ideas on constitutional law to be affected by theoretical approaches alleged to be more common on two continents. This vision of a rich vein of constitutional jurisprudence in the United Kingdom which is in danger of being violated by alien influences is endearing. Anyone familiar with the constitutional jurisprudence in, for example, the United States, and that in the United Kingdom, might well regard with mild surprise the idea that we would suffer by having some outside help. This is more particularly so given that others have had a good deal more experience with the problems of constitutional adjudication pursuant to a Bill of Rights than we have, and given also that such a reform is widely advocated in Britain. The final sense in which Oliver's argument is parochial is *conceptual* in nature. It is ultimately the most important. Her argument as to the sense in which it is possible for a system to be agnostic, or even what it means for a system to 'mix 'n' match', reveals a lack of full awareness of the conceptual issues which underlie any meaningful discussion of citizenship. This is apparent from Oliver's own discussion of the concept.

Oliver properly regards the revival of citizenship as one of the key elements in constitutional reform.[5] It is clear that she intends to discuss the concept in the second and third senses articulated above. Two related matters are evident if one considers this analysis.

One concerns the material which is considered relevant to the discussion. Thus, the work of Marshall,[6] who divided citizenship into political, social and civil aspects, is still regarded by Oliver as the seminal work on the subject.[7] This will not withstand examination. No disrespect is intended to Marshall, but to regard this as the seminal piece ignores those who wrote before and after. In the former category come classics such as Aristotle, Machiavelli and Harrington. If these are for some reason regarded as irrelevant, then those in the latter category would include modern liberal theorists such as Rawls, and the legal and political theory of Dworkin; the work of modern communitarians, such as Sandel or Taylor; and the work of public choice theorists, who have their own distinctive conception of the relationship between citizen and state. All these writers are directly concerned with the normative relationship between individual and the state. Their own arguments would not be altered one jot if the word citizen, which is sometimes used, were always used instead of the word individual. Nor would their respective disagreements be resolved, since it is the precise nature of the rights – social, civil, economic and political – which individuals have, and the priority between them, that is one of the prime distinguishing hallmarks of the different theories.

The other matter that is evident from Oliver's account of citizenship concerns the substance of the respective rights and duties which are said to be encompassed by this concept. The discussion is conducted at a high level of generality, with little specificity being accorded to the rights or duties which are mentioned. Conceptions of citizenship advocated by the political right are juxtaposed piecemeal to conceptions advanced by more centrist or left-wing commentators, with little if any idea as to whether these conceptions can in reality coexist, and if so how. This is mirrored by a general invocation of 'liberal democracy', which is mistakenly thought to be a banner under which all can unite. This is so only as long as that phrase is left at a sufficiently high level of generality, which thereby masks the very real conceptual disagreements that a more detailed invocation of rights and their priority would produce. Phrases such as civic virtue are set out without any overt recognition of the long intellectual history and political theory underlying them. There is a sense that it will somehow be all right on the night, but there is no basis offered for this optimism. Experience from other legal systems, such as those of the United States and, increasingly, Canada, demonstrates that it is precisely when it comes to the *particular conception* of, for example, equality which is to be applied, or the relationship between liberty and equality, or the meaning of property right, or the relation between liberty and the worth of liberty, or the status to be accorded to economic interests, that division exists as to the 'correct' response. That experience also demonstrates that the answer which is forthcoming will, as it must, be strongly influenced by the background theory adopted by different commentators or courts.

The picture of citizenship we are offered by Oliver is neither agnostic nor, as presently stated, a viable 'mix 'n' match'. It is not agnostic both because, as stated above, agnosticism is not possible, and because, even as presently conceived, the picture of citizenship makes a number of particular assumptions about, for example, the status of economic interests. It cannot be considered to be a viable 'mix 'n' match', because many of the topics that are of constitutional contention in other legal systems receive no answer at all.

SOVEREIGNTY: REASONS AND CONCLUSIONS

The more closely one examines the literature on sovereignty, the more apparent it becomes that successive generations of writers have drawn on the conclusions reached by previous writers, while paying scant, if any, attention to the reasoning employed by their 'intellectual ancestors'. The result is that 'authority' for the idea of parliamentary omnipotence has been generated, *inter alia*, by the citation of names from the past, without any reference being paid to the complex reasoning utilized by earlier generations. The process is analogous to the construction of case law precedent for a particular proposition, in which the conclusions of various judgments are brought to bear with little attention being given to the judicial reasoning used over what may be two or three hundred years. That this is so can be readily appreciated by examining the arguments employed by successive generations, beginning with our own. What will also become apparent is that the focus of the current debate is radically different from that of earlier years, in the sense that it largely manages to bypass issues of normative principle which might be deployed to justify sovereignty.

Wade, Positivism and the Modern Debate

Students, and indeed academics, are prone to characterize the current debate over sovereignty as a contest between the traditionalists, represented by Dicey and Wade, and upholders of the new view, represented by Jennings, Heuston and Marshall. However, as will be seen, the species of argument used by Wade is, in fact, very different from that advanced by Dicey, and therefore it is the views of Wade which will be considered in this section. No attempt will be made to consider the detail of the debate between Wade and the advocates of the new view. My own views on this can be found elsewhere.[8] It is the nature of the arguments used in this debate that is of primary interest here. The Wade view of sovereignty is captured in the following quotation:

> An orthodox English lawyer, brought up consciously or unconsciously on the doctrine of parliamentary sovereignty stated by Coke and Blackstone, and enlarged on by Dicey, could explain it in simple terms. He would say that it meant merely that no Act of the sovereign legislature (composed of the Queen, Lords and Commons) could be invalid in the eyes of the courts; that it was always open to the legislature, so constituted, to repeal any previous legislation whatever; that therefore no Parliament could bind its successors. . . . He would probably add that it is an invariable rule that in case of conflict between two Acts of Parliament, the later repeals the earlier. If he were then asked whether it would be possible for the United Kingdom to 'entrench' legislation – for example, if it should wish to adopt a Bill of Rights which would be repealable only by some specially safeguarded process – he would answer that under English law this is a legal impossibility: it is easy enough to pass such legislation, but since that legislation, like all other legislation, would be repealable by any ordinary Act of Parliament the special safeguards would be legally futile. This is merely an illustration of the rule that one Parliament cannot bind its successors. It follows therefore that there is one, and only one, limit to Parliament's legal power: it cannot detract from its own continuing sovereignty.[9]

Three strands of reasoning provide the basis for Wade's view of sovereignty. The first is apparent from the above quotation:

Parliament is sovereign in the sense depicted, because this accords with the reasoning of earlier constitutional writers, such as Coke, Blackstone and Dicey. The actual arguments used by these writers play no further part in Wade's own analysis, and, as will be seen below, they are different in nature from the analysis used by Wade himself.

The second strand of Wade's argument is based upon the case law, and he contends that his view of sovereignty is supported by certain judicial decisions.[10] Whether these decisions do in fact substantiate the quotation adumbrated above, and if so how far, is debatable, but the present chapter is not concerned with this forensic exercise.[11]

The third aspect of the reasoning employed by Wade is more analytical in nature. He is concerned to demonstrate the distinctiveness of the common law rule enjoining judicial obedience to statutes, and thus to rebut an argument advanced by Jennings. The latter had contended that, since statutes could change the common law, a statute might be enacted which altered the procedure by which statutes must be made within a particular area; what was to constitute a statute would, in this particular area, have been altered.[12] Wade's response was to distinguish between the common law 'rule' concerning sovereignty and all other rules of the common law. While it was generally the case that statutes could alter the common law, the 'rule' concerning sovereignty was an exception. Its distinctive feature was that it was the 'top' rule of the system, the source of its authority being historical rather than legal: the authority for the rule that the courts would obey the latest will of Parliament was to be found in the fact that those who operated the system accepted that this would be so. Salmond had concluded that no statute could itself validate the rule that Acts of Parliament have the force of law, since this would be to act on the very power to be conferred.[13] Wade was of like mind and contended that it must also follow that no statute could alter or abolish this rule. The top rule of the system could only be altered by revolution, not by legislation.[14] Such a revolution could be 'quiet and legal' in nature, whereby those who operated the system came to recognize a top rule which was different in content from that which presently existed; or the revolution could be real, with the same consequence. In either event, a statute could not, in itself, alter the content of the top rule, *and* the ultimate deciders as to whether the top rule had altered were the courts, since they could always decide what was a valid Act of Parliament.

The Wade thesis has been vigorously challenged by the proponents of the new view, who have argued that manner and form provisions enacted in a particular statute would be binding, in the sense that a later statute dealing with the same subject matter could alter the earlier statute only if passed in accordance with the provisions of that earlier statute.[15]

The details of these arguments can be found elsewhere.[16] What is of relevance in the present context is the way in which the Wade form of argumentation has coloured the entirety of the current debate. It has had two separate, albeit connected, effects on the way in which the sovereignty issue has been perceived in recent years.

On the one hand, it has allowed Wade, and the supporters of his view, to bypass discussion as to the existence of any normative justification for the sovereign, unlimited, power of Parliament. The issue is conceived of in 'technical' terms, relating to the content of the ultimate legal principle or rule of recognition, which might be said to exist within society at any one point in time. While it is recognized that there might be a different top rule from that which we are presently said to have, there is no argument put as to whether the current rule is normatively justifiable. This absence of any principled justification for the status quo is mirrored by the way in which the courts are said to go about their task as interpreters of the content of the top rule. Thus the process of decision-making facing the South African courts in the *Harris* case[17] is described in the following terms by Wade:

> They must therefore seek 'ultimate legal principles' of their own – and they must invent them, for they have to fill a vacuum. They have to decide for themselves – for no legislation can direct them – what they will recognise as the proper expression of the new sovereign legal power. In this they have a perfectly free choice, for legally the question is ultimate.[18]

The same reasoning can be found throughout the analysis. The South African courts are said to be at 'the ultimate boundary of the legal system', having to 'make a political decision'.[19] The positivism that lies at the root of the analysis comes through clearly in these quotations. The courts will make a political choice at the point where the law 'stops'. There is no need for the courts to engage in a principled discourse as to the 'correct' answer to this question at any particular point in time, since the issue is never perceived in these terms. Academic constitutional lawyers, as commentators on judicial decisions, are likewise absolved of responsibility in this regard. If the courts are essentially making political choices at the point where the law stops, then the academic can abnegate responsibility for evaluating whether the particular choice was correct, by arguing

316

that the evaluation of such options is the preserve of those operating within a different discipline.

On the other hand, the way in which the argument is presented by Wade has, somewhat paradoxically, influenced the mode of counter-argument utilized by the advocates of the new view. This is, in some ways, unsurprising, since they are reacting to the traditionalist view. This reactive posture has a 'price', however. It means that their counter-arguments are also conducted in a manner that minimizes the import of any normative arguments which might be presented for the limitation of sovereign power. It might well be true that they would favour rights-based limits on governmental power, which would thereby further the cause of an empowered citizenry, but this is never the focus of their response. This response is, rather, principally framed in terms that seek to rebut the argument that manner and form provisions would not survive a later repeal by simple majority. The battle between the traditionalist–Wade view and the new view of sovereignty is fought on terrain marked out by the former. It is a battle in which the traditionalist has demarcated the terms of the engagement. The acceptance, by the proponents of the new view, of these terms for the constitutional discourse has, moreover, a further, paradoxical twist. The very labels used to describe the two sides connote an acceptance that the Wade view has the more ancient pedigree, and an implicit acceptance also that the ground on which the issue is fought is of centrality to the topic as a whole. However, as will be seen below, both these assumptions are contestable. While assertions of parliamentary sovereignty can, of course, be found over the preceding centuries, the form of argument used to sustain this assertion has not been in any way identical to that which has characterized what has now become known as the traditionalist view. The constitutional discourse of previous generations reveals an awareness of the need for normative, principled justifications for the existence of sovereign power, in a way which has been largely forgotten. The advocates of the new view must accept their share of responsibility for this, by the very fact that they have accepted the terms of the debate laid down by their opponents.

Pluralism and the Neglected Challenge to Sovereignty

It is only necessary to turn the clock back a mere 60 or 70 or years to find a challenge to the picture of the omnipotent state depicted above. This challenge has been largely neglected in recent years, and this neglect is unwarranted. The nature of this challenge is particularly apposite for the purposes of the present argument, since it is based on arguments of principle which have been largely absent from the present debate described above.

The challenge emanated from the pluralists, who attacked many of the propositions articulated by writers such as Dicey. Space precludes any thorough analysis of what is a complex set of arguments, the precise configuration of which could differ between different writers. A more detailed discussion can be found elsewhere,[20] but some idea of the central themes can be given here. One such theme was the challenge to the conception of the all-powerful state, and an account of the origins of that idea. The pluralists were, therefore, directly concerned with the types of reasons given for the existence of this central power and with evaluating those reasons in order to determine whether they were sustainable.

They argued that this conception of the state was born of an age of crisis, during the turmoil of the sixteenth century. Writers such as Hobbes and Bodin were concerned about the possible fragmentation of the state, from religious discord, civil unrest or external threat. A prominent part of the response to this threat was to assert the supremacy of the state over all other institutions. It was lawyers who later provided conceptual support for this supremacy by developing the notion of unlimited sovereignty, in its Austinian or Diceyan forms.

This vision of the state was questioned in both descriptive and normative terms. From a descriptive perspective, pluralist writers pointed to the very real constraints that associations or groups could place upon the freedom of state action. This was reinforced by the normative argument, which manifested itself in a distinction between state and society. The state was not regarded as the origin or fount of all rights existing in society. Groups existed and had rights even before the evolution of the state. Decentralization of power was desirable in normative terms, while concentration of authority in an omnipotent, centralized state was held to be a threat to liberty, and also operated to stifle diversity and creativity.[21]

There is scant, if any, attention paid to the views of the pluralists in the 'modern' debate on sovereignty depicted in the previous section. This is true even of the proponents of the new view considered above. Such comment as exists is critical. Thus, Marshall takes Laski to task on the ground that the latter was insufficiently precise in his criticism of sovereignty, and that the consequences Laski ascribed to sovereignty did not always follow therefrom.[22] Whether Laski really was guilty of ambiguity or lack of analytical rigour cannot be considered here.[23] This type of critique does, none the less, miss the force of the general argument put by the pluralists. The merits of their argument reside in the fact that they asked

318

important questions as to the *reasons* why sovereignty had ever become part of constitutional discourse, and that they were willing to question whether this degree of power, located in either the 'state' or the 'government', was *normatively justified*.

Dicey and the Self-correcting Constitution

It was argued above that it is mistaken to treat Dicey and Wade as if they both employed the same species of argument. The conclusions that were reached may well have been similar, but the manner of arriving at those conclusions was significantly different. Dicey's own analysis was a blend of the empirical and the normative.

Dicey's empirical reasoning in support of sovereignty was eclectic. It was based partly on the writings of jurists, such as Coke and Blackstone, partly on examples of the exertion of parliamentary authority in the past, as exemplified by the Acts of Union and the Septennial Act, and partly on instances where Parliament had exercised authority over private rights.[24] This positive side of the argument was complemented by a negative, in which Dicey dismissed other possible sources of legislative power, such as the monarch; and in which he also dismissed the possibility of other institutions, such as the courts, placing limitations on what Parliament could do.[25]

This empirical side of the analysis was, however, complemented by a normative argument, which was designed to show that it was sound, in terms of *principle*, for Parliament to have this unlimited power. Dicey realized that the empirical argument could not, by itself, sustain the case for parliamentary sovereignty. He also realized that even though he had quoted from Blackstone, he could not simply draw on the species of normative argument used by the latter, since, as will be seen below, it would not have been applicable, without substantial modifications, to the changed conditions of the nineteenth century in which Dicey was writing. Dicey, therefore, set about constructing his own normative argument to justify the parliamentary sovereignty he had empirically described.

The essence of the argument was that a Parliament, duly elected on the extended franchise, represented the most authoritative expression of the will of the nation. The Parliament thereby elected should therefore be able to carry out any action. Moreover, Dicey believed that the Parliament would control the executive and that the Members of Parliament would not pass legislation that was contrary to the interests of those who elected them. Constitutional protections against the exercise of parliamentary power were not therefore required, since, in the words of Dicey, 'the permanent wishes of the representative portion of Parliament can hardly in the long run differ from the wishes of the English people, or at any rate of the electors; that which the majority of the House of Commons command, the majority of English people usually desire.'[26] The normative argument was, therefore, apparently simple. The British system of democracy was founded upon a channel of authority flowing from the bottom upwards. The expanded electorate chose representatives. The Parliament thus chosen had legitimacy because of the extended franchise and should therefore have all-embracing powers. The elected MPs articulated the views of those who had chosen them, and they controlled the executive. Legislation which was constitutionally questionable would not, therefore, be passed, or would be repealed expeditiously. A central concern of the Diceyan thesis was, in this way, designed to show that the existence of parliamentary sovereignty would not place the rights of individual citizens in jeopardy.

The defects in this mode of argument have been examined in detail elsewhere.[27] Suffice it to say for the present that Britain's system of democracy probably never operated in this self-correcting way, and that this vision of the relationship between electors, Parliament and the executive certainly does not accord with present reality. That reality is better described as one in which the Parliament is controlled by the executive, rather than vice versa, and as one in which it is perfectly possible for a government, elected on what might be a minority of the votes cast, to promulgate legislation which is deleterious to the rights or interests of a certain section of the population.

Notwithstanding the flaws in the Diceyan analysis, it is the structure of that analysis which is of importance for the present argument. Dicey's argument has little, if anything, in common with the Wade mode of analysis considered above. The Diceyan argument is structured as a blend of the empirical and the normative, and is based on the realization that there must be some principled justification for the existence of parliamentary sovereignty. That we have lost sight of this in the modern debate on sovereignty is to be much regretted.

Blackstone and the Balanced Constitution

Blackstone is, almost without exception, regarded as one of the principal architects of the traditional vision of sovereignty. He is perceived as one of the classical authorities who articulated the idea of unlimited parliamentary sovereignty. The 'famous' quotation from Blackstone, set out below, has been oft repeated. However, as will be seen, this picture of Blackstone represents a serious distortion of what is a far more interesting thesis. The use made of Blackstone's quotation, severed from the totality of that author's analysis, exemplifies the danger of not doing something really quite important, and really quite simple: reading the actual reasoning of the author in question. Let us begin with that 'famous' quotation:

> The power and jurisdiction of parliament, says sir Edward Coke is so transcendent and absolute, that it cannot be confined, either for causes or persons, within any bounds. . . . It hath sovereign and uncontrollable authority in the making, confirming, enlarging, restraining, abrogating, repealing, reviving and expounding of laws, concerning matters of all possible denominations, ecclesiastical or temporal, civil, military, maritime, or criminal: this being the place where that absolute despotic power, which must in all governments reside somewhere, is intrusted by the constitution of these kingdoms. All mischiefs and grievances, operations and remedies, that transcend the ordinary course of the laws are within the reach of this extraordinary tribunal. . . . It can in short, do everything that is not naturally impossible; and therefore some have not scrupled to call its power, by a figure rather too bold the omnipotence of parliament. True it is, that what the parliament doth, no authority upon earth can undo. So that it is most essential to the liberties of this kingdom, that such members be delegated to this important trust, as are most eminent for their probity, their fortitude, and their knowledge.[28]

Blackstone continues in the same vein by disagreeing with the Lockean argument that would enable the people to remove or alter the legislature, if the latter had abused the trust reposed in it. Blackstone is firmly of the view that no legal steps could be taken to execute such a plan.[29]

Now the reader may justifiably feel that this does not, at present, appear to represent an image of balanced constitutionalism. This is clearly true if one stops at this juncture. To do so is, however, misleading. The quotation adumbrated above appears nearly twenty pages into a chapter on Parliament, and that quotation is explicitly prefaced by the statement that the object is 'to examine the laws and customs relating to Parliament, thus united together and considered as one aggregate body'.[30] It is readily apparent that this serves as a reference to the entirety of the discussion which has preceded the quote, since, as will be seen, that discussion is concerned precisely with the manner in which the Parliament is perceived to operate. What then is the constitutional vision of the parliamentary process which underpins Blackstone's thought?

The vision is of a balanced constitutional order, and the Parliament which is sovereign in the sense depicted above is a Parliament which is meant to function in the manner he describes. The nature of this balanced order can now be set out.

Blackstone begins his analysis of Parliament by focusing on a central and important theme. Tyrannical governments were those in which the power of making and enforcing laws was vested in the same person. Things were different where the legislative and executive authority was in different hands, since 'the former will take care not to entrust the latter with so large a power as may tend to the subversion of its own independence, and therewith the liberty of the subject'.[31] In England power was thus divided. The legislative branch was the Parliament, which consisted of the King, lords and commons; the executive branch consisted of the King alone.[32] The relationship that is intended to operate between them is made clear by Blackstone:

> It is highly necessary for preserving the balance of the
> constitution, that the executive power should be a branch,
> but not the whole, of the legislative. The total union of
> them, we have seen, would be productive of tyranny; the
> total disjunction of them, for the present, would in the end
> produce the same effects, by causing that union against which
> it seems to provide. The legislature would soon become
> tyrannical, by making continual encroachments, and
> gradually assuming to itself the rights of the executive
> power.[33]

Blackstone picks up the same theme a little later:

> And herein indeed consists the true excellence of the English
> government, that all the parts of it form a mutual check
> upon each other. In the legislature, the people are a check on
> the nobility, and the nobility a check upon the people; by
> the mutual privilege of rejecting what the other has resolved:
> while the king is a check upon both, which preserves the
> executive power from encroachments. And this very executive
> power is again checked and kept within due bounds by the
> two houses, through the privilege of inquiring into,
> impeaching, and punishing the conduct (not indeed of the
> king, which would destroy his constitutional independence
> but, which is more beneficial to the public), of his evil and
> pernicious counsellors. Thus every branch of our civil polity,
> supports and is supported by the rest: for the two houses
> naturally drawing in two directions of opposite interest, and
> the prerogative in another still different from them both,

they mutually keep each other from exceeding their proper limits; while the whole is prevented from separation, and artificially connected together by the mixed nature of the crown, which is part of the legislative, and the sole executive magistrate.[34]

It is only after this discourse that the famous quotation appears, and the body 'thus united' to which Blackstone refers at the beginning of that quotation is the body functioning in the manner described above.

The substance of Blackstone's reasoning and, indeed, the language of his analysis contain echoes of earlier discourse on balanced government, most notably that of Harrington and the republican tradition. The emphasis placed by Blackstone on balanced government, and the form which that balance should assume, demonstrates an attachment, in some part at least, to the earlier ideas. These stressed the ideal of a balanced government, consisting of the one, the few and the many, which would coexist and ensure a stable, well-organized polity. Blackstone's vision of the equilibrium achieved through the combination of the king, the nobility and the commons reflects this same theme. The same impression is conveyed in other parts of the work. Thus Blackstone speaks of the nobility as a natural bridge between the people and the king, and as the middle tier of a pyramid which rises from a 'broad foundation' until it reaches the king at the apex.[35] Moreover, the Harringtonian theme, that a property holding was a necessary qualification for the suffrage, in order to ensure that the voter really had a will of his own and could not simply be bought by those with wealth, occupies a central place in Blackstone's own thesis.[36]

Whether the assumptions on which Blackstone reasoned truly represented the reality of eighteenth-century government is beyond the scope of the present work.[37] The answer to this enquiry is not, however, vital for the present discussion. What is of importance is that Blackstone reasoned on the assumptions set out above. His 'famous' quotation was not written in a legal or political vacuum. He realized that the existence of a sovereign Parliament, with all-embracing power, must have some normative justification if it was to prove acceptable. For Blackstone this principled justification was to be found in the vision of a balanced constitutional order, in which the component parts thereof would operate as a check on each other and act for the public good.

Blackstone's quotation was drawn on by later writers, such as Dicey,[38] and presented as one of the principal foundations for his own vision of sovereignty. However, Dicey utilized Blackstone's views without any apparent realization of the constitutional framework in which the latter reasoned, or at the very least without any allusion to that framework. Yet it is readily apparent that the very foundations of Blackstone's analysis had almost certainly ceased to operate by the late nineteenth century, and have certainly ceased to do so in the modern day. It was perhaps for this reason that Dicey sought to devise a different normative justification for the sovereignty of Parliament. The vision of a balanced constitution, in which the House of Commons checked and was checked by the Lords, in which both checked and were checked by the King, and in which the King was the repository of executive power, and thereby able to counterbalance the power of Parliament, clearly does not represent an accurate picture of constitutional reality in the late nineteenth or twentieth centuries. The differences are manifest. The current position, in which the executive is formed from the governing party and controls the Commons, and in which the counterweights to the Commons power, in terms of the Lords and the Monarch, have fallen away, is a far cry from the ideal of balanced order on which Blackstone premised his thesis.

Sovereignty: Re-evaluating Our Constitutional Foundations

Many of the present discussions of constitutional reform are premised on the idea that a way round the 'traditional' view of parliamentary sovereignty must be found, in order to ensure, for example, that an entrenched Bill of Rights is not overturned by a later simple majority. Many of these analyses do, however, leave the principle of parliamentary omnipotence intact, while seeking tactical devices through which to circumvent it. Such exercises are often ingenious, and nothing in this chapter should be taken to be against the pursuit of such ideas. A more direct attack on what is taken to be the traditional conception of sovereignty can, none the less, be ventured, by drawing on the arguments adumbrated above. This may well be of importance, precisely because the way in which we deal with the sovereignty issue is foundational. The more secure are the foundations, the greater is the likelihood that we can build a constitutional jurisprudence which is satisfactory. We should not subject future generations to the 'fear' that a conception of unlimited sovereign power will reawaken, breaking the tactical ties that have sought to keep it constrained, and thereby endangering hard-won constitutional protections for the citizen. There are two modes of more direct attack open to us.

The more obvious technique would be to undermine what is taken to be the status quo from within, by using the language and methodology of positivism. The general thrust of the argument would be straightforward. Insofar as the vision of sovereignty propounded

by Wade can be taken to be the ultimate legal principle, or rule
of recognition, it is based ultimately on acceptance as such by those
who operate the system, including Parliament and the courts. The
rule of recognition can, however, alter. This can assume the form of
a technical legal revolution, by and through which the 'players' in
the system come to modify the status quo. A modification of the
principle articulated by Wade could therefore come about, with the
consequence that the rule of recognition might henceforth read that
Parliament could not in fact do anything by simple majority in
instances where there was an entrenched Bill of Rights. Moreover, the
players might be convinced that this form of alteration was desirable,
because the previous orthodoxy was based on a series of normative
assumptions which may not have been true at the time they were
propounded, and were certainly not correct now.

The other mode of attack may, to some, appear less plausible, but
it is worth pursuing, both because of its intrinsic importance, and also
because the potential implications of this form of challenge are
far-reaching.

The second mode of challenge is to consider sovereignty from a
Dworkinian perspective of interpretation. The outlines of the argument which might be made are as follows. Dworkin's theory of
adjudication is based on the idea of law as integrity:

> According to law as integrity, propositions of law are true if
> they figure in or follow from the principles of justice,
> fairness, and procedural due process that provide the best
> constructive interpretation of the community's legal practice.[39]

Space precludes any extended exegesis on the foundations of the
Dworkinian thesis, but certain aspects of it must be touched on here
in order that its application to the problem before us can be properly
appreciated. It is particularly important to note the role that history
does and does not play in this form of analysis. Law as integrity *does
not* demand consistency in principle 'over all historical stages of a
community's law'.[40] It *does* require a horizontal as opposed to a
vertical consistency of principle across the 'range of standards the
community now enforces'.[41] The law must be held to consist of not
only the rights and duties which the community now enforces, but
also the scheme of principles necessary to justify them:

> Law as integrity, then, begins in the present and pursues the
> past only so far as and in the way the contemporary focus
> dictates. It does not aim to recapture, even for present law,
> the ideals or practical purposes of the politicians who first
> created it. It aims rather to justify what they did . . . in an

325

overall story worth telling now, a story with a complex claim: that present practice can be organized by and justified in principles sufficiently attractive to provide an honorable future. . . . When a judge declares that a particular principle is instinct in law, he reports not a simple-minded claim about the motives of past statesmen, a claim a wise cynic can easily refute, but an interpretative proposal: that the principle both fits and justifies some complex part of legal practice, that it provides an attractive way to see, in the structure of that practice, the consistency of principle integrity requires.[42]

It is evident from the above quotation that ideas of 'fit' and 'justification' are essential aspects of the concept of law as integrity. The former provides 'a rough threshold requirement that an interpretation of some part of the law must meet if it is to be eligible at all'.[43] This threshold serves to eliminate interpretations which ignore the 'brute facts of history', and also serves to to 'limit the role any judge's personal convictions of justice can play' in reaching a particular decision.[44] The latter element, that of justification, is engaged when the threshold test of fit is passed. At this stage there may still be more than one possible interpretation which has passed the threshold test. At this juncture the judge 'must choose between eligible interpretations by asking which shows the community's structure of institutions and decisions – its public standards as a whole – in a better light from the standpoint of political morality'.[45] The process at this second stage is itself interpretative, in the sense that there may be interpretations which surmount the threshold test but do not fit perfectly with all elements of past practice. This does not place an impossible hurdle in the path of the judge:

When an interpretation meets the threshold, remaining defects of fit may be compensated, in his overall judgment, if the principles of that interpretation are particularly attractive, because then he sets off the community's frequent lapses in respecting these principles against its virtue in generally observing them.[46]

It is apparent from the preceding discussion that the Dworkinian analysis is designed to determine what the current law actually is; it is not an elaborate structure for deciding what the law ought to be. An interpretation of sovereignty using the Dworkinian framework, *and* using the historical material set out above, might take the following form. Let us postulate three possible interpretations of the concept of sovereignty.

The first interpretation would be the formulation taken from Wade which was set out above.[47] The second interpretation would be as follows. In the United Kingdom, the Parliament has sovereign power, in the sense that it can pass laws which cover any subject matter or issue, subject to the qualification that the courts will exercise a power of constitutional review and formally invalidate legislation, should Parliament thereby trespass on certain individual rights. A third interpretation might be presented in the following way. In the United Kingdom, the Parliament has sovereign power, in that it has competence to legislate on any issue. This omnipotence is, however, conditioned, in the sense that the very existence of this authority is premised on certain assumptions as to how the power will be exercised, which assumptions are designed to provide the requisite normative justification for that power. Which of these interpretations provides the best fit and justification in relation to the concept of sovereignty?

The second of the possible interpretations can be ruled out on the threshold test of fit, since it is clear that there is no plausible reading of Britain's constitutional jurisprudence which would support it, even though it might be desirable.

The first interpretation is that which is regarded as the 'traditional' conception of sovereignty. It might seem, therefore, that it must pass the threshold test and be in a good position to 'win' any 'competition' based on justification. Neither of these assumptions is self-evident. Whether this interpretation, as stated, really does fit Britain's past constitutional discourse is, in fact, highly contestable. This is precisely because it misses the entirety of the principled reasoning used in that discourse, which was designed to provide the normative justification for the existence of parliamentary omnipotence. The principled reasoning was an integral part of such analyses. It cannot be severed and forgotten. Even if this first interpretation does pass the threshold test of fit, a more severe test is awaiting at the level of justification. The reason for this is not hard to find: as currently presented this interpretation offers no normative justification at all for the existence of unlimited parliamentary power. The interpretation offered to us is simply a statement about the existence of power. All forms of power must be justified in some manner, and the greater the alleged scope of power the more convincing must be the justification. Now it might of course be open to someone to present all manner of purported rationales for illimitable sovereignty. These could range from the allegedly 'logical', that a body which is sovereign simply cannot be limited, to the allegedly anti-democratic argument, that it is somehow inconsistent with democracy for there to be any checks on what the current parliamentary majority can achieve. The soundness or otherwise of these rationales could then be assessed. It should, however, be recognized that in presenting the argument in this fashion the first interpretation is, in reality, coming to ape the third. The proponent of the first interpretation is then faced with a dilemma. He can stick to that formulation as presented, and then lose any contest based on justification since none is offered. Or he can attempt to furnish such justification, at the cost of transforming the interpretation into something closely resembling the third interpretation.

It would seem, therefore, that it is the third interpretation which provides the best principled basis on which to construct future constitutional discussion, but only if this interpretation could be said to pass the threshold test of fit. The discussion of Britain's constitutional heritage adumbrated above gives ample basis for an affirmative answer to this question, without in any way straining the material. Indeed, as indicated above, it is this third interpretation that comes closest to capturing the type of argument presented by constitutional writers of previous generations.

It might be argued, by way of opposition, that this third interpretation does not 'fit' the practice of the courts, and that such judicial practice is only consonant with the first option. Space precludes any detailed examination of the case law, which I have undertaken elsewhere.[48] Suffice it to say, for present purposes, that the case law normally cited for the first option was never in any way concerned with the 'modern' scenario of an entrenched Bill of Rights being contravened by legislation passed by a simple majority; that in any event the correct interpretation of those cases is open to question; and that more recent judicial decisions in the context of the EC suggest that the courts might well be ready to accept some limits on what is taken to be the traditional view of sovereignty.[49]

If the third interpretation does indeed meet the test of fit, it is, as stated above, superior on the test of justification. Adoption of this interpretation could provide a fitting foundation for the development of a constitutional jurisprudence which is more appropriate to the needs of the modern day. It would leave the way open for an argument to be made that no normative justification can in fact be found for the existence of legally untrammelled parliamentary power in the present day. In reasoning in this way it could be justly contended that the courts were thereby drawing on a vein of constitutional principle which goes back over three hundred years. At the very least, it would serve to frame the issue in these terms, and thereby place the justificatory onus on those who believe that normative reasons can be found for unlimited sovereign power. If that onus is not discharged it would then be open to us to contend that, for example, rights-based constitutional guarantees enshrined in a Bill of Rights and policed by a form of constitutional review are actually justified. Such guarantees provide one species of requisite normative check on the exercise of governmental authority.

CONCLUSION

No attempt will be made to summarize the entirety of the preceding discussion. Two further comments which are of general relevance can, however, be ventured.

The first is as follows. The application of a principled/rights-based approach has been a feature of the work of other public lawyers, including, for example, Jowell and Lester, and Allan. Such writers have drawn on Dworkin for support. It is evident from the foregoing that I am in sympathy with this general theme. The implications of pursuing such an approach must, none the less, be borne in mind. The interpretative technique espoused by Dworkin requires, as seen above, judgments to be made about fit and justification. These will often be controversial, particularly the latter. In order to reach any conclusion in a particular case it will often be necessary to delve deeply into differing conceptions of justice and fairness. This will entail the examination of differing political theories, which may well recognize the same right, but accord it a very different interpretation; or the distinctive theories may have a different hierarchy of rights; or they may posit the relationship between the rights that are recognized and the general social good, in various ways. That this is so is evident from Dworkin's own work. Thus his analysis of the problem of affirmative action in the *Bakke* case is grounded in a certain conception of equality, which is itself posited on more basic assumptions concerning the extent to which an individual has a moral claim to the rewards produced by attributes such as intelligence.[50] Now one may agree or disagree with Dworkin's conception of equality, which is a cornerstone of liberal political theory. That conception of equality has, however, been the subject of extensive discussion by those who do not accept the precepts on which this reasoning is based.[51] This does not, of course, mean that Dworkin's conception is wrong. It does mean that an understanding of the arguments on both sides is a precondition for making any rational evaluation. Precisely the same point can be made with respect to Dworkin's view as to the principle which underlines the common law.[52] At a more general level, this point is exemplified by considering rival conceptions of public law in other countries. Thus, the debate between pluralist and republican theories in the United States is, at one level, a debate between rival schools of thought which claim that their vision of the constitution offers both the best fit and the best interpretation/justification of the rights contained therein.[53] If, therefore, one wishes to pursue this approach to public law, it must be undertaken with the realization that it can only be done properly if one understands the contestable issues of justice and political theory that underlie the resolution of particular problems.

The second comment is a corollary of the first. It is readily apparent from the foregoing that I believe that meaningful constitutional interpretation will entail just such evaluative, normative choices as those considered above. It will be a *necessary* facet of public law. No one has, however, maintained that it provides answers to every detailed issue of, for example, institutional design or competence that can arise within public law discourse, though it may well provide the conceptual frame within which these issues are resolved.[54] Thus, the very meaning to be ascribed to concepts such as accountability will be affected by the background principles underlying the system as a whole.

The conclusion, therefore, sounds the same note as the introduction. Public law will entail normative choices, whether these be founded on a particular background theory, or on some mixture of theories. Attempts to 'understand' public law without addressing these issues lead to statements being made about important issues without any apparent realization that the statements are controversial and of dubious validity. Thus, the assertion that rights-based constitutional review entails an 'important check on democracy', by conferring power on an unelected body of judges,[55] is uttered as if this were a self-evident and straightforward proposition. It is, of course, nothing of the kind. It is based on an implicit conception of democracy, in which the whole essence of that concept is captured by the notion of majoritarianism. This certainly does not capture the totality of almost any sophisticated exposition of democracy, whether it be modern or classical in nature.[56] Examples of this type can be combined with others in which a particular construction is accorded to a concept, such as participatory democracy, without revealing the contestable assumptions which underlie that construction.[57] An overt disavowal of theory will, therefore, not surprisingly normally be attended by an implicit set of assumptions which serve to bring particular theoretical constructs in by the back door. Use of the front door is to be preferred.

NOTES AND REFERENCES

1 See A. Dummett and A. Nicol, *Subjects, Citizens, Aliens and Others* (1990).
2 P. P. Craig, *Public Law and Democracy in the United Kingdom and the United States of America* (1990).
3 See note 2, e.g. p. 214. See Brazier (1990) 107 LQR 680, 681.
4 [1991] PL 623.
5 D. Oliver, *Government in the United Kingdom: The Search for Accountability, Effectiveness and Citizenship* (1991), pp. 22–41.
6 T. H. Marshall, *Citizenship and Social Class* (1950).
7 Note 5, p. 34.
8 P. P. Craig, 'Parliamentary sovereignty of the United Kingdom Parliament after *Factortame*', forthcoming in the *YBEL*.
9 H. W. R. Wade, 'The basis of legal sovereignty' [1955] CLJ 172, 174.
10 *Ibid.*, pp. 175–9. Wade relies upon *Vauxhall Street Estates Ltd* v. *Liverpool Corporation* [1932] 1 KB 733; *Ellen Street Estates Ltd* v. *Minister of Health* [1934] 1 KB 590; *British Coal Corporation* v. *The King* [1935] AC 500.
11 For a discussion of this issue, see Craig, note 8.
12 Sir I. Jennings, *The Law of the Constitution* (5th edn, 1967), Chapter 4.
13 Sir J. Salmond, *Jurisprudence* (10th edn, 1947), p. 155.
14 Note 9, pp. 187–96.
15 Jennings, note 12; R. F. V. Heuston, *Essays in Constitutional Law* (2nd edn, 1964), Chapter 1; G. Marshall, *Constitutional Theory* (1971), Chapter 3.
16 Craig, note 8.
17 *Harris* v. *Minister of the Interior* [1952] 1 TLR 1245.
18 Note 9, p. 192.
19 *Loc. cit.*
20 P. P. Craig, *Public Law and Democracy in the United Kingdom and the United States of America* (1990), Chapters 5 and 6.
21 See, e.g., H. J. Laski, *Studies in the Problem of Sovereignty* (1917); *Authority in the Modern State* (1919); *The Foundations of Sovereignty* (1921); E. Barker, *Reflections on Government* (1942); A. D. Lindsay, *The Essentials of Democracy* (1929).
22 Marshall, note 15, pp. 39–40.
23 I remain unconvinced by many of the examples given, which are often stripped of the textual context in which they were written.
24 A. V. Dicey, *An Introduction to the Study of the Law of the Constitution* (10th edn, 1967), pp. 41–50.
25 *Ibid.*, pp. 50–70.
26 *Ibid.*, p. 83.
27 Craig, note 20, Chapter 2.
28 Sir W. Blackstone, *Commentaries on the Law of England* (16th edn, 1825), Vol. I, Book 2, pp. 160–1.
29 *Ibid.*, pp. 161–2.
30 *Ibid.*, p. 160.
31 *Ibid.*, p. 146.

32 *Ibid.*, pp. 146–7.
33 *Ibid.*, pp. 153–4.
34 *Ibid.*, pp. 154–5.
35 *Ibid.*, p. 158.
36 *Ibid.*, p. 170. For a discussion of the republican tradition, see J. G. A. Pocock, *The Machiavellian Moment: Florentine Political Thought and the Atlantic Republican Tradition* (1975); J. Harrington, 'The Commonwealth of Oceana', in *The Political Works of James Harrington* (ed. J. G. A. Pocock, 1977).
37 See, e.g., B. Kemp, *King and Commons 1660–1832* (1957).
38 Note 24, pp. 41–2.
39 R. Dworkin, *Law's Empire* (1986), p. 225.
40 *Ibid.*, p. 227.
41 *Loc. cit.*
42 *Ibid.*, pp. 227–8.
43 *Ibid.*, p. 255.
44 *Loc. cit.*
45 *Ibid.*, p. 256.
46 *Ibid.*, p. 257.
47 See above, p. 314.
48 See note 8.
49 *Loc. cit.*
50 Note 39, pp. 393–7.
51 See Craig, note 2, Chapters 8 and 9.
52 Note 39, Chapter 8.
53 *Ibid.*, Chapters 3, 4 and 10.
54 This is made clear in the very first quote in Craig, note 2, p. 4. The quotation is taken from Dworkin.
55 See G. Ganz, *Understanding Public Law* (1987), p. 106.
56 See further Dworkin, note 39, pp. 369–79.
57 Ganz, note 55, pp. 87, 115–16.

Select Bibliography

Andrews, Geoff (ed.), *Citizenship* (Lawrence & Wishart, 1991).

Barendt, Eric, *Freedom of Speech* (Clarendon Press, 1987).

Beddard, R. and Hills, D., *Economic, Social and Cultural Rights: Progress and Achievement* (Macmillan, 1992).

Birkinshaw, Patrick, *Freedom of Information: The Law, the Practice and the Ideal* (Weidenfeld and Nicolson, 1988).

Birkinshaw, Patrick, *Reforming the Secret State* (Open University Press, 1991).

Blackburn, Robert and Taylor, John (eds), *Human Rights for the 1990s* (Mansell, 1991).

Brazier, Margaret, *Medicine, Patients and the Law* (Penguin, 2nd edn, 1992).

Citizens' Britain: Policies for a People's Charter (Liberal Democratic Party, (1991).

Citizen's Charter: Labour's Better Deal for Consumers and Citizens (Labour Party, 1991).

The Citizen's Charter: Raising the Standard, Cm 1599 (HMSO, 1991).

Coote, Anna (ed.), *The Welfare of Citizens Developing New Social Rights* (IPPR, 1992).

Council of Europe, *Convention for the Protection of Human Rights and Freedoms* (Council of Europe, 1991).

Craig, Paul, *Administrative Law* (Sweet and Maxwell, 2nd edn, 1989).

Craig, Paul, *Public Law and Democracy in the United Kingdom and the United States of America* (Oxford University Press, 1991).

Dahrendorf, R. 'Citizenship and modern social conflict', in Holme, R. and Elliott, M. (eds), *1688–1988: Time for a New Constitution* (Macmillan, 1988).

Dicey, A. V., *Law of the Constitution* (Macmillan, 10th edn, 1985).

Dummett, A. and Nicol, A., *Subjects, Citizens, Aliens and Others* (Weidenfeld & Nicolson, 1990).

Dworkin, R. M., *Taking Rights Seriously* (Duckworth, 1977).

Elias, P. and Ewing, K. D., *Trade Union Democracy: Members' Rights and the Law* (Mansell, 1988).

Ewing, K. D. and Gearty, C. A., *Freedom under Thatcher: Civil Liberties in Modern Britain* (Oxford University Press, 1990).

Ewing, K. D., *The Right to Strike* (Oxford University Press, 1991).

Griffiths, A., Grimes, R. and Roberts, G., *The Law and Elderly People* (Routledge, 1990).

Hart, H. L. A., *Law, Liberty and Morality* (Oxford University Press, 1962).

Hayek, F. A., *The Constitution of Liberty* (Routledge, 1960).

Heater, D., *Citizenship: The Civil Ideal in World History* (Longman, 1990).

Institute for Public Policy Research, *A Written Constitution for the United Kingdom* (Mansell, 1993).

Justice, *The Citizen and the Administration* (Justice, 1961).

Justice/All Souls Report, *Administrative Justice: Some Necessary Reforms* (Oxford University Press, 1988).

Laski, Harold J., *A Grammar of Politics* (George Allen & Unwin, 1925).

Laski, Harold J., *Liberty in the Modern State* (Penguin, 1937).

Lester, Anthony, and Bindman, Geoffrey, *Race and Law* (Penguin, 1972).

Lister, R., *The Exclusive Society: Citizenship and the Poor* (CPAG, 1990).

Marshall, Geoffrey, *Constitutional Theory* (Clarendon Press, 1971).

Marshall, T. H., *Citizenship and Social Class* (Cambridge, 1950).

Mason, J. K., and Smith, A. McC. (eds), *Law and Medical Ethics* (Butterworths, 3rd edn, 1991).

Mead, I., *Beyond Entitlement* (Free Press, 1986).

Mill, J. S., *On Liberty* (reprinted Penguin, 1974).

Oldfield, A., *Citizenship and the Community: Civil Republicanism and the Modern World* (Routledge, 1990).

Oliver, Dawn, *Government in the United Kingdom: The Search for Accountability, Effectiveness and Citizenship* (Open University Press, 1991).

Oliver, M., *The Politics of Disablement* (Macmillan, 1990).

Plant, Raymond, *Citizenship, Rights and Socialism* (Fabian Society, 1988).

Raz, Joseph, *The Morality of Freedom* (Oxford University Press, 1986).

Robertson, Geoffrey, *Freedom the Individual and the Law* (Penguin, 6th edn, 1989).

Sieghart, Paul, *The Lawful Rights of Mankind* (Oxford University Press, 1985).

Speaker's Commission on Citizenship, *Encouraging Citizenship* (HMSO, 1990).

Stone, D. A., *The Disabled State* (Macmillan, 1984).

Thornton, Peter, *Decade of Decline: Civil Liberties in the Thatcher Years* (Liberty, 1989).

Turner, B., *Citizenship and Capitalism* (Allen and Unwin, 1986).

United Nations, *Universal Declaration of Human Rights; International Covenant on Economic, Social and Cultural Rights; International Covenant on Civil and Political Rights* (United Nations, 1988).

Walker, John, *The Queen Has Been Pleased* (Secker and Warburg, 1986).

Wedderburn, Lord, *The Worker and the Law* (Penguin, 1986).

White, Robin, *The Administration of Justice* (Blackwell, 1992).

Index